Lonely Planet Publications
Melbourne | Oakland | London

P9-CIV-162

Damian Harper &
David Eimer

Beijing

Life in Běijīng

Tea-pouring display,
Lao She Teahouse (p147)

INTERVIEW 1:
I Hope to Make My Fortune

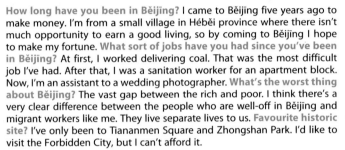

NAME	Wang Ruihai
AGE	25
OCCUPATION	Migrant worker
RESIDENCE	Dōngchéng

How long have you been in Běijīng? I came to Běijīng five years ago to make money. I'm from a small village in Héběi province where there isn't much opportunity to earn a good living, so by coming to Běijīng I hope to make my fortune. **What sort of jobs have you had since you've been in Běijīng?** At first, I worked delivering coal. That was the most difficult job I've had. After that, I was a sanitation worker for an apartment block. Now, I'm an assistant to a wedding photographer. **What's the worst thing about Běijīng?** The vast gap between the rich and poor. I think there's a very clear difference between the people who are well-off in Běijīng and migrant workers like me. They live separate lives to us. **Favourite historic site?** I've only been to Tiananmen Square and Zhongshan Park. I'd like to visit the Forbidden City, but I can't afford it.

'I think there's a very clear difference between the people who are well-off in Běijīng and migrant workers like me. They live separate lives to us.'

Garden wall, Summer Palace (p102)

INTERVIEW 2:
In China's Creative Capital

NAME	Han Qing
AGE	40
OCCUPATION	Artist
RESIDENCE	Wàngjìng

'I think Běijīngers have changed. They're more open now and less conservative than before.'

Best thing about your neighbourhood? It's very close to my studio and lots of other artists live there too. **How has Běijīng changed since you've been living here?** I think Běijīng is getting better and better, especially the nightlife. Also, I think Běijīngers have changed. They're more open now and less conservative than before. Young people in Běijīng put the same emphasis on work and pleasure now; before it was all about work. **What do you think of the way so much of Běijīng's heritage has been demolished?** I think it's a pity that the *hútòng* are disappearing, but it's an inevitable part of China's progress. **Favourite historic site?** The Forbidden City. Although, I don't think it has much to do with people's lives now. **Favourite street snack?** I'm from Sìchuān and the street food you get there is much better than anything you can find in Běijīng! **Best and worst things about living in Běijīng?** The best thing is the chance to have cultural exchanges with other artists from abroad. The worst things are the weather and the pollution. But I don't worry about it too much.

Young artists' displays at the Red Gate Gallery (p79)

Artists' brushes for sale, Panjiayuan Market (p163)

INTERVIEW 3:
Across the Decades

NAME	Feng Guangju
AGE	65
OCCUPATION	Retired typesetter
RESIDENCE	Xuǎnwǔ

Best thing about your neighbourhood? It's a good location. It's near two parks, a supermarket and there are lots of buses. **How has Běijīng changed over the years?** The changes have been so fast that it's hard to keep up. But our lives have improved a lot since I was young. For me, just going to school was a luxury. But now, my son and his wife are already saving money so my grand-daughter can study abroad when she's older. **What do you think about the demolition of so much of Běijīng's heritage?** I grew up in a *hútòng* near here. It was narrow and dirty and had very poor facilities. It's better it was knocked down. I don't have good memories of living there. **Favourite historic site?** I like the Summer Palace. There's water and hills nearby and the Long Corridor is very beautiful. **Favourite street snack?** I like all Běijīng food. But I especially like *lǔ zhǔ huǒ shāo* (a local stew of pig intestines and lung with herbs and *nang* bread). **Best thing about living in Běijīng?** It's clean, the infrastructure is good and I like the lights at night. **Worst thing?** I don't like to see people spitting or quarrelling on the street and using bad words.

'The changes have been so fast that it's hard to keep up. But our lives have improved a lot since I was young.'

Lanterns near Qianhai Lake (p117)

Prayer offerings at Dongyue Temple (p94)

Nine Dragon Screen, Beihai Park (p84)

BĚIJĪNGERS' FAVOURITE HISTORIC SIGHTS

Forbidden City (p87) The magnificent Forbidden City, so called because it was off-limits to commoners for 500 years, occupies a primary position in the Chinese psyche.

Summer Palace (p102) The huge regal encampment of the Summer Palace in the northwest of Běijing is one of the city's principle attractions.

Drum Tower (p86) The Drum Tower was first built in 1272 and marked the centre of the old Mongol capital Dàdū.

Bell Tower (p85) Fronted by a Qing dynasty stele, the Bell Tower – originally built in 1272 – sits along an alley behind

INTERVIEW 4:
Like-Minded Friends

NAME	Lin Gu
AGE	33
OCCUPATION	Journalist
RESIDENCE	Qiánmén

Best thing about your neighbourhood? It's a place where both apartments and *hútòng* co-exist. Around here, people still connect and share a sense of community, instead of being strangers to each other. **How has Běijīng changed since you've been living here?** In the eight years I've been here, Běijīng never sleeps. The whole city is a mega construction site. Eight years ago, Běijīng was a more intimate place. **What do you think about the demolition of so much of Běijīng's heritage?** If Běijīng continues to allow its *hútòng* to be demolished, the city will be transformed into a faceless concrete city, instead of a combination of the ancient and the modern. **Favourite historic site?** The Summer Palace. It's a rare thing to feel both nature and history in a place so close to downtown Běijīng. **Best and worst things about living in Běijīng?** In Běijīng you can bump into people from all over the world and you can always find like-minded friends. It's heaven for a journalist, because there's so much going on. The worst thing is that sometimes you can feel alienated living in such a huge city.

'Around here, people still connect and share a sense of community, instead of being strangers to each other.'

Crossing a bridge over the Golden Stream, Forbidden City (p87)

Many Different Facets

NAME	Zhen Ying
AGE	30
OCCUPATION	Freelance writer and translator
RESIDENCE	Dōngzhímén

'I love the energy; it's such a dynamic city.

Best thing about your neighbourhood? It's convenient. The traffic is so bad that it's good to be close to a subway stop. **Do you think it's a bad thing that so much of Běijīng's heritage has been demolished?** I don't think it's bad. *Hútòng* are nice for visitors to walk through, but you wouldn't want to live in one. **Favourite historic site?** I like the Forbidden City. It's an amazing place when you think about all the history that has happened there. **Favourite street snack?** *Yángròu chuàn* (lamb skewers). **Do you worry about the pollution?** Nowhere is perfect. The city, the whole country, is still developing. The pollution is part of that. I think things will be better in the future; the city will be better managed. **Best and worst things about Běijīng?** It's like a diamond, it has so many different facets. You can see something different every day. I love the energy; it's such a dynamic city. The worst thing is the gap between the rich and poor. A lot of people in Běijīng don't respect those who are worse off than them. That bothers me a lot.

Local transport in the historic *hútòng* (p106)

Contents

Published by Lonely Planet Publications Pty Ltd
ABN 36 005 607 983

Australia Head Office, Locked Bag 1, Footscray,
Victoria 3011, ☎ 03 8379 8000, fax 03 8379 8111,
talk2us@lonelyplanet.com.au

USA 150 Linden St, Oakland, CA 94607,
☎ 510 893 8555, toll free 800 275 8555,
fax 510 893 8572, info@lonelyplanet.com

UK 72–82 Rosebery Ave, Clerkenwell, London,
EC1R 4RW, ☎ 020 7841 9000, fax 020 7841 9001,
go@lonelyplanet.co.uk

The Authors

Damian Harper

A growing penchant for taichi and a meandering career in bookselling (London, Dublin, Paris) persuaded Damian to opt for a four-year degree in Chinese at London's School of Oriental and African Studies. A year of study in Běijīng and employment in Hong Kong further honed his irrepressible tendencies for wandering, inclinations that have led Damian to contribute to over a dozen guidebooks for Lonely Planet, including *Beijing, Shanghai, Hong Kong, China* and *Malaysia, Singapore & Brunei*. Married with two children, Damian and his family divide their time between Honor Oak Park in southeast London and China.

David Eimer

When David made his first trip to China in 1988, he had no idea that he would end up living and working there. After graduating with a law degree from University College London, he abandoned the idea of becoming a barrister for a career as a freelance journalist. That took him from London to LA for five years, where he wrote for a variety of newspapers and magazines including the *London Sunday Times*, the *Mail on Sunday* and the *Guardian*.

Back in London, David became intrigued by the world's increasing focus on China. Returning there for the first time in 14 years, he found a country that had changed almost beyond all recognition. He moved to Běijīng in early 2005 and now contributes to the *Independent on Sunday* and the *South China Morning Post*. This is his first book for Lonely Planet.

DAVID'S TOP BĚIJĪNG DAY

I'll start with a strong cup of tea to wake me up and get me out of the apartment and then an early morning bike ride through the *hútòng* (p106) in Dongsishitiao Qiao, with a stop at a street stall (p122) for a *ròubing* (a bread bun full of finely chopped meat) for breakfast. Then I'll push my bike across one of the *tiānqiáo* (pedestrian bridge) over Chaoyangmen Dajie and ride to the Friendship Store (p162) on Jianguomenwai Dajie to pick up a newspaper. From there, I'll head to nearby Ritan Park (p95) to read the paper by the ornate fish pond where hopeful middle-aged anglers sit all day.

If there's shopping to be done, then it's a short hop to the malls at either Guomao or Wangfujing Dajie (p161). If I'm feeling feisty, a trip to the hectic atmosphere of the Silk Street (p164) or Alien's Street Market (p166) offers the chance to improve my bartering skills and to pick up a few bargains. By the time I'm all haggled out I'm hungry again, so it's time for a quick lunch of *jiǎozi* (dumplings) in a nearby restaurant.

After a morning in Běijīng's commercial emporiums, an afternoon spent contemplating spiritual matters at one of the capital's surviving temples seems in order. I could carry on heading south to the Temple of Heaven Park (p79), but more likely I'll turn around and head back north to the oasis of serenity that is Lama Temple (p91). There I'll join Běijīng's Buddhists as they meditate, pray or just sit gazing into space.

In the evening, it's time to jump into a taxi and head to Sanlitun in Cháoyáng (p132) to catch up with friends over a meal. From there, we'll head to one of the many nearby bars (p143) for a few drinks.

CONTRIBUTING AUTHORS

DR TRISH BATCHELOR
Dr Trish Batchelor is a general practitioner and travel medicine specialist who works at the CIWEC Clinic in Kathmandu, Nepal. She is also a medical advisor to the Travel Doctor New Zealand clinics. Trish teaches travel medicine through the University of Otago and is interested in underwater and high-altitude medicine. She has travelled extensively through Southeast and East Asia. Trish wrote the Health section in the Directory chapter.

JASPER BECKER
British writer Jasper Becker arrived in Běijīng in 1985 to report for the *Guardian* and left after the Tiananmen Square 'incident'. In 1995 he arrived to work for the *South China Morning Post* and has now lived in Běijīng for 16 years. He has written six books including *Hungry Ghosts, The Chinese,* and most recently *City of Heavenly Tranquillity – Peking and the History of China* which is being published in 2007. Jasper wrote the History chapter.

JULIE GRUNDVIG
Julie first travelled to mainland China in the early 1990s where she hitchhiked her way from Yúnnán to Xīnjiāng. Several years after that she moved to Běijīng and eventually Xī'ān where she studied Chinese art and literature. Later came an MA in classical Chinese and a stint in Běijīng teaching English and working in an art gallery.

She is associate editor for the journal *Yishu: Journal of Contemporary Chinese Art* and co-author/contributor of several Lonely Planet titles including *Taiwan, China* and *Beijing.* She currently lives in Vancouver, BC, Canada. Julie co-authored the Arts & Architecture and Food & Drink chapters.

LIN GU
Lin Gu recently left a position as Běijīng-based writer for *China Features* and joined the Graduate School of Journalism at University of California, Berkeley as a visiting scholar. In eight years covering China, he has reported on a number of issues, including social migration and environmental protection. Lin was a regular contributor to the radio talk programmes which replaced Alistair Cooke's 'Letter from America' after Alistair's death. He has also written and presented on current affairs in China for the BBC. Lin has a master's degree in social anthropology from Cambridge University and was the two-time recipient of the Developing Asia Journalism Award for his coverage of the AIDS crisis in China and the controversy over genetically modified rice in the country. He wrote the 'Home' boxed text in the City Life chapter.

PHOTOGRAPHER

Phil Weymouth
Australian born, Phil's family moved to Iran in the late 1960s. They called Tehran home until the revolution in 1979. Phil then studied photography in Melbourne, and returned to the Middle East to work as a photographer in Bahrain. Phil's Lonely Planet commissions include guides to *Beijing, Hong Kong, Shanghai, Dubai, Kyoto* and *Singapore.*

Introducing Běijīng

Capital of the country set to dominate the 21st century, Běijīng is the indestructible heart of China. Just as all roads used to lead to Rome, now the world is beating a path to Běijīng to discover the city that holds the key to the planet's most populous nation.

Běijīng is a city rushing towards the future so fast that it's easy to forget that this ancient capital has been home to Mongol, Ming and Qing emperors. Few cities can boast a history as dramatic or turbulent as Běijīng's. Ruled by emperors and warlords, invaded by everyone from Genghis Khan to the former colonial powers, Běijīng has been razed to the ground many times yet has always risen from the ashes, shaken off the dust and reasserted its authority as the capital of a far-flung country that's now home to 1.3 billion people.

Despite all that history, Běijīng is now in the spotlight as never before. With China's economy roaring like an unstoppable machine and the Olympics on their way, the world's attention is focused on this enigmatic city as never before. For so long shrouded from view from the West, whether because of the capricious whims of emperors, or the bamboo curtain that descended after the 1949 Communist Revolution, Běijīng has thrown open its doors to the outside world. The response has been overwhelmingly enthusiastic and Běijīngers are growing accustomed to the ever-increasing number of foreigners who are coming to see what all the fuss is about.

What they find is a city that seems too large to comprehend. Located on a vast plain that reaches as far south as the Yellow River, the city's chessboard flatness reinforces a sense that it goes on forever. This flat topography, coupled with broad, sweeping avenues, huge open spaces and one-storey *hútòng* (alleyway) architecture, traditionally gave the city a stumpy skyline. Now, high-rise apartment blocks and gleaming office towers of steel and glass are sprouting up everywhere, redefining the city's perspective.

First-time visitors will be dazzled by the contrasts available in Běijīng. New buildings appear almost overnight, the roads are jammed with the latest cars and the streets are full of fashionably dressed men and women with mobile phones clamped to their ears. Business people wheel and deal in the multimillions, vast shopping malls are home to exclusive foreign brands and the city's clubs jump to the latest Western sounds.

But turn off the main roads into the *hútòng* that crisscross the heart of Běijīng and it's as if you've stepped back in time. Hawkers still ride through the alleys on bicycle carts shouting their wares, old men and women step out in their Mao suits and people squat by the roadside to eat bowls of steaming noodles, to get their hair cut, to socialise or just to watch the endless parade of humanity going by.

The mix of past and present is visible everywhere in Běijīng. Although many of the city's historic buildings have been demolished in the rush to modernise the capital, including the old city walls, thousands of temples and *hútòng*, Běijīng is still home to some of China's most stunning and essential sights. It's here that you'll find the Forbidden City, the Summer Palace, Temple of Heaven Park, the Lama Temple and the Great Wall, to name just a few. Beyond Běijīng, excursions to the erstwhile imperial encampment at Chéngdé and the Great Wall's finale at the sea at Shānhǎiguān add additional historical allure.

As the city's fabric is being transformed, so Běijīng is shaking off its reputation as a conservative metropolis. The numerous bars, clubs and restaurants are packed and, after an inevitable period when they were content to ape their Western equivalents, they are now discovering their own identity. New places open every week, a reflection of both the amount of cash floating around and of the desire of Běijīngers to enjoy their newfound prosperity.

Nevertheless, Běijīng is still very much a work in progress and not all the city's residents have embraced the changes. The elderly and those excluded from Běijīng's boom, such as migrant workers and the middle-aged unemployed, can only look on as the younger generation enjoys the fruits of Běijīng's ongoing transformation from dowdy communist capital to truly international world city. The roads of the inner city might be clogged with new cars, but on the outskirts of Běijīng some people still travel to work on donkey-drawn carts. Many Běijīngers are caught in the abyss that separates the free market and the old state-controlled economy and, with no real safety net provided by the government, their prospects are bleak.

Běijīngers though, are a pragmatic, unpretentious, forthright bunch and nothing fazes them. The revolutionary zeal inspired by Mao Zedong and his rhetoric is history for everyone; Běijīngers have been there, done that and moved on. If they can seem a little dour at times, then they make up for that by being overwhelmingly friendly and welcoming people who mock pomposity and cherish candour. They're still curious about life in the West too and equally eager to hear what foreigners think of their hometown.

The short autumn is probably the best time to visit Běijīng. Spring is sandstorm season, while the hot and humid summers can be brutal. The consolation for the heat is that the city's population takes to the streets until the small hours, which makes for a fascinating spectacle. In contrast, the winters are bitterly cold. Nevertheless, there's an icy grandeur to the old sections of Běijīng in January and February as the lakes freeze over and snow clings to the *hútòng* roofs. But whenever you come, you'll be able to experience Běijīng's unique energy and see a city that is changing by the day. It's never boring here. Enjoy your visit.

LOWDOWN

Population 15.4 million

Time zone GMT + 8 hours

Coffee Y20-30

Subway ticket Y3-5

Three-star hotel room Y400-600

Number of cars 2.8 million

Number of taxis 63,000

Number of construction sites 9000+

Expat population 70,000

City Life

City Life

BĚIJĪNG TODAY

New arrivals to Hong Kong or Shànghǎi come primed by both cliché and high expectations, thanks to the shared colonial pasts of these cities. In contrast, many first-timers to Běijīng arrive with a hazy picture of their destination in their minds. Such confusion is perhaps understandable as airlines still slap a label on Běijīng-bound luggage that says 'PEK', a reference to Běijīng's previous incarnation as Peking.

But while Běijīng has changed its name many times, it has been the focal point of Chinese identity since the Yuan dynasty. From the 13th century, while Shànghǎi was still a fishing village and Hong Kong a backwater port, Běijīng was the capital of one of the largest empires the world has ever seen. Very little remains of that era in present-day Běijīng, but that's to be expected in a city that has reinvented itself so many times. That urge for change is one of the first things any visitor notices. A skyline lined with cranes as far as the eye can see, and buildings under construction that seem to grow a storey a day, compete for attention with a ground-level view of millions of people pushing and striving for a better life. Communism and capitalism have met head on in Běijīng and the collision has produced a unique vitality. There has never been such an exciting time to visit Běijīng.

The 2008 Olympics have provided the latest motivation for Běijīng to regenerate itself once again. Just a few years ago, Běijīng was a city dominated by sterile, Soviet-inspired architecture, where monolithic government buildings and drab apartment blocks proliferated. There are still plenty of such structures around, but joining them now are inspiring buildings designed by some of the world's cutting-edge architects. Along with the US$34 billion Běijīng is spending on upgrading its infrastructure, this speak volumes about Běijīng's desire to transform itself into a capital fit to take its place alongside the world's major cities.

It's not just new architecture and subway lines that are driving the changes in Běijīng. The contemporary art scene is the world's most vibrant, and the government is putting US$63 million into renovating artistic and cultural venues, while some of the fortunes being made are being ploughed back into bars, cafés, clubs and restaurants. Fifteen years ago, Běijīngers went to bed early because there was nothing else to do. Now, the capital is increasingly a 24-hour city whose residents play as hard as they work.

A swelling middle and white-collar class has totally redefined the socioeconomic make-up of town. Fashion – once a symbol of the decadent West and a household taboo – is now an indispensable lifestyle fad and not just for the young. Owning a car has become the goal of nearly all Běijīngers and there are 2.8 million of them on Běijīng's jammed roads, a number increasing by 1000 a day. The economic boom has also seen the return of age-old vices that were thought to have been stamped out forever. Prostitution, drugs and crime are back in a big way, despite the best efforts of the police.

Amid all the shiny new developments and the young hipsters walking the streets, it's easy to forget that Běijīng is still a very uneven mix of old and new and rich and poor. For every person benefiting from the soaring economy, there are many more struggling to get by. There's also a big generational gap. Běijīng is home to an increasingly elderly population, almost 11% of Běijīngers are over 60, and while the youth of the city can take advantage of Běijīng's boom, many middle-aged people are resentful about how privatisation has meant

HOT CONVERSATION TOPICS

- Money, money, money
- The newest, best restaurant to spend some of the above in
- The latest pirated Hollywood DVD to hit the streets
- The terrible traffic
- Rumour-mongering about TV and movie stars and just how they got so famous so quick
- Why Běijīng is better than Shànghǎi

HOME *Lin Gu*

Wang Ruihai will never eat instant noodles again. He survived on the cheap noodles in the winter of 2003, when he couldn't find himself a job in Běijīng. Rather than being unemployed, the 25-year-old enrolled in a two-month computer-hardware maintenance course, believing that ignorance about computers was even worse than illiteracy. All he had left after tuition and rent of a room with a broken window and no heating (shared with three other trainees), was Y200 (about US$25).

Wang first came to Běijīng in the winter of 1999. 'Do you want to find something to do in Běijīng?' his father had asked him one day when they were toiling in the fields. Like most of his former schoolmates who were dashing off to the Chinese capital for work or college, the answer was obvious. Together with his uncle, Wang left his family and headed for the big city, more than six hours from his village in Héběi province. They landed in a briquette factory, where Wang's job was to transport the honeycomb-shaped fire starters on a flat-board tricycle into factory storage. He earned Y700 (about US$90) a month, and life there was harsh. He almost lost a thumb on an assembly line. Less than three months passed before the Spring Festival and the traditional time for family reunion, so Wang happily went home to the countryside.

Yet Běijīng kept calling to him. In 2001 Wang returned and worked for a cleaning company in a new apartment compound of 14 buildings in the northwest of the city, where the bulk of the residents were college teachers, foreign students and IT professionals. Every morning he got up at 3am, collected garbage from three apartment buildings by 5am and transported it to the processing station by 8am. His work clothes were often stained with sewage. Once, when Wang was about to share an elevator with a resident, the tenant frowned and covered her nose; at other times, they simply waited for the next elevator.

Wang doesn't blame them. 'The key to solving the problem of discrimination is in our own hands, as long as we try to make the best of ourselves.' All of Wang's workmates were rural migrants like himself, no city resident had the least interest in their line of work. As everyone knows, all the dirty jobs in Běijīng are done by rural migrants.

Běijīng became a ghost city in the spring of 2003 when SARS evacuated the capital. Few dared to linger in public spaces, but there were some exceptions: a team of volunteers came to Wang's workplace, distributing thermometers and gauze masks as preventive measures against SARS. Later, they organised a party for lonely workers, and told Wang about a newly established cultural centre that was tailored to rural migrants just like him.

The city's four million rural migrants have five nongovernment organisations that manage such gathering places. Out of 1.3 billion Chinese, an estimated 150 million at any one time are on the move, mostly from the countryside to the cities, in search of work.

What motivates this giant mobile camp is the widening gap between rural and urban, poor and wealthy. There has long been an outcry for equal treatment for rural migrants in terms of rights to work, medical care and education, with reports of injustices often occupying mainland newspaper headlines. For millions of hard-working women and men like Wang, their lot seems unlikely to change anytime soon. But small, incremental improvements are always possible.

Wang's most recent migration to Běijīng was in March 2005, when he became a photography assistant at a Taiwanese-owned wedding photo studio in downtown Běijīng, based on his one year as a trainee photographer in a small city in Héběi province. The normal pay is about Y1000 (about US$125) per month, but it can rise up to Y1700 (about US$215) at peak season. It's the first step on the ladder.

Wang's boss, a young photographer called Zhang, was impressed by Wang. 'Glamorous as it may appear, this is a place where people with a lower-class background can possibly grab a chance,' Zhang says. 'You may speak Mandarin with an accent, but so what? As long as you have guts!'

Wang now finds his feelings for Běijīng are changing. Today, it's more than just a paying gig. He witnesses constant injustice against migrant workers, and yearns to do something about it. He joins other volunteers in visiting hospitalised migrants, and performs skits in schools for migrant children and at construction sites. He's also organised a photography team, where fellow migrants exchange their ideas about photography while improving their photographic skills.

'Taking photos isn't just for fun. It's a way of documenting our lives,' he says. On a day off work, Wang likes to ride across the city on his bicycle, with his camera at his side. The remnants of an ancient courtyard being demolished by bulldozers, a gang of construction workers on lunch break taking in the shade – these are the typical targets of his lens.

A little timid and, at 1.7m, none too tall, Wang Ruihai is above all a good listener. He smiles as others exchange gossip at the cultural centre. The best moment for him, he says, is when they all sit down to eat together: 'It's like coming home.'

they have lost their secure, relatively well-paid jobs in state-run enterprises, and they are disillusioned by their paltry pensions.

Běijīng has also paid a high price for its rapid development in recent years, with the city's heritage taking a thrashing. As late as 1950, Běijīng was still, essentially, a medieval walled city. The magnificent walls were unceremoniously levelled to make way for the Second Ring Rd in the 1950s, along with numerous *páilou* (decorative archways; see the boxed text, p37). Today, the residents of many *hútòng* (alleyways) which crisscross central Běijīng are being moved on as property developers bulldoze their homes to make way for uniform high-rise apartment blocks for the new moneyed class. As the *hútòng* go, so do huge pockets of history.

There is a growing awareness of the need to protect what is left of old Běijīng. Some *hútòng* are now under government protection and other ancient sites are being rebuilt. But in Běijīng, as in all of China, heritage will always take second place to the demands of business.

Nor, despite the dazzling GDP figures, has the nature of the government changed much. Běijīng is still the capital of a communist state, albeit one which preaches 'Socialism with Chinese Characteristics', a euphemism for combining rigid control of the population with a liberal capitalist economy. In its bid to survive, the government has made great concessions, but it knows that reform can only go so far before the seeds of its own extinction are sown. There are limits to reform.

The tremendous strides that Běijīng has made since the early 1980s are awesome, but they conceal the limping progress of other development indicators, such as democratic reform, effective anti-corruption measures, freedom of the press and freedom of speech.

CITY CALENDAR

China follows both the Gregorian *(yánglì)* and the lunar calendar *(yīnlì)*. Traditional Chinese festivals and holidays (p223) are calculated according to the lunar calendar and fall on different days each year according to the Gregorian calendar.

JANUARY & FEBRUARY
SPRING FESTIVAL
Chūn Jié
7 Feb 2008; 26 Jan 2009
Also known as Chinese New Year, this festival is the high point of the year, kicking off on the first day of the first lunar month. The festival usually falls sometime between late January and mid-February and ushers in a new year marked by one of the 12 animals of the Chinese zodiac. The weeks in the build-up to the festival are an explosion of colour, with *chūnlián* (spring couplets) pasted on door posts, door gods brightening up *hútòng* and shops glistening with red and gold decorations. Work colleagues and relatives present each other with red envelopes *(hóngbāo)* of money, the streets ring with cries of '*gōngxǐ fācái*' ('congratulations – make money') and at night they echo to the sound of fireworks going off non-stop. The White Cloud Temple (p97), the Lama Temple (p91) and other temples in Běijīng stage entertaining temple fairs *(miàohuì)*. Celebrations are also held in parks such as Ditan Park (p86). In 2000, the holiday was officially lengthened from three days to seven, and legions of Chinese use it to head

to the provinces to visit relatives. Despite that, and the fact that it can be bitterly cold, the Spring Festival can be a fascinating time to be in Běijīng. However, air and rail transport is booked solid, hotel accommodation is harder to come by and many businesses shut up shop for a week or so.

LANTERN FESTIVAL
Yuánxiāo Jié
21 Feb 2008; 9 Feb 2009
Celebrated two weeks after the first day of the Spring Festival, this festival (also known as Dēng Jié or Shàngyuán Jié) is not a public holiday, but can be a very colourful time to visit Běijīng. The Chinese visit *dēnghuì* (lantern shows) in the evening and devour gorgeous *yuánxiāo* (glutinous rice dumplings with soft, sweet fillings).

MARCH & APRIL
GUANYIN'S BIRTHDAY
Guānshìyīn Shēngrì
5 Apr 2008; 25 Mar 2009
The birthday of Guanyin (Sanskrit Avalokiteshvara), the Buddhist Goddess of Mercy, is a fine time to visit Buddhist temples,

many of which have halls dedicated to the divinity. Puning Temple (p205) in Chéngdé province is entirely dedicated to Guanyin and sees important celebrations on the occasion of her birthday, held on the 19th day of the second moon.

TOMB SWEEPING DAY
Qīng Míng Jié
5 Apr (4 Apr in leap years)
A day for worshipping ancestors, the festival falls near the date of Easter; people visit and clean the graves *(sǎomù)* of their departed relatives. The Chinese often place flowers on tombs and burn ghost money for the departed. There may be increased vigilance in Tiananmen Square during the festival, as public displays of mourning for the dead of 4 June 1989 remain prohibited.

SEPTEMBER & OCTOBER
MID-AUTUMN FESTIVAL
Zhōngqiū Jié
25 Sep 2007; 14 Sep 2008
Also known as the Moon Festival, this festival is marked by eating tasty *yuèbǐng* (moon cakes), gazing at the full moon and gathering together with relatives for family reunions. It is also a traditional holiday for lovers and takes place on the 15th day of the eighth lunar month.

BIRTHDAY OF CONFUCIUS
Kǒngzi Shēngrì
27 Oct 2007; 27 Oct 2008
The great sage has his birthday on the 27th day of the eighth lunar month, an occasion marked by celebrations at Confucian temples.

CULTURE
CONNECTIONS

China is a country where *guānxì* (connections) is all important. With too many people competing for too few desirable jobs, as well as services, those who have *guānxì* usually get what they want because the connections network is, of course, reciprocal.

Obtaining goods or services through connections is informally referred to as 'going through the back door' *(zǒu hòu mén)*. *Guānxì* is lavishly cultivated by way of banquets, fuelled by drinking *báijiǔ* (white spirits), and by the giving of gifts. As foreign investment in China has grown, gift giving for *guānxì* has become more and more wasteful. Cadres and officials are very well placed for this activity and there is a thin line between exploiting *guānxì* and corruption.

IDENTITY

Běijīng has repeatedly been the source of tempestuous historical events, from the May Fourth Movement to the Cultural Revolution and the student democracy movement of 1989. Despite that, Běijīng is – unlike buzzing Hong Kong or Shànghǎi – a city of slowly brewing latent energy that gradually accumulates before spilling over.

Běijīngers know that they live in the cultural, political and psychological centre of China. They are not only *Zhōngguórén* (Chinese), they are *shǒudūrén* (citizens of the capital) and in the top spot. Throughout the land the Chinese chat in *Pǔtōnghuà* (based on the Běijīng dialect), set their watch according to Beijing Time *(Běijīng Shíjiān)* and act on enigmatic directives from the capital.

Because they live so close to the centre of power, Běijīngers regard themselves as more politically astute than other Chinese and the city's taxi drivers will always have an opinion on the latest issues. Confident of their pre-eminence, they feel superior *(gāorén yīdèng)* to those unfortunate enough to live outside town. They think *Běijīnghuà* – the local dialect – is infinitely superior to *Pǔtōnghuà* and they revel in the complexities of the Běijīng dialect and how it instantly distinguishes outsiders. To be a Běijīnger is to be the genuine article, while everyone else, Chinese included, is a *wàidìrén* (someone from outside town) or even worse, a *tǔbāozi* (country bumpkin).

Běijīngers have a reputation among their fellow Chinese for being blunt and straightforward *(zhíjié liǎodàng)*, honest, well-read and cultivated, if just a bit conservative. Běijīngers scorn the calculating *(suànji)* shrewdness of Hong Kong Chinese and the notorious stinginess of the Shànghǎinese. They take pride in being generous *(dàfang)* and amicable *(yǒushàn)*, and this is nowhere more evident than when dining out. Běijīngers will fight to pay for the bill with loud choruses of *'wǒ lái, wǒ lái, wǒ fù qián'* ('I'll pay') and will never split the bill (as may happen in Shànghǎi). Běijīngers are also prone to excess, cooking more than they need and binning the rest. It's all part of their big-hearted mindset. Although Běijīngers tend to frown on ostentatious displays of wealth, that's beginning to change. Nevertheless, they are far less flash than the Shànghǎinese and generally more modest than the Hong Kong Chinese.

LIFESTYLE

Changes in the way of life of Běijīng residents have matched the city's economic transformation over the past 20 years. Modern Běijīng offers young people a new and exciting world of fashion, music, sport, new slang and lifestyle experimentation. Many over the age of 40, however, often feel trapped between the familiar expectations of their generation and the widening horizons of the city's youth. The unpleasantness of the Cultural Revolution encourages parents in this age group to protect their children from strife and unexpected misfortune.

With the One-child policy enforced strictly in Běijīng, most families only have the one child, unless they are rich and are willing to pay the fine for having a second child, or have serious *guānxì*. The 'Little Emperor' syndrome, where the only child is spoiled rotten by his parents and his grandparents, is very common. Many children continue living with their parents long after leaving school. The high price of real estate in Běijīng means it's still standard for married couples to be living with one or other set of their parents. Many Běijīngers rely on their parents to provide child care for their children.

In part, that's because the Chinese work long hours. Saving money, whether to provide for their child's university education, to finance a move to a bigger apartment or to buy that car, is an obsession with Běijīngers. But if the adults are out working, then life can be equally stressful for the kids. Chinese parents have high expectations for their children and place great faith in university education as a route to a better life. Consequently, if the kids aren't at school, then they're at home studying.

The older generation meanwhile, are out and about and most often can be found in their local park. From dawn till dusk, Běijīng's parks are full of elderly Běijīngers practising taichi, holding dance classes, playing Chinese chess, cards and mah jong, or just hanging out with each other.

CHINESE ETIQUETTE

The Chinese are very polite and will naturally appreciate it if you are polite in return. Reserved in their behaviour and expression, the Chinese eschew public displays of emotion and grand gestures. Saving face (avoidance of shame) is important to the Chinese psyche and forcing a Chinese person to back down prompts loss of face.

Meals are important occasions where friendships and business deals are often forged. The host – or the person sitting next to you – is likely to serve you food and ensure your glass is refilled. Relentless toasting is common, often performed standing up and accompanied by a chorus of *'gānbēi (cheers)'*, which is the signal for you to drain your glass. But if you can only handle half a glass, say *'gān bànbēi'* which literally means 'drink half a glass'. Don't forget to do a toast in return, a few minutes after you have been toasted. Even if you have been invited out make a gesture to pay the bill. It will be appreciated but refused. Don't, however, insist on paying the bill as your host will need to pay. For reasons of face, it is terribly important for Chinese to settle the bill as a sign of generosity and hospitality. Smoking at meal time is generally OK, as it can establish a rapport among smokers, but make sure you offer your smokes around.

A landmine to be wary of is political discussion. The Chinese may secretly agree with you that the Communist Party is a band of good-for-nothings, but these are sentiments they probably won't want to voice. This works both ways, so say you don't want to talk politics (if you are being grilled on US foreign policy, for example) unless there is quid pro quo.

Even if you are not on business, name cards are very important, so make sure you have a stack printed up with Chinese on one side and English on the reverse. The Chinese present and receive business cards with the fingers of both hands.

In the evenings everyone gathers for a meal together. Then they disperse: grown-up children to meet friends, younger ones to MSN their classmates on the computer, the grand-parents to chat with the neighbours, the parents to watch TV and relax. With whole families living in cramped apartments, the streets are always crowded in the evenings, especially in summer, as people go in search of a bit more space. They set up stools or chairs by the roadside, bring out their tea or bottles of beer and chat for hours. The *hútòng* in particular are always lively and are fascinating places to stroll through after dusk.

For those people too exhausted after work to go out, it's the TV that's the main source of entertainment. Korean soap operas are hugely popular, as are soaps from Taiwan. Reality TV shows such as *Supergirls*, the Chinese version of *Pop Idol,* draw massive audiences too and have caught the imagination of the younger generation who feverishly cast votes for their favourites. But if there's a big NBA game or soccer game on, then there'll be a tussle over who watches what.

FASHION

The fashion industry in Běijīng has exploded over the past 10 years. The annual Beijing Fashion Week, featuring increasingly individual and China-centric creations from home-grown designers, has become a fixture on the international fashion circuit, albeit one with a considerably lower profile than Milan or Paris.

While it's unlikely that Běijīng will ever match Hong Kong or Shànghǎi for style or es-tablish itself as a leading fashion city, it does have over 20 schools and colleges with fashion departments and some Běijīngers do take what they wear seriously.

Unsurprisingly, the younger generation lead the way in individual style. With more and more people tuning into the NBA, thanks to the presence of China's basketball star Yao Ming, hip-hop culture is a real influence on male teenagers. Younger women too, increasingly look to the prevalent street fashion trends in the West, while spending a lot on skin-whitening creams, the most popular cosmetics in China. There's also a growing market for plastic surgery. Devotees of rock and punk music, club culture and skateboard-ing dress accordingly.

For the rich it is label worship all the way. But for everyone else fashion means less. Many elderly people still take to the streets in their old Mao jackets, while men dress in conservative black, grey or brown suits and are unselfconscious about carrying man-bags or having mobile-phone holsters on their belts. Traditional Chinese-style clothes, especially jackets and *qípǎo* (traditional, full-length Chinese dress), are still in vogue with women, sometimes after being given a modern twist by local designers.

MEDIA

China is the world's largest producer of daily newspapers; there are over 2200 of them on sale each day. The problem is that few of them contain anything worth reading. Papers in China stick to a diet of good news: the booming economy and sporting success, while avoiding writing about anything that might offend the government. The media, as well as the internet, is closely monitored by the authorities and every year China features near the bottom of Reporters Without Borders annual World Press Freedom Index.

As a consequence of this many newspapers have adopted a tabloid tone, with graphic pictures of car crashes competing with celebrity gossip. The capital's papers are no excep-tion. The most reputable is the *Beijing News*. But unless you read Chinese your newspaper reading will be limited to the government's English-language flagship, the anodyne *China Daily* (see p227 for more on newspapers and magazines). It's a similar story with the state-run CCTV, China Central Television. Their English-language outlet is the equally bland CCTV 9. Other stations, like BTV (Beijing TV), offer an uninspiring mix of soap operas, reality TV, game shows and sport. Just like in the West really, only with censored news.

If the print and TV media are a lost cause, then hope can be found in the blogosphere. With the world's second-largest internet population, the Chinese are fanatical bloggers. There were some 35 million blogs out there at the last count and they're written by everyone from movie stars to schoolkids. It's through reading the blogs that you can get a sense of what people in this vast country are preoccupied with, angry about and what their hopes for the future are. There are websites which provide English translations of the most popular ones; www.danwei.org has a list of these.

Unsurprisingly, the authorities are moving to try and control the blogosphere. At the time of writing, proposals to make all bloggers register their blogs under their real names were being mooted. But despite the much-vaunted 'Great Firewall of China', the government's grip on cyberspace is not nearly as tight as is sometimes assumed. Proxy servers enable people to access those sites, like Wikipedia and the BBC, that are routinely blocked, while a number of file-sharing websites offer free downloads of foreign TV shows that would never pass the censors.

ECONOMY & COSTS

He who is not in charge of it does not interfere in its business.

Confucius

Běijīng is the capital of the world's fastest growing economy. Already the fourth largest in the world, the economy continues to grow at a rate of over 10% a year and, if it sustains its current momentum, sometime in the next 25 years or so China will have the world's largest economy.

With the Olympics in the bag, the local government has seized the nettle to activate a vast investment blueprint that will shake up Běijīng. US$6.7 billion is to be spent on Běijīng's public transport system and road construction, US$4.4 billion is earmarked for environmental protection and US$18.2 billion is planned for the expansion of manufacturing and high-tech industries. Further down the line, there are plans to build a ring of satellite towns around Běijīng to house the city's ever-expanding population.

Tourism is becoming an increasingly important source of revenue, with the Chinese tourism industry set to become the second-largest in the world after the USA by 2015. Already, China has the largest domestic tourist market in the world. The tourism sector was expected to be worth US$354 billion in 2006 and with China tipped to be the world's top travel destination by 2020, the potential for further growth is huge.

HOW MUCH?

Bāozi (steamed meat buns) from street stall Y3

Bus ticket Y1

Cinema ticket (for a foreign film) Y60

Large bottle of Yanjing Beer from a shop Y2

1L of petrol Y5

Local SIM card Y100

Newspaper (in Chinese) Y0.5

0.5L bottle of mineral water Y1.5

Taxi rate (for first 3km) Y10

T-shirt from Yashow market Y60

Facts and figures aside, Běijīng remains China's political heart rather than its economic frontline and its pulse is more measured than, say, Shànghǎi's. Vigilant about its affairs and scrupulous at reigning in more strident trends nationwide, the economic environment of Běijīng is far from laissez faire, despite the seemingly random nature of some of the housing developments going up. Regularly published paeans to China's robust economy may paint a different picture, but much of Běijīng's economic development is propelled by state investment and large scale public works programmes rather than by market forces. Many of the labour intensive and high investment programmes that will shape the Beijing Olympic Economy fall into this category.

A similar formula powers much of China's spectacular GDP growth. The conspicuous manifestations of such development – high-rise towers, chic designer-clothing stores and Bentley showrooms – are eye catching, but much of the economy remains under the control of the socialist state and its army of bureaucrats.

Several major obstacles to growth exist, some of which represent local problems, while others are part of larger national dilemmas. All of them impinge on the city's economic performance, discourage investment and hamper Běijīng's efforts to become a major international financial centre.

Běijīng has a largely unfavourable geographical location – neither on the coast nor on a major waterway – and never developed a great trading economy like that of Shànghǎi or Hong Kong.

Water and land are two natural resources that are being rapidly depleted, which restricts Běijīng's development potential. At the same time, the combination of millions of migrant workers moving to the capital in search of work and a huge upsurge in the number of graduates seeking jobs in Běijīng means that unemployment is a problem for both the educated and uneducated. In 2006, the official unemployment rate in Běijīng was 2.5%, a figure predicted to rise in the next few years. With no real social security system in the PRC, an anomaly for such an avowedly socialist country, prospects for the unemployed are bleak.

Běijīng is investing considerable sums in transport infrastructure, building new roads and widening existing ones, while expanding the subway system and over-ground rail services. But economic development itself has revealed the limitations of Běijīng's road and transport systems. The number of vehicles on the city's roads was 2.8 million in late 2006 and, with the government reluctant to rein in the demand for car ownership, and prices for both cars and fuel artificially cheap, gridlock is perhaps just down the road. There is little doubt that congestion charging will have to be introduced in the near future.

Corruption not only erodes China's GDP but is one of the major causes of public dissatisfaction with the government. One of the principal complaints of the 1989 Tiananmen demonstrators, the problem of corruption has not been solved, despite the arrest, imprisonment and, in a few cases, the execution of high-ranking cadres. In June 2006, Běijīng's vice-mayor Liu Zhihua, who was in charge of overseeing the construction of all Olympic venues, was removed from his post for corruption and dissolute behaviour. Liu had been taking bribes from property developers, while maintaining multiple mistresses.

> ### BĚIJĪNG'S ECONOMIC STATS
>
> - Běijīng's GDP US$84 billion (2005)
> - Total retail expenditure US$35.7 billion (2005)
> - Expenditure on real estate US$22.7 billion (2005)

As a city hell-bent on modernising, Běijīng can be shockingly expensive. You can pay criminal prices: up to Y45 (US$5.50) for a coffee or Y50 (US$6) for a bowl of noodles at Capital Airport; Y1.2 million (US$150,000) for a bottom-rung Porsche or US$8500 a month for a plush three-bedroom apartment.

Foreigners (and the Chinese nouveau riche) are targeted for their hard-earned cash, so don't just dish it out. Look around, learn to get savvy and get a feel for where locals shop, and quickly try to get a sense of proportion. Working with a new currency, take your time to accurately convert prices.

Hotels are going to be the biggest expense, but food and transport can add up quickly too. Excluding the cost of getting to Běijīng, ascetics can survive on as little as US$15 per day – that means staying in dormitories, travelling by bus or bicycle rather than taxi, eating from street stalls or small restaurants and refraining from buying anything. At the time of writing, the cheapest dorm bed was Y15 and a basic meal in a run-of-the-mill streetside restaurant cost around Y20.

At the opposite end of the spectrum, five-star hotel rooms can reach US$300 per day and upmarket restaurant meals around US$50. And there is an increasing number of expensive department stores. If you want to spend money you won't have a problem.

Beer at corner shops (xiǎomàibù) – often buried down hútòng – should cost around Y2 for a bottle of Beijing or Yanjing Beer. Drinking at bars is much more expensive, where a small bottle of Tsingtao will cost around Y15 to Y25. Unlike cigarettes in countries such as the UK, where prices for cigarettes are by and large the same, there is great variation in Chinese cigarette prices (Y3 to Y70 per pack).

Pirate DVDs usually retail for around Y7 to Y10, but be warned that quality is often a problem (see also the Lost in Translation boxed text, p168).

GOVERNMENT & POLITICS

A revolution is not a dinner party, or writing an essay, or painting a picture, or doing embroidery; it cannot be so refined, so leisurely and gentle, so temperate, kind, courteous, restrained and magnanimous. A revolution is an insurrection, an act of violence by which one class overthrows another.

Mao Zedong

Běijīng is the seat of political power in China and all the important decisions that affect the rest of the land are made here.

Little is known about the inner workings of the Chinese government, but what is clear is that the entire monolithic structure, from grass roots work units to the upper echelons of political power, is controlled by the Chinese Communist Party (CCP) and its power base is Běijīng.

The highest authority rests with the Standing Committee of the Politburo of the CCP. Including the president, Hu Jintao, and premier, Wen Jiabao, its nine members are in effect China's cabinet. Beneath them are another 25 members and below them is the 210-member Central Committee, made up of younger party members and provincial party leaders. At the grass roots level the party forms a parallel system to the administrations in the army, universities, government and industries. Real authority is exercised by the party representatives at each level in these organisations. They, in turn, are responsible to the party officials in the hierarchy above them, thus ensuring strict central control.

The day-to-day running of the country lies with the State Council, which is directly under the control of the CCP. The State Council is headed by the premier and beneath the premier are four vice-premiers, 10 state councillors, a secretary-general, 45 ministers and various other agencies. The State Council implements the decisions made by the Politburo.

Approving the decisions of the CCP leadership is the National People's Congress (NPC), the principal legislative body that convenes in the Great Hall of the People (p77). It comprises a 'democratic alliance' of party members and non-party members including intellectuals, technicians and industrial managers. In theory they are empowered to amend the constitution and to choose the premier and State Council members. The catch is that all these office holders must first be recommended by the Central Committee, thus the NPC is only an approving body.

The Chinese government is also equipped with a massive bureaucracy. The term 'cadre' is usually applied to bureaucrats, and their monopoly on power means that wide-ranging perks are a privilege of rank for all and sundry – from the lowliest clerks to the shadowy puppet masters of Zhōngnánhǎi. China's bureaucratic tradition is a long one.

The wild card in the system is the armed forces, the People's Liberation Army (PLA). Comprising land forces, the navy and the air force, it has a total of around 2.3 million members.

TOP BOOKS ON THE ECONOMY & POLITICS

- **China Shakes the World: The Rise of a Hungry Nation** (James Kynge; Weidenfeld; 2006) How China's emergence as an economic superpower affects the rest of the world.
- **Chinese Lessons: Five Classmates and the Story of the New China** (John Pomfret; Henry Holt; 2006) A former Běijīng bureau chief for the Washington Post, Pomfret gives an invaluable insight into the reality of life in present-day China from Nanjing University over the last 25 years, offering a moving narrative of what happened to five of his 1981 classmates
- **Mao: The Unknown Story** (Jung Chang & Jon Halliday; Jonathan Cape; 2005) Hugely controversial biography of Mao that paints a picture of a man consumed by egoism and indifferent to the fate of the Chinese people. Banned in China.
- **Mr China: A Memoir** (Tim Clissold; Constable & Robinson; 2004) Amusing and readable account of a British businessman's misadventures in China in the 1990s.
- **The Tiananmen Papers** (compiled by Zhang Liang, edited by Andrew Nathan & Perry Link; Public Affairs; 2001) A two-inch thick compilation of Politburo memos, minutes and documents, this publication blows away the smoke screen hanging over 4 June 1989.

Another 1.1 million serve in the People's Armed Police. China is divided into seven military regions, each with its own military leadership – in some cases with strong regional affiliations.

China's president, Hu Jintao, is also chairman of the Central Military Commission and so head of the PLA. Along with his status as the General-Secretary of the CCP, it means that Hu holds the three most powerful positions in China. Born in 1942 in Anhui province and trained as an engineer (like many of China's most senior politicians) at Běijīng's prestigious Tsinghua University, Hu is the first of China's presidents to have joined the CCP after the 1949 revolution.

Although Hu, who is said to have a photographic memory and to be a keen ballroom dancer, often appears enigmatic in his public appearances, he has consistently shown his ability to out-manoeuvre his political opponents. Having inherited a government packed with previous President Jiang Zemin's supporters, known as the 'Shanghai Gang' (because so many of them rose to power in Shànghǎi), Hu has edged some of them out while promoting his own protégés who, like him, had begun their careers in the Communist Youth League.

He has also shown a fierce determination to reinforce the CCP's dominant position in China, as well as promoting his vision of a 'Harmonious Society', something which owes much to the teachings of Confucius. In 2006, he launched the 'Eight Honours and Eight Disgraces' (Bā Rong Bā Chi) campaign in an effort to restore the Chinese people's faith in the CCP. The campaign calls on party members to avoid greed and corruption, while thinking always of society's needs rather than those of the individual.

That the CCP's 70 million members need an image overhaul is obvious. Rising discontent over official corruption, along with anger over illegal land seizures and damage to the environment, routinely spills over into violence. There were 74,000 violent protests across China in 2004 according to the government. That number declined by 22% in 2005, but included one protest over the construction of a power station in Guangdong province that saw members of the People's Armed Police open fire on demonstrators for the first time since the student protests in Tiananmen Square in June 1989.

While such a harsh reaction is uncommon, the authorities continue to be ruthless in their treatment of those they regard as their enemies. Environmental activists, crusading lawyers, investigative journalists and members of banned groups such as the Falun Gong all risk imprisonment because of their activities. But thanks to mobile phones and the spread of the internet, it is now far harder for the government to prevent news of protests from leaking out. And with an ever-growing gap between the rich and the poor fuelling discontent, it will only get harder for the CCP to maintain its grip on China.

ENVIRONMENT

China's breakneck economic growth over the past few decades has both depleted resources and generated vast quantities of pollution. Long-distance train travellers through China will be familiar with a bleak landscape of fields and trees choked with shredded non-biodegradable plastic bags. Successful economic renewal provides the CCP with a tenuous mandate to rule, so green issues and sustainable development policies have long taken a back seat to short-term political planning. More and more Chinese are becoming aware of the need to protect what is left of the environment – there are now over 2000 environmental groups in China – but the laws for protecting the environment are often not rigorously enforced, or are flouted at the local level by corrupt cadres.

Běijīng is under tremendous pressure to clean itself up for the 2008 Olympics. Various measures have been introduced to clean the air, including encouraging the use of natural gas and electricity rather than the traditional circular coal briquettes (fēngwōméi) for winter heating, replacing diesel buses with ones powered by natural gas, and closing heavily polluting industries, or moving them out of the city. But Běijīng still consumed 55 million tonnes of coal in 2005 and along with the burgeoning number of cars on the roads, and the dust from thousands of construction sites, it demonstrates that air pollution is as bad, if not worse, than ever.

For the Olympics, drastic temporary measures will be taken to ensure that the athletes don't have to compete in a haze of smog. Construction sites will be closed down two months before the Games start, as will polluting industries, while private cars are likely to be banned

DUST DEVIL

You've heard of the Gobi and you may have heard of the Takla Makan, but did you know that Běijīng may one day be another of China's deserts? The Gobi Desert is just 150km from Běijīng and winds are blowing the sands towards the capital at a rate of 2km a year, with dunes up to 30m high wriggling ever closer.

In 2006, Běijīng was hit by eight major sandstorms that coated the city in choking yellow dust. One particularly vicious storm dumped 330,000 tonnes of dust on the capital. Experts blame overgrazing and deforestation; without grassland and tree cover, and with a dropping water table, the deserts are on a roll, overwhelming villages in northern China. The Gobi Desert is expanding towards the south at a rate of 2.4% per year, extinguishing the grasslands. Every month, 200 sq km of arable land in China becomes desert.

According to the United Nation's Office to Combat Desertification and Drought (UNSO), a third of China is subject to desertification – the process by which previously semi-arable or arable land gradually becomes depleted of plant and animal life.

The Chinese government has been jolted into pledging a massive US$6.8 billion to stop the spread of the sand. A green wall, which will eventually stretch 5700km – longer than the Great Wall – is being planted in northeastern China to keep back the sand, though some experts argue that it is not tree but grass cover that best binds the soil.

from the roads for the duration of the Games. The capital's 160 parks, oases of green in a mostly concrete city, are being renovated and prettified ahead of the Olympics too.

Apart from air pollution, Běijīng's most pressing environmental problem is the lack of water. The occasional summer rainstorm aside, Běijīng is badly dehydrated. It is so arid that old anti-aircraft guns positioned around the city are routinely used to fire shells containing rain-inducing chemicals into the clouds. This 'cloud seeding' will be used during the Olympics to wash away the haze.

Běijīng and much of north China now faces an acute water shortage, with dropping water tables and shrinking reservoirs. Increased water use in and around Běijīng – and upstream along the Yellow River – has resulted in more and more water being extracted from the ground. Crisis point will come in 2010 when Běijīng's population is expected to top 17 million, three million more than available resources can supply. Although the gargantuan south–north water transfer project will start supplying the city with water directly pumped from the flood-prone Yangtze River in 2008, Běijīngers face the very real possibility of water rationing in the future.

Běijīng is the most polluted of the major cities, using measurements of the number of micrograms of particles of pollution dust per cubic metre. Beijing's level is 142 micrograms, compared to the averages of Paris (22), London (24) and New York (27). The World Health Organization (WHO) guideline is 20.

URBAN PLANNING

The demands of a rapidly increasing population and ballooning vehicle numbers have put Běijīng's transport and housing infrastructure under duress. But netting the 2008 Olympics has given the city a chance to grab the bull by the horns. Millions of square feet of real estate space are under construction, with the total amount of office space expected to double by 2008. The subway is undergoing a massive extension and roads are being widened, with the Chinese character *chāi* (for 'demolition') daubed in white on condemned buildings city-wide.

But Běijīng's metamorphosis is not all roses – huge building projects have relocated over 100,000, often elderly, urban residents. Some have moved willingly while others have tried to resist, but with the state owning all property in Běijīng, protesters can do little to confront police. A third of Běijīng's *hútòng* within the Second Ring Rd have been demolished and, because the remainder sit on immensely valuable land, they continue to be demolished, albeit not at the rapid rate they once were. Before 1949, Běijīng had 3600 *hútòng;* now there are just 500.

Běijīng planners say that it's easy for foreign observers to condemn the destruction, remarking that Běijīng needs to modernise like any other city. Nonetheless, the identity of the city is undergoing an irreversible transformation. At the time of writing, there was an increasing awareness of the need to protect what is left of *lǎo* (old) Běijīng and a halt had been called to major demolition projects ahead of the Olympics. But once the Games have been and gone, no one is sure what will happen.

Arts & Architecture

Arts & Architecture

ARTS

The arts scene in Běijīng has come a long way in the past two decades, with a once underground arts movement now firmly established above ground. Following alongside China's dizzying social and economic transformation, Běijīng artists are riding a wave of creative energy that's putting many of them on the international map. With its excellent cinema, theatre, music and visual arts venues, the capital serves as the most important meeting place for artists in China and is an excellent place to see for yourself the enduring vitality of Chinese traditional and contemporary arts.

LITERATURE

Běijīng has been home to some of China's towering literary figures, including such heavyweights as Lao She, Lu Xun, Mao Dun and Guo Moruo. Over the past 100 years, Běijīng writers have penned their stories of sorrow, fears and aspirations amid a context of ever-changing trends and political upheaval. Nowadays, with the explosion of the internet and popular culture, there's an enormous flurry of literary activity, ranging from politics to pulp, from blogs to porn. Běijīng remains one of China's most important literary centres, with a dynamic group of writers, many young and upcoming, who are turning the Chinese writing scene on its head.

Contemporary Chinese literature is commonly grouped into two stages: pre-1989 and post-1989. After China came under the control of the communists, most writing in 20th-century China tended to echo the Communist Party line, with dull, formulaic language and humdrum plotlines. Writers were required to fill their work with stock phrases such as 'the great, glorious, correct Communist Party' and create cardboard characters that embodied political ideals. Writing was banal and unimaginative, with little allowance for creative embellishment.

After Mao's death in 1976, Chinese artists and writers threw off political constraints and began to write more freely, exploring new modes of literary expression. Western books began to appear in translation, including works by authors such as Faulkner, Woolf and Hemingway. The Chinese also developed a taste for more mainstream fare like Kurt Vonnegut and even Jackie Collins. This deluge of Western writing had a great impact on many Chinese authors who were exposed for the first time to a wide array of literary techniques and styles.

An important writer to emerge during this period is Zhang Jie, who first drew the attention of literary critics in the late 1970s with the publication of her daring novella *Love Must Not Be Forgotten* (1979). The book challenged the traditional structure of marriage with its intimate portrayal of a middle-aged woman and her love of a married man. Chinese authorities disparaged the book, calling it morally corrupt, but the book was extremely popular with readers and won a national book award. Zhang went on to write the novels *Heavy Wings* (1980) and *The Ark* (1981). *The Ark*, about three women separated from their husbands, established Zhang as China's 'first feminist author'. Shen Rong was another talented female author to appear during the 1980s. Her novella *At Middle Age* (1980), tells the plight of a Chinese intellectual during the Cultural Revolution who must balance her family life with her career as a doctor.

Several literary movements appeared during the late 1970s and 1980s, including a movement called 'Scar Literature', in which writers for the first time dared to explore the traumatic events of the Cultural Revolution. Another literary movement that also emerged was called 'New Realism', which explored issues that were previously taboo, such as AIDS, party corruption and other contemporary social problems. One of the most controversial novels to appear in the 1980s was *Half of Man is Woman*, by Zhang Xianliang and translated into English by Martha Avery. The novel gives a candid exploration of sexuality and marriage in contemporary China and Zhang's book became an international bestseller. Another of Zhang's works that has been translated into English is *Getting Used to Dying* (1989), about a writer's new-found sexual freedom, also translated by Martha Avery.

After the tragic events of 1989 the desire for a more 'realist' type of literature grew in China, paving the way for a new group of writers, such as the now internationally recognised 'hooligan author' Wang Shuo, a sailor turned fiction writer, who has become known for his satirical stories about China's underworld and political corruption. Wang's stories, which are dark, gritty and take jabs at just about every aspect of contemporary Chinese society, have made him none too popular among Chinese authorities, who believe him to be a 'spiritual pollutant' and a bad influence on his readers. One of Wang's most contentious novels, *Please Don't Call Me Human*, first published in 1989, was written after the events of Tiananmen Square and provides a mocking look at the failures of China's state security system. Wang's works appeal to a broad spectrum of Chinese society, despite being banned. He has written over 20 books as well as screenplays for TV and film. Books available in English include *Playing for Thrills* (2000) and *Please Don't Call Me Human* (1998), both translated by Howard Goldblatt.

The literature that came out of the 1990s was certainly a far cry from the Maoist tracts of earlier years. The 1990s saw an explosion of experimental writing, with many works probing the boundaries of risky and often controversial subjects. Wang Meng, former minister of culture, became famous for his stream-of-consciousness style of writing and his satirical take on everything from politics to Chinese medicine. His collection of short stories, *The Stubborn Porridge and Other Stories* (1994), translated by Zhu Hong, is a smart, scathing look at modern Chinese society. The composer, playwright and author Liu Sola, who began writing in the mid-1980s, became internationally recognised a decade later with her novel *Chaos and All That* (1994), translated by Richard King, about a Chinese woman in London who writes a novel about growing up in Běijīng during the Cultural Revolution.

BĚIJĪNG BOOKSHELF

- *Diary of a Madman and Other Stories* (1990) – by Lu Xun, translated by William Lyell. Lu Xun is considered the father of modern Chinese literature and this classic was the first of its kind to be written in a first-person narrative. The story is a criticism of Confucian repression in pre-revolutionary China. *Diary of a Madman* was also the first short story written in *baihua* (colloquial speech) apart from its first paragraph.
- *Camel Xiangzi* (1981) – by Lao She, translated by Shi Xiaoqing. A masterpiece by one of China's most beloved authors about a rickshaw puller living in early-20th-century China.
- *Blades of Grass: The Stories of Lao She* (2000) – translated by William Lyell. This collection contains 14 stories by Lao She – poignant descriptions of people living through times of political upheaval and uncertainty.
- *Beijinger in New York* (1993) – by Glen Cao, translated by Ted Wang. The author's own immigrant story about a young Běijīng couple in New York and their difficult transition to life in the West.
- *Black Snow* (1993) – by Liu Heng, translated by Howard Goldblatt. Liu Heng, author of the story that formed the basis for the film, *Ju Dou*, wrote this compelling novel about workers in contemporary Běijīng. A superbly written book and a fine translation.
- *Empress Orchid* – Anchee Min (2004). Historical novel about Empress Cixi and her rise to Empress of China during the last days of the Qing dynasty. Good historical background of Běijīng and entertaining to read.
- *Peking Story: The Last Days of Old China* (2003) – David Kidd. This is a true story of a young man who marries the daughter of an aristocratic Chinese family in Běijīng two years before the 1949 Communist Revolution. The writing is simple, yet immersive.
- *Beijing: A Novel* (2003) – by Philip Gambone. A well-written account of an American working in a medical clinic in Běijīng who falls in love with a local artist. One of the few books out there to explore in depth the intricacies of Běijīng gay subculture.
- *The Noodle Maker* (2004) – by Ma Jian, translated by Flora Drew. A collection of interconnected stories as told by a state-employed writer during the aftermath of Tiananmen Square. Bleak, comical and unforgettable.
- *Sounds of the River: A Young Man's University Days in Beijing* (2003) – by Da Chen. A humorous account of the author's life as a student in Běijīng. The writing is lyrical and uplifting.
- *Lake with No Name* (2004) – by Diane Wei Liang. An intelligent memoir of a young woman's involvement in the events leading up to 4 June 1989. The author writes movingly of her relationships with many of the activists involved.
- *Foreign Babes in Beijing: Behind the Scenes of a New China* (2005) – by Rachel Dewoskin. An easy-going account of a young woman's five years spent in Běijīng during the mid-1990s.

China's rampant commercialisation and excessive materialism have given an emerging generation of authors a new platform. Younger authors, who remember nothing about the Cultural Revolution and to whom the events at Tiananmen Square remain a vague memory, are writing instead about the loneliness and decadence of modern city life. Escapism is a common theme in contemporary novels, often through sex, drugs and alcohol. The provocative novel *Beijing Doll* (2004), by Chun Shu (Sue), translated by Howard Goldblatt, is written by a high school dropout who lives a life of sex, drugs and alcohol. Called a 'punk memoir', the book is currently banned in China for its disturbing account of teenagers caught up in Běijīng's dark underbelly. Annie Wang's *The People's Republic of Desire* (2006) also holds nothing back with its candid exploration of sexuality in modern Běijīng. The acclaimed novelist Ma Jian also picks up on the theme of escapism, but infuses his work with a sense of nostalgia. *Red Dust* (2004) by Ma Jian, translated by Flora Drew, is a poignant story of the author's three-year trek through Guizhou, Burma and Tibet. One of the most moving works to appear in English within the past few years is *A Thousand Years of Good Prayers* (2006) by Yiyun Li. The short stories in this collection, told in haunting prose, reveal the lives of ordinary Chinese caught up in the sweeping cultural changes of the past twenty years. This book won the Guardian First Book Award in 2006.

Over the past several years the internet has given rise to a vibrant, alternative literary scene. A large number of established and wannabe authors are posting their poetry,

CHINA'S CONTEMPORARY ART SCENE David Eimer

When Brian Wallace arrived in China as a backpacker in 1984 there was no visible contemporary art scene. Artists were viewed with suspicion and were frequently subject to harassment and worse by the authorities. They showed their work to each other and their friends only inside the safety of their own homes. But just as China has transformed itself into an economic powerhouse, so Chinese artists have made the long march from obscurity to global recognition and their work has become prized by both mainland Chinese art collectors and foreigners.

Part of that success is due to Wallace, an Australian who grew up in a small country town in New South Wales. Having returned to China to live in 1986, he opened the **Red Gate Gallery** (p79), Běijīng's first space devoted to contemporary art, in the imposing Southeast Corner Watchtower in 1991. In 2005, he opened his second gallery in the flourishing 798 Art District in Dashanzi (p103).

Wallace represents, or has represented, just about every contemporary Chinese artist of note. His role in helping develop China's booming art scene means he's often referred to as the 'father of contemporary Chinese art'. 'Other people have said that. I would never say it,' protests the amiable, bearded Wallace. In fact, when he started out in the late '80s, it was a simple case of helping out mates. 'My friends were artists and in those days there were no galleries, so we started to organise exhibitions for them.'

Things have changed dramatically since then. Paintings by artists like Fang Lijun, Zhang Xiaogang and Yue Minjun can fetch US$1 million at auction, as the advent of mainland Chinese buyers has helped drive prices up. 'In the last couple of years, galleries overseas have started to pick up on contemporary Chinese artists, museums have started to buy and now the auction houses have kicked in. Their job is to talk up the market of course, which they've been doing quite well,' says Wallace.

Painters and sculptors are the artists who've benefited the most from the boom. 'The more traditional forms are the most popular. The market for photography has eased off a bit. Mainland buyers, who make up 20% of our customers, are more conservative than overseas buyers. They like the contemporary work, but they stick to paintings rather than the more conceptual stuff,' points out Wallace. Nor have female artists prospered as much as the men. 'I think it's more difficult for women artists. They don't necessarily hold up half the sky in the art world.'

In the past, Chinese artists were often accused of being derivative and in thrall to their Western contemporaries. Wallace believes that's no longer the case. 'They went through a period where they absorbed everything, but now they're much more confident and appreciative of the attention they're getting. The stamp of approval gives them a lot of confidence. There's a lot of gutsy stuff out their now.'

While China's filmmakers and writers are still subject to stringent censorship, the visual arts have been treated more leniently. 'The government has accepted, or realised, that young artists aren't going to bring down the country,' says Wallace. 'But we know the political limits and we have had to take shows down in the past when they've been over-the-top politically.'

With an ever-increasing range of art available, visitors to Běijīng who want to buy a piece can find something to suit every taste and price range. 'You can get some very valuable prints by very important artists for hundreds of dollars, or we can sell you a large oil painting for US$200,000', says Wallace. With the demand for Chinese art set to continue, you could end up with a bargain.

personal diaries and even novels on the internet and attracting huge numbers of readers. It's estimated that there are over 17 million blogs in China and that number is growing. Government censors find it difficult to control works on the 'net, in contrast to the tight editorial controls on print media. Authors often blog away about controversial topics such as sex and politics without too much fear of political repercussion. Lin Qianyu is the latest in a number of internet celebrities. He's a 19-year-old high school dropout whose fantasy novel *Carefree: A Crusade Legend* won the grand prize in Sina.com's (www .sina.com; the largest Chinese-language web portal in the world) online writing competition. Writer Ning Ken's story *The Veiled City* was posted online and landed him the Lao She Literary Award, one of the most prestigious awards in China.

VISUAL ARTS

With scores of private and state-run galleries and a booming art market, Běijīng is a fantastic place to witness the changing face of contemporary art in China. While traditional Chinese art is still practised in the capital, Běijīng is also home to a large community of artists practising a diverse mix of art forms including performance art, installation, video art and film. Běijīng artists commonly compete internationally in art events, and joint exhibitions with European and North American artists are common. The capital plays host to a number of art festivals, including the Dashanzi International Arts Festival, held every spring, and the Běijīng Biennale, held every two years in September/October, which attract artists, dealers and critics from around the world. Greater freedom from government control and international recognition has helped many Běijīng artists reach new levels of economic success and some have even entered the pop cultural mainstream.

Similar to what was happening in the Chinese literary scene, Chinese artists experienced a creative renaissance after the death of Mao in 1976. Some painters began using the realist techniques they learned in China's art academies to portray the harsh realities of Chinese peasant life in modern day China. Others broke away from the confines of 'socialist realism' and moved into broader territory, experimenting with a variety of contemporary forms. Many turned to the West for inspiration and tried to incorporate Western ideas into their works.

One such group of artists, the Stars, found inspiration in Picasso and German Expressionism. The short-lived group was very important for the development of Chinese art in the 1980s and 1990s, leading the way for the New Wave movement that appeared in 1985. New Wave artists were greatly influenced by Western art, especially Marcel Duchamp, and through their work challenged traditional Chinese aesthetics. One New Wave artist, Huang Yongping, became known for destroying his works at exhibitions, in an effort to escape from the notion of 'art'. Some New Wave artists transformed Chinese characters into abstract symbols while others used graphic images in their work in order to shock viewers.

Performance art also became popular, with many artists wrapping themselves in plastic or tape to symbolise the repressive realities of modern day China.

The pivotal turning point for contemporary Chinese art came in 1989. In February of that year, Běijīng's China Art Museum (p85) sponsored an exhibit devoted exclusively to Chinese avant-garde art for the first time, inviting all of the important artists of the past decade to exhibit. On the opening day of the exhibition, artists Tang Song and Xiao Lu fired pistol shots at their own installations and the exhibition closed. Both artists were arrested but released several days later.

The upsetting events that followed June 1989 caused many artists to become disillusioned with the current political situation in China and idealism soon soured into cynicism. This attitude is reflected through the 1990s and artworks are permeated with feelings of loss, loneliness and social isolation. Many artists left China to find greater artistic freedom in the West. Two of the most important Běijīng artists to characterise this period of 'Cynical Realism' are Fang Lijun and Yue Minjun. Both created grotesque portraits of themselves and friends that convey a sense of boredom and mock joviality.

Experiments with American-style pop art were another reaction to the events of 1989. Inspired by Warhol, some artists took symbols of socialist realism and transformed them into kitschy visual commentary. Images of Mao appeared against floral backgrounds and paintings of rosy-cheeked peasants and soldiers were interspersed with ads for Canon cameras and Coca-Cola. Artists were not only responding to the tragedies of the Tiananmen massacre but also to the rampant consumerism that was sweeping the country.

Reaction to the rapid modernisation that is affecting Běijīng as well as other Chinese cities has been a current theme of much of the art from the 1990s to the present day. Urban development and accompanying feelings of isolation and dislocation are themes of Běijīng video artist Zhu Jia. In his video titled 'Double Landscape', a man is being served coffee by a mannequin dressed as a woman. The banality of the video and its lack of drama or narrative are meant to be representative of the meaninglessness of urban existence. The artist Yin Xiuzhen has become internationally renowned for her artistic commentaries (eg visual installations) on globalisation, urban waste and the destruction of Běijīng's traditional architecture.

Throughout the 1990s, artists who felt marginalised from the cultural mainstream found escape from political scrutiny by setting up their own exhibitions in non-official spaces outside of state-run institutions. Many relied on the financial support of foreign buyers to continue working. Despite political pressure from authorities, some artists began to receive international attention for their art, sparking a worldwide interest in Chinese art. A defining moment for artists was in 1999, when 20 Chinese artists were invited to participate in the Venice Biennale for the first time.

In just a few short years, the art climate in Běijīng has changed dramatically. Many artists who left China in the 1990s have returned, setting up private studios and galleries. Government censorship remains, but authorities often turn a blind eye to work once considered politically subversive. It's estimated that in 2006, there were more than 300 art galleries in Běijīng, the majority opened after 2001. Half of these galleries are Chinese-owned, and as well there are dozens of foreign galleries that have opened branches in Běijīng.

Dashanzi, a factory-turned-gallery zone in northeastern Běijīng is a favourite destination for artists and buyers. Created in 2001, this once quiet enclave has transformed into a thriving neighbourhood of lofts, galleries, bookshops, design studios, cafés and bars, all tucked into a small section of Dashanzi called 798 Art District (p103) – named after Factory 798, a disused electronics factory complex built in the 1950s by East German architects. Here, Mao's ideals are reinterpreted through the artistic works of China's new visionaries, resulting in a lively, enigmatic and sometimes controversial community that attracts artists, dealers and critics from around the world. For an excellent behind-the-scenes look at the vibrant Dashanzi art community, be sure to get your hands on *Beijing 798: Reflections on Art, Architecture and Society in China,* edited by Běijīng artist Huang Rui.

TOP TEN BĚIJĪNG ART GALLERIES

- Courtyard Gallery (p86) – This contemporary Chinese art gallery has recently relocated from its Forbidden City location to Caochandi, a few kilometres northeast of the 798 Art District.
- Red Gate Gallery (p79) – Founded by an Australian, this gallery has a focus on contemporary Chinese art.
- 25000 Cultural Transmission Center – Also known as 'The Long March Space,' the 25000 Cultural Transmission Center promotes artistic works often excluded from Běijīng's mainstream art scene.
- Wan Fung Art Gallery (p77) – Gallery representing contemporary artists working in traditional painting, oil painting, watercolour painting, sculpture and mixed media.
- 798 Art Space (p103) – German Bauhaus warehouse (gallery within 798 Art District) with over 1200 sq metres of art space exhibiting works of Chinese contemporary artists.
- China Art Archives and Warehouse – Exhibition space devoted to experimental art in China.
- L.A. Gallery Beijing – Gallery dedicated to cultural exchange between artists internationally.
- Chinese Contemporary Art Gallery – This gallery shows mainly group exhibitions of contemporary Chinese artists.
- Millennium Art Museum – Also called the World Art Museum, this museum exhibits ancient and modern art from around the globe.
- China Art Museum (p85) – This was the first gallery in Běijīng to exhibit modern Western artworks and remains a pivotal institution in China's contemporary art scene.

TRADITIONAL CHINESE PAINTING

The origins of Chinese painting lie in the Bronze Age, beginning with representational figures of humans, animals and demons inscribed on bronze vessels. The emphasis on brushwork and line in these works was and remains the defining element of traditional Chinese painting. In fact, the character *hua*, 'to paint', represents a brush tracing the boundaries of a field. While Western painting values colour, composition and texture, the quality of a Chinese painting has shown from early on the great importance placed on brush technique.

Painting flourished during the Tang dynasty (AD 618–907). The most painted subjects were scenes of court life, as well as animals. The Tang also saw a rise in the popularity of landscape painting. The idyllic natural worlds depicted in Tang landscapes are beautifully detailed in brilliant washes of blues and greens.

During the Northern (AD 960–1127) and Southern Song (1127–1279) dynasties landscape painting rose to new heights of excellence. Song painters preferred moody, romantic landscapes with mist-covered mountains and imaginary locales.

With the Mongol invasion in the 13th century, Yuan dynasty (1279–1368) painting took on a much different tone to that of the Song dynasty. Yuan paintings have large empty spaces and are quite austere compared to those of the Tang and Song.

The Ming (1368–1644) and Qing dynasties (1644–1911) saw a return to earlier styles of painting. Conventional subject matter was conveyed in startling new ways, with more emphasis on patterns and bright colours.

MUSIC

In 1986 during a 'World Peace' music concert held in Běijīng, a young trumpet player named Cui Jian walked on stage, strapped on a guitar and played a song that would forever change the sound and look of Chinese popular music. With its distinctly abrasive vocal style and lyrics describing feelings of loneliness and alienation, 'Nothing To My Name' ('Yi Wo Suo You') was unlike any song ever performed by a mainland Chinese musician.

For early Chinese rock bands like Tang Dynasty and Black Panther, the riffs and power chords of heavy metal from the '70s and '80s (ie Led Zeppelin and Rush) provided the inspiration to pick up guitars, grow long hair and start a band. This 'First Generation' of Chinese rockers took inspiration from classic rock, heavy metal, and punk's aggression and abrasiveness.

Since those early days, Chinese rock has continued to flourish and Běijīng has gained the reputation as China's rock-music mecca. Acts like ambient breakbeaters Supermarket, post-punk outfit SUBS, metal groups Spring and Autumn (Chunqiu), Suffocation (Zhixi) and Ritual Day (Shijiao Ri), and the Nirvana- and Doors-influenced Cold Blooded Animals, share the stage at Běijīng's numerous live-music venues (see p148) with rockers Black Panther, Sand (Shazi), Xiao He, the highly popular Second Hand Roses (Ershou Meigui) and more established acts. Look out also for hip-hop acts Dragon Tongue, CMBC and MC Da Kuan.

DJ culture has also come to China with Běijīng's new wave of clubs. Club-goers can now get their grooves on to the booming sounds of hip-hop, house, drum-and-bass, techno and trance in addition to the popular sounds of home-grown Chinese house music.

This infusion of new styles and sounds has left an indelible impression on Chinese society, especially its youth culture. Today the sight of a long-haired Běijīng homeboy with a guitar strapped to his back is about as common as that of a cigarette vendor or taxi driver. TV music programmes and radio shows play songs by rock acts almost as frequently as they do pop crooners and divas, while even hotel bars feature rock bands on a regular basis. Indeed, with such an infusion of new sounds and styles it appears that Chinese rock is here to stay.

Rock festivals worth looking out for include the open-air MIDI Music Festival at the Beijing MIDI School of Music (☎ 6259 0101, 6259 0007) – held every October (changed from May) when a vast array of heavy metal, punk and jazz bands perform live. Another excellent festival is the Beijing Pop Festival (www.beijingpopfestival.com/music) held every September in Chaoyang Park. In 2006, the venue sold 12,000 tickets and featured the international acts Supergrass, Placebo, Norway's Don Juan Dracula, and local hard rockers AK47 and Muma.

For classical music and opera lovers, the five-day International Music Festival is held every May and attracts internationally renowned composers from China and abroad. Performances are held at the Central Conservatory of Music and the Beijing Concert Hall (p150). The Beijing Music Festival (www.bmf.org.cn) is held for around 30 days during the months of October and November and features musical performances by opera, jazz and classical artists from around the world. For live music venues, see p148.

TRADITIONAL CHINESE MUSIC

The Chinese believed that the chimes of the large sets of bells (seen in Confucian temples and at the Great Bell Temple in Běijīng) corresponded with the *dào* (way). A concordant pitch would signify all was well between heaven and earth. Similarly, the Chinese believe that all music influences the equilibrium of the *dào*.

Historically, music served a ceremonial or religious function, rather than as entertainment. Confucian students studied music not to rouse the emotions, but to seek inner quietude and balance. The *Book of Songs (Shījīng)* and the *Book of Rites (Lǐjì)*, two books of the Confucian canon, dwell on song, the rhythms of life and the function of music. It fell to folk song traditions to reflect the musical enjoyment of the common people and China's rich ethnic mix.

Traditional Chinese musical instruments include the two-stringed fiddle (*èrhú*) – famed for its desolate wail – the two-stringed viola (*húqín*), the vertical flute (*dòngxiāo*), the horizontal flute (*dízi*), the four-stringed lute (*pípa*) and the Chinese zither (*zhēng*).

To appreciate traditional music in Běijīng, catch performances at the **Lao She Teahouse** (p147) or the **Sanwei Bookstore** (p148).

CINEMA & TV

The cinematic output of Fifth Generation directors, whose works were received with standing ovations worldwide in the 1980s and 1990s, was a high-point for Chinese film. *Farewell My Concubine* (1993), directed by Chen Kaige, and *Raise the Red Lantern* (1991), directed by Zhang Yimou, were garlanded with praise and reaped several major film awards. The lavish tragedies, starring icons such as Gong Li, radiated a beauty that entranced Western audiences and made their directors the darlings of Cannes.

Sixth Generation film directors shunned the exquisite beauty and lush palette of the Fifth Generation and rendered instead the angst and grimness of modern urban Chinese life. Their independent, low-budget works put an entirely different spin on mainland Chinese filmmaking, but their dour subject matter and harsh film style (frequently in black and white) left many Western viewers cold.

The Beijing Film Academy graduate Zhang Yuan set a precedent for gritty, independent filmmaking with *Mama* (1990), a beautiful but disturbing film about a mother and her autistic child. This small film, created without government sponsorship, had a large influence on future filmmakers. Zhang followed up *Mama* with *Beijing Bastards* (1993), which focussed on the preoccupations and drug-taking lifestyle of Běijīng's youth. Another important film, *Frozen* (1995), directed by Wang Xiaoshuai, also strayed into controversial territory with its disturbing examination of suicide. *Beijing Bicycle* (2001), also directed by Wang Xiaoshuai and inspired by De Sica's *Bicycle Thieves*, is a tale of a Běijīng youth seeking to recover his stolen bike.

Today, except for a few directors who are able to attract domestic and overseas investments, such as Zhang Yimou and Chen Kaige, Chinese filmmakers are constantly dealing with a shortage of funds, small audiences and high ticket prices. To cap it all, many Sixth Generation films went unseen inside China. Both Fifth and Sixth Generation directors have constantly run into problems with the authorities and the most controversial were clipped by the censors or banned outright. Other retaliatory measures included revoking their passports so they could not attend foreign film festivals. Regardless, the movie industry carries on, producing surprisingly high-quality films on tiny budgets.

Some of the most intriguing movies of the past few years include the films of Feng Xiaogang, known for *Big Shot's Funeral* (2001, starring Donald Sutherland) and most recently *The Banquet* (2006), a lavish historical epic starring China's new leading lady Zhang Ziyi. On a much simpler note, Zhang Yuan's *Little Red Flowers* (2006) is a poignant story of a young boy adapting to the rigid conformity of Chinese kindergarten and is well-worth seeing. A film that caused a buzz at international film festivals is Jia Zhangke's *The World* (2005), which follows the lives of youth and migrant workers employed at a Běijīng theme park. A good place to screen Chinese films by established and emerging directors is at the Beijing Student Film Festival, a 20-day event held every April. Films are shown at various venues around the city – you can check *That's Beijing* (www .thatsbj.com) for screen times.

On TV, most Chinese prefer to watch contemporary sitcoms and soaps imported from South Korea or Japan (collectively called *rìhánjù*, literally 'series from Japan and South Korea') or films made in Hong Kong and Taiwan (collectively called *gǎngtáipiàn*), rather than those produced locally. Chinese productions portraying contemporary life fail to depict the world realistically, but Chinese viewers lap up the ubiquitous Chinese historical costume dramas.

PERFORMING ARTS
Theatre

As spoken drama is a recent introduction to China and opera traditionally took the place of storytelling, theatre remains an emergent art. An increasing number of theatrical companies are coming to Běijīng from abroad, however, and local theatre companies are staging more and more productions, many of which are influenced by Western technique and content. For stage events in Běijīng, consult the stage listings of *That's Beijing*.

Opera

Beijing opera is still regarded as the *crème de la crème* of all the opera styles prevalent in China and has traditionally been the opera of the masses. Intrigues, disasters or rebellions usually inspire themes, and many have their source in the fairy tales and stock characters and legends of classical literature.

The music, singing and costumes are products of the opera's origins. Formerly, opera was performed mostly on open-air stages in markets, streets, teahouses or temple courtyards. The orchestra had to play loudly and the performers had to develop a piercing style of singing, which could be heard over the throng. The costumes are a garish collection of sharply contrasting colours because the stages were originally lit by oil lamps.

The movements and techniques of the dance styles of the Tang dynasty are similar to those of today's opera. Provincial opera companies were characterised by their dialect and style of singing, but when these companies converged on Běijīng they started a style of musical drama called *kunqu*. This developed during the Ming dynasty, along with a more popular variety of

---

BEST FILMS ABOUT BĚIJĪNG

- *Beijing Bicycle* (2001) – Eschewing the lavish colour of Fifth Generation directors and observing Běijīng through a realist lens, Wang Xiaoshuai's film follows young and hapless courier Guo on the trail of his stolen mountain bike.
- *The Last Emperor* (1987) – Bernardo Bertolucci's celebrated (seven Oscars including best director, best costume design and best cinematography) and extravagant epic charts the life of Henry Puyi during his accession and the ensuing disintegration of dynastic China.
- *Beijing Bastards* (1993) – Starring rocker Cui Jian, Yuan Zhang's documentary-style cinematography tags along with a rock band in Běijīng, grittily capturing the energy of Běijīng's alienated and discontented youth.
- *The Gate of Heavenly Peace* (1995) – Using original footage from the six weeks preceding the Tiananmen massacre, Richard Gordon and Carma Hinton's moving three-hour tribute to the spirit of the student movement and its annihilation is a must-see.
- *Farewell My Concubine* (1993) – Charting a dramatic course through 20th-century Chinese history from the 1920s to the Cultural Revolution, Chen Kaige's film is a sumptuous and stunning narrative of two friends from the Beijing opera school whose lives are framed against social and political turmoil.
- *The Making of Steel* (1998) – Lu Xuecheng directed this intriguing film about a rebellious young man and his involvement in Běijīng's underground music scene during the 1970s and 1990s.
- *The World* (2005) – Jia Zhangke's social commentary on the effects of globalisation is set in a Běijīng theme park called 'World Park', where workers and visitors play out their lives among replicas of the world's monuments.
- *Blooming Flowers in Springtime* (2002) – This exquisitely beautiful short film by Chang Zheng tells the story of a young deaf-mute couple in Běijīng and the trials of bringing up their hearing son.
- *Shower* (1999) – Though at times overly sentimental, this endearing film about a bathhouse owner and his sons warmed the hearts of both Chinese and foreign audiences. Directed by Zhang Yang.
- *For Fun* (1992) – Directed by Ning Ying, China's most renowned female filmmaker, this film follows the life of a retired custodian at a Beijing opera theatre and his humorous attempts to transform a group of grumpy senior citizens into opera singers.

THE WHO'S WHO OF BEIJING OPERA

There are four types of actors' role: the *shēng*, *dàn*, *jìng* and *chǒu*. The *shēng* are the leading male actors and they play scholars, officials, warriors and the like. They are divided into the *laoshēng*, who wear beards and represent old men, and the *xiǎoshēng*, who represent young men. The *wénshēng* are the scholars and the civil servants. The *wushēng* play soldiers and other fighters, and because of this are specially trained in acrobatics.

The *dàn* are the female roles. The *lǎodàn* are the elderly, dignified ladies such as mothers, aunts and widows. The *qīngyī* are aristocratic ladies in elegant costumes. The *huādàn* are the ladies' maids, usually in brightly coloured costumes. The *dǎomǎdàn* are the warrior women. The *cǎidàn* are the female comedians. Traditionally, female roles were played by male actors, but now they are almost always played by females.

The *jìng* are the painted-face roles and they represent warriors, heroes, statesmen, adventurers and demons. Their counterparts are the *fújìng*, ridiculous figures who are anything but heroic.

The *chou* is basically the clown. The *cǎidàn* is sometimes the female counterpart of this male role.

play-acting pieces based on legends, historical events and popular novels. These styles gradually merged by the late 18th and early 19th centuries into the opera we see today.

The musicians usually sit on the stage in plain clothes and play without written scores. The *èrhú*, a two-stringed fiddle that is tuned to a low register and has a soft tone, generally supports the *húqín*, a two-stringed viola tuned to a high register. The *yùeqín*, a sort of moon-shaped four-stringed guitar, has a soft tone and is used to support the *èrhú*. Other instruments are the *shēng* (a reed flute) and the *pípa* (lute), as well as drums, bells and cymbals. Last but not least is the *ban*, a time-clapper that virtually directs the band, beats time for the actors and gives them their cues.

Apart from the singing and the music, the opera also incorporates acrobatics and mime. Few props are used, so each move, gesture or facial expression is symbolic. A whip with silk tassels indicates an actor riding a horse. Lifting a foot means going through a doorway. Language is often archaic Chinese, music is ear-splitting (bring some cotton wool), but the costumes and make-up are magnificent. Look out for a swift battle sequence – the female warriors involved are trained acrobats who leap, twirl, twist and somersault into attack.

There are numerous other forms of opera. The Cantonese variety is more 'music hall', often with a 'boy meets girl' theme. Gaojia opera is one of the five local operatic forms from the Fújiàn province and is also popular in Taiwan, with songs in the Fújiàn dialect but influenced by the Beijing opera style.

If you get bored after the first hour or so, check out the audience antics – spitting, eating apples, plugging into a transistor radio (important sports match perhaps?) or loudly slurping tea. It's lively audience entertainment fit for an emperor. For recommended theatres that stage performances of Beijing opera see p147.

ARCHITECTURE

Běijīng today is an eye-popping fusion of old and new. On every street corner there's the buzz of jackhammers as streets are torn up and traditional buildings are razed to make way for new roads, hotels, restaurants and office complexes – all in preparation for the 2008 Olympics, where officials hope to showcase the city as a model of material success. Authorities have planned an entire makeover of the city, with construction in the works for a new light rail and subway system, a new expressway and the expansion of streets in the downtown urban core. Don't despair – even under all the noise and construction, parts of the old city still remain; architectural masterpieces like the Forbidden City and the Temple of Heaven are off limits to developers and remain one of the best reasons to visit China's sprawling, enigmatic capital.

Traditional architecture in Běijīng is a legacy of the Ming and Qing dynasties (1368–1911), as seen in the magnificent Forbidden City, Summer Palace and the remaining *hútòng*, small alleys and courtyard style homes, in the centre of the city. Few buildings now stand in Běijīng that predate the Ming dynasty. Because early buildings were constructed with wood and paper, most were not meant to last very long. The longest standing structure in Běijīng is the Great Wall, built in 3 BC though what you'll mainly see today around town are Ming dynasty rebuilds. One of the best places to see the ancient architecture of China is at the **Beijing Ancient Architecture Museum** (p83), which has exhibits of architecture ranging from early mud huts to examples of Ming and Qing palaces.

Chinese architecture normally falls into four categories: residential, imperial palaces, temples and recreational. Residences in Běijīng were once *sìhéyuàn*, houses situated on four sides of a courtyard. The houses were aligned exactly – the northern house was found directly opposite the southern, the eastern directly across from the western. *Sìhéyuàn* can still be found in a few remaining pockets in central Běijīng, though most have disappeared.

Traditionally the Chinese followed a basic ground plan when they built their homes. In upper class homes as well as in palaces and temples, buildings were surrounded by an exterior wall and designed on a north–south axis, with an entrance gate and a gate built for spirits that might try to enter the building. Behind the entry gates in palaces and residential buildings was a public hall and behind this were private living quarters built around a central court with a garden. The garden area of upper-class gentry and imperial families spawned an entire subgenre of 'recreational architecture', which included gardens, pavilions, pagodas, ponds and bridges. The Forbidden City (p87) and Summer Palace (p102) remain the finest examples of imperial architecture remaining in Běijīng. In fact, the Forbidden City is the largest architectural complex in China, covering over 72 hectares. Fine examples of temple architecture can be seen at Beihai Park (p84), the Lama Temple (p91) and at Chéngdé (p203).

Běijīng's building mania accelerated in the 1990s, with a housing renovation policy that resulted in thousands of old-style homes and Stalinist concrete structures from the 1950s being torn down and replaced by modern apartment buildings. During the 1990s Běijīng destroyed so much of its architectural heritage it was denied a World Heritage listing in

BĚIJĪNG'S DECORATIVE ARCHWAYS

Many of Běijīng's streets, alleys and place names are named after temples, city gates, markets and bridges, some of which have survived to the present, but many have not. Chaoyangmen Nandajie and Chaoyangmen Beidajie in Cháoyáng district mean, respectively, 'the street south of Chaoyang Gate' and 'the street north of Chaoyang Gate'. Nothing remains of Chaoyang Gate as it was pulled down in the 1950s; it survives in road names alone. Baiyun Lu is named after its namesake Taoist temple, the White Cloud Temple (Báiyún Guàn; p97), which survives to this day. Tiānqiáo, Hǔfángqiáo and Gānshíqiáo are place names that remember now-vanished bridges (*qiáo*).

The etymology of such street names may be easy to trace, but not many Běijīng youngsters know how Xisi, Dongsi, Xidan and Dongdan came to be named. In fact, they recall the now-levelled *páilou*, or decorative arches, that used to stand there.

Páilou, still visible along the street that runs just south of the Confucius Temple (p85) on Guozijian Jie, were erected at entrances to numerous streets and alleys of note in Běijīng. Also known as *páifáng*, *páilou* served a decorative rather than a practical function, and were adorned with a horizontal inscription board. Few survive today, but at one time Běijīng had more *páilou* than any other city in China.

Dongdan and Xidan, which respectively mean 'East Single' and 'West Single' recall the individual *páilou* that stood there. Dongsi and Xisi, which mean 'East Four' and 'West Four', refer to the four *páilou* that were erected at the crossroads at each spot. At both the Dongsi and Xisi crossroads, four wooden *páilou* were constructed, facing the four points of the compass. The *páilou* survived until the 1950s, when they came down to make way for road widening. The single *páilou* that existed at Dongdan and Xidan – each three bays wide and supported by four huge pillars – dated to the reign of Ming emperor Yongle. They were similarly levelled for road widening.

The Arrow Tower and Zhengyang Gate at today's Front Gate (p76) can still be seen, but a huge *páilou* once stood there as well. Some older Běijīng residents still refer to Qianmen as Wǔpáilou (five *páilou*), referring to the now-vanished five-bay Ming dynasty archway that rose up south of Zhengyang Gate. The *páilou* was torched when Qianmen was set on fire as foreign troops entered Běijīng in 1900 to quell the Boxer uprising. The archway was reconstructed when Cixi returned to Běijīng in 1901, but came down for good in the 1950s when Qianmen Dajie was widened. Other *páilou* that have disappeared include the three archways that stood outside the Dagaoxuan Temple (p118).

Apart from those on Guozijian Jie and a marvellous glazed archway in the Imperial College (p85) itself, several other *páilou* survive in today's Běijīng. The archway in Zhongshan Park (p83) is a three-bay, four-pillar *páilou*, tiled in blue with triple eaves. It used to stand at the western entrance to Xizongbu Hutong in Dongdan, before being moved to the park in 1919. Three *páilou* stand in front of the Lama Temple (p91), a vast *páilou* can be seen in front of the White Cloud Temple (p97) and across from the entrance to Dongyue Temple (p94), on the far side of Chaoyangmenwai Dajie.

2000 and 2001. This prompted the government to establish 40 protection zones throughout the older parts of the city to protect the remaining heritage buildings. Despite these attempts at protection, Unesco claims that since 2003 a third of the 62km square area that makes up the central part of the old city has now been destroyed, displacing close to 580,000 people. Since Běijīng was awarded the Olympics, demolition has increased dramatically.

One of the hardest hit areas is the central neighbourhood of Qianmen, once the home of scholars and Beijing opera singers. The area has been rundown for years and with the Games on the horizon, residents believe that officials are afraid of foreigners seeing the area as an eyesore. Preservationists and residents have petitioned for government protection but even after a new resolution was passed in 2005 to protect Běijīng's historic districts, many places like Qianmen weren't included because they were approved for demolition before the order was passed.

The Olympic building frenzy has stirred up plenty of controversy in other areas too. Some local architects are resentful of foreign architectural firms hired to design the Olympic buildings and many wonder how the city will ever pay for the elaborate structures, which include the Beijing National Stadium, National Gymnasium, Olympic Aquatic Park, Convention Center, Olympic Village, and the Wukesong Cultural and Sports Center.

Some of the buildings planned for the Olympics are more contentious than others. The National Stadium, dubbed a 'bird's nest' by locals, was designed by the Swiss architectural firm Herzog & de Meuron. Bowl shaped and covered with an interlocking web of steel bars and beams, the building is regarded by many Chinese as positively associated with nature (and bird's nest soup – a luxury treat). The National Stadium will be the site of the Opening Ceremony and Closing Ceremony as well as track and field events and soccer finals.

Sitting alongside the National Stadium is the National Aquatics Center, a fantastic-looking shimmering 'cube' of water, designed by the Australian firm PTW. Winner of the 2006 Popular Science 'Best of What's New in Engineering' prize, its watery appearance is meant to balance the 'fiery' characteristics of the bird's nest next door.

By far, the most controversial buildings is the new National Grand Theater, designed by French architect Paul Andreu, which is being built on the west side of Tiananmen Square. Despite the designer's claim that the building's unique design is in harmony with nature – dome shaped with a circular roof and sitting on a square-shaped lake – locals have disparagingly dubbed it an 'egg'. Many see the building as an outlandish example of foreign architectural madness, an eyesore compared to the traditional architecture of the Forbidden City nearby.

BĚIJĪNG'S TOP TEN MOST NOTABLE BUILDINGS

- **Forbidden City (p87)** – to many, this elegant Ming dynasty palace is the symbol of Běijīng. Its grand scale and traditional architecture provide a marvellous glimpse into China's imperial history.
- **Summer Palace (p102)** – with its majestic halls, gardens and galleries painted with scenes from Chinese mythology, this is one of the loveliest spots in the city to see traditional Chinese architecture.
- **Peking University** – designed in 1919 by an American architect, the university follows traditional Chinese design, combined with Western features such as a pitched roof and large windows.
- **Peace Hotel** – built in 1953, this hotel is regarded as the first modern building in Běijīng. It launched an era of Soviet-influenced architecture that lasted through the 1950s.
- **Great Hall of the People (p77)** – one of many buildings erected during Mao's Great Leap Forward. Its massive size is meant to symbolise the power and strength of the Chinese people.
- **CCTV Building** – designed by Rem Koolhaas, this futuristic building is shaped like a gigantic 'Z' and has generated an unprecedented amount of controversy over its shape – to many Chinese it resembles a person kneeling.
- **National Aquatics Center (above)** – this iridescent 'cube' of water has won international awards for its innovative design, including 'The Most Accomplished Work in Atmosphere' at the 2004 Venice Biennale.
- **National Stadium (above)** – this building, with its translucent lattice-like mesh of steel bars, is one of the most unique Olympic buildings to be built for the 2008 Olympics.
- **National Grand Theater (above)** – the most controversial building of all, Paul Andreu's 'egg' shaped dome hasn't won any awards from Běijīng residents for its radical, but to some, outlandish, design.
- **National Gymnasium** – to many, this striking building looks like a traditional Chinese folding fan. There are plans to turn it into a fitness centre for locals after the Olympics.

Food & Drink

Food & Drink

Běijīng today offers a dazzling array of local and global cuisines served with a flavour and fervour on par with most international cities. The city has something for everybody – from inexpensive food stalls to five-star gourmet restaurants.

Běijīng cuisine combines the best of cuisines from around China, with a preference for warm, filling dishes, due to its northerly location. Many dishes reflect the influence of the Mongols, with an emphasis on mutton and flat breads. Wheat-based noodles, buns and dumplings are preferred over rice and, of course, Běijīng's most famous dish is Peking duck (see the Story of the Duck boxed text on p127), a must-try for anyone visiting the capital.

Eating well in Běijīng doesn't have to break the bank. Budget eats can be found in the night markets and down small sidestreets where a bowl of noodles or dumplings will cost very little. A formal restaurant, with tablecloths and waiting staff, will be more expensive but provide more choices. Restaurants featuring international cuisine will be the priciest. Regardless of the establishment, always verify prices before ordering. Prices for certain items like seafood can vary from place to place and you don't want a shock when you see the bill.

Most top-end restaurants in Běijīng have some kind of English menu, although translations from Chinese are often literal and rather amusing (anyone for 'fried pig stomach on cabbage'?). Smaller restaurants will provide a menu in Chinese or have placards posted on the wall featuring daily specials. For help with Chinese menus check out the Menu Decoder (p48) or go with Chinese friends and let them order. In general, it's better to eat Chinese food in a group as you'll be served a wider variety of dishes.

CULTURE
ETIQUETTE

At first glance, Chinese food etiquette may seem like a minefield, but in fact today's Chinese are quite tolerant of tableside misdemeanours, especially as the meal unfolds. Meals can commence in Confucian fashion – with good intentions, a harmonic arrangement of chopsticks and a clean tablecloth – before spiralling into a Taoist mayhem, fuelled by incessant *báijiǔ* (白酒; white spirits) toasting and furious smoking all round. Large groups in particular often wreak havoc wherever they dine and vast quantities of food can be left strewn across the table at the end of a meal. However, there are some basic rules to follow when eating with Běijīng friends or colleagues that will make things at the table go as smoothly as possible.

Everyone receives an individual bowl and a small plate and teacup. If food contains bones or seeds, park them on your side dish (or even on the tablecloth, unless the restaurant is smart). The rule of thumb and the best trick in the book is to observe what your Chinese co-diners are doing and follow suit. Chinese waiting staff may hover annoyingly at the elbow while you ponder the menu, but there's nothing wrong with asking them to go away for a while.

It's good form to occasionally drop some food into your neighbour's plate as they will appreciate it and reciprocate the gesture. Also remember to fill your neighbours' tea cups when they are empty, as yours will be filled by them. You can thank the pourer by tapping your middle finger on the table gently. On no account serve yourself tea without serving others first. When your teapot needs a refill, signal this to the waiter by taking the lid off the pot or say *jiāshuǐ* (加水; 'add water').

Chopstick skills are a necessary means of survival when eating out. If you haven't mastered the tricky art of eating with two sticks you could find yourself on a crash diet without even trying! Don't despair if at first much of the food lands on the table or in your lap and not in your bowl or mouth. Eating in this way takes practice and most Chinese are understanding when it comes to foreigners and chopstick problems. They certainly have their own problems when it comes to steak knives and forks. When eating from communal dishes, don't use your chopsticks to root around in a dish for a piece of food. Find a piece by sight and go directly for it without touching anything else. And remember that while dropping food is OK, never drop your chopsticks as this is considered bad luck.

It's perfectly acceptable to smoke during the meal, unless you find yourself in a no-smoking zone. If you do smoke, hand your cigarettes around as Chinese smokers (virtually all male) are naturally generous and stinginess will raise eyebrows. As in other neighbouring Asian countries, toothpick (牙签; *yáqiān*) etiquette is for one hand to shield the mouth while the other excavates the teeth with the tool.

The arrival of the bill is an excuse for selfless histrionics. The Chinese – especially the Běijīng Chinese – pride themselves on unwavering generosity in public. Unless you are the host, you should at least make an attempt – however feeble and futile – to pay, but you will be thrust aside by the gaggle of hands gesturing for the bill. If you insist on paying, you could prompt loss of face to the host, so only go so far and then raise your hands in mock surrender. Going Dutch is almost unheard of in Běijīng, so if you invite someone out for dinner, be prepared to foot the bill.

BANQUETS

The banquet is the apex of the Chinese dining experience. Virtually all significant business deals in China are clinched at the banquet table.

Dishes are served in sequence, beginning with cold appetisers and continuing through 10 or more courses. Soup, usually a thin broth to aid digestion, is generally served after the main course.

The idea is to serve or order far more than everyone can eat. Empty bowls imply a stingy host. Rice is considered a cheap filler and rarely appears at a banquet – don't ask for it, as this would imply that the snacks and main courses are insufficient, causing embarrassment to the host.

It's polite to wait for some signal from the host before beginning to eat. You will most likely be invited to take the first taste. Often your host will serve it to you, placing a piece of meat, chicken or fish in your bowl. If a whole fish is served, you might be offered the head, the cheeks of which are considered to be the tastiest part. Try and at least take a taste of what was given to you.

Refrain from drinking alone. Imbibing is conducted via toasts, which will usually commence with a general toast by the host, followed by the main guest reply toast, and then settle down to frequent toasts to individuals. A toast is conducted by raising your glass in both hands in the direction of the toastee and crying out *gānbēi* (干杯), literally 'dry the glass'. Drain your glass in one hit. It is not unusual for everyone to end up very drunk, though at formal banquets this is frowned upon. Raising your tea or water glass in a toast

---

EATING DOS & DON'TS

- Don't wave your chopsticks around or point them at people. This is considered rude.
- Don't drum your chopsticks on the side of your bowl – only beggars do this.
- Never stick your chopsticks vertically into your rice as they will resemble incense sticks in a bowl of ashes and will be considered an omen of death.
- Wait to be seated when entering a restaurant.
- Don't discuss business or unpleasant topics at dinner.
- Do try and sample all dishes, if possible.
- Don't let the spout of a teapot face towards anyone. Make sure it is directed outward from the table or to where nobody is sitting.
- Never flip a fish over to get to the flesh underneath. If you do so, the next boat you pass will capsize.

is not very respectful so, unless you have deep-rooted convictions against alcohol, it's best to drink at least a mouthful.

Don't be late for a formal banquet; it's considered extremely rude. The banquet ends when the food and toasts end – the Chinese don't linger after the meal.

HOW BĚIJĪNG PEOPLE EAT

To the Chinese, eating is an excuse to socialise and forge friendships across the dinner table. Chinese restaurants are bright, garrulous and crowded places where people get together with family and friends to unwind and enjoy themselves. A social lubricant, dining also provides the nouveaux riches with an opportunity to flaunt their wealth, so ostentation is a common ingredient. Friends in the West may go out for a beer, but the Chinese will opt for a *rènào* (热闹; 'hot and noisy') meal punctuated with increasingly vociferous shots of *báijiǔ*.

Typically, the Chinese sit at a round table and order dishes from which everyone partakes; ordering a dish just for yourself would be treasonable. It's not unusual for one person at the table to order on everyone's behalf. Usually among friends only several dishes will be ordered, but if guests are present the host will order at least one dish per person, possibly more. At formal dinners, be prepared for a staggering amount of food, far more than anyone could possibly eat.

Epicureans advise that the key to ordering is to request a variety and balance of textures, tastes, smells, colours and even temperatures. Most Chinese meals start with some snacks, perhaps some peanuts or pickled vegetables. Following the little titbits come the main courses, usually some meat and vegetable dishes. Soup is often served at the end of the meal as well as noodles or rice.

Most Chinese eat early, often as early as 11am for lunch and 5pm for dinner, but lots of trendy late-night Běijīng eateries buzz for 24 hours. Breakfast is the one meal that many foreigners have problems with. Chinese breakfasts generally include dumplings, *yóutiáo* (fried breadsticks), *congee* (rice porridge), pickled vegetables, peanuts and soya-bean milk: all worth bearing in mind as you get excited about your gratis two-star hotel buffet breakfast. If you can't face it, Western breakfasts are widely available in hotels and cafés around town.

Chinese restaurants may not be everyone's cup of *chá*: bright, brash and noisy, they are rarely spots for romantic meals, unless you steer yourself very upmarket. For most Chinese the quality of the food is paramount and eating is enjoyed as an overt display, rather than the Western preference for privacy. Service can be gauche and sometimes little attempt is made to make your meal an overall experience.

STAPLES

NOODLES 面条

In Běijīng, *miàntiáo* (noodles) are eaten more than rice, which is a more common staple of south China. Noodles can be made by hand or by machine but many agree that hand-pulled noodles *(拉面; lā miàn)* are the tastiest and the spectacle of their manufacture is almost as great a treat as eating them. First the cook stretches the dough in his hands, shakes it gently up and down and swings it so the dough twists around itself many times before becoming firm. The dough is pulled and stretched until it becomes very fine.

Noodles are thought to have originated in northern China during the Han dynasty (206 BC–AD 220), when the Chinese developed techniques for large-scale flour grinding. Not only were noodles nutritious, cheap and versatile, they were portable and could be stored for long periods. Legend credits Marco Polo with introducing noodles to Italy in 1295 after his experiences in China.

The Chinese like to eat noodles on birthdays and during the New Year because their long thin shape symbolises longevity: this is why it's bad luck to break noodles before cooking them. The other popular staple of Běijīng and north China is *mántou* (馒头), dense and rapidly-filling steamed buns.

RICE 大米

There's a saying in Chinese that 'precious things are not pearls or jade but the five grains'. An old legend narrating the origin of rice claims it was a gift from the animals. The fable tells how China was once overwhelmed by floods that destroyed the crops and caused massive famine. One day some villagers saw a dog running towards them with bunches of long yellow seeds on its tail. When the villagers planted the seeds, rice grew and hunger vanished.

The Chinese revere rice not only as their staff of life but also for its aesthetic value. With a mellow aroma not unlike bread, its texture when properly done – soft yet offering some bite, the grains detached – sets off the textures of the foods that surround it. Flavours are enhanced by its simplicity – rice is the great unifier of the table, bringing other dishes into harmony.

Rice comes in many different preparations – as porridge (粥; *zhōu*) served with savouries at breakfast, fried with tiny shrimps, pork or vegetables and eaten at lunch or as a snack. But plain steamed white rice (白饭; *báifàn*) – fragrant yet neutral – is what you should order at dinner.

REGIONAL CUISINES

All of China's cuisines converge on Běijīng, from far-flung Tibet to the hardy northeast, the arid northwest and the fecund south. The most popular cooking styles are from Sìchuān, Shànghǎi, Hong Kong, Guǎngdōng (Cantonese) and Běijīng, but if you want to explore China's full compendium of cooking styles, the capital is *the* place to start.

BĚIJĪNG 京菜

Běijīng cuisine is classified as a 'northern cuisine' and typical dishes are made with wheat or millet, whose common incarnations are as steamed dumplings (饺子; *jiǎozi*) or noodles, while arguably the most famous Chinese dish of all is Peking duck. Vegetables are limited, so there is a heavy reliance on freshwater fish and chicken; cabbage and turnips are some of the most ubiquitous vegetables found on menus as well as yams and potatoes.

Not surprisingly, the influence of the Mongols is felt most strongly in Běijīng and two of the region's most famous culinary exports – Mongolian barbecue and Mongolian hotpot – are adaptations from Mongol field kitchens. Animals that were hunted on horseback could be dismembered and cooked with wild vegetables and onions using soldiers' iron shields on top of hot coals as primitive barbecues. Alternatively, each soldier could use his helmet as a pot, filling it with water, meat, condiments and vegetables to taste. Mutton is now the main ingredient in Mongolian hotpot.

Roasting was once considered rather barbaric in other parts of China and is still more common in the northern areas. The main methods of cooking in the northern style, though, are steaming, baking and 'explode frying' (*bàochǎo*; 爆炒) – a rapid method of cooking in which the wok is superheated over a flame and the contents tossed in for a swift stir-frying. The last of these is the most common, historically because of the scarcity of fuel and, more recently, due to the introduction of the peanut, which thrives in the north and produces an abundance of oil. Although northern-style food has a reputation for being salty and unsophisticated, it has the benefit of being filling and therefore well-suited to the region's punishing winters.

SÌCHUĀN 川菜

Famed as China's fieriest cuisine, approach the menu with caution and flagons of chilled H2O. A concoction of searing red chillis (introduced by Spanish traders in the early Qing dynasty), star anise, peppercorns and pungent 'flower pepper' (花椒; *huājiāo*) – a numbing herb peculiar to Sìchuān cooking – dishes are simmered to allow the chilli peppers time to seep into the food. Meats are often marinated, pickled or otherwise processed before cooking, which is generally by stir- or explode-frying.

Landlocked Sìchuān is a long way from the coast, so pork, poultry, legumes and *dòufu* (豆腐; tofu) are commonly used, and supplemented by a variety of wild condiments and mountain products, such as mushrooms and other fungi, as well as bamboo shoots. Seasonings are heavy: the red chilli is often used in conjunction with Sìchuān peppercorns, garlic, ginger and onions. Hallmark dishes include camphor-smoked duck, Granny Ma's tofu and spicy chicken with peanuts.

CANTONESE 粤菜

This is what non-Chinese consider 'Chinese' food, largely because most émigré restaurateurs originate from Guǎngdōng (Canton) or Hong Kong. Cantonese flavours are generally more subtle than other Chinese styles – almost sweet – and there are very few spicy dishes. Sweet-and-sour and oyster sauces are common. The Cantonese are almost religious about the importance of fresh ingredients, which is why so many restaurants are lined with tanks full of finned and shelled creatures. Stir-frying is by far the most favoured method of cooking, closely followed by steaming. Dim sum (点心; *diǎnxīn),* now a worldwide Sunday

DUMPLINGS, UNWRAPPED

There's an old saying that 'nothing tastes better than dumplings'. In fact, the Chinese have been eating this tasty home-style food since the Han dynasty! Dumplings have traditionally been eaten during Chinese New Year, their half-moon shape thought to resemble ancient gold ingots and bring good luck. Nowadays, you can get them at any time of year but they're the most popular in the north. Try this recipe for your own version of this tasty dish. (Makes 35 to 40 dumplings).

Chinese Dumplings

1 pack dumpling wrappers
300g (10 oz) ground pork
150g (5 oz) minced Napa cabbage
2 bunches of chopped coriander (cilantro)
1 bunch of chopped spring (green) onions
100 g (3½ oz) chopped ginger
2 cloves of finely chopped garlic
1 tbsp dark soy sauce
1 tbsp sesame oil

Sauce

4 tbsp light soy sauce
1 tbsp sesame oil
1 tbsp vinegar
Chilli oil to taste
2 cloves of chopped garlic

Combine the ingredients for the filling.

Moisten the edges of a dumpling wrap and put a small amount of filling in the centre.

Fold the wrap over and pinch together in a crescent shape, making a tight seal.

Place the dumplings one at a time into a large pot of boiling water. When the water comes to a hard boil, pour in one cup of cold water. Wait for the water to come to a boil again and repeat with the cold water. Do this one more time. When the dumplings rise to the top, drain and transfer to a large plate. Don't overcook or the dumplings will fall apart.

Mix all the ingredients together for the sauce and serve in small, individual bowls.

institution, originated in this region; to go *yám cha* (饮茶; Cantonese for 'drink tea') still provides most overseas Chinese communities with the opportunity to get together at the weekend. Dim sum can be found in restaurants around Běijīng.

Expensive dishes – some that are truly tasty, others that appeal more for their 'face' value – include abalone, shark's fin and bird's nest. Pigeon is a Cantonese specialty served in various ways but most commonly roasted.

SHÀNGHǍI 上海菜

Shànghǎi cuisine is generally sweeter and oilier than China's other cuisines. Unsurprisingly, Shànghǎi cuisine features plenty of fish and seafood, especially cod, river eel and shrimp.

Fish is usually *qīngzhēng* (清蒸; steamed) but can be stir-fried, pan-fried or grilled. Crab roe dumplings are another Shanghainese luxury.

Several restaurants specialise in cold salty chicken, while drunken chicken gets its name from being marinated in Shàoxīng rice wine. *Bāo* (煲; claypot) dishes are braised for a long time in their own casserole dish. Shànghǎi's most famous snack is *xiǎolóngbāo* (小笼包), small dumplings containing a meaty interior bathed in a scalding juice.

Vegetarian dishes include *dòufu*, cabbage in cream sauce, *mèn* (焖; braised) bean curd and various types of mushrooms, including *xiānggū báicài* (香菇白菜; mushrooms surrounded by baby bok choy). Tiger-skin chillies are a delicious dish of stir-fried green peppers seared in a wok and served in a sweet chilli sauce. Fried pine nuts and sweet corn is another common Shanghainese dish.

Dàzháxiè (大闸蟹; hairy crabs) are a Shànghǎi speciality between October and December. They are eaten with soy, ginger and vinegar and downed with warm Shàoxīng rice wine. They are delicious but can be fiddly to eat. The body opens via a little tab on the underside (don't eat the gills or the stomach).

UYGHUR 新疆菜

The Uyghur style of cooking reflects the influences of Xīnjiāng's chequered past. Yet, despite centuries of sporadic Chinese and Mongol rule, the strongest influence on ingredients and methods is still Turkic or Middle Eastern, which is evident in the reliance on mutton for protein and wheat for the staple grain. When rice is eaten, it is often in the Central Asian version of pilau (*plov*). Nevertheless, the influence of Chinese culinary styles and ingredients makes it probably the most enjoyable region of Central Asia in which to eat.

Uyghur bread resembles Arabic *khoubz* (Indian naan) and is baked in ovens based on the *tanour* (Indian tandoor) model. It is often eaten straight from the oven and sprinkled with poppy seeds, sesame seeds or fennel. Uyghur bakers also make excellent *girde nan* (bagels). Wheat is also used for a variety of noodles. *Laghman* are the most common: noodles cooked *al dente,* thick and topped with a combination of spicy mutton, peppers, tomatoes, eggplant, green beans and garlic. *Suoman* are noodle squares fried with tomatoes, peppers, garlic and meat, sometimes quite spicy. *Suoman goshsiz* is the vegetarian variety.

Kebabs are common, as they are throughout the Middle East and Central Asia, both shashlik- and tandoori-style. *Samsas* or *samsis* are the Uyghur version of samosas: baked envelopes of meat. Meat often makes an appearance inside *chuchura* (dumplings), which can be steamed or fried.

VEGETARIAN 素菜

China has a long history of Daoist and Buddhist philosophers who abstained from eating animals, and vegetarianism can be traced back over 1000 years. The Tang dynasty physician Sun Simiao extolled the virtues of vegetarianism in his 60-volume classic, *Prescriptions Worth a Thousand Pieces of Gold*. Legend has it that Sun lived to the ripe old age of 101. However, try telling this to your waiter who brings out a supposedly pristine veggie or tofu dish decorated with strips of pork or chicken. The majority of Chinese have little understanding of vegetarianism and many consider it a strange Western concept.

Because of China's history of poverty and famine, eating meat is a status symbol, and symbolic of health and wealth. Many Chinese remember all too well the famines of the 1950s and 1960s when having anything to eat was a luxury. Eating meat (as well as milk and eggs) is a sign of progress and material abundance. Even vegetables are often fried in animal-based oils and soups are most commonly made with chicken or beef stock. Saying you don't eat meat confuses many Chinese who may interpret this to mean seafood is OK, or even chicken or pork. Trying to explain the reasons behind why you don't eat meat brings even more confusion. Men especially are looked down upon because not eating meat is thought to decrease sexual virility.

However, in larger cities such as Běijīng, Shànghǎi or Guǎngzhōu, vegetarianism is slowly catching on and there are new chic vegetarian eateries appearing in fashionable restaurant districts. Buddhist temples also often have vegetarian restaurants.

Buddhist vegetarian food often consists of 'mock meat' dishes made from tofu, wheat gluten and vegetables. Some of the dishes are quite fantastic to look at, with vegetarian ingredients sculpted to look like spare ribs or fried chicken. Sometimes the chefs go to great lengths to create 'bones' from carrots and lotus roots. Some of the more famous vegetarian dishes include vegetarian 'ham', braised vegetarian 'shrimp' and sweet and sour 'fish'.

SNACKS 小吃

Snacking in Běijīng is great fun and a good way to explore the local cuisine. A tasty Muslim treat is lamb kebabs (烤羊肉串; *kǎo yángròu chuàn*), often sold in night markets or outdoor restaurants.

Běijīng has plenty of tasty breads, such as bread stuffed with leeks and eggs (韭菜饼; *jiǔ cài bǐng*), thin and crunchy pancakes (煎饼; *jiān bǐng*) and bread filled with diced pork (*ròu bǐng*; 肉饼). During winter it's common to see people eating sugar-coated crab apples on a stick and roasted sweet potatoes (红薯; *hóngshǔ*), which are sold by the roadside. For more information on snacks see the Street Food Běijīng Style boxed text, p122.

DESSERTS & SWEETS 甜点

The Chinese do not generally eat dessert, but fruit is considered to be an appropriate end to a good meal. Western influence has added ice cream to the menu in some restaurants, but in general sweet stuff is consumed as snacks and is seldom available in restaurants.

One exception to the rule is caramelised fruits, including apples (拔丝苹果; *básī pínggǔo*) and bananas (拔丝香蕉; *básī xiāngjiāo*), which you can find in a few restaurants. Other sweeties include shaved ice and syrup (冰沙; *bīngshā*); a sweet, sticky rice pudding known as Eight Treasure Rice (八宝饭; *bābǎofàn*); and various types of steamed bun filled with sweet bean paste.

DRINKS

NONALCOHOLIC DRINKS 无酒精饮料

A fundamental part of Chinese existence, tea is celebrated by an ancient saying as one of the seven basic necessities of life, alongside fuel, oil, rice, salt, soy sauce and vinegar. The Chinese were the first to cultivate tea (茶; *chá*), and the art of brewing and drinking tea – popular since the Tang dynasty (AD 618-907) – shows few signs of losing steam.

China has three main types of tea: green (绿茶; *lùchá*) or unfermented; black tea (红茶; *hóng chá*), which is fermented; and wulong (乌龙茶; *wūlóngchá*), or semi-fermented. But there are numerous varieties, from jasmine (茉莉花茶; *mòlìhuāchá*) and chrysanthemum (菊花茶; *júhuā chá*) to pu'er (普洱茶; *pǔerchá*), Iron Guanyin (铁观音; *tiěguānyīn*) and beyond. Cheap restaurants often serve on-the-house pots of weak jasmine or green tea. Higher quality brands of tea are available in teashops and supermarkets. Traditionally,

DRINKING IN THE CITY

Beer (啤酒; *píjiǔ*) is Beijing's favourite tipple, but besides imported brands, you'll have to settle for the Chinese beers, of which Yanjing Beer, Beijing Beer and Tsingtao are the bestselling labels. Canned and bottled in brown and green bottles, Yanjing Beer is both watery and unremarkable, but it is extraordinarily cheap.

China's drinkers are slowly developing a taste for wine (葡萄酒; *pútaojiǔ*), but prices at restaurants can be outrageously expensive. China furthermore ferments its own wine, with Dynasty and Great Wall some of the better known. Many Chinese brands, however, are very sweet and cling to the teeth.

To aid digestion and get rapidly sozzled, Chinese men often drink *báijiǔ* with lunch and dinner. Despite being loosely translated as wine, the potent potion is in fact a clear spirit fermented from sorghum (a type of millet). *Báijiǔ* is used for toasts at banquets; if you are invited to *gānbēi* (literally 'dry the glass') you will be expected to drain your glass. The drink is a searing, eye-wateringly strong tipple that will quickly have you sliding off your seat and taking the tablecloth with you, so go easy on it. Rice wine (*mǐjiǔ*) is intended more for cooking than drinking.

Chinese hard-core drinkers sociably congregate in packs and are the last to be bundled out of restaurants as the shutters crash down. Chinese finger-guessing games require little intelligence and become the last resort of the seriously drunk in eateries the land over.

Chinese would never put milk or sugar in their tea but things are changing. Now 'milk tea' (奶茶; *nǎi chá*) is available everywhere in Běijīng, often served cold with a whopping amount of sugar. Thirst-quenching bubble tea (珍珠奶茶; *zhēnzhū nǎichá*), a hot or cold concoction sold in a variety of sweet flavours, is also widely available.

Coffee (咖啡; *kāfēi*) long ago took Běijīng by storm and cafés of wildly varying quality have covered town like a rash, with even the bastion of the Forbidden City being controversially breached by Starbucks. Prices are on a par with the West, with cups of coffee costing around Y25 to Y30. Note that McDonalds offer free coffee refills – ask the staff to *xùbēi kāfēi* (续杯咖啡).

Soft drinks (汽水; *qìshuǐ*) can be found at every turn, along with bottled water. Milk (牛奶; *niúnǎi*) and yoghurt (酸奶; *suānnǎi*) are available from supermarkets and convenience stores, along with powdered milk (奶粉; *nǎifěn*).

ALCOHOLIC DRINKS 酒精饮料

Beer (啤酒; *píjiǔ*) – once anathema to Chinese alcohol-lovers – is now embraced as the alcoholic drink of choice in town. China's most famous beer is Tsingtao, a German inheritance from the early days of the 20th century, still brewed up in the namesake port town of Qīngdǎo. Among locally-brewed labels are Běijīng Beer and Yanjing Beer; a bottle will normally cost Y2 to Y3 in street shops and small bottles of beer retail for around Y15 to Y25 in bars. Most of China's beers are uniform in taste and strength, but a wide selection of foreign brands – both brewed in China and imported – line the shelves of Western bars and supermarkets.

China has cultivated vines and produced wine for an estimated 4000 years although wine-producing techniques differ from those in the West. Western producers try to prevent oxidation in their wines, but oxidation produces a flavour that Chinese tipplers find desirable and go to great lengths to achieve.

Many Chinese 'wines' are in fact spirits. Occasionally literally translated as 'white wine', *báijiǔ* (see the boxed text, above) is a heady spirit with a sharp, sweet smell hovering somewhere between nail polish remover and turpentine. The most expensive and prestigious is Maotai, but Běijīng's most popular white spirit is the locally distilled Erguotou – a cheap and utilitarian path to inebriation.

Chinese diners also appreciate wines with herbs and creatures soaked in them, which they drink for their health and for restorative or aphrodisiac qualities. Wine fortified with dead bees or pickled snakes is also desirable for its alleged tonic properties – in general, the more poisonous the creature, the more potent the tonic effects. Hejie Jiu (lizard wine) is produced in the southern province of Guǎngxī; each bottle contains one dead lizard suspended perpendicularly in the clear liquid.

MENU DECODER
USEFUL WORDS & PHRASES

I don't want MSG.	*Wǒ bú yào wèijīng.*	我不要味精
I'm vegetarian.	*Wǒ chī sù.*	我吃素
Not too spicy.	*Bú yào tài là.*	不要太辣
menu	*càidān*	菜单
bill (cheque)	*mǎi dān/jiézhàng*	买单/结帐
set meal (no menu)	*tàocān*	套餐
Let's eat!	*Chī fàn!*	吃饭
Cheers!	*Gānbēi!*	干杯

THE BASICS

rice	*báifàn*	白饭
noodles	*miàntiáo*	面条
salt	*yán*	盐
pepper	*hújiāo*	胡椒
sugar	*táng*	糖
soy sauce	*jiàngyóu*	酱油
chilli	*làjiāo*	辣椒
egg	*jīdàn*	鸡蛋
beef	*niúròu*	牛肉
pork	*zhūròu*	猪肉
chicken	*jīròu*	鸡肉
lamb	*yángròu*	羊肉
vegetables	*shūcài*	蔬菜
potato	*tǔdòu*	土豆
broccoli	*xīlánhuā*	西兰花
carrots	*húluóbo*	胡萝卜
sweet corn	*yùmǐ*	玉米
green peppers	*qīngjiāo*	青椒
soup	*tāng*	汤
chopsticks	*kuàizi*	筷子
knife	*dāozi*	刀子
fork	*chāzi*	叉子
spoon	*sháozi*	勺子
hot	*rède*	热的
ice cold	*bīngde*	冰的

STAPLES
Rice Dishes

jīdàn chǎofàn	鸡蛋炒饭	fried rice with egg
jīchǎofàn	鸡炒饭	fried rice with chicken
jīdàn mǐfàn	鸡蛋米饭	steamed white rice
shūcài chǎofàn	蔬菜炒饭	fried rice with vegetables
xīfàn/zhōu	稀饭/粥	watery rice porridge *(congee)*

Noodle Dishes

húntun miàn	馄饨面	wontons and noodles
jīsī chǎomiàn	鸡丝炒面	fried noodles with chicken
jīsī tāngmiàn	鸡丝汤面	soupy noodles with chicken

májiàng miàn	麻酱面	sesame paste noodles
niúròu chǎomiàn	牛肉炒面	fried noodles with beef
niúròu miàn	牛肉面	soupy beef noodles
ròusī chǎomiàn	肉丝炒面	fried noodles with pork
shūcài chǎomiàn	蔬菜炒面	fried noodles with vegetables
tāngmiàn	汤面	noodles in soup
xiārén chǎomiàn	虾仁炒面	fried noodles with shrimp
zhájiàng miàn	炸酱面	bean and meat noodles

Bread, Buns & Dumplings

cōngyóu bǐng	葱油饼	spring onion pancakes
guōtiē	锅贴	pot stickers/pan-grilled dumplings
mántou	馒头	steamed buns
ròu bāozi	肉包子	steamed meat buns
shāobǐng	烧饼	clay-oven rolls
shuǐjiān bāo	水煎包	pan-grilled buns
shuǐjiǎo	水饺	boiled dumplings
sùcài bāozi	素菜包子	steamed vegetable buns

Soup

húntun tāng	馄饨汤	wonton soup
sān xiān tāng	三鲜汤	three kinds of seafood soup
suānlà tāng	酸辣汤	hot and sour soup

CUISINES
Běijīng & Other Northern-style Dishes

běijīng kǎoyā	北京烤鸭	Peking duck
jiāo zhá yángròu	焦炸羊肉	deep-fried mutton
qīng xiāng shāo jī	清香烧鸡	chicken wrapped in lotus leaf
sān měi dòufu	三美豆腐	sliced beancurd with Chinese cabbage
shuàn yángròu	涮羊肉	lamb hotpot
sì xǐ wánzi	四喜丸子	steamed and fried pork, shrimp and bamboo shoot balls
yuán bào lǐ jǐ	芫爆里脊	stir-fried pork tenderloin with coriander
zāo liū sān bái	糟溜三白	stir-fried chicken, fish and bamboo shoots
jiǎozi	饺子	dumplings
mántou	馒头	steamed buns
ròu bāozi	肉包子	steamed meat buns

Shànghǎi Dishes

xiánjī	咸鸡	cold salty chicken
xiāngsū jī	香酥鸡	crispy chicken
zuìjī	醉鸡	drunken chicken
sōngzǐ yā	松子鸭	duck with pine nuts
xièfěn shīzitóu	蟹粉狮子头	lion's head meatballs with crab

sōngrén yùmǐ	松仁玉米	Fried pine nuts and sweet corn
hǔpíjiānjiāo	虎皮尖椒	tiger skin chillies
xiǎolóngbāo	小笼包	small dumplings containing a meaty interior bathed in a scalding juice

Cantonese Dishes

bái zhuó xiā	白灼虾	blanched prawns with shredded scallions
dōngjiāng yánjú jī	东江盐焗鸡	salt-baked chicken
gālí jī	咖喱鸡	curried chicken
háoyóu niúròu	蚝油牛肉	beef with oyster sauce
kǎo rǔzhū	烤乳猪	crispy suckling pig
mì zhī chāshāo	蜜汁叉烧	roast pork with honey
shé ròu	蛇肉	snake
tángcù lǐjǐ	糖醋里脊	sweet and sour pork fillets
tángcù páigǔ	糖醋排骨	sweet and sour spare ribs

Sìchuānese Dishes

bàngbàng jī	棒棒鸡	shredded chicken in a hot pepper and sesame sauce
dàsuàn shàn duàn	大蒜鳝段	stewed eel with garlic
gānshāo yán lǐ	干烧岩鲤	stewed carp with ham and hot and sweet sauce
gōngbào jīdīng	宫爆鸡丁	spicy chicken with peanuts
huíguō ròu	回锅肉	boiled and stir-fried pork with salty and hot sauce
málà dòufu	麻辣豆腐	spicy tofu
mápó dòufu	麻婆豆腐	Granny Ma's tofu
shuǐ zhǔ niúròu	水煮牛肉	fried and boiled beef, garlic sprouts and celery
yúxiāng ròusī	鱼香肉丝	'fish-resembling' meat
zhàcài ròu sī	榨菜肉丝	stir-fried pork or beef tenderloin with tuber mustard
zhāngchá yā	樟茶鸭	camphor tea duck

Beef Dishes

háoyóu niúròu	蚝油牛肉	beef with oyster sauce
hóngshāo niúròu	红烧牛肉	beef braised in soy sauce
niúròu fàn	牛肉饭	beef with rice
tiěbǎn niúròu	铁板牛肉	sizzling beef platter
gānbiān niúròu sī	干煸牛肉丝	stir-fried beef and chilli

Chicken & Duck Dishes

háoyóu jīkuài	蚝油鸡块	diced chicken in oyster sauce
hóngshāo jīkuài	红烧鸡块	chicken braised in soy sauce
jītuǐ fàn	鸡腿饭	chicken leg with rice

níngméng jī	柠檬鸡	lemon chicken
tángcù jīdīng	糖醋鸡丁	sweet and sour chicken
yāròu fàn	鸭肉饭	duck with rice
yāoguǒ jīdīng	腰果鸡丁	chicken and cashews

Pork Dishes

biǎndòu ròusī	扁豆肉丝	shredded pork and green beans
guōbā ròupiàn	锅巴肉片	pork and sizzling rice crust
gūlǔ ròu	咕噜肉	sweet and sour pork
háoyóu ròusī	蚝油肉丝	pork with oyster sauce
jiàngbào ròudīng	酱爆肉丁	diced pork with soy sauce
jīngjiàng ròusī	京酱肉丝	pork cooked with soy sauce
mùěr ròu	木耳肉	wood-ear mushrooms and pork
páigǔ fàn	排骨饭	pork chop with rice
qīngjiāo ròu piàn	青椒肉片	pork and green peppers
yángcōng chǎo ròupiàn	洋葱炒肉片	pork and fried onions

Seafood Dishes

gélì	蛤蜊	clams
gōngbào xiārén	宫爆虾仁	diced shrimp with peanuts
háo	蚝	oysters
hóngshāo yú	红烧鱼	fish braised in soy sauce
lóngxiā	龙虾	lobster
pángxiè	螃蟹	crab
yóuyú	鱿鱼	squid
zhāngyú	章鱼	octopus

Vegetable & Bean Curd Dishes

báicài xiān shuānggū	白菜鲜双菇	bok choy and mushrooms
cuìpí dòufu	脆皮豆腐	crispy skin bean curd
hēimù'ěr mèn dòufu	黑木耳焖豆腐	bean curd with wood-ear mushrooms
jiāngzhī qīngdòu	姜汁青豆	string beans with ginger
lǔshuǐ dòufu	卤水豆腐	smoked bean curd
shāguō dòufu	砂锅豆腐	clay pot bean curd
tángcù ǒubīng	糖醋藕冰	sweet and sour lotus root cakes
hóngshāo qiézi	红烧茄子	red cooked aubergine
sùchǎo biǎndòu	素炒扁豆	garlic beans
sùchǎo sùcài	素炒素菜	fried vegetables
yúxiāng qiézi	鱼香茄子	'fish-resembling' aubergine
jiācháng dòufu	家常豆腐	'home style' tofu

DRINKS

píjiŭ	啤酒	beer
báijiŭ	白酒	white spirits
kěkŏu kělè	可口可乐	Coca-Cola
yézi zhī	椰子汁	coconut juice
nǎijīng	奶精	coffee creamer
kāfēi	咖啡	coffee
niúnǎi	牛奶	milk
kuàngquán shuǐ	矿泉水	mineral water
hóng pútáo jiŭ	红葡萄酒	red wine
mǐjiŭ	米酒	rice wine
qìshuǐ	汽水	soft drink (soda)
dòujiāng	豆浆	soya bean milk
chá	茶	tea
kāi shuǐ	开水	water (boiled)
bái pútáo jiŭ	白葡萄酒	white wine
suānnǎi	酸奶	yoghurt

History ■

History *Jasper Becker*

THE RECENT PAST

The rebuilding of Běijīng is the greatest urban project attempted in China since the 14th century, when the great Ming Emperor Yongle (1360–1442) made Běijīng his capital. After former President Jiang Zemin launched the project in 1998, China spent at least US$200 billion, not counting more than US$40 billion specifically for the 2008 Summer Olympic Games. By lavishing three times the amount Athens spent on hosting the 2004 Games, the 2008 Games will be the costliest in Olympics history. Yet China can proudly show off a new capital with a modern infrastructure and eye-catching designs, created by the top names in international architecture. All worthy of a great global power.

Yet, on the other hand, the losses are incalculable. China's leaders have comprehensively destroyed the historical fabric of Běijīng, and the damage to the collective memory of the Chinese has been immense. This city has been home to five dynasties, including two of the greatest – the Ming and the Qing – and most of the greatest events in the nation's turbulent modern history have played out here. Four dynasties (Liao, Jin, Yuan, Qing) belonged to 'barbarians,' although it is not politically correct to say so anymore. Only one dynasty, the Ming, was truly Chinese. This is also where the project to modernise China was born, where the first Chinese republic was born and where, later, Chairman Mao Zedong realised his ambition to recast Chinese society by so thoroughly erasing the 'feudal Confucian legacy' and turn the Chinese – as Mao said – into a 'blank sheet of paper'.

The new Běijīng is thus intended to symbolise how the Chinese Communist Party has fulfilled its mission to build a new China. The historical legacy now consists of a handful of buildings and streets, islands in a forest of glass and concrete towers. With the relocation of over three million residents from the city centre, communities who have lived in the capital for centuries have gone and been replaced by newcomers – some ignorant of its traditions and customs.

FROM THE BEGINNING

As a youth in the 14th century, the future Emperor Yongle was sent by his father to live as the Prince of Yan in the abandoned ruins of the former capital of the Yuan dynasty (present-day Běijīng), established by Kublai Khan. The Mongols called the city Khanbalik, and it was from here that the descendants of Genghis Khan ruled over the largest land empire in history. This is where Marco Polo, one of many thousands of foreigners drafted to help the Mongols govern China, came to serve as an official. Běijīng was really only the winter capital for Kublai Khan (1215–1294), who chose to spend the summer months at Běijīng's sister city, Xanadu, which lay to the north, 6000ft up on the steppes. This was called the 'upper capital', or 'Shàngdū' in Chinese, while Běijīng was 'Dàdū' or great capital.

At first sight, Běijīng seems a curious place to select as the capital of the Yuan empire, or indeed any empire. For one thing, it lacks a river or access to the sea. It is on the very outer edge of the great northern plain, and very far indeed from the rich rice granaries in the south and the source of China's lucrative exports of tea, silk and porcelain. Throughout history the Han Chinese considered this barbarian territory, home to a series of hostile predatory dynasties like the Liao (907–1125) and the Jin (1115–1234). To this day Chinese historians describe these peoples as primitive 'tribes' rather than nations, perhaps a prejudice from the ancient antipathy between nomadic pastoralist peoples and the sedentary farmers who are the Chinese.

TIMELINE	500,000BC	pre-11th century BC	8th century–3rd century BC
	Peking Man inhabits Běijīng region	First Chinese record of settlements in Běijīng area	Yànjīng, capital of the state of Yan, located near Běijīng

Běijīng first became a walled settlement in AD 938 when the Khitans, one of the nomadic 'barbarian tribes', established it as an auxiliary southern capital of their Liao dynasty. It was sometimes called Yànjīng, or the 'city of swallows' and this is still the name of a beer produced by a local brewery. When they were overthrown by Jurchens from Manchuria, the progenitors of the Manchus, it became Zhōngdū or 'middle capital'. Each of these three successive barbarian dynasties enlarged the walled city and built palaces and temples, especially Buddhist temples. They secured a supply of water by channelling streams from the dry limestone hills around Běijīng, and stored it in the lakes which still lie at the heart of the city.

The Khitans relied on the Grand Canal to ship goods like silk, porcelain, tea and grain from the Yangtze Delta. Each successive dynasty shortened the Grand Canal. It was originally 2500km long when it was built in the 5th century by the Chinese Sui dynasty to facilitate the military conquest of northeast China and Korea. From the 10th century it was used for a different purpose: to enable these northern peoples to extract the wealth of central China. Běijīng's role was to be the terminus.

For 1000 years, half a million peasants spent six months a year hauling huge barges from Hángzhōu up the Grand Canal to Běijīng. You can still see the canal after it enters the city from Tōngzhōu, now a suburb of Běijīng, and then winds around the Second Ring Rd. The tax or tribute from central China was then stored in huge warehouses, a few of which still remain. From Běijīng, the goods were carried out of the West Gate or Xizhimen, and taken up the Tanqin Gorge to Bādálǐng (p193), which once marked the limits of the Chinese world. Beyond this pass, the caravans took the road to Zhāngjiākǒu, 6000ft above sea level where the grasslands of Inner Asia begin. The Mongols referred to Zhāngjiākǒu as Kalgan; 'the Gate'.

This pass was also the favourite route chosen by invaders like Genghis Khan who wanted to attack China. The ultimate aim of Khitans, Jurchen, Mongols and Manchus was to control the lucrative international trade in Chinese-made luxuries. Chinese dynasties like the Song faced a choice of paying them off or staging a bloody resistance. The Southern Song did attack and destroy Běijīng, but when it failed to defeat the Liao dynasty of the Khitans it resorted to a strategy of 'using the barbarian to defeat the barbarian'. It made a pact with the Jurchen, and together they captured Běijīng in 1125. But instead of just helping to defeat the Khitans, the Jurchen carried on south and took the Song capital at Kāifēng. The Jurchens, however, chose not to try to govern China by themselves and instead opted to milk the Southern Song dynasty. The Mongols became the first 'barbarian' tribe to attempt to rule China. They ruled from Běijīng for just short of a century, from 1272 to 1368.

MING DYNASTY BĚIJĪNG

Běijīng can properly be said to be a Chinese city only during the Ming dynasty (1368–1644), when the Emperor Yongle – whose name means perpetual happiness – used over 200,000 prisoners of war to rebuild the city, construct its massive battlements, rebuild the imperial palace and establish the magnificent Ming tombs. He forced tens of thousands of leading Chinese families to relocate from Nánjīng, the capital founded by his father, and unwillingly settle in what they considered an alien land at the extremity of the Chinese world. Throughout the Ming dynasty it was constantly under attack by the Mongols, and on many occasions the

AD 938	1153	1215
Běijīng established as auxiliary capital of the Liao dynasty; city walls first built	Běijīng becomes Jin dynasty capital; city walls expanded	The Mongols, under Genghis Khan, sack Běijīng

horsemen reached the very gates of Běijīng. Mongol bandits roamed the countryside or hid out in the marshes south of the city, threatening communications with the empire.

Everything needed for this gigantic enterprise, even tiles, bricks and timber, had to be shipped up the Grand Canal, but in time Běijīng grew into a city of nearly a million residents. Although farms and greenhouses sprang up around the city, it always depended on the Grand Canal as a life-line. Most of the canal was needed to ship the huge amounts of food needed to supply the garrison of more than a million men which Yongle press-ganged into building and manning the new Great Wall (p191). This Wall, unlike earlier walls, was clad in brick and stone, not pounded earth, and the Ming emperors kept enlarging it for the next 250 years, adding loops, spurs and watchtowers. For long stretches, the fortifications run in two parallel bands.

Běijīng grew from a forward defence military headquarters into an administrative centre staffed by an elite corps of mandarins. They had to pass gruelling examinations which tested candidates' understanding of classical and Confucian literature. Then they were either assigned to the provinces or selected to work in the central government ministries, situated in what is now Tiananmen Square, south of the Meridian Gate and the entrance to the Forbidden City (p87). Each day the mandarins and the generals entered the 'Great Within' and kowtowed at an audience before the emperor. He lived inside like a male version of a queen bee, served by thousands of women and eunuchs. Ming emperors were the only males permitted to live in the palace. Yongle established rigid rules and dreary rituals, and many of his successors rebelled against the constrictions of the heavily controlled life.

Under later Ming emperors, the eunuchs came to be more trusted and more powerful than the mandarins. There were 100,000 by the end of the Ming dynasty – more than any other civilization in history. A few became so powerful they virtually ruled the empire, but many died poor and destitute. Some used their wealth to build grandiose residences and tombs, or patronised temples and monasteries located in hills outside the walls. The eunuchs tended to be Buddhists (while the mandarins honoured Confucius), as it gave them hope they would return as whole men in a future reincarnation.

Over time Běijīng became the most important religious centre in Asia, graced by more than 2000 temples and shrines. Daoists and Buddhists vied for the favour of the emperor who, as a divine being, was automatically the patron of every approved religious institution in the empire. As the residence of the emperor, the Chinese regarded Běijīng as the centre of the universe. The best poets and painters also flocked to Běijīng to seek court patronage. The Forbidden City required the best porcelain, furniture, and silverware, and its workshops grew in skill and design. Literature, drama, music, medicine, mapmaking, astrology and astronomy flourished too, so the imperial city became a centre for arts and sciences.

Although early visitors complained about the dust and the beggars, as they do now, most were awed and inspired by its size, magnificence and wealth. Ming culture was very influent in Japan, Korea, Vietnam and other neighbours. By the close of the 15th century the Ming capital, which had started out as a remote and isolated military outpost, had become a wealthy and sophisticated Chinese city.

Despite the Great Wall, the threat from the north intensified. The Manchus, (formerly the Jurchens) established a new and powerful state based in Shěnyáng, (currently the capital of Liáoníng province) and watched as the Ming empire decayed. The Ming had one of the most elaborate tax codes in history but corrupt eunuchs abused their growing power. Excessive taxation sparked a series of peasant revolts. Silver, the main form of exchange, was devalued by the import of silver from the new world, leading to inflation.

One peasant rebel army, led by Li Zicheng (1606–45), actually captured Běijīng. The last Ming emperor, Chongzhen (1611–44), called on the Manchus for help, and after crossing the Great Wall at Shānhǎiguān (p200), helped rout Li Zicheng's army. They then marched on Běijīng, where Emperor Chongzhen hung himself on a tree on Coal, or Prospect, Hill (p91), which overlooks the Forbidden City. Chongzhen lies buried in the Ming tomb a short distance from the grander Ming tomb complex, and now there's a small artificial snowfield near his tomb.

1260	1368	1368–1644
The first Yuan emperor, Kublai Khan, transforms the city and names it Dàdū	Zhu Yuanzhang takes Běijīng and founds the Ming dynasty	City wall reshaped; Great Wall rebuilt; basic layout of modern Běijīng established

QING DYNASTY BĚIJĪNG

The Manchus established their Qing dynasty in 1664, although it took several decades before they completed the conquest of the Ming empire. As a foreign dynasty, they took great pains to present themselves as legitimate successors to the Chinese Ming dynasty. For this reason they kept Běijīng as their capital and changed very little, effectively preserving Yongle's city. The Manchu imperial family, the Aisin Gioro Clan, moved in to the Forbidden City, and imperial princes took large courtyard palaces.

Soon the Aisin Gioro family began to feel that living inside the confines of the Forbidden City was claustrophobic. The great Emperor Kangxi (1654–1722) effectively moved the court to what is now called the Old Summer Palace (p101), a vast parkland of lakes, canals and palaces linked to the city by the Jade Canal. The Manchus, like the Mongols, enjoyed hunting, riding, hawking, skating and archery. In summer, when Běijīng became hot and steamy, the court moved to Chéngdé (p203; formerly Jehol or Rehol), a week's ride to the north. At Jehol the court spent three months living in felt tents (or yurts) in a walled parkland.

The Manchu army was divided into regiments called banners, so the troops were called bannermen *(qírén)*. Each banner had a separate colour by which it was known and settled in a particular residential area in Běijīng. The Embroidered Yellow Bannermen, for example, lived near the Confucius Temple (p85), and a few are still there today. Only a minority were actually ethnic Manchus – the rest were Mongols or Han Chinese.

Běijīng was a Manchu city and foreigners used to call it the 'Tartar City': 'Tartars' being the label given to any nomadic race from Inner Asia. The Han Chinese, forced to wear their hair in a queue (pigtail) as a symbol of their subjugation, lived in the 'Chinese city' to the south of Tiananmen Square. It was the liveliest, most densely populated area, packed with markets, shops, theatres, brothels, guild houses and hostels for provincial visitors. If Chinese people wanted to get to north Běijīng, they had to go all the way round the outside walls. The Bannermen posted at all the gates prevented anyone from entering without permission. Right up to 1900, the state provided all Bannermen families with clothing and free food that was shipped up the Grand Canal and stored in grain warehouses.

It was the Manchu Bannermen who really created a Běijīng culture. They loved Beijing opera, and the city once had over 40 opera houses and many training schools. The sleeveless *qípǎo* dress is really a Manchu dress. The Bannermen, who loved animals, raised songbirds and pigeons and bred exotic-looking goldfish and miniature dogs like the Pekinese. And after the downfall of the Qing Empire, they kept up traditional arts like painting and calligraphy.

Through the centuries of Qing rule, the Manchus tried to keep themselves culturally separate from the Chinese, speaking a different language, wearing different clothes and following different customs. For instance, Manchu women did not bind their feet, wore raised platform patens (raised shoe), and wore their hair coiled in distinctive and elaborate styles. All court documents were composed in the Manchu script; Manchu, Chinese and Mongolian script were used to write name signs in places like the Forbidden City.

At the same time, the Qing copied the Ming's religious and bureaucratic institutions. The eight key ministries (Board of Works, Board of Revenue, Board of State Ceremonies, Board of War, Board of Rites, Board of Astronomy, Board of Medicines, and Prefecture of Imperial Clan Affairs) continued to operate from the same buildings in what is now Tiananmen Square. The Qing dynasty worshipped their ancestors at rites held in a temple which is now in the Workers Cultural Palace (p82), south of the Forbidden City. They also built a second ancestral temple devoted to the spirits of every Chinese emperor that ever ruled. Until recently it was a girls' school but has since been turned back into a museum.

They encouraged the study of Confucius in order to strengthen the loyalty of the mandarins employed by the state bureaucracy. And they carried out the customary rituals at the great state temples like the Temple of Heaven (p79). By inclination, however, many of the Manchu emperors were either shamanists or followers of Tibetan Buddhism. The Shamanist shrines have disappeared, but Běijīng is full of temples and stupas connected with Tibetan Buddhists. The

1403–25	1644	1850–68
Reign of Emperor Yongle sees construction of Forbidden City and Temple of Heaven	Founding of the Qing dynasty	Taiping Rebellion

Emperor Qianlong considered himself the incarnation of the Bodhisattva Manjusri and culti-vated strong links with various Dalai Lamas and Panchen Lamas. Many visited – a round trip usually lasted three years, and special palaces were built for them. The Dalai Lama's ex-palace is now rented out by the government of the Tibet Autonomous Region. The Manchus deliberately fostered the spread of Tibetan Buddhism among the warlike Mongols in the hope of pacifying them. Běijīng therefore developed into a holy city attracting pilgrims of all kinds.

EMPRESS DOWAGER CIXI & THE FOREIGN DEVILS

Of course, the arrival of the first Jesuits and other Christians made Běijīng an important centre of Christianity in China. Emperor Qianlong employed many Jesuits who, among other things, built for him the baroque palaces and stone ruins that can still be seen in the Old Summer Palace (Yuánmíng Yuán; the Garden of Perfect Happiness), which was burnt down in 1860 by a combined force of British and French troops.

After the military defeats of the Opium Wars (1839–42 and 1856–60), the Western na-tions forced the Qing emperors to allow them to open formal embassies or legations in the capital. Hitherto, the emperor had had no equal in the world – foreign powers could only send embassies to deliver tribute, and they were housed in tributary hostels.

The British legation was the first to open after 1860. It lay on the east side of Tiananmen Square and stayed there until the 1950s when its grounds were taken over by the Ministry of State Security. By 1900, there were a dozen legations in an odd foreign ghetto with an ec-lectic mixture of European architecture. The Foreign Legation Quarter (p76) never became a foreign concession like those in Shànghǎi or Tiānjīn but it had banks, schools, shops, post offices, hospitals and military parade grounds. Much of it was reduced to rubble when the army of Boxers besieged it in the summer of 1900. It was later rebuilt.

The last of these foreign embassies did not leave until 1967, and, though much of the Lega-tion Quarter has been destroyed during the past decade, it is still worth a visit. You can see the lion and unicorn above the entrance to the British legation, and the French legation is still there, even though it has been given to Cambodia's Prince Sihanouk as his residence.

The Empress Dowager Cixi (1835–1908), a daughter of a Bordered Blue Bannerman, was a young concubine when the original Summer Palace was burned down. Cixi allowed the Old Summer Palace to fall into decay, associating it with a humiliation, and instead built herself the new Summer Palace (Yíhé Yuán, p102). She was left with a profound hatred and distrust of the Western barbarians and their ways.

Over the four decades in which she ruled China 'from behind the curtain' through a series of proxy emperors, she resisted pressure to change and reform. After a naval defeat at the hands of the Japanese in 1895, young Chinese officials put forward a modernisation program. She had some of them executed outside Běijīng's walls then imprisoned their patron and her nephew, Emperor Guangxu (1871–1908). She encouraged the Boxers, a quasi-religious cult, to attack Westerners, especially foreign missionaries in northern China, and when Boxers besieged the Foreign Legation Quarter in 1900, she stood by. When the allied forces marched in to Běijīng to end the siege, she fled in disguise, an ignominious retreat that marked the final humiliation that doomed the Qing dynasty. When Cixi returned in disgrace a year later, China's moderni-sation had begun in earnest, but it was too late to save the Qing dynasty – it fell in 1911.

REPUBLICAN CHINA

After 1900, the last tribute barges arrived in Běijīng and a railway line ran along the traditional invasion route along the Juyong Pass to Bādálǐng. You can see the handsome clocktower and sheds of Běijīng's first railway station (Qian Men Railway Station, p76), recently restored, on the southeast corner of Tiananmen Square. Běijīng never became an industrial or commercial centre – that role went to nearby Tiānjīn, as it lies on the coast. Yet it remained the leading political and intellectual centre of China until the late 1920s. China's first (and only) parlia-

1900	1908	1911
Boxer Rebellion and siege of the Foreign Legation Quarter	Empress Dowager Cixi bequeaths power to two-year-old Puyi, the last emperor	Collapse of the Qing dynasty; Sun Yat-sen declared president of the Republic of China

ment was established in Běijīng in what was once the imperial elephant house, now out of sight in the sprawling headquarters of Xinhua, the state news agency.

In the settlement imposed after 1900, China had to pay the victors heavy indemnities. Some of this money was returned to China and used to build the first modern universities, including what are now the Oxford and Cambridge of China – Qinghua and Peking Universities. Běijīng's university quarter is in the Hǎidiàn district, near the Old Summer Palace (some campuses are actually in the imperial parkland). Intellectuals from all over China continued to gravitate to Běijīng, including the young Mao Zedong, who arrived to work as a librarian in 1921.

Běijīng students and professors were at the forefront of the 1919 May Fourth Movement. This was at once a student protest against the Versailles Treaty, which had awarded Germany's concessions in China to Japan, and an intellectual movement to jettison the Confucian feudal heritage and Westernise China. Mao himself declared that to modernise China it was first necessary to destroy it. China's intellectuals looked around the world for models to copy. Some went to Japan, others to America, Britain, Germany or, like Deng Xiaoping and Zhou Enlai, France. Many, of course, went to study Marxism in Moscow.

As the warlords marched armies in and out of Běijīng, the almost medieval city began to change. Temples were closed down and turned into schools. The last emperor, Puyi, left the Forbidden City in 1924 with his eunuchs and concubines. As the Manchus adapted to the changes, they tried to assimilate and their presence faded. Western-style brick houses, shops and restaurants were built. City gates were widened and new ones added, including one at Jianguomenwai to make way for the motorcar. Běijīng acquired nightclubs, cinemas, racecourses and a stock exchange; brothels and theatres flourished. Despite political and diplomatic crises, this was a period when people had fun and enjoyed a unique period of individual freedom.

Generalissimo Chiang Kaishek united most of the country under Chinese National Party (KMT or Kuomintang in Chinese) rule and moved the capital to Nánjīng. Even after 1928, Běijīng's romantic air of decaying grandeur attracted Chinese and Western writers and painters trying to fuse Western and Chinese artistic traditions. Some of 20th-century China's best literature was written in Běijīng in the 1920s and 1930s by the likes of Lao She, Lin Huiyin, Xu Zhimou, Shen Congwen and Qian Zhongshu.

It all came to end when Japan's Kwantung Army moved down from Manchuria and occupied Běijīng in 1937. By then most people who could had fled – some to Chóngqìng in Sìchuān province, which served as Chiang Kaishek's wartime capital. Others joined Mao Zedong in his communist base in Yan'an. Many universities established campuses in exile in Yúnnán province. And the collection of imperial treasures was secretly removed, eventually ending up in Taiwan where it can still be seen in a Taipei museum.

The Japanese stayed in Běijīng for eight years and, before their WWII defeat in 1945, had drawn up plans to build a new administrative capital in an area to the west of the city walls near Gongzhufen. It was a miserable time for Běijīng, but the architecture was left largely untouched by the war. When the Japanese surrendered in August 1945, Běijīng was 'liberated' by American marines. The city once again became a merry place famous for its parties – the serious events took place elsewhere in China. When the civil war broke out in earnest between nationalists and communists in 1947 the worst fighting took place in the cities of Manchuria.

In 1948, the Communist Eighth Route Army moved south and encircled Běijīng. General Fu Zuoyi, Commander-in-Chief of the Nationalists Northern China Bandit Suppression Headquarters, prepared the city for a prolonged siege. He razed private houses and built gun emplacements and dug-outs along the Ming battlements. Nationalist planes dropped bags of rice and flour to relieve the shortages, some hitting skaters on the frozen Beihai Lake. Both sides seemed reluctant to fight it out and destroy the ancient capital. The rich tried to flee on the few planes that took off from a runway constructed at Dongdan on Changan Avenue (Changan means 'avenue of eternal peace'). Another airstrip was opened at the Temple of Heaven by cutting down 20,000 trees, including 400 ancient cypresses.

On 22 January 1949 General Fu signed a surrender agreement, and on 31 January his KMT troops marched out and the People's Liberation Army (PLA) entered. A truck drove up

1926	1928	1937
The Kuomintang embark on the Northern Expedition to unify China	Capital moved to Nánjīng	Japanese occupation of Běijīng

Morrison St (now Wangfujing Dajie) blasting a continuous refrain to the residents of Běijīng (or Peiping as it was know then): 'Welcome to the Liberation Army on its arrival in Peiping! Congratulations to the people of Peiping on their liberation!' Behind it marched 300 soldiers in battle gear. A grand victory parade took place on 3 February with 250 assorted military vehicles, virtually all American-made and captured from the KMT over the previous two years.

AFTER 1949

In the spring of 1949 Mao Zedong and the communist leadership were camped in the Western suburbs around Badachu, an area which is still the headquarters of the PLA. On 1 October 1949, Mao Zedong mounted the Gate of Heavenly Peace (p76) and declared the founding of the People's Republic of China, saying the Chinese people had stood up. He spoke only a few words in one of the very few public speeches he ever made.

Mao then moved into Zhōngnánhǎi, part of the chain of lakes and gardens dating back to Kublai Khan. Marshal Yuan Shikai (1859–1916) had lived there too during his short-lived attempt to establish his own dynasty after 1911. During his final two decades Mao lived in a courtyard house on an island in the lake called Yingtai where the Empress Dowager had her nephew, Emperor Guangxu, locked up after 1897. Mao spent much of his time sprawled across a huge double bed surrounded by shelves of books, many about Ming history.

Nobody is quite sure why he chose Běijīng as his capital – nor why he failed to carry out his intention to raze the Forbidden City and erect new party headquarters on the site. Designs were drawn up in the late 1960s but never implemented. The Forbidden City was closed for nearly 10 years and became overgrown with weeds.

After 1949 many of new China's top leaders followed Mao's cue and moved their homes and offices into the old princely palaces (*wángfǔ*) – inadvertently preserving much of the old architecture. Mao wished to turn Běijīng from a 'city of consumption into a city production.' 'Chairman Mao wants a big modern city: he expects the sky there to be filled with smoke-stacks,' said Peng Zhen, the first Party Secretary of Běijīng, to China's premier architectural historian, Liang Sicheng, as they stood on the Gate of Heavenly Peace looking south.

Thousands of factories sprang up in Běijīng and quite a few were built in old temples. In time Běijīng developed into a centre for steel, chemicals, machine tools, engines, electricity, vinegar, beer, concrete, textiles, weapons – in fact everything that would make it an economically self-sufficient 'production base' in case of war. By the 1970s Běijīng had become one of the most heavily polluted cities in the world.

The move to tear down the city's walls, widen the roads, demolish the distinctive *páilou* (ceremonial arches) started immediately after 1949, but was fiercely contested by some intellectuals, including Liang Sicheng, who ran the architecture department of Qinghua University. So in the midst of the demolition of so many famous landmarks, the municipal authorities earmarked many buildings and even old trees for conservation. However, it was all to no avail – Mao's brutal political purges silenced all opposition. In the 1958 Great Leap Forward, the last qualms about preserving old Běijīng were abandoned. A new plan was approved to destroy 80% of the old capital. The walls were pulled down, but a series of ring roads were never built.

Those intellectuals who escaped persecution in the 1950s were savagely dealt with during the Cultural Revolution (1966–76). Qinghua University became the birthplace of the Red Guards. In the 'bloody August' of that year, Běijīng's middle-school students turned on their teachers, brutally murdering some of them. In August and September of 1966, a total of 1772 people were killed in the capital, according to a report published by the *Beijing Daily* after 1979. The numbers exclude those beaten to death as they tried to escape Běijīng on trains – their registration as residents of Běijīng was suddenly cancelled. The headquarters of the Cultural Revolution in Běijīng had been in the Jianguomenwai area, and has since been demolished. The site is now occupied by the Si-tech Department Store.

By 1969 Mao had fallen out with Moscow and he prepared China for a nuclear war. The remaining population was turned out to build tunnels and nuclear fall-out shelters. Bricks from

1949	1950s	1966
Communist victory over the Kuomintang; founding of the People's Republic of China	Most of Běijīng's city walls and gates are levelled to make way for roads	The Cultural Revolution is launched

the city walls and even the Old Summer Palace were used to build these. You can still visit the tunnels and shelters built during those years in many places, such as Ditan Park (p86), where the tunnels are used as an ice rink, and the Beijing Underground City (p74). At Yuetan Park the tunnels have been converted into a shopping arcade. This underground city is connected by road and rail tunnels, which still allow the top leadership to move around Běijīng in secret.

In Mao's time the geomantically inspired symmetry of Běijīng was radically changed. The north–south axis of the Ming City was ruined by widening Changan Ave into a 10-lane, east–west highway. This was used for huge annual military parades or when visiting dignitaries arrived and the population was turned out to cheer them. In the 1950s, the centre was redesigned by Soviet architects and modelled on Moscow's Red Square. Three major gates and many other Ming buildings, including the former government ministries, were demolished, leaving the concrete expanse you see today.

Mao used the square to receive the adulation of the millions of Red Guards who flocked to Běijīng from 1966 to 1969 but, from 1976, it became the scene of massive anti-government protests. After 1969 Mao exiled the Red Guards along with 20 million 'educated youth' to the countryside, but in 1976, when Premier Zhou Enlai died, there was a large and apparently spontaneous protest on the square which was put down by the police. In 1976, Mao himself died.

Deng Xiaoping (1904–97), backed by a group of veteran generals, seized power in a coup d'etat and threw Mao's widow, Jiang Qing (1914–91), and her ultra-leftist cronies into the notorious Qincheng prison outside the city, where Mao had incarcerated so many senior Party veterans. This still exists not far from the Ming Tombs.

At the third plenum of the 11th Party Congress, Deng consolidated his grip on power and launched economic reforms. At the same time thousands of people began putting up posters, along a wall west of Zhōngnánhǎi, complaining of injustices under the 'Gang of Four' (Jiang Qing and her three associates) and demanding democracy. The Democracy Wall in Xidan has now disappeared and been replaced by a shopping mall. Deng initially appeared to back political reforms, but soon the activists were thrown in jail, some in the Beijing No 1 Municipal Prison. This famous prison no longer exists, it was demolished in the mid-1990s.

Many of the activists were former Red Guards or the exiled educated youth. After 1976 they drifted back to the city but could only find jobs in the new private sector running small market stalls, tailor shops or restaurants. After the universities opened conditions remained poor and the intelligentsia continued to be treated with suspicion. Frustrations with the slow pace of reforms prompted fresh student protests in the winter of 1986. Peasants did well out of the first wave of reforms, but in the cities many people felt frustrated. Urban life revolved around 'work units' to which nearly everyone was assigned. The work unit distributed food, housing, bicycles, travel permits and almost everything else. Běijīng was still a rather drab dispiriting place in the 1980s; there was much more to eat but everything else was in a lamentable state. For 30 years, there had been little investment in housing or transport.

In January 1987 the Party's conservative gerontocrats ousted the pro-reform Party chief Hu Yaobang and, when he suddenly died in the spring of 1989, Běijīng students began assembling on Tiananmen Square. Officially they were mourning his passing but they began to raise slogans for political reform and against corruption. The protests snowballed as the Communist Party leadership split into rival factions, causing a rare paralysis. The police stood by as the protests spread across the country and workers, officials and ordinary citizens took to the streets. When the military tried to intervene, Běijīngers surrounded the tanks. The students set up tents on Tiananmen Square and went on a hunger strike. When the premier Li Peng held a dialogue with the students that was aired live on TV, student leaders sarcastically upbraided him.

The students created the first independent student union since 1919 and celebrated the anniversary of the May Fourth Movement with a demonstration in which over a million took to the streets. For the first time since 1949, the press threw off the shackles of state censorship and became independent. When Soviet leader Mikhail Gorbachev entered on a state visit, and was enthusiastically welcomed as a symbol of political reform, it seemed as if the Chinese Communist Party, too, would embrace political change. Party General Secretary Zhao Ziyang

1976	1979	1980s
Death of Mao; death of Premier Zhou Enlai sparks spontaneous protests	Deng Xiaoping's reformist agenda commences	Temples and monuments restored for tourism; construction boom begins

led the reformist faction, but the older-generation leaders, led by Deng Xiaoping, feared the worst. They decided to arrest Zhao and retake the city with a military assault. On the night of 3 June, tens of thousands of troops backed by tanks and armoured personnel carriers entered the city from four directions, bulldozing aside the hastily erected barricades.

Many people died, and by the early hours of 4 June the troops were in control of Tiananmen Square. In the crackdown that followed across the country, student leaders escaped abroad while the Party arrested thousands of students and their supporters. In the purge of Party members that followed, China's reforms seemed to be going into reverse.

The 1989 pro-democracy protests were the largest political demonstrations in Chinese history. Since then Běijīng has seen only one major protest when, in 1999, the followers of the Falun Gong movement surrounded Zhōngnánhǎi.

Things only began to change when Deng Xiaoping emerged from the shadows and set off in 1991 on a so-called 'southern tour', visiting his special economic zones in the south and calling for more and faster change. Despite opposition in the Party, he won the day. China began a wave of economic reforms, but, today, the political system remains unchanged. Reforms transformed urban China and brought new wealth and opportunities to most urban residents. At the same time some 40 million workers in state-owned factories lost their jobs. Deng's reforms pulled in a tide of foreign investment, creating two economic booms, after 1992 and 1998. Stock markets reopened, state companies privatised, and private enterprise began to flourish, especially in the service sector, creating millions of new jobs. Over 100 million peasants left the countryside to work on construction sites or in export-processing factories. The factories were moved out of Běijīng, a city which has once again become a 'centre of consumption'.

The economy was given a huge impetus by decisions to rebuild all major cities virtually from scratch, privatise housing, and sell 50- or 70-year land leases to developers. There was resistance by Party Secretary Chen Xitong to the destruction of Běijīng's centre. During the '80s and early '90s, Chen approved redevelopment plans that aimed to preserve and restore Běijīng's historic centre and characteristic architecture. Chen had earlier helped persuade many army and civilian work units to vacate historical sites they'd occupied during the '70s. However, in 1995, he was ousted by Jiang Zemin who in 1995 had him imprisoned on corruption charges.

Once the Beijing Party apparatus was under his direct control, President Jiang approved plans to completely rebuild Běijīng and replace its inhabitants. This was part of the nationwide effort to rebuild the dilapidated and neglected infrastructure of all Chinese cities. The 'trillion-dollar' economic stimulus package has been carried out with remarkable speed. In Běijīng more than a million peasants, housed in dormitories on the construction sites, have worked round the clock. By 1999, new shopping malls, office blocks, hotels and luxury housing developments were being thrown up at astonishing speed. Nothing so fast or on so vast a scale could ever have happened in any other country in the world. Only an absolute dictatorship with the vast human and industrial resources of China at its command could ever have achieved this.

Jiang wanted to turn Běijīng into another Hong Kong, with a forest of glass-and-steel skyscrapers. The new municipal leadership threw out the old zoning laws, which limited the height of buildings within the Second Ring Rd. It revoked existing land deeds by declaring old buildings to be dilapidated slums. Such regulations enabled the state to force residents to abandon their homes and move to new housing in satellite cities. Under the new plan, only a fraction of the 67-sq km Ming city is being preserved. The city still boasted more than 3679 *hútòng* (historic residential alleyways) in the 1980s, but only 430 were left according to a field survey carried out in 2006 by the Beijing Institute of Civil Engineering and Architecture.

Some see this as a collective punishment on Běijīng for its 1989 rebellion, but others see it as the continuing legacy of Mao's Cultural Revolution and the late Qing dynasty reformers. Many in the current leadership are engineers and ex-Red Guards, including President Hu Jintao, who graduated from Qinghua University during the Cultural Revolution. They are determined to jettison everything from the past and bury recent history. Běijīng's new architecture is designed to embody their aspiration to create a new, forward-looking, hi-tech society, and mark the realisation of the goal of a new modern China.

1989	1997	2001
Tiananmen Square massacre	Death of Deng Xiaoping; reconstruction of Běijīng launched	Běijīng chosen to host the 2008 Olympic Games

The Olympics ▪

The Olympics

That Běijīng is hosting the Olympics just 28 years after China first took part in the Games is a remarkable achievement. Having refused to participate in the Olympics from 1949 until 1980 because Taiwan was allowed to compete under the name Republic of China, the Chinese are now eagerly counting down the days till the 2008 Games begin on 8 August.

For the Chinese, the Olympics will be a massive coming out party, the most potent demonstration yet of China's arrival on the world stage as a genuine superpower. With events being staged in Hong Kong, Qīngdǎo, Qínhuángdǎo, Shànghǎi, Shěnyáng and Tiānjīn as well as Běijīng, there's a very real feeling that the 2008 Olympics belong to all of China and not just Běijīng.

But it is Běijīng that will be the focus of attention. Since 2003, the capital has been turned upside down as venues are constructed and the city's infrastructure completely overhauled. This transformation has come at a huge price. It's estimated that the total cost of hosting the Games will be US$40 billion, making the 29th Olympiad by far the most expensive ever held.

OLYMPICS HISTORY: ANCIENT TO MODERN

The history of the Olympic Games dates back to 776 BC. Held every four years in honour of the Olympian gods, the Games were staged at Olympia in Greece and were open to all free Greek males. Later, the Romans were allowed to compete. Women were barred from both participating in and watching the Games.

Conceived as a test of body, mind and will, winners received a wreath made of olive leaves. Winning didn't just mean individual glory, but was an honour for the athlete's birthplace. This led to corruption, in the form of bribing judges. In AD 66, the first in a long line of Olympic scandals took place, when a drunken Emperor Nero was declared winner of a chariot race, despite failing to finish the course.

The rise of Christianity put an end to the ancient Olympics. They were abolished in AD 393 by the Christian Emperor Theodosius as part of a purge of pagan festivals.

The Games were revived in 1896 thanks to the efforts of a Frenchman, Baron Pierre de Coubertin. Distressed by the effects of the Franco-Prussian War, de Coubertin hit on the idea of using sport as a way to foster goodwill between nations. He organised a world sports congress in Paris in 1894, which gave birth to the International Olympic Committee (IOC), and two years later the Games were staged once more. Fittingly, Athens was the site of the first modern Olympics.

Despite the Baron's hopes, the Olympics have failed dismally as a deterrent to wars. The outbreak of WWI saw the cancellation of the 1916 Games, while the 1936 Berlin Olympics,

LOCAL VOICES

Liu Qianwen knows exactly where she was when she heard that Běijīng had been awarded the 2008 Olympics. 'I was in a taxi when the result was announced on the radio,' she recalls. 'I was happy and excited, but not very surprised. We lost out last time, so it should have been us this time. We deserved it.'

A 23-year-old engineering student from Běijīng, Liu's university, the Beijing Institute of Technology, is one of the venues for the Games. The judo and tae kwon do events will be held in the university's gymnasium and Liu is hoping to attend.

Like most Běijīngers, she's pleased with the work that's been done to improve Běijīng's infrastructure and thinks the disruption to everyday life is a small price to pay. 'The transport system in particular is going to be much better,' she says. Above all, Liu believes the Olympics will offer foreigners an insight into her hometown. 'The world will know much more about Běijīng after the Olympics.'

MASCOTS: IT'S ALL IN THE NAME

In Chinese they are *Fúwá*, literally 'good luck dolls', but to the rest of the world they are the official Olympic mascots. Initially called 'The Friendlies', until someone decided that sounded too close to 'friendless', the five cartoon characters, two females and three males, will tour the world before the Games kick off.

Bèibei, Jīngjing, Huānhuan, Yíngying and *Nīni* were unveiled at an elaborate ceremony in Běijīng in November 2005. Each one represents an animal or element, respectively a fish, giant panda, fire, Tibetan antelope and swallow, as well as particular sports and each of the five Olympic rings.

But there is far more to them than that. Each *Fúwá* has a double syllable name because that is a common way to form affectionate nicknames in Mandarin. And when the first syllables of each *Fúwá* are joined together you get the phrase *Běijīng huānyíng nǐ,* or 'Běijīng welcomes you'.

the last before WWII, turned into a showcase for the Nazi regime. It would be 12 years before they were held again. By then women, allowed into the Olympics in 1900, were competing in more and more events.

Throughout the Cold War era the Olympics were increasingly politicised, as nations used the high profile of the Games to protest the Soviet invasions of Hungary, Czechoslovakia and Afghanistan, Britain's intervention in the 1956 Suez crisis, and the apartheid policies of South Africa. The protests hit a peak in 1980, when the USA boycotted the Moscow Olympics in response to the Soviet invasion of Afghanistan. The Soviets and many of their East European allies responded four years later by boycotting the Los Angeles Olympics. But the low point of Olympic history came at the 1972 Munich Games, when 11 Israeli athletes were murdered by Palestinian terrorists.

The end of the Cold War coincided with professional athletes being allowed to compete in the Olympics. At the same time, the use of drugs to boost performance became widespread – an issue that has affected the Games credibility, as have allegations of corruption within the IOC. A number of IOC members and organisers of the 2002 Salt Lake City Winter Games were sanctioned, after it emerged that bribes had been offered to IOC officials.

Corruption and drugs aside, perhaps the biggest threat to the future of the Games is their very success. The Olympics have become so vast and expensive to stage that few nations can afford to host them.

THE BĚIJĪNG OLYMPICS

When Běijīng was awarded the 2008 Olympics on 13 July 2001, having previously lost to Sydney for the chance to host the 2000 Games, it was the cue for wild rejoicing across not just Běijīng but all China. Bids to stage the Olympics from both past and future hosts from the developed world, such as Barcelona and London, have sparked furious debate over the cost of hosting the Games and their potential benefits. However, there has been no such dissent in China.

Běijīng's passion for the Games was demonstrated when the call for the 70,000 volunteers needed went out; 43,000 people applied in the first 48 hours. Běijīngers have also responded enthusiastically to the way their city is being upgraded for the Games. New subway lines and improved roads will join the 12 venues being constructed for the Olympics as a lasting legacy of 2008.

SEX PLEASE, WE'RE ATHLETES

In the ancient Olympics, athletes competed in the nude to better show off their muscled bodies. Times have changed, but if the example of recent Olympics is anything to go by, then for some of the 10,500 athletes who will call the Olympic Village in the north of Běijīng home for two weeks, the Games are an excuse for a bacchanalian-like celebration.

The combination of adrenalin, toned bodies and the close proximity of fellow competitors inspires a vigorous social life amongst Olympic athletes. At the Athens Olympic Games in 2004, one company supplied 130,000 condoms to the Olympic Village but more were needed. 250,000 condoms were handed out at the 2002 Winter Olympics in Salt Lake City, while the Sydney Olympic Games ran out of condoms so quickly that the organisers had to arrange extra supplies. Běijīng organisers have been silent on their plans for this issue, but clearly they need to be prepared.

OLYMPIC DEVELOPMENTS

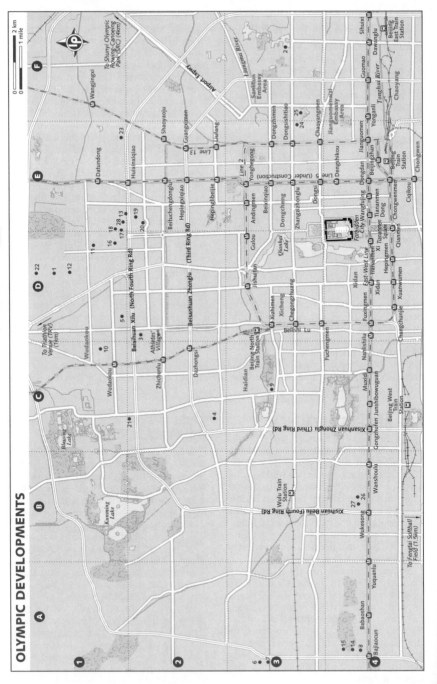

Of the new sites, the most impressive are the centrepiece National Stadium (the 'bird's nest', p38), and the National Aquatics Center (p38), known as the 'water cube' for its shape and bubble-like exterior. The 'bird's nest' and the 'water cube' were both designed by foreign firms, but there has been little public anger over this. Chinese architects have been employed as junior partners in all the foreign-designed projects and the desire of the Chinese to create an Olympics to remember means that nationalistic concerns have been put to one side.

This, however, won't be the case when it comes to the crowds who will fill every one of the 30 venues staging the Olympics in Běijīng. China only won its first Olympic gold medal in 1984, but has made no secret of its desire to top the medals table in 2008. The slogan of the 2008 Games might be 'One World, One Dream', but the Běijīngers watching them will be fiercely partisan and patriotic.

TOP VANTAGE POINTS

With most of the events taking place inside stadiums and university gymnasiums, the only Olympic event that people are guaranteed to enjoy for free is the cycling road race. Scheduled to take place on 9 August, one day after the Games open, the 200km course will start at Tiananmen Square (p81). After heading north through the city, the world's top cyclists will ride to the Great Wall. The riders then face seven punishing circuits of the nearby hills, which will be a great place to catch some of the action.

Although no details had been confirmed at the time of writing, it is likely that giant video screens will be set up at various places around town for people to watch the Games. Ritan Park (p95) is one possible central location. Check local expat magazines (see p227) for more details.

THE PRACTICALITIES

The Games run from 8–24 August 2008. The start time of 8pm on the eighth month of the eighth year of the 21st century was carefully chosen as a particularly auspicious day for the Olympics to begin. Eight is the luckiest number in Chinese culture and is traditionally associated with prosperity.

Tickets have been available since early 2007. Prices are much lower than those of recent Games: 58% of the seven million tickets that went on sale cost Y100 or less. Tickets for the opening ceremony range from Y200 to Y5000. For the preliminary rounds of events, they go from Y30 to Y300, for finals, Y60 to Y1000. Fourteen per cent of tickets have been reserved at a discounted rate for students. The official website for the 2008 Olympics (http://en.beijing2008.com) has details of how to buy tickets.

Sights ▪

Sights

The neighbourhoods of Běijīng, a flat city of largely uniform character uninterrupted by major waterways or hilly terrain, are not clearly delineated by distinct boundaries or physical features, yet the city is divided into numerous historical districts.

The Forbidden City acts as the cartographic and physical focus of Běijīng, the bull's-eye around which the city's notable historic sights cluster and the city's five ring roads radiate concentrically. Běijīng's most historic quarters surround the Forbidden City and Tiananmen Square, within the looping boundary of the Second Ring Rd and subway Line 2.

Xīchéng (West City) is the district to the west of the Forbidden City and the Drum Tower. Dōngchéng (East City) is conversely the neighbourhood to the east of these points. Both Xīchéng and Dōngchéng are the city's core districts, containing Běijīng's most ancient monuments, famous lakes and *hútòng* (alleyways) and enclosing the former Imperial City.

For all practical purposes, north and south Běijīng are divided by Chang'an Jie (divided into Dongchang'an Jie and Xichang'an Jie; becoming Jianguomennei Dajie and Jiang

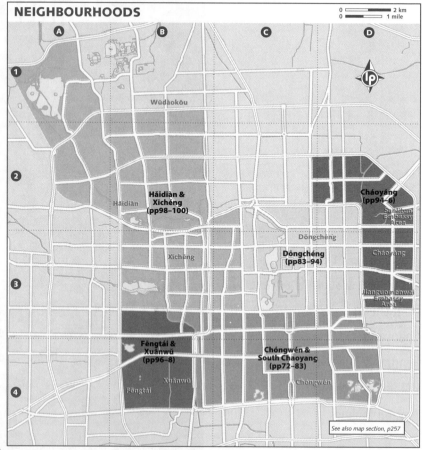

NEIGHBOURHOODS

0 — 2 km
0 — 1 mile

Wǔdàokǒu

Hǎidiàn

Hǎidiàn & Xīchéng (pp98–100)

Cháoyáng (pp94–6)

Sānlǐtún Embassy Area

Xīchéng

Dōngchéng

Dōngchéng (pp83–94)

Cháoyáng

Jiānguomenwài Embassy Area

Fēngtái & Xuānwǔ (pp96–8)

Chóngwén & South Chaoyang (pp72–83)

Xuānwǔ

Fēngtái

Chóngwén

See also map section, p257

uomenwai Dajie in the east and Fuxingmennei Dajie and Fuxingmenwai Dajie in the west), along which runs Line 1 of the subway. The district of Chóngwén, containing the Temple of Heaven, lies south of Dōngchéng, and Cháoyáng is a huge neighbourhood to the north, east and southeast of both Dōngchéng and Chóngwén.

South of Xīchéng and Dōngchéng is the district of Xuānwǔ, largely enclosed within the Second Ring Rd, and the huge district of Fēngtái which covers a huge swathe of southwest Běijīng. The colossal district of Hǎidiàn, sprawling west and north of Xīchéng, is the preserve of some of Běijīng's premier sights, including the Summer Palace, the Old Summer Palace and Fragrant Hills Park.

ITINERARIES

One Day

The **Forbidden City** (p87) is Běijīng's obligatory sight, so devote at least a morning to the palace and the sights of nearby **Tiananmen Square** (p81). Hop on the subway from Tiananmen Xi to **Wangfujing Dajie** and lunch at **Quanjude Roast Duck Restaurant** (p131) or **Wangfujing Snack Street** (p124). Walk off your meal browsing shops along Wangfujing Dajie before taking a taxi to the **Temple of Heaven Park** (p79) for a few hours. Try to squeeze in a performance of Chinese acrobatics at the Chaoyang Theatre (p152) before rounding off the evening by wining and dining in **Sanlitun** (p132).

Three Days

The **Forbidden City** (p87) and the monuments of **Tiananmen Square** (p81) can easily occupy an entire morning, before lunch at the **Liqun Roast Duck Restaurant** (p126) or other roast duck eateries in the vicinity of Qianmen. In the afternoon, follow our walking tours around the **Foreign Legation Quarter** (p114) and **Wangfujing Dajie** (p115). Dine perched next to the east gate of the Forbidden City at **Courtyard** (p131) or hoover up snacks along **Donghuamen Night Market** (p128). To round off the day, take a taxi to **Sanlitun** (p143) or **Nanluogu Xiang** (p141) and find a bar.

On day two take a day trip to the **Great Wall** (p191) and the **Ming Tombs** (p197). Back in Běijīng, spend the evening enjoying **Beijing opera** (p147) at one of the city's numerous theatres and dine at **Xiao Wang's Home Restaurant** (p126).

On day three make an early morning visit to the **Temple of Heaven Park** (p79) before browsing the stalls and bric-a-brac shops of **Liulichang** (p167). In the afternoon, journey to the **Summer Palace** (p102); alternatively, walk along the restored **Ming City Wall** (p78) from Chongwenmen to the **Southeast Corner Watchtower** (p79) and then, if you have the time, the **Lama Temple** (p91) or Běijīng's **hútòng** (p106) can be explored. Cap the day dining at **Bookworm** (p135).

One Week

Follow the three-day schedule above but bump exploration of the **Summer Palace** (p102) to day four and devote an entire day to the complex. A comprehensive appraisal of the **798 Art District** (p103) should occupy the morning of the fifth day, leaving the afternoon free for our bike ride around Běijīng (p118), which threads through much of the city's **hútòng** heartland. On day six take a trip to **Chéngdé** (p203) or **Shānhǎiguān** (p200), where you can either return the same day or spend the night. Alternatively, devote the entire day to exploring the Great Wall vestiges at **Huánghuā** (p196), where you can also overnight. Make day seven a shopping day, with trips to **Silk Street** (p164), the **Sanlitun Yashow Clothing Market** (p167), **Oriental Plaza** (p163) and the shops of **Dashilar** (p161); if it's a weekend, rise early to sift through the goods at **Panjiayuan Market** (p163).

ORGANISED TOURS

Tours in and around Běijīng and to other parts of China can be arranged through several companies. The recommended China Culture Club (☎ 6432 9341, ext 18; www.chinese cultureclub.org; 29 Liangmaqiao Lu) offers a range of fascinating tours geared to expats and foreign tourists. Destinations range from Běijīng to off-the-beaten-track locations around China and they also offer a variety of stimulating courses on Chinese language and culture. Panda Tour (☎ 6522 2991; 36 Nanlishi Lu) offers tours to popular sights in and around town, including trips around *hútòng*, acrobatic shows and other performances. Panda Tour can also be found at hotel counters including at St Regis (p182), Kempinski (p186) and Shangri-La (p188). Numerous outfits run tours around Běijīng's *hútòng*, see the Historic Hútòng chapter (p106) for details. The short '*hútòng*-style' bus tours that run from the south end of pedestrianised Wangfujing Dajie are uninteresting and best avoided. China International Travel Service (CITS; ☎ 8511 8522; www.cits.com .cn; Rm 1212, CITS Bldg, 1 Dongdan Beidajie) and China Travel Service (CTS; ☎ 6464 6400, ext 6448/6422; 2 Beisanhuan Donglu) both run tours, but are generally aimed at Chinese tourists. CTS is at hotel counters including at the Hilton and the Novotel. The Beijing Tourist Information Centers (p231) dotted around Běijīng can also link you up with tours; also ask at your hotel, which should offer tours to the big sights.

> ## TOP FIVE BĚIJĪNG MUSEUMS
>
> - Avidly explore the imperial acreage of the **Palace Museum** (the Forbidden City, p87).
> - Find time for Běijīng's snappily designed **Capital Museum** (p96).
> - Catch up with the long arm of the law at the **Beijing Police Museum** (p74).
> - Peruse the exhibition commemorating the Imperial City at the **Imperial City Exhibition** (p77).
> - Savour the elegant collection of the **Poly Art Museum** (p95).

CHÓNGWÉN & SOUTH CHAOYANG

崇文、朝阳南

Eating p124; Shopping p161; Sleeping p180

This segment of Běijīng embraces the historic swathe south and southeast of the Forbidden City, largely within the loop of the Hùchénghé (City Moat) and the footprint of the now vanished Chinese City Wall. It also incorporates parts of Dōngchéng, Xīchéng and Xuānwǔ districts.

The area north of Qianmen Xidajie and Qianmen Dongdajie and within the Second Ring Rd was the historic Manchu sector of Běijīng. Within the southern extents of the old Tartar City are the Gate of Heavenly Peace and artefacts of the Imperial City, including the Supreme Temple and the Imperial Archives.

Not surprisingly, this core district also contains the city's brashest Communist Party symbols, including the imposing portrait of Mao Zedong and his mausoleum, the Great Hall of the People and Tiananmen Square itself. This is also where the foreign powers chose to establish their legation quarters (p76) in the 19th century.

The area south of Qianmen Xidajie and Qianmen Dongdajie traditionally belonged to the old Chinese quarter, south of the Qing dynasty Tartar City Wall and well beyond the exclusive imperial zone. Historically an enclave of the *lǎobǎixìng* (common people), this was a typically more down-at-heel and shabby neighbourhood, threaded by small *hútòng* and home to the shops and bazaars of Dashilar and the *hóngdēngqū* (red light district). Yet this district also belongs in the south, an aspect facing the sun and indicative of *yáng* (the male and positive principle). Blessed with such positive attributes, it is not surprising that the principle imperial shrine of Běijīng, the Temple of Heaven, is also located here. A considerable amount of investment has been ploughed into prettifying the shops around Qianmen Dajie in the lead-up to the 2008 Olympic Games, although Dashilar has also suffered much destruction.

The subway stations of Qianmen, Chongwenmen and Jianguomen recall some of the Tartar City Wall's vast and imposing gates, of which only the Front Gate (p76) and the Southeast Corner Watchtower (Dongbianmen; p79) to the southeast, survive. The road looping south from Jianguomen station, following the line of the city moat, marks the outline of the levelled Chinese City Wall, whose gates survive only in street names, such as Guangqumen Nanbinhe Lu, Zuo'anmen Xibinhe Lu and Yongdingmen Dongbinhe Lu.

ANCIENT OBSERVATORY Map pp268-9
Gǔ Guānxiàngtái 古观象台

☎ 6524 2202; adult Y10; ☽ 9.30-11.30am &
1-4.30pm, sometimes closed on Monday;
Ⓜ Jianguomen

Star-gazing is perhaps on the back foot in
today's Běijīng – it may take a supernova to
penetrate the haze that frequently blankets
the nocturnal sky – but the Chinese capital
has a sparkling history of astronomical
observation.

The observatory – today mounted on the
battlements of a watchtower lying along
the line of the old Ming City Wall – originally
dates back to Kublai Khan's days when it lay
north of the present site. Khan – like later
Ming and Qing emperors – relied heavily
on astrologers to plan military endeavours.
The present observatory – the only surviving
example of several constructed during the
Jin, Yuan, Ming and Qing dynasties – was
built between 1437 and 1446 to facilitate
both astrological predictions and seafaring
navigation.

At ground level is a pleasant courtyard –
perfect for parking yourself on a bench
and recharging – flanked by halls housing
displays (with limited English captions),
including China's Ancient Astronomical
Achievements Exhibition. Also within the
courtyard is a reproduction-looking armillary sphere supposedly dating to 1439,
supported by four dragons. At the rear is an
attractive garden with grass, sundials and
another armillary sphere.

Climb the steps to the roof and see an
array of Jesuit-designed astronomical instruments, embellished with sculptured bronze
dragons and other Chinese flourishes – a
unique mix of East and West. The Jesuits,
scholars as well as proselytisers, arrived in
1601 when Matteo Ricci and his associates
were permitted to work alongside Chinese
scientists. Outdoing the resident calen-
dar-setters, they were given control of the
observatory and became the Chinese court's
official advisers. Instruments on display
include an Azimuth Theodolite (1715), an
Altazimuth (1673) and an Ecliptic Armilla
(1673); of the eight on view, six were designed and constructed under the supervi-
sion of the Belgian priest Ferdinand Verbiest.
It's not clear which instruments on display
are the originals.

During the Boxer Rebellion, the instru-
ments disappeared into the hands of the
French and Germans. Some were returned
in 1902, and others were returned after
WWI, under the provisions of the Treaty of
Versailles (1919).

BEIJING NATURAL HISTORY
MUSEUM Map pp268-9
Běijīng Zìrán Bówùguǎn 北京自然博物馆

☎ 6702 4431; 126 Tianqiao Nandajie; adult Y30;
☽ 8.30am-4.30pm Tue-Sun, last entry 4pm;
Ⓜ Qianmen

The main entrance to this overblown,
creeper-laden museum is hung with
portraits of the great natural historians,
including Darwin and Linnaeus (here spelt
Linnacus). Escort kiddies to the revamped
dinosaur hall facing you as you enter, which
presents itself with an overarching skeleton
of a *mamenchisaurus jingyanensis* – a vast
sauropod that once roamed China – and a
much smaller *protoceratops*. Creepy crawlies
are consigned to the second floor, there's
an aquarium with Nemo-esque clown fish
and an exhibition on the origins of life on
earth, but the lack of English captions is
baffling. Some of the exhibits, such as the
spliced human cadavers and genitalia in the
notorious Hall of Human Bodies are best
reserved for those with strong constitu-
tions, while visiting with munchkins could
subject them to months of vivid nightmares
and nocturnal disturbances. Visiting exhibitions are occasionally staged, again without
English explanations. Some halls were being
revamped at the time of writing.

BEIJING PLANNING EXHIBITION
HALL Map pp268-9
Běijīngshì Guīhuà Zhǎnlǎnguǎn
北京市规划展览馆

☎ 6701 7074; 20 Qianmen Dongdajie; admission
Y30; ☽ 9am-5pm Tue-Sun; Ⓜ Qianmen

This little-visited exhibition hall takes
particular pains to present Běijīng's gut-
wrenching, *hútòng*-felling metamorphosis
in the best possible light. English labelling
is sadly scarce; the only exhibits of note
are a detailed bronze map of the town in
1949 – ironically the very year that sealed
the fate of old Peking – and a huge, detailed diorama of the modern metropolis.
The rest of the exhibition is a paean to
modern city planning and the unstoppable advance of the concrete mixer, while
3-D films trumpet 'The New Běijīng'.

BEIJING MUSEUM PASS 博物馆通票

This pass (Bówùguǎn Tōngpiào) is a fantastic investment that will save you both money and queuing for tickets. For Y80 you get either complimentary access or discounted admission (typically 50%) to almost 90 museums, temples or tourist sights in and around Běijīng. Attractions covered include a section of the Great Wall at Bādálǐng, Confucius Temple and the Imperial College, the Bell Tower, the Imperial City Exhibition, Miaoying Temple White Dagoba, Dongyue Temple, Zhihua Temple, Fayuan Temple, Wanshou Temple, the Beijing Planetarium, the Beijing Natural History Museum, the Xu Beihong Museum and many others. Not all museums are worth visiting, but many are worthwhile and you only have to visit a small selection of museums to get your money back. The pass comes in the form of a booklet (Chinese with minimal English), valid from 1 January to 31 December in any one year. The pass can be picked up from participating museums and sights. It is sometimes hard to find (especially as the year progresses), so phone (☎ 6222 3793 or 8666 0651; you may need a Chinese speaker) or consult www.bowuguan.bj.cn (in Chinese) to locate stocks.

BEIJING POLICE MUSEUM Map pp268-9
Běijīng Jǐngchá Bówùguǎn 北京警察博物馆
☎ 8522 5018; 36 Dongjiaomin Xiang; adult Y5;
🕑 9am-4pm Tue-Sun; Ⓜ Qianmen
Infested with propaganda perhaps, but some riveting exhibits make this a fascinating exposé of Běijīng's dà gài mào (local slang for the constabulary). Learn how Běijīng's first Public Security Bureau (PSB) college operated from the Dongyue Temple (p94) in 1949 and find out how officers tackled the 'stragglers, disbanded soldiers, bandits, local ruffians, hoodlums and despots….' planted in Běijīng by the Kuomintang (KMT). There are also eye-opening accounts of how KMT spies Li Andong and Yamaguchi Takachi planned to mortar the Gate of Heavenly Peace (p76), and a welcome analysis of how the Běijīng PSB was destroyed during the 'national catastrophe' of the Cultural Revolution. Altogether 9685 policemen were dismissed from their posts during the paroxysms of violence – spot the yawning gap among portraits of PSB directors from June 1966 to June 1977. The museum covers grisly business: there's Wang Zhigang's bombing of Beijing Train Station on 29 October 1980, an explosion at Xidan Plaza in 1968, while upstairs the museum gets to grips with morbid crimes and their investigations.

BEIJING UNDERGROUND CITY
Map pp268-9
Běijīng Dìxiàchéng 北京地下城
62 Xidamochang Jie; adult Y20; 🕑 8am-6pm;
Ⓜ Chongwenmen
By 1969, as the USA landed on the moon, Mao had decided the future for Běijīng's people lay underground. Alarmist predictions of nuclear war with Russia dispatched an army of Chinese beneath Běijīng's streets to burrow a huge warren of bombproof tunnels. The task was completed Cultural Revolution–style – by hand – with the finishing touches made in 1979, just as Russia decided to bog down in Afghanistan instead.

A section of tunnels enticingly known as the Beijing Underground City can be explored. English-language tours guide you along parts of this mouldering warren, past rooms designated as battlefield hospitals, a cinema, arsenals, other anonymous vaults and portraits of Mao Zedong. There's even a rudimentary elevator, flood-proof doors and a ventilation system to expel poisonous gases. Most of the tunnels are around 8m below ground, so it's cold and very damp, with the humidity increasing the deeper you go (sections at greater depths are flooded). Clad in combat gear, the guide waves down dark and uninviting tunnels, announcing their end points: one leads to the Hall of Preserving Harmony in the Forbidden City, another winds to the Summer Palace, while yet another reaches Tiānjīn (a mere 130km away), or so the guide insists. A tiresome detour to an underground silk factory concludes the trip – pass on the pricey duvet covers and pillow cases and make for the door and daylight. Emerging from the exit, head east and take a peek down the first alley on your right – Tongle Hutong – one of Běijīng's narrowest.

CENTRAL ACADEMY OF FINE ARTS GALLERY Map p262
Zhōngyāng Měiyuàn Měishùguǎn
中央美院美术馆
☎ 6527 7991; 5 Xiaowei Hutong; admission Y5;
🕑 9.30am-4pm Tue-Sun; Ⓜ Wangfujing
A short stroll from Wangfujing Dajie and part of the Central Academy of Fine Arts, this

rather old-fashioned but centrally located exhibition hall displays a selection of Chinese art in a variety of media over three floors.

CHAIRMAN MAO MEMORIAL HALL
Map pp268-9
Máo Zhǔxí Jìniàntáng 毛主席纪念堂
Southern side of Tiananmen Square; admission free, bag/camera storage Y2-10/2-5; 8.30-11.30am Tue-Sun, 2-4pm Tue & Thu, not open pm in Jul & August; Tiananmen Xi, Tiananmen Dong or Qianmen
An obligatory place of pilgrimage for China's proletariat and a must-see for those breezing around Tiananmen Square or on the trail of Běijīng's rare freebies, this mausoleum should not be missed. Mao Zedong died in September 1976, and his mausoleum was constructed shortly after on the site of Zhonghua Gate (Zhonghua Men p82).

Easy as it now is to vilify his excesses, many Chinese still show deep respect when confronted with the physical presence of the man. You are reminded to remove your hat and you can fork out Y3 for a flower to lay at the foot of a statue of Mao. Further on, the Great Helmsman's mummified corpse lies in a crystal cabinet, draped in an anachronistic red flag emblazoned with hammer and sickle, as guards in white gloves impatiently wave the hoi-polloi on towards further rooms, where a riot of Mao kitsch – lighters, bracelets, statues, key rings, bottle openers, you name it – ensues. Don't expect to stumble upon Jung Chang signing copies of her *Mao, the Unknown Story* (see p24). At certain times of the year the body requires maintenance and is not on view. Bags need to be deposited at the building east of the memorial hall across the road from Tiananmen Square (if you leave your camera in your bag you will be charged for it).

CHINA NATIONAL MUSEUM
Map pp268-9
Zhōngguó Guójiā Bówùguǎn 中国国家博物馆
Eastern side of Tiananmen Square; admission Y30, audio tour Y30; 8.30am-4.30pm; Tiananmen Dong
Housed in a sombre 1950s edifice, this museum is a work in progress, suffering from chronic lighting, a tawdry layout and sporadic English captions. At the time of writing only three halls were open, the most absorbing of which houses the gorgeous bronzes and ceramics of the Selected Treasures of the National Museum of China – look out for the Bronze Rhino-Shaped *Zun* inlaid with gold and silver designs from the Western Han. The cheesy waxworks museum is mildly diverting.

DUAN GATE Map pp268-9
Duān Mén 端门
North of Gate of Heavenly Peace; admission Y10; 8.30am-4.30pm; Tiananmen Xi or Tiananmen Dong
Sandwiched between the Gate of Heavenly Peace and Meridian Gate, Duan Gate was stripped of its treasures by foreign forces quelling the Boxer Rebellion. The hall today is hung with photos of old Běijīng, but steer your eyes to the ceiling, wonderfully painted in its original colours and free of the cosmetic improvements so casually inflicted on so many of China's other historic monuments – including, it must be added, the slap-dash red paintwork on the exterior walls of Duan Gate itself.

TRANSPORT

Subway Line 1: Tiananmen Xi and Tiananmen Dong subway stops serve Tiananmen Square, the Forbidden City, the Imperial City Exhibition and the Imperial Archives; Wangfujing subway stop serves Wangfujing Dajie, and you can backtrack into the Foreign Legation Quarter from here; get off at the Jianguomen stop (both Line 1 and Line 2) for the Ancient Observatory, Southeast Corner Watchtower and the restored Ming City Wall Ruins Park. Line 2: The Qianmen stop is right by Front Gate; Chongwenmen takes you to the Ming City Wall Ruins Park that leads to the Southeast Corner Watchtower; alight at the Beijingzhan stop for Beijing Train Station. Line 2 intersects with Line 1 at Jianguomen. Line 5: Still under construction at the time of writing, the north–south Line 5 intersects with Line 1 at Dongdan and with Line 2 at Chongwenmen, running south to Ciqikou, Tiantandongmen and Puhuangyu.

Bus Services along Chang'an Jie include buses 1 and 4, travelling from Sihuizhan along Jianguomenwai Dajie, Jianguomennei Dajie and Chang'an Jie; bus 20 journeys from Tianqiao via Qianmen to Wangfujing, Dongdan and Beijing Train Station.

FOREIGN LEGATION QUARTER
Map pp268-9

⊕ Chongwenmen, Qianmen or Wangfujing

As James Ricalton described the Foreign Legation district in the days after the Boxer Rebellion:

Here the fire was as hot as anywhere. A cannon ball came through the wall of this legation and carried off the head of Mr Wagener, a gentleman in the customs service. I was told by good authorities that this burned district, destroyed ruthlessly and uselessly, represented, at a low estimate, five million dollars' worth of property.

The former Foreign Legation Quarter, where the 19th century foreign powers flung up their embassies, schools, post offices and banks, lay east of Tiananmen Square. Stroll around Taijichang Dajie and Zhengyi Lu which still suggest its former European flavour (see the Tiananmen Square & Foreign Legation Quarter Walk p114). On the northern corner of Taijichang Toutiao's intersection with Taijichang Dajie survives a brick in the wall engraved with the road's former foreign name: **Rue Hart**.

The district was turned into a war zone during the famous legation siege during the Boxer Rebellion (1899–1901). Probably the greatest cultural loss was the torching of the Hanlin Academy, the centre of Chinese learning and literature. Ricalton noted:

'The Classics of Confucius inscribed on tablets of marble were treasured there; these are gone; the 20,000 volumes of precious literature are gone; and this venerable institution, founded a thousand years before the Christian era...is a heap of ruins. The loss of thousands of volumes of ancient records recalls the destruction of the Alexandrian Library as an irreparable loss; not so many precious books, perhaps, yet the Hanlin College antedated the Alexandrian Library by nearly seven hundred years.'

The library was burnt down by Muslim Huí troops in a disastrous bid to flush out besieged Westerners.

At the junction of Taijichang Dajie and Dongjiaomin Xiang stands the gaunt twin-spired **St Michael's Church**, facing the buildings of the former **Belgian Embassy**. Along the western reaches of Dongjiaomin Xiang you'll pass the former **French Legation** (behind bright red doors), the former **French post office** (now the Jingyuan Sichuan Restaurant) and the fascinating **Beijing Police Museum** (p74).

FRONT GATE Map pp268-9
Qián Mén 前门

☎ 6525 3176; adult Y10; ⏱ 8.30am-4pm;
⊕ Qianmen

Front Gate actually consists of two gates. The northernmost of the two, the 40m-high **Zhengyang Gate** (正阳门; Zhèngyáng Mén) dates from the Ming dynasty and was the largest of the nine gates of the inner city wall separating the inner, or Tartar (Manchu), city from the outer, or Chinese, city. Partially destroyed in the Boxer Rebellion, the gate was once flanked by two temples that have since vanished. With the disappearance of the city walls, the gate sits out of context, but you can climb it for views of the square, although at the time of writing the gate was being restored. Similarly torched during the Boxer Rebellion, the **Arrow Tower** (箭楼; Jiàn Lóu) to the south also dates from the Ming and was originally connected to Zhengyang Gate by a semicircular enceinte (demolished last century). To the east is the old British-built Qian Men Railway Station (老车站; Lǎo Chēzhàn), now housing shops and restaurants, while to the south extends Qianmen Dajie, undergoing wholesale repackaging for 2008.

GATE OF HEAVENLY PEACE Map pp268-9
Tiānānmén 天安门

North of Tiananmen Square; adult Y15; ⏱ 8.30am-4.30pm; ⊕ Tiananmen Xi or Tiananmen Dong

Hung with a vast likeness of Mao, the double-eaved Gate of Heavenly Peace is a potent national symbol. Built in the 15th century and restored in the 17th century, the gate was formerly the largest of the four gates of the Imperial City Wall (皇城; Huáng Chéng). Called Chengtian Men during the Ming dynasty, it was renamed Tianan Men during Emperor Shunzhi's reign during the Qing dynasty. The gate is guarded by two pairs of Ming stone lions; one of the creatures apocryphally blocked the path of Li Chuangwang as he invaded Běijīng at the end of the Ming dynasty. Li fended the lion off by stabbing its belly with his spear while on horseback, leaving a mark that can still be seen. Other locals dispute this story, arguing that it is a bullet hole from allied force guns, when troops entered Běijīng to quell the Boxer Rebellion.

There are five doors to the gate, fronted by seven bridges spanning a stream. Each of these bridges was restricted in its use, and only the emperor could use the central door and bridge. The soldiers performing the punctilious daily flag raising and lowering ceremony on Tiananmen Square (p81) emerge through the gate.

Today's political coterie watch mass troop parades from here, and it was from this gate that Mao proclaimed the People's Republic on 1 October 1949. The dominating feature is the gigantic portrait of the ex-chairman, to the left of which runs the poetic slogan 'Long Live the People's Republic of China' and to the right 'Long Live the Unity of the Peoples of the World'.

You pass through the gate on your way to the Forbidden City if entering the palace from the south. Climb up for excellent views of Tiananmen Square, and peek inside at the impressive beams and overdone paintwork. There's no fee for walking through the gate, but if you climb the gate you'll have to buy an admission ticket and pay (Y1-6) to store your bag at the kiosk about 30m northwest of the ticket office. As it's a state symbol, security at the gate can be intense.

GREAT HALL OF THE PEOPLE

Map pp268-9

Rénmín Dàhuìtáng 人民大会堂

Western side of Tiananmen Square; adult Y30, bag deposit Y2-5; 🕙 **usually 8.30am-3pm (times vary);** Ⓜ **Tiananmen Xi**

On a site previously occupied by Taichang Temple, the Jinyiwei (Ming dynasty secret

service) and the Ministry of Justice, the Great Hall of the People is the venue of the legislature, the National People's Congress (NPC). The 1959 architecture is monolithic and intimidating, and a fitting symbol of China's remarkable political inertia. The tour parades visitors past a choice of 29 of its lifeless rooms named after the provinces of the Chinese universe. Also here is the banquet room where US President Richard Nixon dined in 1972, and the 10,000-seat auditorium with the familiar red star embedded in a galaxy of ceiling lights. The Great Hall of the People is closed to the public when the People's Congress is in session. The ticket office is down the south side of the building. Bags need to be checked in but cameras are admitted.

IMPERIAL ARCHIVES Map pp268-9

Huángshǐ Chéng 皇史宬

136 Nanchizi Dajie; admission free; 🕙 **9am-7pm;** Ⓜ **Tiananmen Dong**

Tucked away on the right-hand side of the first road to the east of the Forbidden City is the former Imperial Archives, repository for the imperial records, decrees, the 'Jade Book' (the imperial genealogical record) and huge encyclopaedic works, including the *Yongle Dadian* and the *Daqing Huidian*. You can peer through the closed door and make out the chests in which the archives were stored. With strong echoes of the splendid imperial palace, the courtyard contains well-preserved halls and the **Wan Fung Art Gallery** (www.wanfung.com.cn; 🕙 noon-6pm Mon & 10am-6pm Tue-Sun).

IMPERIAL CITY EXHIBITION Map pp268-9

Huáng Chéng Yìshùguǎn 皇城艺术馆

☎ **8511 5104; www.huangcheng.org; 9 Changpu Heyan; adult Y20, audio tour Y50;** 🕙 **10am-5.30pm;** Ⓜ **Tiananmen Dong**

Substantial portions of Běijīng survive solely in a twilight world of fading nostalgia. This fascinating museum is devoted to one of the city's most splendid creations: the Imperial City (皇城; Huáng Chéng), which – beyond its fragmented constituent parts – exists in name alone. Centrepiece of the only extant chunk of the Imperial City Wall, the museum is within the **Changpu River Park** (Chāngpú Hé Gōngyuán), a delightful, if contrived, formula of marble bridges, rock features, paths, a stream, willows, magnolias, scholar and walnut trees north of Dongchang'an Jie.

The museum functions as a memorial to the demolished wall, gates and buildings of the Imperial City. A **diorama** in the museum reveals the full extent of the yellow-tiled Imperial City Wall, which encompassed a vast chunk of Běijīng nearly seven times the size of the Forbidden City. In its heyday, 28 large temples could be found in the Imperial City alone, along with many smaller shrines. Many of these can be observed on the diorama, including a large temple in the northwest of the Imperial City with a double-eaved hall similar to the Hall of Prayer for Good Harvests (p81) at the Temple of Heaven Park. Period photos of the old gates of Běijīng and images of the halls and pavilions in Zhōngnánhǎi are hung on the walls.

Further galleries have exhibits of imperial ornaments such as *ruyi* (sceptres), porcelain and enamelware, and the weapons and armour of the imperial guards. There are also small exhibitions on Běijīng's *hútòng* and, downstairs, a bookshop and a rotating exhibition of paintings.

MING CITY WALL RUINS PARK
Map pp268-9
Míng Chéngqiáng Yízhǐ Gōngyuán
明城墙遗址公园
Chongwenmen Dongdajie; 24hr;
Chongwenmen
Topped with saplings, trees and a healthy head of vegetation, the last surviving slice of the Ming Inner City Wall (originally 40km in length) runs along the length of the northern flank of Chongwenmen Dongdajie, attached to a slender and pleasant strip of park. Levelled in the 1950s to facilitate transport and compromise the legacies of earlier dynasties, the city wall is perhaps Běijīng's most conspicuous chunk of lost heritage.

South of Beijing Train Station, the park runs from the former site of Chongwen Men (Chongwen Gate; one of the nine gates of the inner city wall) to the Southeast Corner Watchtower (opposite). You can walk the park's length, taking in its higgledy-piggledy contours and the interior layers of stone in parts of the wall that have collapsed. The restored sections run for 2km, rising to a height of around 15m and interrupted every 80m with buttresses *(dun tai)* extending to a maximum depth of 39m. The most interesting sections of wall are those closer to their original and more dilapidated state and some of the bricks have bullet holes. You can find a fur-

ther section of original, collapsing wall if you follow Jianguomen Nandajie north of the Southeast Corner Watchtower. The dishevelled wall runs to your left as you walk north up Jianguomen Nandajie. Take a left onto Beijingzhan Dongjie where you can see the wall come to a halt as it meets the pavement.

MONUMENT TO THE PEOPLE'S HEROES Map pp268-9
Rénmín Yīngxióng Jìniànbēi 人民英雄纪念碑
Tiananmen Square; Tiananmen Xi, Tiananmen Dong or Qianmen
North of Mao's mausoleum, the Monument to the People's Heroes was completed in 1958. The 37.9m-high obelisk, made of Qīngdǎo granite, bears bas-relief carvings of key patriotic and revolutionary events (such as Taiping rebels and Lin Zexu destroying opium at Hǔmén), as well as calligraphy from communist bigwigs Mao Zedong and Zhou Enlai. Mao's eight-character flourish proclaims 'Eternal Glory to the People's Heroes'. The monument is illuminated at night.

SONGTANGZHAI MUSEUM Map pp268-9
Sōngtángzhāi Mínjiān Diāokè Bówùguǎn
松堂斋民间雕刻博物馆
14 Liulichang Dongjie; admission by voluntary donation; 9am-6pm Tue-Sun; Hepingmen
This small **museum** on Liulichang Dongjie has few English captions, but it's one of the few places you can see traditional Chinese carvings gathered together. Well worth popping into if wandering Liulichang (p167). Seek out the gateway from Jiāngxī with its elaborate architraving, examine drum stones, Buddhist effigies, ancient pillar bases and stone lions.

SOUTHEAST CORNER WATCHTOWER & RED GATE GALLERY Map pp268-9

Dōngnán Jiǎolóu & Hóngmén Huàláng
东南角楼、红门画廊

☎ 8512 1554; Dongbianmen; adult Y10;
🕑 9am-5pm; Ⓜ Jianguomen or Chongwenmen

This splendid fortification, with a green-tiled, twin-eaved roof rising up imperiously south of the Ancient Observatory, dates back to the Ming dynasty. Clamber up the steps for views alongside camera-wielding Chinese trainspotters eagerly awaiting rolling stock grinding in and out of Beijing Train Station. Mounting the battlements, two forlorn stumps of flag abutments and a cannon or two can be seen, but really worth hunting out are the **signatures** etched in the walls by allied forces during the Boxer Rebellion. Look for the brass plaque in Chinese and a sheet of Perspex nailed to the wall near the top of the steps. You can make out the name of a certain P Foot; 'USA' is also scrawled on the brickwork. The international composition of the eight-nation force that relieved Běijīng in 1900 is noted in names such as André, Stickel and what appears to be a name in Cyrillic. One brick records the date 'Dec 16 1900'. Allied forces overwhelmed the redoubt after a lengthy engagement. Note the drainage channels poking out of the wall along its length. You can reach the watchtower from the west through the **Railway Arch**, which was built for the first railway that ran around Běijīng.

The watchtower is punctured with 144 archers' windows, and attached to it is a 100m section of the original inner city wall, beyond which stretches the restored **Ming City Wall** (opposite), extending all the way to Chongwenmen. Inside the highly impressive interior is some staggering carpentry: huge red pillars surge upwards, topped with solid beams. The 1st floor is the site of the **Red Gate Gallery** (☎ 6525 1005; www.redgategallery.com; admission free; 🕑 10am-5pm), one of Běijīng's long-established modern art galleries; the 2nd-floor gallery has an exhibition on the watchtower, the city gates and the history of Chóngwén district, while the 3rd-floor gallery contains more paintings. Say you're visiting the Red Gate Gallery and the Y10 entry fee to the watchtower will be waived.

TEMPLE OF HEAVEN PARK Map pp268-9

Tiāntán Gōngyuán 天坛公园

Tiantan Donglu; low season Y10-30, high season Y15-35, audio tour available at each gate Y40;
🕑 park 6am-9pm, sights 8am-6pm; Ⓜ Chongwenmen, Qianmen, or Tiantandongmen

The most perfect example of Ming architecture, Tiāntán – literally 'Altar of Heaven' but commonly called temples – has come to symbolise Běijīng.

The temple originally served as a vast stage for the solemn rites performed by the emperor, the Son of Heaven (天子; Tiānzǐ), as he sought good harvests, divine clearance and atonement for the sins of the people. The complex of halls is set in a 267-hectare park with gates at each point of the compass and bounded by walls.

The Temple of Heaven's unique architectural features will delight numerologists, necromancers and the superstitious – not to mention acoustic engineers and carpenters. Shape, colour and sound combine to take on symbolic significance. Seen from above the temples are round and the bases square, a pattern deriving from the ancient Chinese belief that heaven is round and earth is square. Thus the northern end of the park is semicircular and the southern end is square. The **Temple of the Earth**, also called Ditan (see Ditan Park p86), in the north of Běijīng is on the northern compass point, and the **Temple of Heaven** is on the southern.

The most important ceremony of the year was performed just before the winter solstice when the emperor and his enormous entourage passed down Qianmen Dajie in total silence to the **Imperial Vault of Heaven**. Commoners were not permitted to view the ceremony and remained cloistered indoors. The procession included elephant and horse chariots and long lines of lancers, nobles, officials and musicians dressed in their finest, with flags fluttering. The next day the emperor waited in a yellow silk tent at the southern gate while officials moved the

TOP FIVE BĚIJĪNG PARKS

- Size up the imposing grandeur and cosmic overtones of **Temple of Heaven Park** (right).
- Explore the lakeside temple architecture of **Beihai Park** (p84) in low gear.
- Clamber to the top of **Jingshan Park** (p91) for astonishing views over the Forbidden City.
- Make an expedition to **Fragrant Hills Park** (p101).
- Ponder the fate of Běijīng's city walls at **Ming City Wall Ruins Park** (opposite).

TEMPLE OF HEAVEN PARK 天坛公园

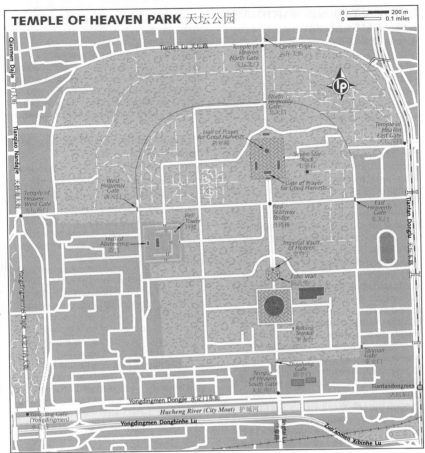

sacred tablets to the **Round Altar**, where the prayers and sacrificial rituals took place. It was thought that this ritual decided the nation's future; hence a hitch in any part of the proceedings was regarded as a bad omen.

Although the park can be entered through any of the gates at the cardinal points, the imperial approach to the temple was via **Zhaoheng Gate** (昭亨门; Zhāohēng Mén) in the south, and that is reflected in our ordering of the principal sights below.

Full of old cypresses, the park remains an important meeting place. Get here at 6.30am (before the temple structures are open) to see *tàijíquán* (also known as taichi), dancing to Western music and various other games being played. This is how Běijīng awakens; by 9am it becomes just another Chinese park.

Round Altar 圜丘

The 5m-high Round Altar (Yuán Qiū) was constructed in 1530 and rebuilt in 1740. Assembled from white marble arrayed in three tiers, its geometry revolves around the imperial number nine. Odd numbers were considered heavenly, and nine is the largest single-digit odd number. The top tier, thought to symbolise heaven, contains nine rings of stones. Each ring has multiples of nine stones, so that the ninth ring has 81 stones. The middle tier – earth – has the 10th to 18th rings. The bottom tier – humanity – has the 19th to 27th rings. The number of stairs and balustrades are also multiples of nine. If you stand in the centre of the upper terrace and say something, the sound bounces off the marble balustrades, making your voice sound louder (by nine times?).

Echo Wall 回音壁

Just north of the altar, surrounding the Imperial Vault of Heaven, is the Echo Wall (Huíyīn Bì), 65m in diameter. Its form has unusual acoustic properties, enabling a whisper to travel clearly from one end to the other – unless a tour group gets in the way. In the courtyard are the **Triple-Sounds Stones** (三音石; Sānyīn Shí). It is said that if you clap or shout standing on the stones, the sound is echoed once from the first stone, twice from the second stone and thrice from the third stone. Queues can get long at this one.

Imperial Vault of Heaven 皇穹宇

The octagonal Imperial Vault of Heaven (Huáng Qióng Yǔ) was built at the same time as the Round Altar, and is structured along the same lines as the older Hall of Prayer for Good Harvests. It used to contain spirit tablets used in the winter solstice ceremony.

Proceeding north from the Imperial Vault is a walkway called the Red Stairway Bridge (丹陛桥; Dānbì Qiáo), leading to the Hall of Prayer for Good Harvests.

Hall of Prayer for Good Harvests 祈年殿

The crowning structure of the whole complex is the Hall of Prayer for Good Harvests (Qínián Diàn), magnificently mounted on a three-tiered marble terrace and capped with a triple-eaved umbrella roof. Built in 1420, it was burnt to cinders in 1889 and heads rolled in apportioning blame (although lightning was the most likely cause). A faithful reproduction based on Ming architectural methods was erected the following year, the builders choosing Oregon fir for the support pillars, as explained by Lucian S Kirtland in *Finding the Worthwhile in the Orient* (1926):

When it was desired to rebuild the temple, and the Manchus were determined to copy in detail the building which had been destroyed, it was found that China's forests were bereft of timbers which could uphold the heavy tiled roof. After much argument with themselves, the necromancers of the court finally decided that pine logs from the forests of Oregon would constitute proper feng-shui. This decision very happily corresponded with the best engineering advice, and the New World furnished the pillars which you now see.

The four central pillars symbolise the seasons, the 12 in the next ring denote the months of the year, and the 12 outer ones represent the day, broken into 12 'watches'. Embedded in the ceiling is a carved dragon, a symbol of royalty. The patterning, carving and gilt decoration of this ceiling and its swirl of colour is a dizzying sight.

All this is made more amazing by the fact that the wooden pillars ingeniously support the ceiling without nails or cement – quite an accomplishment for a building 38m high and 30m in diameter. The hall underwent large-scale restoration in 2006.

TIANANMEN SQUARE Map pp268-9
Tiān'ānmén Guǎngchǎng 天安门广场

Ⓜ **Tiananmen Xi, Tiananmen Dong or Qianmen**
The world's largest public square at 440,000 sq metres, Tiananmen Square is a vast desert of paving stones at the heart of Běijīng and a poignant epitaph to China's hapless democracy movement. It may be a grandiose Maoist tourist trap, but there's more than enough space to stretch a leg. And the view can be breathtaking, especially on a clear day and at nightfall when the square is illuminated. Kites flit through the sky, children stamp around on the paving slabs and Chinese out-of-towners huddle together for the obligatory photo opportunity with the great helmsman's portrait. On National Day (1 October), Tiananmen Square is packed.

The square is laid out on a north–south axis. Threading through the **Front Gate** (p76) to the south, the square's meridian line is straddled by the **Chairman Mao Memorial Hall** (p75), cuts through the **Gate of Heavenly Peace** (Tiān'ānmén; p76) – the gate that lends its name to the square – to the north, and cleaves through the **Forbidden City** (p87).

In the square, one stands in the symbolic centre of the Chinese universe. The rectangular arrangement, flanked by halls to both east and west, to some extent echoes the layout of the Forbidden City. As such, the square employs a conventional plan that pays obeisance to traditional Chinese culture, but its ornaments and buildings are largely Soviet-inspired. What is noticeable is the low level of the skyline – there are no high-rises here in the very centre of the city – which maximises the dome of the sky.

Tiananmen Square as we see it today is a modern creation and there is precious little sense of history. During Ming and Qing times part of the Imperial City Wall (皇城; Huáng Chéng) called the Thousand Foot Corridor (Qiānbù Láng) poked deep into the space today occupied by the square, enclosing a section of the imperial domain. The wall took the shape of a 'T', emerging from the two huge, and now absent, gates that rose up south of the Gate of Heavenly Peace – Chang'an Zuo Gate and Chang'an You Gate – before running south to the vanished Daming Gate (Daming Men). Called Daqing Gate during the Qing dynasty and Zhonghua Gate during the Republic, the Daming Gate had three watchtowers and upturned eaves and was guarded by a pair of stone lions. It was pulled down after 1949, a fate similarly reserved for Chang'an Zuo Gate and Chang'an You Gate. East and west of the Thousand Foot Corridor stood official departments and temples, including the Ministry of Rites, the Ministry of Revenue, Honglu Temple and Taichang Temple.

Mao conceived the square to project the enormity of the Communist Party, so it's all a bit Kim Il-Sungish. During the Cultural Revolution, the chairman, wearing a Red Guard armband, reviewed parades of up to a million people here. In 1976 another million people jammed the square to pay their last respects to Mao. In 1989 army tanks and soldiers forced pro-democracy demonstrators out of the square. Although it seems likely that no one was actually killed *within* the square itself, possibly thousands were slaughtered *outside* the square. Despite being a public place, the square remains more in the hands of the government than the people; it is monitored by closed circuit TV cameras, and plainclothes police are primed to paralyse the first twitch of dissent.

West of the **Great Hall of the People** (p77), the future **National Grand Theater** – with its controversial styling and out-of-place looks – was approaching completion at the time of writing. Outside the China National Museum (p75), a LED clock counts down the seconds to the 2008 Olympic Games.

If you get up early you can watch the **flag-raising ceremony** at sunrise, performed by a troop of People's Liberation Army (PLA) soldiers drilled to march at precisely 108 paces per minute, 75cm per pace. The soldiers emerge through the Gate of Heavenly Peace to goosestep faultlessly across Chang'an Jie as all traffic is halted. The same ceremony in reverse is performed at sunset. Ask at your hotel for flag-raising/lowering times so you can get there early, as crowds can be quite intense.

Unless you want a map you'll have to sidestep determined map-sellers and their confederates – the incessant learners of English – and just say no to the 'poor' art students press-ganging tourists to view their exhibitions; fending them off can be draining.

Bicycles cannot be ridden across Tiananmen Square (apparently tanks are OK), but you can walk your bike. Traffic is one way for north–south avenues on either side of the square.

BEIJING WANGFUJING PALEOLITHIC MUSEUM Map pp268-9

Běijīng Wángfǔjǐng Gǔrénlèi Wénhuà Yízhǐ Bówùguǎn
北京王府井古人类文化遗址博物馆
W1P3 Oriental Plaza, 1 Dongchang'an Jie; adult Y10;
🕙 10am-4.30pm Mon-Fri, 10am-6.30pm Sat & Sun;
🚇 Wangfujing

Archaeologists and anthropologists will be rewarded at this simple museum detailing the tools and relics (stone flakes, bone scrapers, fragments of bone etc) of Late Pleistocene Man who once inhabited Běijīng. The discoveries on display were unearthed during the construction of Oriental Plaza in 1996. To find the museum, take exit 'A' from the Wangfujing metro station.

WORKERS CULTURAL PALACE
Map pp268-9
Láodòng Rénmín Wénhuà Gōng
劳动人民文化宫
Northeast of the Gate of Heavenly Peace; adult Y2;
🕙 6.30am-7.30pm; 🚇 Tiananmen Dong

On the Forbidden City's southeastern flank opposite Zhongshan Park and away from the frantic hubbub is the Workers Cultural

Palace. Despite the unappealing name, this was the emperor's premier place of worship, the **Supreme Temple** (太庙; Tài Miào). If you find the Forbidden City either too colossal or crowded, the temple halls here (all undergoing renovation at the time of writing) are a cheaper and more tranquil alternative; there is also a **tennis court** (☎ 6512 2856) here if you want to practise your backhand within earshot of the Forbidden City. The huge halls of the temple remain, their roofs enveloped in imperial yellow tiles, beyond a quiet grove of ancient cypresses and enclosed within the **Glazed Gate** (琉璃门; Liúlí Mén). Rising up to the splendid **Front Hall**, the scene of imperial ceremonies of ancestor worship, are three flights of steps. Only gods could traverse the central plinth; the emperor was consigned to the left-hand flight. The plaque above the Front Hall is inscribed in both Chinese and Manchu. Sadly this hall, as well as the **Middle Hall** and **Rear Hall** behind, is inaccessible. As with Zhongshan Park, the northern perimeter of the park abuts the palace moat (tǒngzi hé), where you can find a bench and park yourself in front of a fine view. Take the northwest exit from the park and find yourself just by the Forbidden City's Meridian Gate and point of entry to the palace.

XIANNONG ALTAR & BEIJING ANCIENT ARCHITECTURE MUSEUM
Map pp268-9
Xiānnóng Tán & Běijīng Gǔdài Jianzhù Bówùguǎn
先农坛、北京古代建筑博物馆
21 Dongjing Lu; admission Y15; ⊙ 9am-4pm;
🚇 Qianmen

Dating to 1420, this altar – to the west of the Temple of Heaven – was the site of solemn imperial ceremonies and sacrificial offerings. Glance at any pre-1949 map of Běijīng and you can gauge the massive scale of the altar; today, many of its original structures survive, but what remains is a tranquil and little-visited constellation of relics. Located within what is called the Hall of Jupiter (太岁殿; Tàisuì Diàn) – the most magnificent surviving hall – is the excellent **Beijing Ancient Architecture Museum** (⊙ 9am-4pm) which informatively narrates the elements of traditional Chinese building techniques. Brush up on your dǒugǒng brackets and sǔnmǎo joints, get the lowdown on Běijīng's courtyard houses, while eyeballing detailed models of standout temple halls and pagodas from across the land. English captions.

ZHONGSHAN PARK Map pp268-9
Zhōngshān Gōngyuán 中山公园
West of Tiānānmén; adult Y3; ⊙ 6am-9pm;
🚇 Tiananmen Xi

This pleasant park sits west of the Gate of Heavenly Peace, with a section hedging up against the Forbidden City moat. A refreshing prologue or conclusion to the magnificence of the adjacent imperial residence, the park was formerly the sacred Ming-style Altar to the God of the Land and the God of Grain (Shèjìtán), where the emperor offered sacrifices. The square altar (wǔsè tǔ) remains, bordered on all sides by walls tiled in various colours. Near the park entrance stands a towering dark blue tiled páilou (decorative archway) with triple eaves that originally commemorated the German Foreign Minister Baron von Ketteler, killed by Boxers in 1900. In the eastern section of the park is the **Forbidden City Concert Hall** (p150). Take the northeastern exit from the park and find yourself by the Forbidden City's **Meridian Gate**; from here you can reach the **Supreme Temple** and the **Workers Cultural Palace** (opposite).

DŌNGCHÉNG 东城

Eating p127; Shopping p164; Sleeping p182

Bounded to the north and east by the Second Ring Rd and by Chang'an Jie to the south, Dōngchéng (East City) is one of Běijīng's most historic districts. Formerly marking the centre of Yuan dynasty Běijīng, a city whose east-west axis later shifted south, the Drum and Bell Towers rise up from an area riddled with charming hútòng and lanes. In fact, hútòng crisscross the entire district, and wandering in the resulting maze is one of the best ways to appreciate the city.

The centrepiece of this district, however, is the Forbidden City, which forms a massive and imperious chunk of the southwest. At the heart of the former Imperial City (a large part of which belongs to Dōngchéng), the rectangular outline of the imperial palace and its moat imprints itself on the rest of Dōngchéng. Progressively larger squares and parallelograms of streets radiate out from the Forbidden City, culminating in the boxlike boundary of the Second Ring Rd.

The top right corner of the old Imperial City, the eastern boundary of which ran along Donghuangchenggen Nanjie and Donghuangchenggen Beijie and then west along Dianmen Dongdajie and Dianmen

Xidajie, is in Dōngchéng. None of the four gates of the Imperial City Wall survive, but a few fragments of Dongan Men (p86) can be seen near the Forbidden City's east gate (Donghua Men). Also part of the erstwhile Imperial City, Jingshan Park and Beihai Park have strong imperial connections. Qianhai Lake, across the road north from Beihai Park, lay just outside the Imperial City. The area around the lake, which is also called Shíchàhǎi (Sea of the Ten Buddhist Temples, presumably denoting the shrines that once stood here), has developed an ever-growing bar and café industry thriving on its picturesque and historic ambience.

Běijīng's finest temple, the Lama Temple, lies just within the Second Ring Rd to the northeast, and a short walk south is Běijīng's Confucius Temple.

Dōngchéng also hosts Běijīng's premier shopping street: Wangfujing Dajie, with its host of top-name shops and malls.

BEIHAI PARK Map p262
Běihǎi Gōngyuán 北海公园
Northwest of the Forbidden City; adult Y5, through ticket to sights Y20; ☺ 6.30am-8pm, buildings to 4pm; ⊕ Tiananmen Xi, then 🚌 5

A relaxing opportunity to amble about, grab a snack, sip a beer, rent a rowing boat, or admire calligraphers scribbling Chinese characters on paving slabs with water and fat brushes, Beihai Park is largely lake, or more specifically the lake of Beihai (which literally means 'North Sea'). The associated South and Middle Seas to the south together lend their name to the nerve centre of the Communist Party west of the Forbidden City, Zhōngnánhǎi.

The park, covering an area of 68 hectares, was the former playground of the Yuan emperors. Jade Islet in the lower middle is composed of the heaped earth scooped out to create the lake – some attribute this to Kublai Khan.

The site is associated with the Great Khan's palace, the navel of Běijīng before the Forbidden City replaced it. All that remains of the Khan's court is a large jar made of green jade dating from 1265 in the Round City (Tuán Chéng; admission Y1) near the park's southern entrance. Also within the Round City is the Chengguang Hall (Chéngguāng Diàn), where a white jade statue of Sakyamuni from Myanmar can be found, its arm wounded by the allied forces

that entered Běijīng in 1900 to quash the Boxer Rebellion.

Dominating Jade Islet on the lake, the 36m-high White Dagoba was originally built in 1651 for a visit by the Dalai Lama, and was rebuilt in 1741. You can reach the dagoba through the Yongan Temple (included in the through ticket). Enter the temple through the Hall of the Heavenly Kings, past the Drum and Bell Towers to the Hall of the Wheel of the Law, with its central effigy of Sakyamuni and flanked by Bodhisattvas and 18 luóhàn. At the rear is a bamboo grove and a steep flight of steps up through a decorative archway, emblazoned with the characters 'Long Guang' on one side. Head up the steps to the Zhengjue Hall, which contains a statue of Milefo and Weituo. Pu'an Hall, the next hall, houses a statue of Tsong Khapa, founder of the Yellow Hat sect of Tibetan Buddhism, flanked by statues of the fifth Dalai Lama and the Panchen Lama. Eight golden effigies on either flank include Tantric statues and the goddess Heinümu, adorned with a necklace of skulls. The final flight of steep steps brings you to the dagoba.

On the northeastern shore of the islet is the handsome, double-tiered Painted Gallery (Huàláng). Near the boat dock is the Fangshan Restaurant (p131), a restaurant that prepares imperial recipes favoured by Empress Cixi, who was partial to 120-course dinners with about 30 kinds of desserts.

Xītiān Fànjìng, on the lake's northern shore, is one of the city's most interesting temples (admission is included in your park ticket). Taichi (tàijíquán) practitioners can frequently be seen practising outside the main entrance. The first hall, the Hall of the Heavenly Kings, takes you past Milefo, Weituo and the four Heavenly Kings. The Dacizhenru Hall dates to the Ming dynasty and contains three huge statues of Sakyamuni, the Amithaba Buddha and Yaoshi Fo (Medicine Buddha). The golden statue of Guanyin at the rear is sadly unapproachable. The hall is supported by huge wooden pillars (nánmù), and you can make out where the original stone pillars existed. At the very rear of the temple is a glazed pavilion and a huge hall that are both unctrified out of bounds.

The nearby Nine Dragon Screen (Jiǔlóng Bì; included in the through ticket), a 5m-high and 27m-long spirit wall, is a glimmering stretch of coloured glazed tiles.

BELL TOWER Map p262

Zhōnglóu 钟楼

9 Zhonglouwan Linzi, north end Dianmenwai Dajie; adult Y15; ⏰ **9am-5pm;** 🚌 **5, 58 or 107**

Fronted by a Qing dynasty stele, the Bell Tower – originally built in 1272 – sits along an alley directly north behind the Drum Tower. The tower burnt down during the reign of Yongle and was rebuilt in 1420, only to succumb once again to flames; the present tower dates to 1745. Clamber up the steep steps and marvel at its massive bell (Chinese bells have no clappers but are instead struck with a stout pole), weighing 63 tons and suspended within a pleasantly unrestored interior. Augment visits with rooftop drinks at the Drum & Bell (p142), located between its namesake towers.

CHINA ART MUSEUM Map p262

Zhōngguó Měishùguǎn 中国美术馆

☎ **6401 7076/2252; 1 Wusi Dajie; adult Y5;** ⏰ **9am-5pm, last entry 4pm;** 🚌 **103, 104, 106 or 108 to Meishu Guan stop**

This revamped museum has received a healthy shot of imagination and flair, with absorbing exhibitions from abroad promising doses of colour and vibrancy. Běijīng's art lovers have lapped up some top notch presentations here, from the cream of Italian design to modern artworks from the Taipei Fine Arts Museum, the latter offering a chance to compare contemporary mainland Chinese art – with its burdensome political baggage and endlessly recurring themes – with the light-footed, invigorating and more universalist conceptions from the island across from Fújiàn. English captions can be sporadic, but this is a first-rate place to see modern art from China and abroad and, just as importantly, to watch the Chinese looking at art. Lifts allow for disabled access.

CONFUCIUS TEMPLE & IMPERIAL COLLEGE Map p262

Kǒng Miào & Guózǐjiàn 孔庙、国子监

13 Guozijian Jie; adult Y10; ⏰ **8.30am-5pm;** 🚇 **Yonghegong**

Long neglected like a discarded piece of unloved bric-a-brac, the arid Confucius Temple offers a quiet sanctuary from Běijīng's congested, smoggy streets and snarling traffic. In a bid to clear the dust

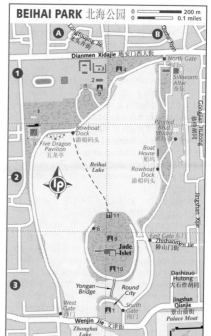

BEIHAI PARK 北海公园

SIGHTS & ACTIVITIES	
Chengguang Hall 承光殿	1 B3
Dacizhenru Hall 大慈真如殿	2 A1
Glazed Pavilion 琉璃阁	3 A1
Jingxin House 静心斋	4 B1
Nine Dragon Screen 九龙壁	5 A1
Pavilion of Calligraphy 阅古楼	6 A2
Small Western Paradise 小西天	7 A2
White Dagoba 白塔	8 B3
Xitiān Fànjìng 西天梵境	9 A1
Yongan Temple 永安寺	10 B3

EATING 🍴	
Fangshan Restaurant 仿膳饭庄	11 B2

that perennially swathes its cypresses and pavilions, China's second largest Confucian temple has restored its main hall, which houses a statue of the sage, Kongzi (Confucius). Some of Běijīng's last remaining *páilou* bravely survive in the *hútòng* outside (Guozijian Jie).

Many of the temple's stele pavilions are bricked up alongside gnarled cypresses that claw at the sky. At the rear, a forest of 190 stelae records the 13 Confucian classics in 630,000 Chinese characters. Also inscribed on stelae are the names of successful candidates of the highest level of the official Confucian examination system. It was the ambition of every scholar to see his name engraved here, but it wasn't easy. Each candidate was locked in one of about 8000 cubicles, measuring roughly 1.5 sq metres, for a period of three days. Many died or went insane during their incarceration.

Like everywhere in town, skeletons lurk in the temple cupboard and a distasteful footnote lurks unrecorded behind the tourist blurb. Běijīng writer Lao She (p93) was dragged here in August 1966, forced to his knees in front of a bonfire of Beijing opera costumes to confess his anti-revolutionary crimes, and beaten. The much-loved writer drowned himself the next day in Taiping Lake.

West of the Confucius Temple stands the Imperial College (Guózǐjiān), where the emperor expounded the Confucian classics to an audience of thousands of kneeling students, professors and court officials – an annual rite. Built by the grandson of Kublai Khan in 1306, the former college was the supreme academy during the Yuan, Ming and Qing dynasties. On the site is a marvellous glazed, three-gate, single-eaved decorative archway, called a liúli páifāng (glazed archway). The Biyong Hall beyond is a twin-roofed structure with yellow tiles surrounded by a moat and topped with a gold knob.

Religious artefact and souvenir shops are scattered around the vicinity of the Lama Temple (p91) and Guozijian Jie, stocking effigies of Buddhist deities and Bodhisattvas along with Buddhist keepsakes and talismans (hùshénfú).

COURTYARD GALLERY Map pp258-9
四合院画廊
☎ 6526 8882; www.courtyard-gallery.com; 319 Caochangdi, Chaoyang; admission free; 🚌 735 or 402
Recently relocated from its famous location in the basement of the namesake restaurant (p131) just east of the Forbidden City, this gallery is a trendy component of the flourishing contemporary art scene in Caochandi, a few kilometres northeast of the 798 Art District (p103).

DITAN PARK Map p262
Dìtán Gōngyuán 地坛公园
East of Andingmenwai Dajie; park Y2; altar Y5; 🕙 6am-9pm; 🚇 Yonghegong
Cosmologically juxtaposed with the Temple of Heaven (Tiāntán; p79), the Altar of the

Moon (Yuètán), the Altar of the Sun (Rìtán; p95) and the Altar to the God of the Land and the God of Grain (Shèjìtán; p83), Ditan is the Temple of the Earth. The park, site of imperial sacrifices to the Earth God, lacks the splendour of the Temple of Heaven Park but is worth a stroll if you've just been to nearby Lama Temple. During Chinese New Year, a temple fair is held here, and in winter, a sparkling ice festival is staged. The park's large altar (fāngzé tán) is square in shape, symbolising the earth. Within the park, the art gallery One Moon (Yīyuè Dāngdài Yìshù; ☎ 6427 7748; www.onemoonart.com; 🕙 11am-7pm Tue-Sun) displays thoughtful contemporary Chinese art from a 16th-century-dynasty temple hall, a funky meeting of the Ming and the modern. If visiting the art gallery alone (admission free), the entrance fee to the park should be waived.

DONGAN MEN REMAINS Map p262
Míng Huáng Chéng Dōngānmén Yízhǐ
明皇城东安门遗址
Imperial Wall Foundation Ruins Park, intersection of Donghuamen Dajie & Beiheyan Dajie; 🕙 24 hr; 🚇 Tiananmen Dong
In an excavated pit on Beiheyan Dajie sits a pitiful stump, all that remains of the magnificent Dongan Men, the east gate of the Imperial City. Before being razed, the gate was a single-eaved, seven-bay wide building with a hip and gable roof capped with yellow tiles. The remnants of the gate – just two layers of 18 bricks – may make for dull viewing but of more interest are the accompanying bricks of the excavated Ming dynasty road that used to run near Dongan Men. The road is around 2m lower than the current road level, its expertly made bricks typical of precisely engineered Ming dynasty brickwork. The remains are located in the Imperial Wall Foundation Ruins Park, a thin strip of park that follows much of the course of the eastern side of the Imperial City Wall.

DRUM TOWER Map p262
Gǔlóu 鼓楼
Gulou Dongdajie; adult Y20; 🕙 9am-5.30pm; 🚌 5, 58 or 107
The Drum Tower was first built in 1272 and marked the centre of the old Mongol capital Dàdū. Originally constructed of wood, the structure went up in flames and was rebuilt in 1420, since then it has been repeatedly

destroyed and restored. Stagger up the incredibly steep steps for wide-ranging views over Běijīng's rooftops. The drums of this later Ming dynasty version were beaten to mark the hours of the day – in effect the Big Ben of Běijīng. Time was kept with a water clock and an idiosyncratic system of time divisions. On view is a large collection of drums, including the large and dilapidated **Night Watchman's Drum** (*gēnggǔ; gēng* being one of the five two-hour divisions of the night) and a big array of reproduction drums. Originally there were 25 watch drums here, and damage to the drums is blamed on allied forces that quelled the Boxers back in 1900. There is also an analysis of the ancient Chinese seasonal divisions and an exhibition relating to old Běijīng. When ascending or descending the Drum Tower, watch out for slippery steps.

FORBIDDEN CITY Map p262
Zǐjīn Chéng 紫禁城

☎ 6513 2255; www.dpm.org.cn; adult Y40 Nov-Mar, Y60 Apr-Oct, Clock Exhibition Hall & Hall of Jewellery Y10 each; ⏲ 8.30am-4pm May-Sep, 8.30am-3.30pm Oct-Apr; ◉ Tiananmen Xi or Tiananmen Dong

The magnificent Forbidden City, so called because it was off limits to commoners for 500 years, occupies a primary position in the Chinese psyche. To the Han Chinese, the Forbidden City is a contradictory symbol. It's a politically incorrect yarn from a pre-revolutionary dark age, but it's also one spun from the very pinnacle of Chinese civilisation. It's not therefore surprising that more violent forces during the Cultural Revolution wanted to trash the place. Perhaps hearing the distant tinkle of the tourist dollar, Premier Zhou Enlai did the right thing by stepping in to keep the Red Guards at bay.

This gargantuan palace complex – China's largest and best preserved cluster of ancient buildings – sheltered two dynasties of emperors, the Ming and the Qing, who didn't stray from their pleasure dome unless they absolutely had to. A bell jar dropped over the whole spectacle maintaining a highly rarefied atmosphere that nourished its elitist community. A stultifying code of rules, protocol and superstition deepened its otherworldliness, perhaps typified by its twittering band of eunuchs. From here the emperors governed China, often erratically and haphazardly, with authority occasionally drifting into the hands of opportunistic court officials and eunuchs. It wasn't until 1911 that revolution eventually came knocking at the huge doors, bringing with it the last orders for the Manchu Qing and dynastic rule.

Its mystique diffused (the Běijīng authorities insist on prosaically calling the complex the Palace Museum or *gùgōng bówùguǎn*; 故宫博物馆), entry to the palace is no longer prohibited. In former ages the price for uninvited admission would have been instant death; these days Y40-60 will do.

Ignore unscrupulous characters who insist that you must have an official guide to see the palace; it isn't true. For Y40, rent a funky automatically activated audio tour instead.

Don't confuse the Gate of Heavenly Peace (p76) with the Forbidden City entrance. Some visitors purchase a Gate of Heavenly Peace admission ticket by mistake, not realising that this admits you only to the upstairs portion of the gate. The Forbidden City ticket booths are on either side of the Meridian Gate – walk north until you can't walk any further without paying and you will spot the queues nearby.

Restaurants and, controversially, a branch of Starbucks can be found within the Forbidden City, as well as toilets. Exterior photography is no problem, but photographing the interior of halls is often prohibited. Wheelchairs (Y500 deposit) are free to use as are strollers (Y300 deposit). At the time of writing, several palace halls, including the Gate of Supreme Harmony, were undergoing restoration and were inaccessible, shrouded and out of view.

History
Constructed on the site of a palace dating to Kublai Khan and the Mongol Yuan dynasty, the Ming emperor Yongle established the basic layout of the Forbidden City between 1406 and 1420. The grandiose emperor employed battalions of labourers and crafts workers – by some estimates there may have been up to a million of them – to build it. The palace lay at the heart of the Imperial City, a much larger, walled enclosure reserved for the use of the emperor and his personnel. The wall enclosing the Forbidden City – assembled from 12 million bricks – is the last intact surviving city wall in Běijīng.

Most of the buildings you see now are post-18th century: the largely wooden palace was a tinderbox and fire was a constant hazard – a lantern festival combined with a sudden gust of Gobi wind would easily send flames dancing in unexpected directions, as would a fireworks display. Fires were also deliberately lit by court eunuchs and officials who could get rich off the repair bills.

It wasn't just the buildings that went up in flames, but also rare books, paintings and calligraphy. Libraries and other palace halls and buildings housing combustible contents were tiled in black; the colour represents water in the five-element (wǔxíng) theory, and its symbolic presence was thought to prevent conflagrations. In the 20th century there were two major lootings of the palace by Japanese forces and the Kuomintang. Thousands of crates of relics were removed and carted off to Taiwan, where they remain on display in Taipei's National Palace Museum (worth seeing). Some say this was just as well, since the Cultural Revolution reduced much of China's precious artwork to confetti.

Layout

Ringed by a picturesque 52m-wide moat that freezes over in winter, the palace is so unspeakably big (over 1 million sq metres, with 800 buildings and 9000 rooms) that a permanent restoration squad circulates, repainting and repairing. It takes about 10 years to do a full renovation, by which time they have to start repairs again. Many halls have been repainted in a way that the original pigment is concealed; other halls such as the Hall of Mental Cultivation (Yǎngxīn Diàn), however, are more faithful to their former selves. And despite the attentions of restorers, some of the hall rooftops still sprout tufts of grass.

Even though less than half of the palace (430,000 sq metres) is actually open to visitors and it is possible to explore the Forbidden City in a few hours, a full day will keep

you fully occupied and the enthusiast will make several trips. Whatever you do, don't miss the delightful courtyards, pavilions and mini-museums within them on each side of the main complex.

The palace's ceremonial buildings lie on the north–south axis of the Forbidden City, from the Gate of Heavenly Peace in the south to Divine Military Genius Gate (Shénwǔ Mén) to the north.

Restored in the 17th century, Meridian Gate (Wǔ Mén) is a massive portal that in former times was reserved for the use of the emperor. Gongs and bells would sound imperial comings and goings, while lesser mortals used lesser gates: the military used the west gate, civilians the east gate. The emperor also reviewed his armies from here, passed judgment on prisoners, announced the new year's calendar and oversaw the flogging of troublesome ministers.

Through the Meridian Gate, Xihe Gate (Xīhé Mén) to your left leads to a pleasantly green expanse that offers a definitive contrast with much of the rest of the palace grounds that overwhelmingly concerns itself with the affairs of man and heaven. The recently restored Hall of Military Prowess (Wǔyīng Diàn) contains a collection of Ming dynasty paintings and literature.

The Golden Stream (Jīn Shuǐ), delightfully fringed by willows, runs through here and into the courtyard in front of the Gate of Supreme Harmony (Tàihé Mén) where it is shaped to resemble a Tartar bow and spanned by five marble bridges. The dwarfing courtyard could hold an imperial audience of 100,000 people. At the time of writing the majesty of the gate was neutralised by the scaffolding and green awning completely enveloping the gate, but this should be down by 2008.

Raised on a three-tier marble terrace with balustrades are the Three Great Halls (Sān

Dàdiàn), the heart of the Forbidden City. The **Hall of Supreme Harmony** (Tàihé Diàn) is the most important and the largest structure in the Forbidden City. Built in the 15th century and restored in the 17th century, it was used for ceremonial occasions, such as the emperor's birthday, the nomination of military leaders and coronations. Bronze vats – once full of water for dousing fires – stand in front of the hall; in all 308 such vats were dotted around the Forbidden City with fires lit under them in winter to keep them from freezing over. The large bronze turtle in the front symbolises longevity and stability. It has a removable lid, and on special occasions incense was lit inside it so that smoke billowed from its mouth. Within the **Hongyi Pavilion** (Hóngyì Gé) to the west is an exhibition of the ceremonial music system of the imperial palace.

To the west of the terrace is a small pavilion with a bronze grain measure and to the east is a sundial; both are symbolic of imperial justice. On the corners of the hall's roof, as with other buildings in the city, there's a mounted figure with his retreat cut off by mythical and actual animals, a story relating to a cruel tyrant hanged from one such eave.

Inside the Hall of Supreme Harmony is a richly decorated **Dragon Throne** (Lóngyǐ) from which the emperor would preside over trembling officials. The entire court had to touch the floor nine times with their foreheads (the custom known as kowtowing) in the emperor's presence. At the back of the throne is a carved Xumishan, the Buddhist paradise, signifying the throne's supremacy.

Behind the Hall of Supreme Harmony is the smaller **Hall of Middle Harmony** (Zhōnghé Diàn), which was used as the emperor's transit lounge. Here he would make last-minute preparations, rehearse speeches and receive close ministers. On display are two Qing dynasty sedan chairs, the emperors' mode of transport around the Forbidden City. The last of the Qing emperors, Puyi, used a bicycle and altered a few features of the palace grounds to make it easier to get around.

The third hall is the **Hall of Preserving Harmony** (Bǎohé Diàn), used for banquets and later for imperial examinations. The hall has no support pillars, and to its rear is a 250-tonne marble imperial carriageway carved with dragons and clouds, which was transported into Běijīng on an ice path. The emperor was conveyed over the carriageway in his sedan chair as he ascended or descended the

terrace. The outer housing surrounding the Three Great Halls was used for storing gold, silver, silks, carpets and other treasures.

Halls west of the Three Great Halls exhibit treasures from the palace. Running from south to north the exhibitions cover: **scientific instruments** (astronomical devices, telescopes etc) and details of Jesuit scientists who attended the Qing court, **articles of daily use** (including imperial hunting guns, chessboards and ceramics), **objects presented as tribute** and **objects made by the imperial workshop**.

The basic configuration of the Three Great Halls is echoed by the next group of buildings. Smaller in scale, these buildings were more important in terms of real power, which in China traditionally lies at the back door or, in this case, the back gate.

The first structure is the **Palace of Heavenly Purity** (Qiánqīng Gōng), a residence of Ming and early Qing emperors, and later an audience hall for receiving foreign envoys and high officials.

Immediately behind it is the **Hall of Union** (Jiāotài Diàn), which contains a clepsydra – a water clock made in 1745 with five bronze vessels and a calibrated scale. There's also a mechanical clock built in 1797 and a collection of imperial jade seals on display.

At the northern end of the Forbidden City is the **Imperial Garden** (Yù Huāyuán), a classical Chinese garden with 7000 sq metres of fine landscaping, including rockeries, walkways, pavilions and ancient, carbuncular and deformed cypresses. Before you reach the large Divine Military Genius Gate (Shénwǔ Mén), note the pair of bronze elephants whose front knees bend in an anatomically impossible fashion.

The western and eastern sides of the Forbidden City are the palatial former living quarters, once containing libraries, temples, theatres, gardens and even the tennis court of the last emperor. Walk east and you can access the **Hall of Jewellery** (Zhēnbǎo Guǎn; admission Y10; �־ 8.30am-4pm summer, 8.30am-3.30pm winter), tickets for which also entitle you to glimpse the **Well of Concubine Zhen** (Zhēn Fēi Jǐng), into which the namesake wretch was thrown on the orders of Cixi, and the glazed **Nine Dragon Screen** (Jiǔlóng Bì). The treasures on view are fascinating: within the **Hall of Harmony** (Yíhé Xuān) sparkle Buddhist statues fashioned from gold and inlaid with gems, and a gold pagoda glittering with precious stones, followed by jade, jadeite, lapis lazuli and crystal

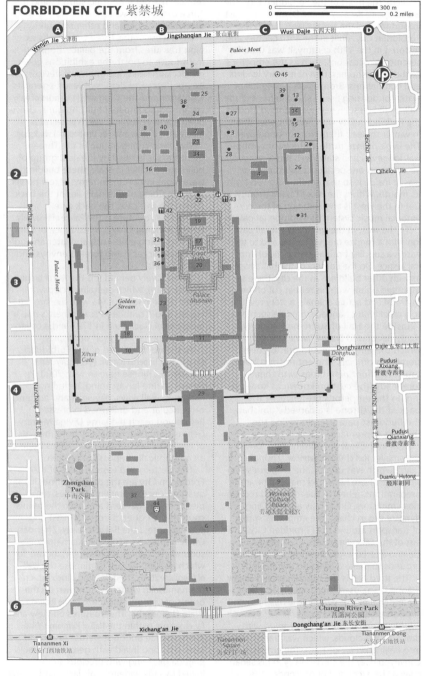

FORBIDDEN CITY 紫禁城

pieces displayed in the **Hall of Joyful Longevity** (Lèshòu Táng). Further objects are displayed within the **Hall of Character Cultivation** (Yǎngxìng Diàn), but at the time of writing the further sequence of halls to the south was empty. The **Changyin Pavilion** (Chàngyīn Gé) to the east was formerly an imperial stage.

The **Clock Exhibition Hall** (Zhōngbiǎo Guǎn) is one of the unmissable highlights of the Forbidden City. Located at the time of writing in the Fengxian Hall (Fèngxiàn Diàn), the exhibition contains an astonishing array of elaborate timepieces, many gifts to the Qing emperors from overseas. Many of the 18th-century examples are crafted by James Cox or Joseph Williamson (both of London) and imported through Guǎngdōng from England; others are from Switzerland, America and Japan. Exquisitely wrought, fashioned into magnificently designed elephants and other creatures, they all display astonishing artfulness and attention to detail. Standout clocks include the 'Gilt Copper Astronomy Clock' equipped with a working model of the solar system and the automaton-equipped 'Gilt Copper Clock with a robot writing Chinese characters with a brush'. The Qing court must surely have been amazed by their ingenuity. Time your arrival with 11am or 2pm to see the clock performance in which choice timepieces strike the hour and give a display to wide-eyed children and adults.

JINGSHAN PARK Map p262
Jǐngshān Gōngyuán 景山公园
Jingshan Qianjie; adult Y2; ⏰ **6am-9.30pm;** 🚇 **Tiananmen Xi, then** 🚌 **5**
Known as Coal Hill by Westerners during legation days, Jingshan Park was shaped from the earth excavated to create the moat of the Forbidden City. The hill supposedly protects the palace from the evil spirits – or dust storms – from the north. Clamber to the top for a magnificent panorama of the capital and princely views over the russet roofing of the Forbidden City.

On the eastern side of the park a locust tree stands in the place where the last of the Ming emperors, Chongzhen, hung himself as rebels swarmed at the city walls.

LAMA TEMPLE Map p262
Yōnghé Gōng 雍和宫
28 Yonghegong Dajie; adult Y25, audio guide Y20; ⏰ **9am-4pm;** 🚇 **Yonghegong**
With three richly worked archways and five main halls (each one taller than the preceding one), revolving prayer wheels, multi-coloured glaze tiles, magnificent Chinese lions, tantric statuettes and hall boards decorated with Mongolian, Manchu, Tibetan and Chinese, the Lama Temple is Běijīng's most magnificent Buddhist temple.

The temple was once the official residence of Count Yin Zhen who became emperor in 1723 and traded up to the Forbidden City. His name was changed to Yongzheng, and his former residence became Yonghe Palace (Yōnghé Gōng). In 1744 it was converted into a lamasery and became home to legions of monks from Mongolia and Tibet.

In 1792 the Emperor Qianlong, having quelled an uprising in Tibet, instituted a new administrative system involving two golden vases. One was kept at the renowned Jokhang Temple in Lhasa, to be employed for determining the reincarnation of the Dalai Lama, and the other was kept at the Lama Temple for the lottery used for choosing the next Panchen Lama. The Lama Temple thus assumed a new importance in ethnic minority control.

The first hall, **Lokapala**, houses a statue of the future Buddha, Maitreya, flanked by celestial guardians. The statue facing the back door is Weituo, guardian of Buddhism, carved from sandalwood. In the courtyard beyond is a pond with a bronze mandala depicting Xumishan, the Buddhist paradise.

The second hall, the huge **Yonghe Hall** (Yōnghé Diàn), presents worshippers with a trinity of gilded effigies representing the past, present and future Buddhas.

The third hall, **Yongyou Hall** (Yŏngyòu Diàn), has statues of the Buddha of Longevity and the Buddha of Medicine (to the left).

The **Hall of the Wheel of the Law** (Fǎlún Diàn) further north contains a large bronze statue of a benign and smiling Tsong Khapa (1357-1419), founder of the Gelukpa or Yellow Hat sect, robed in yellow and illuminated by sunlight from above.

The final hall, **Wanfu Pavilion** (Wànfú Gé), has a stupendous 18m-high statue of the Maitreya Buddha in his Tibetan form, clothed in yellow satin and reputedly sculpted from a single block of sandalwood. Each of the Bodhisattva's toes is the size of a pillow. You may find yourself transported to Tibet, where the wood for this statue originated, thanks to the smoke curling up from yak butter lamps. Galleries can be seen above, but they sadly cannot be climbed up to. Behind the statue is the **Vault of Avalokiteshvara**, from where a diminutive and blue-faced statue of Guanyin peeks out. The Wanfu Pavilion is linked by an overhead walkway to the **Yansui Pavilion** (Yánsuí Gé), which encloses around a huge lotus flower that revolves to reveal an effigy of the longevity Buddha.

An enthralling conclusion to the temple is the collection of bronze Tibetan Buddhist statues within the **Jiètái Lóu**. Most effigies

BEHIND THE WALL

If ceremonial and administrative duties occupied most of the emperor's working hours, it was the pursuit of pleasure behind the high walls of the Forbidden City that occupied much of his attention during the evenings. With so many wives and consorts to choose from, a system was needed to help the emperor choose his bed-time companion. One method was to keep the names of royal wives, consorts and favourites on jade tablets near the emperor's chambers. By turning the tablet over the emperor made his request for the evening, and the eunuch on duty would rush off to find the lucky lady. Stripped naked (and therefore weaponless), the little foot-bound creature was giftwrapped in a yellow cloth, piggybacked over to the royal boudoir and dumped at the feet of the emperor; the eunuch recording the date and time to verify the legitimacy of a possible child.

Aside from the emperor's frolicking, all this activity had a more serious purpose: prolonging the life of the emperor. An ancient Chinese belief that frequent sex with young girls could sustain one's youth even motivated Mao Zedong to follow the same procedure.

Financing the affairs of state probably cost less than financing the affairs of the emperor, and keeping the pleasure dome functioning drew heavily on the resources of the empire. During the Ming dynasty an estimated 9000 maids of honour and 70,000 eunuchs were serving the court. Apart from the servants and prize concubines, there were also the royal elephants to maintain. Pocketing the cash was illegal, but selling elephant dung for use as shampoo was not – it was believed to give hair that extra sheen. Back in the harem the cosmetic bills piled up to 400,000 liang of silver. Then, of course, the concubines who had grown old and were no longer in active service were still supposed to be cared for. Rather than cut back on expenditure, the emperor sent out eunuchs to collect emergency taxes whenever money ran short.

As for the palace eunuchs, the royal chop was administered at the Eunuch Clinic near the Forbidden City, using a swift knife and a special chair with a hole in the seat. The candidates sought to better their lives in the service of the court, but half of them died after the operation. Mutilation of any kind was considered grounds for exclusion from the next life, so many eunuchs carried around their appendages in pouches, believing that at the time of death the spirits might be deceived into thinking them whole.

date from the Qing dynasty, from languorous renditions of Green Tara and White Tara to exotic, tantric pieces (such as Samvara) and figurines of the fierce-looking Mahakala.

Photography is not permitted inside the temple buildings but a mini Lama Temple VCD comes free with your ticket. English-speaking guides can be found in the office to the left of the entrance gate or loitering near the temple entrance. The street outside the temple entrance heaves with shops piled high with statues of Buddha, talismans, Buddhist charms and keepsakes, picked over by pilgrims. Exiting the temple and walking east along Xilou Hutong brings you to the former Bailin Temple (Map p262; 1 Xilou Hutong) at the bend in the alley, its temple halls now converted to offices and its northernmost wall still daubed with the outline of Maoist slogans.

LAO SHE MUSEUM Map p262
Lǎo Shě Jìniànguǎn 老舍纪念馆
☎ 6559 9218; 19 Fengfu Hutong, off Dengshikou Xijie; adult Y10; ⏰ 9am-5pm; ⊕ Tiananmen Dong
This modest courtyard museum is dedicated to one of Běijīng's most popular 20th-century writers. Author of *Rickshaw Boy* and *Tea House*, and former teacher at London's School of Oriental and African Studies, Lao She (1899–1966) tragically committed suicide by throwing himself into a Běijīng lake during the Cultural Revolution (whispers of murder continue). Captions are largely in Chinese, but a large number of first editions are on view, along with photos and personal effects, and Lao She's courtyard home is brimful of simple charm.

MAO DUN FORMER RESIDENCE
Map p262
Máo Dùn Gùjū 茅盾故居
☎ 6404 4089; 13 Houyuan Ensi Hutong, off Jiaodaokou Nandajie; adult Y5; ⏰ 9am-4pm Tue, Thu & Sat; ⊕ Andingmen
Deep in the heart of the historic *hútòng* quadrant southeast of the Drum and Bell Towers is this small and unassuming museum. Mao Dun was the pen name of Shen Yanbing (1896–1981), who was born into an elite family in Zhèjiāng province but educated in Běijīng. In 1920 he helped found the Literary Study Society, an association promoting literary realism. Mao Dun joined the League of Left Wing Writers in

TOP FIVE BĚIJĪNG TEMPLES
- Step into another world at Běijīng's most distinctive Taoist temple, **Dongyue Temple** (p94).
- Relish the colourful pageant of the **Lama Temple** (p91), Běijīng's largest Buddhist temple.
- Weigh up the mysteries of the awesome **Temple of Heaven** (p79).
- Flee the Běijīng traffic and retire to the **Confucius Temple** (p85).
- Make a foray into the huge **White Cloud Temple** (p97) and enter a universe of Taoist myth, faith and superstition.

1930, becoming solidly entrenched in the bureaucracy after the communists came to power. He lay low during the Cultural Revolution, but briefly returned to writing in the 1970s. The museum is typically parsimonious and low-key.

ST JOSEPH'S CHURCH Map p262
Dōng Táng 东堂
74 Wangfujing Dajie; ⏰ 6.30-7am Mon-Sat, 6.30-8am Sun; ⊕ Wangfujing
A crowning edifice on Wangfujing Dajie and one of Běijīng's four principal churches, St Joseph's Church is also known locally as the East Cathedral. Originally built during the reign of Shunzhi in 1655, it was damaged by an earthquake in 1720 and reconstructed. The luckless church also caught fire in 1807, was destroyed again in 1900 during the Boxer Rebellion, and restored in 1904, only to be shut in 1966. Now fully repaired, the church is a testament to the long history of Christianity in China (see boxed text Christianity in China, p94). A large piazza in front swarms with children playing; white doves photogenically flutter about and Chinese models in bridal outfits wait for the sun to emerge before posing for magazine shots.

SCIENCE & TECHNOLOGY MUSEUM
Map pp258-9
Kējìguǎn 科技馆
1 Beisanhuan Zhonglu; ⏰ 9am-4.30pm Tue-Sun; Hall A/B/C Y30/30/20; through ticket Y50; ⊕ Gulou Dajie
Some exhibits at this museum are showing their age, but kids can run riot among the main hall's three floors of hands-on displays. Watch industrial robots perform a flawless taichi sword routine, try chatting with the speech robot who only seems able to say

'对不起 我没有听懂你的话' ('Sorry, I didn't catch you'), follow a maglev train gliding along a stretch of track or test out a bullet-proof vest with a sharp pointy thing. You could spend half the day working through the imaginative and educational displays in the main hall (Hall A), but if you want to make a real go of it, Hall B (astrovision theatre) and Hall C (Children's Scientific Entertainment Hall) offer extra diversions for boffins, young and old. English captions throughout.

CHÁOYÁNG 朝阳

Eating p132; Shopping p166; Sleeping p185

This district covers a vast swathe of Běijīng east and northeast of the Second Ring Rd. As Cháoyáng lay outside the old city walls, it is not a historic district and contains only a few sights of note. But the Sanlitun bar street (Sanlitun Lu) – sections of which have been levelled and are slated for massive redevelopment before the Olympic Games – can be found here, as well as the top-end hotels around the embassy area. The southern part of Cháoyáng, containing the Jianguomenwai Embassy Area and its associated restaurants and hotels, is incorporated on the Chóngwén and South Chaoyang map (pp268–9), and the Cháoyáng map (p264).

CREATION ART GALLERY Map p264
Kěchuàng Míngjiā Yìyuàn 可创铭佳艺苑

☎ 8561 7570; www.creationgallery.com.cn; cnr Ritan Donglu & Ritan Beilu; admission free; ⏱ 10am-7pm Tue-Sun

This well-lit, intimate space off the northeast corner of Ritan Park (opposite) presents an enjoyable array of paintings and sculptures, with a small area for sedentary contemplation of what's on view. Of the 20 or 30 artworks – many contemporary landscapes – several are composed by the gallery owner, Li Xiaoke. Prices start from around US$800.

DONGYUE TEMPLE Map p264
Dōngyuè Miào 东岳庙

☎ 6553 2184; 141 Chaoyangmenwai Dajie; adult Y10; ⏱ 9am-4.30pm Tue-Sun; Ⓜ Chaoyangmen

The morbid Taoist shrine of Dongyue Temple is an unsettling albeit fascinating experience. With its roots poking deep into the Yuan dynasty, what's above ground level

CHRISTIANITY IN CHINA

The explosion of interest in Christianity in China over recent years is unprecedented except for the wholesale conversions that accompanied the tumultuous rebellion of the pseudo-Christian Taiping in the 19th century.

The history of Christianity in China dates to the arrival of Nestorians in the 7th century but it wasn't until the fall of the Qing dynasty in the early 20th century that the religion began to successfully proliferate, as China increasingly drew upon foreign ideologies and practices. The Cultural Revolution and growing secularism of China under the communists was a spectacular reversal, but the faith has flourished in the relatively liberal social climate that followed the death of Mao Zedong.

The economic reforms of the past three decades have brought riches to many urban Chinese, but the spiritual vacuum at the heart of contemporary Chinese life – coupled with the hardships still endured by huge sections of the population – provides an ideal environment for the flourishing of faith. The associations between Christianity and a strong work ethic coupled with the progressive standing of Christian nations around the world have only added to its allure. Christianity is furthermore seen as being tolerant and able to accommodate, and to a degree inspire, scientific endeavour.

It is hard to calculate the total number of Christians in China. Estimates of 70 million Chinese Protestants and up to 20 million Chinese Catholics (the latter including around 10 million members of the state sanctioned church) are hard to verify; what is undeniable however is the huge number of house churches operating in China, attracting legions of adherents. Being free of government control, unregistered house churches attract most worshippers who prefer them to the official state churches. For more details on the Chinese house church movement, click on www.backtojerusalem.com.

Visitors increasingly report being stopped by English-speaking Chinese Christians around China; some are zealously evangelical, an activity that is forbidden. As with the Taiping, whose leader Hong Xiuquan claimed he was the Son of God, the lack of trained priests creates ample room for Christian heresies to appear.

Increasingly concerned about losing ideological ground to a competing system of thought, the Communist Party has responded by closing numerous house churches, but this has done little to stem the tide.

Jesus in Beijing (How Christianity is Changing the Global Balance of Power) by David Aikman argues that China is approaching a tipping point that will transform the land into a largely Christian domain over the next thirty years. However unlikely the scenario, such an achievement would surely owe much to the secularisation of China, which has turned the nation's soul into a blank sheet of paper to be written upon.

has been revived with care and investment. Dedicated to Tài Shān, the most easterly of the five Taoist peaks of China, Dongyue Temple is an active place of worship where Taoist monks attend to a world entirely at odds with the surrounding glass and steel high-rises. Note the temple's fabulous *páifāng* (memorial archway) lying to the south, divorced from its shrine by the intervention of Chaoyangmenwai Dajie.

Stepping through the entrance pops you into a Taoist Hades, where tormented spirits reflect on their wrong-doing and elusive atonement. You can muse on life's finalities in the **Life and Death Department** or the **Final Indictment Department**. Otherwise get spooked at the **Department for Wandering Ghosts** or the **Department for Implementing 15 Kinds of Violent Death**.

It's not all doom and gloom: the luckless can check in at the **Department for Increasing Good Fortune and Longevity**. Ornithologists will be birds of a feather with the **Flying Birds Department**, while the infirm can seek cures at the **Deep-Rooted Disease Department**. The **Animal Department** has colourful and lively fauna. English explanations detail department functions.

Other halls are no less fascinating. The huge **Daiyue Hall** (Dàiyuè Diàn) is consecrated to the God of Tàishān, who manages the 18 layers of hell. Visit during festival time, especially during the Chinese New Year and the Mid-Autumn festival, and you'll see the temple at its most vibrant.

POLY ART MUSEUM Map p264
Bǎolì Yìshù Bówùguǎn 保利艺术博物馆
☎ 6500 8117; www.polymuseum.com; Poly Plaza, 14 Dongzhimen Nandajie; Y50; ⊙ 9.30am-4.30pm Tue, Thu & Sat, group reservations Mon, Wed & Fri; ⊕ Dongsishitiao

Primed to move to new premises (the New Poly Plaza, directly southwest of the current address on the other side of the intersection of Dongzhimen Nandajie and Gongrentiyuchang Beilu), this excellent museum displays Shang and Zhou dynasty bronzes and stone Buddhist effigies sculpted between the Northern Wei and Tang dynasties. It's a sublime display but note the often unaccommodating opening hours for individuals.

PYONGYANG ART STUDIOS Map p264
☎ 6416 7544; Red House Hotel, 10 Chunxiu Lu; ⊕ Dongsishitiao or Dongzhimen

Unsurpassed Communist kitsch delivered straight to your hands from the axis of evil.

TRANSPORT

Subway Line 2: The Poly Art Museum is just north of Dongsishitiao stop, and Dongyue Temple is a 10-minute walk east of Chaoyangmen stop; Dongsishitiao is the closest subway stop to the bars and restaurants of Sanlitun. To save walking take a cab or bus 115. Line 10: When completed, part of Line 10 will run through this district, connecting with Line 1 at Guomao and linking up with Line 5, the Airport Line and Line 13.

Bus Double-decker bus 3 takes you from the Jingguang New World Hotel, past Tuanjiehu Park and the Agricultural Exhibition Center to the Lufthansa Center; bus 110 runs from Chaoyangmen subway station along Chaoyangmenwai Dajie, past the Dongyue Temple and then north along Gongrentiyuchang Donglu via the Workers' Stadium and up Xin Donglu; bus 115 runs east along Gongrentiyuchang Beilu from the Dongsishitiao subway stop to Sanlitun.

Finger maps of Pyongyang and turn over edifying literature ('Towards the Eminence of Socialism'), North Korean ciggies (Y20 per pack), liquor, T-shirts (Y80), posters vilifying America, DRPK flags (Y150), postcards (Y80) and badges (Y30), or grab a second impression of 'The US Imperialists started the Korean War' (Y100) – while stocks last.

RITAN PARK Map p264
Rìtán Gōngyuán 日坛公园
☎ 8563 5038; Ritan Lu; ⊙ 6am-9pm; ⊕ Chaoyangmen

Dating from 1530, this park is one of Běijīng's oldest, established as an altar for ritual sacrifice to the sun. The square altar, typically surrounded by kite flyers and children playing, is ringed by a circular wall, while the rest of the park is given over to pines and quietude.

ZHIHUA TEMPLE Map p262
Zhìhuà Sì 智化寺
5 Lumicang Hutong; adult Y20; ⊙ 8.30am-4.30pm; ⊕ Jianguomen or Chaoyangmen

Běijīng's surviving temple brood has endured slapdash renewal which regularly buries authenticity beneath casual restoration work. This rickety shrine is thick with the flavours of old Peking, having eluded the Dulux treatment that invariably precedes entrance fee inflation and stomping tour groups. You won't find the coffered ceiling of the third hall (it's in the USA) and the Four Heavenly Kings have vanished from Zhihua Gate

(Zhìhuà Mén), but the Scriptures Hall encases a venerable Ming dynasty revolving wooden library and the highlight **Ten Thousand Buddhas Hall** (Wànfó Diàn) is an enticing two floors of niche-borne Buddhas and cabinets for storing sutras. Creep up the staircase at the back of the hall, to visit the Vairocana Buddha seated upon a lotus flower in the upper chamber, before wondering the fate of the 1000-Armed Guanyin that once presided over the Great Mercy Hall at the temple rear.

FĒNGTÁI & XUĀNWǓ
丰台、宣武
Shopping p167; Sleeping p187

Fēngtái and Xuānwǔ occupy the southwest of Běijīng, an area that might not see Běijīng at its prettiest or most historic. But travellers will enjoy rummaging for curios in the stalls and shops of Liulichang (p167), and experiencing the Taoist mysteries of the White Cloud Temple (opposite). The district around the Niujie Mosque (opposite) is distinctive for its Huí (Chinese Muslim) character. The quarter focuses on Niu Jie (Cow St), named after the local Muslim predilection for beef.

CAPITAL MUSEUM Map pp266-7
Shǒudū Bówùguǎn 首都博物馆
☎ 6337 0491; www.capitalmuseum.org.cn;
16 Fuxingmenwai Dajie; admission Y20; ☉ 9am-5pm Tue-Sun; ◉ Muxidi
With Běijīng busily hatching a huge and disparate brood of new and often rather

pointless museums, this modern and sleek addition is a showpiece achievement. Staging a headline-grabbing exhibition in 2006 from the collection of the British Museum, the museum – stunning from the outside – aims at high-profile exhibitions from abroad while maintaining permanent displays of ancient bronzes, Buddhist statues, jade, calligraphy, paintings and ceramics.

CHINA MILLENNIUM MONUMENT
Map pp266-7
Zhōnghuá Shìjì Tán 中华世纪坛
9a Fuxing Lu; admission Y30; ☉ 8.30am-5.30pm;
◉ Junshibowuguan
Vaguely resembling a vast sundial pointing directly south to Beijing West Train Station, this cumbersome monument solidifies Běijīng's triumphant 21st century aspirations in stone. For such a momentous statement, the design is devoid of imagination or artistry, while examination of the stone cladding shows it already requires repair. The **art gallery**, however, is worth perusing (included in the ticket price) and you can pick up boats from the dock (世纪坛码头; Shìjìtán Mǎtou; adult Y70) to the Summer Palace, leaving daily at 10am, 11am, 2pm and 5pm, or go for a stroll in **Yuyuantan Park** (Yùyuāntán Gōngyuán; Map pp260–1) to the north (Y2), where you can also board boats (Y60; return ticket Y80; ☉ 10.10am, 11.10am, 2.10pm and 3.10pm) to the Summer Palace from the Bayi Lake dock (Bāyī Hú Mǎtou; Map pp260–1).

BĚIJĪNG FOR CHILDREN
The weeny ones can dig their heels in and holler when faced with the measureless museum-style torpor of the Forbidden City and the Ming Tombs. Thanks to China's One-child policy, however, Běijīng's sibling-less tykes are spoiled rotten by their parents, and the city is bursting with activities to keep toddler tantrums at bay. **Beijing Aquarium** (p98) is an option for a rainy day, while **Beijing Zoo** (p98) is a fun outing. **ExploraScience** (Suǒní Tànmèng; Map pp268–9; ☎ 8518 2255; 1st fl, Oriental Plaza, Wangfujing Dajie; adult/child Y30/20 ☉ 9.30am-5.30pm Mon-Fri, 10am-7pm Sat & Sun, closed 2nd Mon & Tue every month) is a hands-on foray into the world of science and **Beijing Planetarium** (p98) may take them to the stars. The dinosaurs at the **Beijing Natural History Museum** (p73) may go down well, while the **Science & Technology Museum** (p93) has loads of gadgets and fun displays. Alternatively put your children on ice at **Le Cool Ice Rink** (p154). In the evenings, the **China National Puppet Theatre** (p150) casts a spell over its audience of little (and not-so-little) ones. If your children are fed up with window-shopping, take them along to the **Xin Zhongguo Kid's Stuff** (p165), a huge toy emporium on Wangfujing Dajie. For more toys, try **Kids World** (6th fl, Lufthansa Center Youyi Shopping City), the stalls on the 4th floor of the Sanlitun Yashow Clothing Market (p167) and **Kids Toys Market** (Hóngqiáo Tiānlè Wánjù Shìchǎng; ☉ 8.30am-7pm) in the building behind Hongqiao Market (p162). Events and attractions for children – from plays to arts and crafts events and seasonal parties – are listed in the monthly English-language culture magazine **That's Beijing** (www.thatsmagazines.com). Note that many museums and attractions have a cheaper rate for children, usually applying to children shorter than 1.3m, so ask.

FAYUAN TEMPLE Map pp266-7
Fǎyuán Sì 法源寺

7 Fayuansi Qianjie; adult Y5; ⊗ 8.30-11am & 2-3.30pm Thu-Tue; 🚌 6 to Niu Jie or 10 to Libaisi stop
In a lane east of Niujie Mosque, this temple originally dates back to the 7th century and remains busy with monks and worshippers. Now the **China Buddhism College**, the temple was originally built to honour Tang soldiers who had fallen during combat against the northern tribes. The temple follows the typical Buddhist layout, with drum and bell towers and the usual succession of halls, but look out for its unusual **copper-cast Buddha** seated on a thousand-petal lotus flower in the Pilu Hall (the fourth hall). The Guanyin Hall towards the rear is a pleasant repository for several statues of the Goddess of Mercy. From the entrance of Niujie Mosque, walk left 100m then turn left into the first *hútòng*. Follow the *hútòng* for about 10 minutes, and you'll arrive at Fayuan Temple.

MILITARY MUSEUM Map pp266-7
Jūnshì Bówùguǎn 军事博物馆

9 Fuxing Lu; adult Y20; ⊗ 8am-5pm, last entry 4.30pm; ⊚ Junshibowuguan
This hulking monolith of a building topped with a communist star is purely for military enthusiasts. Cold War–era F-5 fighters, the much larger F-7 and F-8s, tanks, and HQ-2 (Red Flag-2) surface-to-air missiles are down below, while upstairs has further weaponry and a heavy-going gallery of statues of military and political top brass. Other halls include the Hall of Agrarian Revolutionary War and the Hall of the War to Resist US Aggression and Aid Korea, while in the forecourt you can clamber aboard a missile boat (Y5).

NIUJIE MOSQUE Map pp266-7
Niújiē Lǐbài Sì 牛街礼拜寺

☎ 6353 2564; 88 Niu Jie; adult Y10, free for Muslims; ⊗ 8am-sunset; 🚌 6 to Niu Jie or 10 to Libaisi stop
With a history dating back to the 10th century, this recently renovated Chinese-styled mosque is Běijīng's largest. A burial site for a number of Islamic clerics, the grounds of the mosque are given over to a profusion of greenery, flourishes of Arabic, the main prayer hall (only Muslims can enter), women's quarters and the **Building for Observing the Moon** (Wàngyuèlóu), from where the lunar calendar was calculated. Dress appropriately (no shorts or short skirts) and be

TRANSPORT

Subway Line 2: You can reach the South Cathedral at the Xuanwumen stop. Line 1: Get off at the Junshibowuguan stop for the Military Museum and the Muxidi stop for the Capital Museum. Line 4: When completed, Line 4 will connect with Line 1 at Xidan and with Line 2 at Xuanwumen, heading south to Beijing South Train Station.

Bus Double-decker bus 1 runs from Beijing West Train Station, past the Capital Museum and the Military Museum, east past Xidan and onto Tiananmen Square and beyond along Chang'an Jie; bus 10 connects Niu Jie with Wangfujing Dajie, running through Tiananmen, Xidan and Changchun Jie.

particularly respectful on Fridays, or save your visit for another day of the week.

SOUTH CATHEDRAL Map pp266-7
Nántáng 南堂

141 Qianmen Xidajie; ⊗ mass in Latin 6am Sun-Fri, in English 10am Sun; ⊚ Xuanwumen
Běijīng's South Cathedral was built on the site of the house of Matteo Ricci, the Jesuit missionary who introduced Catholicism to China. Since being completed in 1703, the church has been destroyed three times, including being burnt down in 1775, and endured a trashing by anti-Christian forces during the Boxer Rebellion in 1900. The church is now decorated with modern stained glass, fake marbling, portraits of the Stations of the Cross and cream-coloured confessionals.

WHITE CLOUD TEMPLE Map pp266-7
Báiyún Guàn 白云观

☎ 6346 3531; Baiyun Lu; adult Y10; ⊗ 8.30am-4.30pm May-Sep, 8.30am-4pm Oct-Apr; ⊚ Muxidi, then 🚌 708
White Cloud Temple, once the Taoist centre of northern China, was founded in AD 739. It's a lively, huge and fascinating temple complex of shrines and courtyards, tended by Taoist monks with their hair twisted into topknots. Today's temple halls date principally from the Ming and Qing dynasties.

Near the temple entrance, worshippers rub a polished stone carving for good fortune. The halls at the temple, centre of operations for the Taoist Quanzhen School and abode of the China Taoist Association, are dedicated to a host of Taoist officials and marshals. The **Hall of the Jade Emperor** celebrates this most famous of Taoist deities, while Taoist housewives cluster earnestly at the **Hall to the God of Wealth** to divine their financial future. Depictions of the Taoist Hell festoon the walls of the **Shrine Hall for the Saviour Worthy**.

Drop by White Cloud Temple during the Spring Festival (p18) and be rewarded with the spectacle of a magnificent temple fair (*miàohui*). Worshippers funnel into the streets around the temple in their thousands, lured by artisans, street performers, *wŭshù* (martial arts) acts, craft workers, traders and a swarm of snack merchants.

To find the temple, walk south on Baiyun Lu from the Capital Museum and across the moat. Continue along Baiyun Lu and turn into a curving street on the left; follow it for 250m to the temple entrance.

HĂIDIÀN & XĪCHÉNG
海淀、西城

Eating p136; Sleeping p187

Xīchéng occupies the western flank of Běijīng's central district, including part of the Imperial City and sites around the Qianhai and Houhai lake area. Hăidiàn district occupies the northwest of Běijīng, an area noted for the famous Peking and Qinghua Universities; it also incorporates the Zhongguancun high-tech district.

BEIJING PLANETARIUM Map pp260-1
Běijīng Tiānwénguǎn 北京天文馆
138 Xizhimenwai Dajie; Old Bldg Y15, New Bldg Y10, Optical Planetarium Y15, 4-D Theatre Y30, Space Simulator Y30, Digital Space Theatre Y45; 🕑 **10am-5pm Wed-Sun;** 🚇 **Xizhimen, then** 🚌 **104, 205 or 106**

TRANSPORT

Subway Line 2: offers access to the Xu Beihong Museum, the Lu Xun Museum and the Miaoying Temple White Dagoba. Line 4: When completed, Line 4 will connect with Line 2 at Xizhimen before running on to Beijing Zoo and the Old Summer Palace and Summer Palace.

Bus Double-decker bus 4 runs from Beijing Zoo past the Exhibition Center and then south along the Second Ring Rd to Qianmen (for Tiananmen Square); several westbound buses from Xizhimen can get you to the zoo, including buses 104 and 106.

Across from the zoo (below), children will find something to marvel at among the telescopes, models of the planets and the solar system, and the variety of shows in the new building, even though the typical absence of thorough English captions can make full comprehension an astronomical task.

BEIJING ZOO & BEIJING AQUARIUM
Map pp260-1
Běijīng Dòngwùyuán
北京动物园、北京海洋馆
137 Xizhimenwai Dajie; admission Y15 1 Apr-31 Oct, Y10 1 Nov-31 Mar, panda house Y5 extra, English audio guide Y40; 🕑 **7.30am-5.30pm;** 🚇 **Xizhimen, then** 🚌 **104, 205 or 106**

A pleasant spot for a stroll among the trees, grass and willow-fringed lakes, Beijing Zoo is chiefly notable for its pandas (if Sìchuān is not on your itinerary), even if the remaining resident menagerie is cooped up in pitiful cages and enclosures. The **Popular Science Museum** (Y5) within the grounds of the zoo has no English captions so is highly missable, but the small **children's zoo** (Y10; 🕑 9am-5pm) is fun for young zoologists.

The polar bears pin their hopes on graduating from their concrete cosmos to the far more stellar **Beijing Aquarium** (☎ 6217 6655; adult/child Y100/50; 🕑 low season 9am-5.30pm, high season 9am-6pm), a worthwhile diversion in the northeastern corner of the zoo. On view is an imaginative Amazon rainforest (complete with piranha), coral reefs, a shark aquarium (where you can dive with the flesh eaters), and a marine mammal pavilion. The last hosts lively aquatic animal displays. The ticket price to the aquarium includes entry to the zoo; you can buy this ticket at the zoo entrance.

Boats to the Summer Palace depart from the dock in front of the aquarium (☎ 8838 4476; Y40; every hour from 10am-4pm).

East of the zoo is the distinctive **Beijing Exhibition Hall** (Běijīng Zhǎnlǎn Guǎn; Map pp260-1), designed in the days when Chinese architects were party ideologues.

LU XUN MUSEUM Map pp260-1
Lǔ Xùn Bówùguǎn 鲁迅博物馆
19 Gongmenkou Ertiao; adult Y5; 🕑 **9am-4pm Tue-Sun;** 🚇 **Fuchengmen**

Lu Xun (1881–1936), born in Shàoxīng in Zhèjiāng province, is often regarded as the father of modern Chinese literature. As a writer, Lu Xun, who first trained in medicine, articulated a deep yearning for reform by mercilessly exposing the foibles of the Chinese people's character. Hampered by a shortage of English captions, the museum's collection of photos and manuscripts remains largely impenetrable to all but the most erudite.

MEI LANFANG FORMER RESIDENCE

Map pp260-1

Méi Lánfāng Jìniàn Guǎn 梅兰芳纪念馆

☎ 6618 0351; 9 Huguosi Lu; adult Y10; ⏰ 9am-4pm Tue-Sun Apr-Nov; ⓞ Jishuitan

Place of pilgrimage for Beijing opera aficionados, this former *sihéyuàn* (courtyard house) of actor Mei Lanfang is tucked away in a *hútòng* named after the nearby remains of Huguo Temple. Beijing opera (p35) was popularised in the West by Mei Lanfang (1894–1961), who played *dàn* or female roles, and is said to have influenced Charlie Chaplin. His former residence has been preserved as a museum, replete with costumes, furniture, opera programmes and video presentations of his opera performances.

MIAOYING TEMPLE WHITE DAGOBA

Map pp260-1

Miàoyíng Sì Báitǎ 妙应寺白塔

☎ 6616 0211; 171 Fuchengmennei Dajie; adult Y10; ⏰ 9am-4pm; ⓞ Fuchengmen, then 🚌 13, 101, 102 or 103 to Baita Si

The Yuan dynasty white dagoba of the Miaoying Temple is similar to that in Beihai Park (p84). The highpoint of a visit here, however, is the riveting collection of thousands of **Tibetan Buddhist statues**. A population of bronze *luóhàn* figures also inhabits the temple. There is liberal use of English captions.

NORTH CATHEDRAL Map pp260-1

Běitáng 北堂

☎ 6617 5198; Xishiku Dajie; ⓞ Fuchengmen or 🚌 14 or 55 to Xianmen stop, then walk north

Also called the Cathedral of Our Saviour, this august cathedral is one of Běijīng's four main churches and the only one located within the grounds of the Imperial City. Built in 1887, the church was badly damaged during the Cultural Revolution before serving as a factory warehouse. Despite being covered in gaudy grey, flaking paint, the cathedral is well worth a look-see.

PALEOZOOLOGICAL MUSEUM OF CHINA Map pp260-1

Zhōngguó Gǔdòngwùguǎn 中国古动物馆

142 Xizhimenwai Dajie; admission Y20; ⏰ 9am-4.30pm Tue-Sun; ⓞ Xizhimen, then 🚌 104, 205 or 106

A little bit cheesy, with an impressive tally of *zero* English captions, but young palaeontologists can scurry among the dinosaur remains and legions of Chinese schoolchildren, gawping at skeletons of *Tyrannosaurus Rex* and *Tsingtaosaurus* and examining the parrot-like beak of *Psittacosaurus*.

PRINCE GONG'S RESIDENCE

Map pp260-1

Gōngwáng Fǔ 恭王府

☎ 6616 5005; 14 Liuyin Jie; adult Y20; tour Y60 (including opera performance & tea ceremony); ⏰ 8.30am-4.30pm; ⓞ Gulou Dajie then 🚌 60 or taxi

Reputed to be the model for the mansion in Cao Xueqin's 18th-century classic, *Dream of the Red Mansions*, the residence is one of Běijīng's largest private residential compounds. It remains one of Běijīng's more attractive retreats, decorated with rockeries, plants, pools, pavilions and elaborately carved gateways. Performances of Beijing opera are held in the Qing dynasty **Grand Opera House** (☎ 6618 6628; adults Y80-120 ⏰ 7.30-8.40pm, Mar-Oct) in the east of the grounds.

SONG QINGLING FORMER RESIDENCE Map pp260-1

Sòng Qìnglíng Gùjū 宋庆龄故居

☎ 6403 5858; 46 Beiheyan Lu; adult Y8; ⏰ 9am-4pm Tue-Sun; ⓞ Gulou Dajie or Jishuitan

Madam Song is lovingly venerated by the Chinese as the wife of Sun Yat-sen, founder of the Republic of China. Her house is rather dormant and moth-eaten; on display are personal items, pictures, clothing and books. You can find the museum on the northern side of Houhai Lake and within reach of Prince Gong's residence.

WANSHOU TEMPLE & BEIJING ART MUSEUM Map pp260-1

Wànshòu Sì & Běijīng Yìshù Bówùguǎn 万寿寺、北京艺术博物馆

Suzhou Jie; adult Y15; ⏰ 9am-4pm; ⓞ Gongzhufen, then 🚌 944

Ringed by a red wall on the southeastern corner of Suzhou Jie (off the Third Ring Rd), the Ming dynasty Wanshou Temple was originally consecrated for the storage of Buddhist texts. The temple's name echoes the Summer Palace's Longevity Hill (Wànshòu Shān; p103); in fact, from Qing times the imperial entourage would put their feet up here and quaff tea en route to the palace. Wanshou Temple fell into disrepair during the Republic, with the Wanshou Hall burning down in 1937. Things went from bad to worse and during the Cultural Revolution the temple served as an army barracks.

The highlight of a visit to this restored temple is its prized collection of bronze **Buddhist statuary** in the 'Buddhist Art Exhibition of Ming and Qing Dynasties'. The displays guide you through the Buddhist pantheon with statues of Sakyamuni, Manjusri, Amitabha, Guanyin (in bronze and *déhuà*, or blanc-de-Chine porcelain) and exotic tantric pieces. Also look out for the *kapala bowl* made from a human skull, *dorjes* (Tibetan ritual sceptres) and *purbhas* (Tibetan ritual daggers). Further halls are devoted to Ming and Qing porcelain. Also worth noting is the decidedly masculine-looking Guanyin at the rear of the **Mahavira Hall** (she is usually, but not exclusively, female). The pavilion at the rear once housed a 5m-high gold-lacquered brass statue now long gone; in its place is a miniature pagoda alloyed from gold, silver, zinc and lead. Some of China's holy mountains (including Pǔtuó Shān and Éméi Shān) in the form of small rockeries can also be found.

WUTA TEMPLE Map pp260-1
Wǔtǎ Sì 五塔寺
24 Wutasi Cun; adult Y20; audio guide Y5; ☻ 9am-4pm; ◉ Xizhimen, then 🚌 104, 205 or 106
Known also as Zhenjue Temple (真觉寺; Zhēnjué Sì), the distinctive Indian-styled Wuta Temple (Five Pagoda Temple) is topped by its five magnificent namesake pagodas. The exterior of the main hall is decorated with *dorjes* (Tibetan sceptres), hundreds of images of Budda and legions of beasts, amid traces of red pigment that can still be discerned. Facing you as you climb the steps to the five pagodas – themselves carved with a galaxy of Buddhist images – are wall carvings of the feet of Buddha. During Ming times, the temple ranged to at least six halls, all later tiled in yellow during Qing times; the terrace where the Big Treasure Hall once stood can still be seen. The temple, dating from 1473, is reached by the canal bridge

directly opposite the rear exit of Beijing Zoo (p98), also houses the **Carved Stone Museum** (Shíkē Bówùguǎn), with clusters of stone stelae, statues and *bìxì* – mythical tortoise-like dragons often seen in Confucian temples.

XU BEIHONG MUSEUM Map pp260-1
Xú Bēihóng Jìniàn Guǎn 徐悲鸿纪念馆
☎ 6225 2042; 53 Xinjiekou Beidajie; adult Y5; ☻ 9am-4pm Tue-Sun; ◉ Jishuitan
The Chinese artist Xu Beihong (1895–1953), best remembered for his galloping horses that injected dynamism into previously static forms of Chinese brushwork, is commemorated in this intriguing museum. Exposed to foreign (principally European) painting styles, Xu possessed one of 20th-century China's more fertile imaginations. The communists feted Xu, which partly explains the success and longevity of his name. His success is celebrated here in seven halls and remembered in a collection of oils, gouache, pen and ink sketches, and portraits.

AROUND BĚIJĪNG
BEIJING BOTANIC GARDENS
Map pp258-9
Běijīng Zhíwùyuán 北京植物园
☎ 6259 1283; 2km east of Fragrant Hills Park; adult Y5; ☻ 6am-8pm; ◉ Pingguoyuan, then 🚌 318; or 🚌 331 from Summer Palace; or 🚌 360 from Xizhimen (via Beijing Zoo)
The well-tended botanic gardens, set against the backdrop of the Western Hills, make for a pleasant outing among bamboo fronds, pines and lilacs. The **Beijing Botanical Gardens Conservatory** (Y50; ☻ 8.30am-4pm), contains 3000 different types of plants and a rainforest house.

Within the grounds and about a 15-minute walk from the front gate (follow the signs) is **Sleeping Buddha Temple** (Wòfó Sì; adult Y5; ☻ 8am-5pm). The temple, first built during the Tang dynasty, has a huge reclining effigy of Sakyamuni weighing 54 tonnes as a centrepiece, said to have 'enslaved 7000 people' in its casting. On each side of Buddha are arrayed some sets of gargantuan shoes, gifts to Sakyamuni from various emperors in case he went for a stroll.

On the eastern side of the gardens is the **Cao Xueqin Memorial** (Cáo Xuěqín Jìniànguǎn; ☎ 6259 5904; 39 Zhengbaiqi; Y10; ☻ 8.30am-4.15pm) where Cao Xueqin lived in his latter years. Cao (1715–63) is credited with penning the classic *Dream of the Red Mansions*, a vast and prolix family saga set in the Qing period.

FRAGRANT HILLS PARK

Map pp258-9

Xiāng Shān Gōngyuán 香山公园

☎ 6259 1283; adult Y10; ☻ 8am-6pm; ◉ Pingguoyuan, then ☒ 318; or ☒ 331 from Summer Palace; or ☒ 360 from Xizhimen (via Beijing Zoo)

Easily within striking distance of the Summer Palace are the **Xī Shān** (Western Hills), another former villa-resort of the emperors. The part of Xī Shān closest to Běijīng is known as **Fragrant Hills** (Xiāng Shān). Scramble up the slopes to the top of **Incense-Burner Peak** (Xiānglú Fēng), or take the **chairlift** (one way/return Y30/50; ☻ 8.30am-5pm). From the peak you get an all-embracing view of the countryside, and you can leave the crowds behind by hiking further into the Western Hills. Běijīngers flock here in autumn when the maple leaves saturate the hillsides in great splashes of red.

Near the north gate of Fragrant Hills Park is the excellent **Azure Clouds Temple** (Bìyún Sì; adult Y10; ☻ 8am-5pm), which dates back to the Yuan dynasty. The **Mountain Gate Hall** contains two vast protective deities: Heng and Ha, beyond which is a small courtyard and the drum and bell towers, leading to a hall with a wonderful statue of Milefo: it's bronze, but coal black with age. Only his big toe shines from numerous inquisitive fingers.

The **Sun Yat-sen Memorial Hall** contains a statue and a glass coffin donated by the USSR on the death of Mr Sun in 1925. At the very back is the marble **Vajra Throne Pagoda**, where Sun Yat-sen was interred after he died, before his body was moved to its final resting place in Nánjīng. The **Hall of Arhats** is well worth visiting; it contains 500 *luóhàn* statues, each crafted with an individual personality.

Southwest of the Azure Clouds Temple is the Tibetan-styled **Temple of Brilliance** (Zhāo Miào), and not far away is a glazed tile pagoda. Both survived visits by foreign troops intent on sacking the area in 1860 and 1900.

GREAT BELL TEMPLE Map p271

Dàzhōng Sì 大钟寺

☎ 6255 0819; 31a Beisanhuan Xilu; adult Y10; ☻ 8.30am-4.30pm; ◉ Dazhongsi; ☒ 361, 367 or 422

This temple houses a massive Ming dynasty bell, 6.75m tall, weighing in at a hefty 46.5 tonnes, inscribed with Buddhist sutras, comprising more than 227,000 Chinese characters, and decorated with Sanskrit incantations. Clamber up to the circular hall (Y2), where there's a small exhibition on bell casting (with some English captions), and chuck a coin through the opening in the top of the bell for luck.

The bell was cast during the reign of Emperor Yongle in 1406, with the tower built in 1733. To get the bell from the foundry to the temple, a shallow canal was dug, and when it froze over in winter, the bell was shunted across the ice by sled.

OLD SUMMER PALACE

Map pp258-9

Yuánmíng Yuán 圆明园

☎ 6262 8501; 28 Qinghua Xilu; adult Y10, palace ruins Y15; ☻ 7am-7pm; ◉ Yuanmingyuan; ◉ Wudaokou, then ☒ 375 or 726; or minibus from Summer Palace

Located northwest of the city centre, the original Summer Palace was laid out in the 12th century. The ever-capable Jesuits were later employed by Emperor Qianlong to fashion European-style palaces for the gardens, incorporating elaborate fountains and baroque statuary. During the Second Opium War, British and French troops vandalised the palace and sent the booty abroad, an event forever inscribed in Chinese history books as a nadir in China's humiliation by foreign powers. Most of the palace was destroyed, but a melancholic tangle of broken columns and marble chunks remain. The subdued ruins of the European Palace can be mulled over in the **Eternal Spring Garden** (Chángchūn Yuán) in the northeast of the park; entering by the east gate guides you directly to their vestiges. It's here that you can find the **Great Fountain Ruins**, considered the best-preserved relic in the palace.

West of the ruins you can lose your way in an artful reproduction of a former labyrinth called the **Garden of Yellow Flowers**.

The palace gardens cover a huge area – 2.5km from east to west – so be prepared for some walking. Besides the ruins, there's the western section, the **Perfection & Brightness Garden** (Yuánmíng Yuán) and in the southern compound, the **10,000 Springs Garden** (Wànchūn Yuán).

You can take some pleasant trips in the area by public transport. Take bus 332 from the zoo to both the old and new Summer Palaces; change to bus 333 for Fragrant Hills Park; from Fragrant Hills Park change to bus 360 to go directly back to Beijing Zoo.

Another route is to take the subway to Pingguoyuan (the last stop in the west), and from there take bus 318 to Fragrant Hills Park; change to 331 for the Summer Palace, and then bus 332 for the zoo.

SUMMER PALACE Map pp258-9

Yíhé Yuán 颐和园

☎ 6288 1144; admission Y40-50, audio guides Y30; ⏰ 8.30am-5pm; ⊕ Wudaokou, then 🚌 375; or 🚌 332 from zoo; or 🚌 726 from Qianmen

The huge regal encampment of the Summer Palace in the northwest of Běijīng is one of the city's principle attractions. Once a playground for the imperial court eluding the insufferable summer swelter of the For-

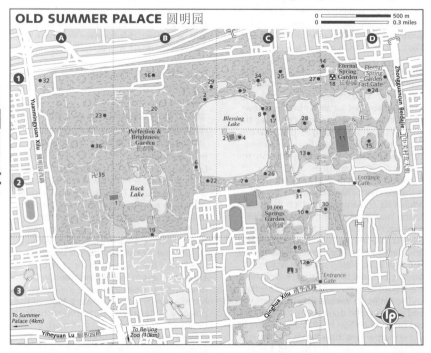

OLD SUMMER PALACE 圆明园

bidden City, today the palace grounds, its temples, gardens, pavilions, lakes and corridors teem with marauding tour groups.

The site had long been a royal garden and was considerably enlarged and embellished by Qing emperor Qianlong in the 18th century. Enlisting 100,000 labourers, he deepened and expanded **Kunming Lake** (Kūnmíng Hú) and reputedly surveyed imperial naval drills from a hilltop perch.

Anglo-French troops badly damaged the buildings during the Second Opium War in 1860. Empress Dowager Cixi began a refit in 1888 with money flagged for a modern navy, indulging herself with the extravagant marble boat on the northern edge of the lake.

Foreign troops, victorious over the Boxers, again rampaged through the palace grounds in 1900, prompting further resto-

ration work. The palace fell into disrepair during the years of the Republic, and a major overhaul began in 1949.

Three-quarters of the park is occupied by Kunming Lake and the most notable structures are near the east gates and on **Longevity Hill** (Wànshòu Shān). The main building is the **Hall of Benevolence & Longevity** (Rénshòu Diàn) by the east gate; it houses a hardwood throne and is fronted by a courtyard decorated with bronze animals, including the mythical *qílín* (a hybrid animal that appeared on earth only at times of harmony). The hall, sadly, is barricaded off so you can only peer in.

Along the lake's northern shore and undergoing restoration at the time of writing, the **Long Corridor** (Cháng Láng) is trimmed with paintings, while the slopes and crest of Longevity Hill behind are decorated with

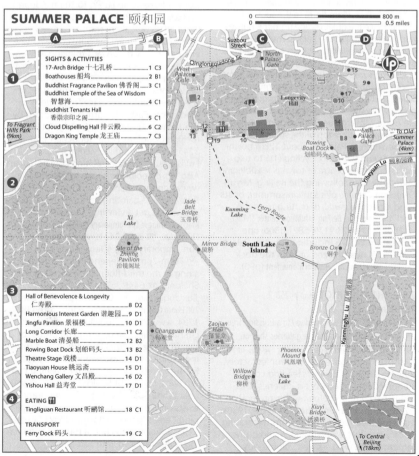

SUMMER PALACE 颐和园

0 — 800 m
0 — 0.5 miles

SIGHTS & ACTIVITIES
17-Arch Bridge 十七孔桥 1 C3
Boathouses 船坞 2 B1
Buddhist Fragrance Pavilion 佛香阁 3 C1
Buddhist Temple of the Sea of Wisdom
智慧海 4 C1
Buddhist Tenants Hall
香崇宗印之阁 5 C1
Cloud Dispelling Hall 排云殿 6 C2
Dragon King Temple 龙王庙 7 C3

To Fragrant
Hills Park
(9km)

Hall of Benevolence & Longevity
仁寿殿 8 D2
Harmonious Interest Garden 谐趣园 9 D1
Jingfu Pavilion 景福楼 10 D1
Long Corridor 长廊 11 C2
Marble Boat 清晏船 12 B2
Rowing Boat Dock 划船码头 13 B2
Theatre Stage 戏楼 14 D1
Tiaoyuan House 眺远斋 15 D1
Wenchang Gallery 文昌殿 16 D2
Yishou Hall 益寿堂 17 D1

EATING
Tingliguan Restaurant 听鹂馆 18 C1

TRANSPORT
Ferry Dock 码头 19 C2

Suzhou
Street

Qinglongqiaodong Jie

West
Palace
Gate

North
Palace
Gate

15

9

17

Longevity
Hill

10

14

East
Palace
Gate

To Old
Summer
Palace
(4km)

Rowing
Boat Dock
划船码头

Yiheyuan Lu 颐和园路

Jade
Belt
Bridge
玉带桥

Xi
Lake

Kunming
Lake

Ferry Route

Site of the
Zhijing
Pavilion
治镜阁址

Mirror Bridge
镜桥

South Lake
Island

Bronze Ox
铜牛

Kunminghu Lu 昆明湖路

Changguan Hall
畅观堂

Zaojian
Hall
藻鉴堂

Phoenix
Mound
凤凰墩

Willow
Bridge
柳桥

Nan
Lake

Xiuyi
Bridge
绣漪桥

To Central
Beijing
(18km)

temples. Slung out uphill on a north–south axis are **Buddhist Fragrance Pavilion** (Fóxiāng Gé; Y10) and **Cloud Dispelling Hall** (Páiyún Diàn), which are connected by corridors. At the crest sits the **Buddhist Temple of the Sea of Wisdom** (Zhì Huìhǎi) with glazed tiles depicting Buddha. Many, sadly, have had their heads obliterated.

The graceful **17-arch bridge** spans 150m to **South Lake Island** (Nánhú Dǎo) from the eastern shore of the lake. Cixi visited the island's **Dragon King Temple** (Lóngwáng Miào) to beseech the temple's statue for rain in times of drought. You can traverse Kunming Lake by boat (Y8) from the island to the northern shore where idles Cixi's **marble boat**, north of which survive some fine Qing boathouses.

Set in a clean and engaging pocket of reproduction Qing architecture, the **Wenchang Gallery** (Wénchāng Yuàn; ☎ 6256 5886, ext 224; adult Y20; ☺ 8.30am-5pm) to the south of the entrance is a quiet escape from the hordes rampaging through the palace. The galleries comprise a porcelain exhibition, a jade gallery and an unusual selection of Qing artefacts (including some of Cixi's calligraphy), plus some decent bronzes. In the north of the grounds is **Suzhou Street** (Sūzhōu Jiē), a fun diversion of riverside walkways, shops and eateries. Purchases are made with antique Chinese coins; exchange your renminbi at the top of the street.

The Summer Palace is about 12km northwest of central Běijīng. Cycling (1½ to two hours) from the centre of town is feasible and taking the road following the Beijing–Miyun Diversion Canal is pleasant. In summer, boats head along the canal, departing from the dock behind the **Beijing Exhibition Center** (Map pp260–1; ☎ 6823 2179, 6821 3366; one way/return Y45/75 including Summer Palace admission) near the zoo or from the dock behind the **China Millennium Monument** (p96).

798 ART DISTRICT Map pp258-9
Yìshù Xīnqū; 798 艺术新区

☎ 6438 4862; 2 & 4 Jiuxianqiao Lu; admission free; ☺ galleries 10am-6pm (some galleries shut on Mondays), bars & bistros open longer; ☒ 403 or 909

A disused and converted electronics factory, 798 Art District is Běijīng's leading concentration of contemporary art galleries. The industrial complex celebrates its proletarian roots in the communist heyday of the 1950s via retouched red Maoist slogans decorating gallery interiors, effigies of Mao and burly, lantern-jawed workers. The voluminous

factory workshops are ideally suited to art galleries that require space for multimedia installations and other ambitious projects. You could easily spend an entire day visiting the complex and its cafés and restaurants, making 798's non-central inaccessibility less of an inconvenience and more of an opportunity for an outing (but note some galleries are shut on Monday). Some galleries are more innovative than others; there is challenging and cutting-edge material, but prepare for hackneyed and technically unaccomplished work. Standout galleries include the impressive **White Space Beijing** (☎ 8456 2054; 2 Jiuxianqiao Lu; ☺ noon-6pm Tue-Sun), **798 Red Gate Gallery** (☎ 6438 1005; 2 Jiuxianqiao Lu) – with its utilitarian and industrial ambience – and the vast **798 Space** (798 Shítài Kōngjiān; ☎ 6438 4862; www.798space .com; 4 Jiuxianqiao Lu ☺ 10.30am-7.30pm). **3818 Cool Gallery** (3818 Kù; ☎ 8688 2525; www.3818coolgallery.com; 4 Jiuxianqiao Lu; ☺ 10.30am-6.30pm Tue-Sun) contains several galleries with forward-thinking artworks and a handy café. Singaporean-owned **China Art Seasons** (Běijīng Jìjié; ☎ 6431 1900; www .artseasons.com.sg; ☺ 11am-7pm Tue-Sun) is a huge warehouse space for modern works from East Asian artists. Supported by the Japan Foundation, **Beijing Tokyo Art Projects** (Běijīng Dōngjīng Yìshù Gōngchéng; ☎ 8457 3245; www.tokyo-gallery.com; 4 Jiuxianqiao Lu) is a huge space exhibiting conceptual art. Also worth looking into are **Long March Space** (www.longmarchspace.com) and **Long March Space B**, where paintings, photos, installations and videos get a viewing, and the wellknown **Chinese Contemporary Beijing** (Zhōngguó Dāngdài; ☎ 8456 2421; www.chinese contemporary.com; 4 Jiuxianqiao Lu; ☺ 11am-7pm). Independent cinema gets an airing at the third-floor **Hart Center of Arts** (Hātè Shālóng; ☎ 6435 3570; www.hart.com.cn; 4 Jiuxianqiao Lu; ☺ 10.30am-7pm Tue-Sun). **798 Photo Gallery** (Bǎinián Yìnxiàng; ☎ 6438 1784; www.798photogallery.cn; 4 Jiuxianqiao Lu) has a collection of intriguing prints for sale from the Cultural Revolution, and rotating exhibitions of fascinating photography. For funky retro clothing with a dashing modern twist, check out **Fengling** (Fēnglíng Fúshì) near White Space Beijing; a further branch exists on the second floor of the 3.3 Shopping Centre (p166). **First Sound Gallery** (☎ 6477 5195; 2 Jiuxianqiao Lu) is a tranquil and relaxing space caressed with soft music.

HISTORIC HÚTÒNG

Classic entrance to one of Běijīng's courtyard residences

HISTORIC HÚTÒNG

Běijīng's very identity as a city centres on its distinctive *hútòng* (胡同) – the characteristic lattice of alleyways that crisscross the centre of town. These lanes are the stamping ground of more than 20% of Běijīng's residents, so immersing yourself here is both a trip back in time and a fascinating way to approach this vibrant community at the heart of the city. As the Chinese saying goes: 'There are 360 *hútòng* with names and as many nameless *hútòng* as there are hairs on a cow.' Even if you get lost, it won't be for long as you'll never be far from a main road.

These enchanting passageways first covered Běijīng in the Yuan dynasty, after Genghis Khan's army reduced the city, then known as Zhōngdū, to rubble. The city was redesigned, with *hútòng* (alleyways) running east–west. By the Qing dynasty, more than 2000 *hútòng* riddled Běijīng, leaping to around 6000 by the 1950s; the figure has again dwindled to around 2000. Among the oldest *hútòng* in Běijīng is 900-year old Sanmiao Jie (三庙街; Three Temple Street) in Xuānwǔ district, which dates to the Liao dynasty (907–1125).

The story of Běijīng's *hútòng* is almost as fascinating as a visit to the lanes themselves. The original meaning of the word '*hútòng*' is hazy. Based on the Mongolian, the name derives from the time when the Khan's horsemen camped in the new Yuan dynasty capital. It might have referred to a passageway between *gers* (or 'yurts', the Russian term). Or it might come from the word '*hottog*' (meaning a well) – wherever there was water in the dry plain around Běijīng, there were inhabitants.

Most *hútòng* lie within the loop of the Second Ring Rd, which largely follows the outline of the flattened Tartar City Wall. The most famous *hútòng* have the oldest and grandest courtyard houses (*sìhéyuàn*), but many lesser *hútòng* are more functionally designed, with little or no ornamentation. *Hútòng* land is consequently a hotchpotch of the old and the new, where Qing dynasty courtyards stand pockmarked with modern brick outhouses and socialist-era conversions, alongside grim apartment blocks.

Some residents may be happy to trade their crumbling dwellings for a newly built high-rise flat on the outskirts of town, but considerable dislocation has accompanied the wholesale felling of *hútòng*.

For a bird's-eye panorama of Běijīng's shrinking *hútòng* universe, and a snapshot of what is still standing, take a look at the diorama of the modern city at the Beijing Planning Exhibition Hall (p73).

The changing face of traditional hútòng – bustling Yandai Xiejie (p118)

Hútòng craftsman fashioning figures from heated sugar

Enjoying a hútòng meal, Dàzhàlan area

Hutong to Highrise (www.hutongtohighrise.com) is a photographic archive of life in Běijīng's dwindling *hútòng* world and its disappearing communities. Also take a look at the website of the Beijing Cultural Heritage Protection Center (www.bjchp.org) and the Dazhalan Project (www.dazhalanproject.org), which focuses on the historic *hútòng* area around Dàzhàlan.

Why not spend the night in a *hútòng* courtyard hotel to experience these delightful lanes to the full? See the boxed text on p185 for a list of Běijīng's top courtyard hotels.

OLD WALLED COURTYARDS 四合院

Old walled courtyards, or *sìhéyuàn*, are the building blocks of this delightful *hútòng* world. Some old courtyards such as the Lao She Museum (p93) have been quaintly mothballed as museums, but many of them remain inhabited and hum with domestic activity. From spring to autumn, men collect outside their gates, drinking beer, playing chess, smoking and chewing the fat. Inside, trees soar aloft, providing shade and a nesting place for birds.

Most old courtyards date from the Qing dynasty, although some have struggled through from the Ming. Particularly historic and noteworthy courtyard homes boast a white marble plaque near the gates identifying them as protected structures.

Prestigious courtyards are entered by a number of gates, but the majority have just a single door. Venerable courtyards are fronted by large, thick red doors, outside of which perch either a pair of Chinese lions or drum stones (*bǎogǔshí*; two circular stones resembling drums, each on a small plinth and occasionally topped by a miniature lion or a small dragon head). A set of square *méndāng* (wooden ornaments) above the gateway is a common sight. You may even see a set of stepping-on stones (上马石; *shàngmǎ shí*) that the owner would use for mounting his steed.

Many of these impressive courtyards were the residences of Běijīng's officials, wealthy families and even princes; Prince Gong's Residence (p99) is one of the more celebrated examples.

Běijīng's more historic courtyard gates are accessed by a set of steps and topped with and flanked by ornate brick carvings. The generosity of detail indicates the social clout of the courtyard's original inhabitants.

Courtyards used to house just one family of the noblesse, but many were appropriated by work units to provide housing to its workforce. Others belong to private owners, but the state ultimately owns all property in China, which helps explain why *hútòng* are knocked down with such ease.

Foreigners long ago cottoned on to the charm of courtyard life and breached this conservative bastion (see the 'Hútòng Life' boxed text, p112). Though many have been repelled by poor heating, no hot water, no cable TV, dodgy sanitation and no place to park the SUV. Some *hútòng* homes still lack toilets, explaining the malodorous public loos strung out along alleyways. But other homes have been thoroughly modernised and sport features such as varnished wooden floors, fully-fitted kitchens, a Jacuzzi and air-conditioning.

Many old courtyard houses have been divided into smaller units, but many of their historical features remain, especially their roofs. Courtyard communities are served by small shops and restaurants strung out along *hútòng*, while children gather at local kindergartens and schools. For informative displays on Běijīng's courtyard houses, visit the Beijing Ancient Architecture Museum at Xiannong Altar (p83).

THE HÚTÒNG OF THE IMPERIAL CITY

The Imperial City failed to survive the convulsions of the 20th century, but the *hútòng* that threaded through the imperial enclave survive. Many bore names denoting their former function during imperial days. Zhonggu Hutong (钟鼓胡同; Bell and Drum Alley) was responsible for the provision of bells and drums to the imperial household. Jinmaoju Hutong (巾帽局胡同; Cloth and Cap Department Alley) handled the caps and boots used by the court, while Zhiranju Hutong (织染局胡同; Weaving and Dying Department Alley) supplied its satins and silks. Jiucuju Hutong (酒醋局胡同; Wine and Vinegar Department Alley) managed the stock of spirits, vinegar, sugar, flour and other culinary articles.

Also scattered within the Imperial City were numerous storehouses, surviving in name only in such alleys as Lianziku Hutong (帘子库胡同; Curtain Storehouse Alley), Denglongku Hutong (灯笼库胡同; Lantern Storehouse Alley) and Duanku Hutong (缎库胡同; Satin Storehouse Alley). Candles were vital items during Ming and Qing times, their supply handled by the Làkù (蜡库胡同; Candle Storehouse), which operated from Laku Hutong. The Cui Ming Zhuang Hotel (p184) sits on the former site of the Cíqìkù (Porcelain Storehouse), which kept the Forbidden City stocked with porcelain bowls, plates, wine cups and other utensils.

West of Beihai Park (p84), the large road of Xishiku Dajie (西什库大街; West Ten Storehouse St) gets its name from the various storehouses scattered along its length during Ming times. Among items supplied to the Imperial City from warehouses here were paper, lacquer, oil, copper, leather and weapons, including bows, arrows and swords.

There are also the *hútòng* named after the craft workers who supplied the Forbidden City with its raw materials, such as Dashizuo Hutong (大石作胡同; Big Stonemason's Alley), where stonemasons fashioned the stone lions, terraces, imperial carriageways and bridges of the Imperial City.

Now-vanished temples are also recalled in *hútòng* names, such as the Guangming Hutong (光明胡同) south of Xi'anmen Dajie, named after the huge Guāngmíng Diàn (Guangming Temple) that is no more.

Auspicious glass symbols for sale in a Dàzhàlan hútòng

Communist mural in a Dōngchéng hútòng

Buddha statues along Wangfujing Snack Street (p124)

WIND-WATER LANES

By far the majority of *hútòng* run east–west, ensuring that the main gate faces south, satisfying feng shui requirements. This south-facing aspect guarantees maximum sunshine and protection from negative forces prevailing from the north. This positioning mirrors the layout of all Chinese temples, which nourishes the *yáng* (the male and light aspect) while checking the *yín* (the female and dark aspect).

Less significant north–south running alleyways link the main alleys. The resulting rectangular waffle-grid pattern stamps the points of the compass on the Běijīng psyche. You may hear a Běijīng local exclaiming, '*wǒ gāoxìng de wǒ bù zhī běi le*', meaning 'I was so happy, I didn't know which way was north' (an extremely disorientating state of joy). In cities without this plethora of parallel roads (eg Shànghǎi), it's far easier to lose your way.

Some courtyards used to be further protected by rectangular stones bearing the Chinese characters for Tài Shān (Mount Tai) to vanquish bad omens. Other courtyards still preserve their screen walls or spirit walls (影壁; *yǐngbì*) – feng shui devices erected in front of the main gate to deflect roaming spirits. Běijīng's two most impressive spirit walls are the Nine Dragon Screens at the Forbidden City (p87) and in Beihai Park (p84).

Trees provide *qì* (energy) and much-needed shade in summer, and most old courtyards have a locust tree at the front, which would have been planted when the *sìhéyuàn* was constructed.

HÚTÒNG NAMES

Some *hútòng* names are christened after families, such as Zhaotangzi Hutong (赵堂子胡同; Alley of the Zhao Family). Other *hútòng* simply took their names from historical figures, temples or local features, while others have more mysterious associations, such as Dragon Whiskers Ditch Alley. Others reflect the merchandise that is for sale at local markets, such as Ganmian Hutong (干面胡同; Dry Flour Alley), while some *hútòng*, such as Gongbei Hutong (弓背胡同; Bow Back Hutong) – have names derived from their shape.

Some rather unusual industries coalesced around the Forbidden City. Wet Nurse Lane was full of young mothers who breast-fed the imperial offspring. These young mothers were selected from around China on scouting trips four times a year. Clothes Washing Lane was where the women who did the imperial laundry lived. The maids, having grown old in the service of the court, were packed off to faraway places until their intimate knowledge of royal undergarments was out of date and no longer newsworthy.

Hútòng Name Changes

During the Cultural Revolution, selected *hútòng* and roads were rechristened in obeisance to the changing political climate. Nanxiawa Hutong (南下洼胡同) was renamed Xuemaozhu Hutong (学毛著胡同), literally 'Study Mao's Writings Hutong'. Doujiaoer Hutong (豆角儿胡同) became Hongdaodi Hutong (红到底胡同), Red to the End Hutong, and Andingmen Dajie (安定门大街) unfortunately became known as Dayuejin Lu (大跃进路) or 'Great Leap Forward Road', a perhaps optimistic prediction of Běijīng's pernicious traffic.

Other *hútòng* names conceal their original names, which were considered either too unsavoury or unlucky, in homophones or similarly sounding words. Guancai Hutong (棺材胡同), 'Coffin Alley', was instead dropped for Guangcai Hutong (光彩胡同), which means 'Splendour Hutong'. Muzhu Hutong (母猪胡同), 'Mother Pig Hutong' or 'Sow Hutong', was elevated to the more poetic Meizhu Hutong (梅竹胡同) or 'Plum Bamboo Hutong'.

HÚTÒNG DIMENSIONS

Despite an attempt at standardisation, Běijīng's alleys have their own personalities and proportions. The longest alley is Dongjiaomin Xiang (东交民巷), which extends for 3km (see the Tiananmen Square & Foreign Legation Quarter Walk, p114), while the shortest – unsurprisingly called Yichi Dajie (一尺大街; One Foot St) – is a very brief 25m. Some people contest that Guantong Xiang (贯通巷; Guantong Alley), near Yangmeizhu Xijie in Xuānwǔ district (east of Liulichang Dongjie), is even shorter at 20m.

Some *hútòng* are wide and leafy boulevards, whereas other *hútòng* are narrow, claustrophobic corridors. Běijīng's broadest alley is Lingjing Hutong (灵境胡同; Fairyland Alley), with a width of 32m, but the aptly named Xiaolaba Hutong (小喇叭胡同; Little Trumpet Alley) is a squeeze at 50cm. And chubby wayfarers could well get wedged in Qianshi Hutong (钱市胡同) situated not far from Qiánmén and Dàzhàlàn – its narrowest reach is a mere 44cm. The alley with the most twists and turns is Jiuwan Hutong (九湾胡同; Nine Bend Alley), while another of Běijīng's oldest *hútòng* is Zhuanta Hutong (砖塔胡同; Brick Pagoda Alley). Dating from Mongol times, it can be found west off Xisi Nandajie.

Hútòng locals playing Chinese poker

Mao Dun Former Residence (p93)

Flying the PRC flag in a Běijīng hútòng

AN INTERVIEW WITH WANG JUN

Wang Jun is author of the bestselling *Story of a City* (Chéngjì; Sanlian Chubanshe; 2003), which documents the destruction of Běijīng's traditional architectural heritage.

Why did you write 'Story of the City'?

To nail down the history of the original layout of Běijīng. One motivation was when I learned of the destruction of the old city walls at the end of the 1960s. Before that I knew nothing about the city, like most new immigrants here. When it was published, the book caused quite a stir, and I'm not surprised. If Venice disappeared from the face of the earth, the world would be shocked; it's the same with Běijīng.

Is there any connection between the felling of hútòng and the 2008 Olympics?

Of course there's a connection. Like Shànghǎi, Běijīng wants to give the impression that it's a well-developed international city and 2008 is a good chance to show the world. But the destruction started way before this.

When did it begin?

Over the past 50 years, Běijīng has gone through two phases of destruction. The first phase happened before 1978, when over 40km of city wall was demolished, as well as most of the *páilou* (ornamental arches). The second phase occurred after 1978, when historic areas formed by *hútòng* and courtyards were knocked down.

And what about Běijīng's hútòng temples?

During the reign of Emperor Qianlong, there were two temples per *hútòng* on average. It's a bit like how churches in Western countries and temples were of course places for prayer, but also places for communities to meet, make friends and discuss things. You perhaps know the alley called Houyuan Ensi Hutong – well, it's named after a local temple, but of course it's not there any more.

HÚTÒNG TOUR

Exploration of Běijīng's *hútòng* is an unmissable experience. Go on one of our walking or cycling tours, such as the Běijīng Bike Ride (p118), and delve deep into this alternately ramshackle and genteel, but always magical, world. Or wander off the main roads in the centre of Běijīng into the alleyways that riddle the town within the Second Ring Rd. Otherwise limit yourself to historic areas, such as around the Drum Tower (p86), the area around Nanluogu Xiang (南锣鼓巷) or the roads branching east and west off Chaoyangmen Nanxiaojie, east of Wangfujing Dajie. Most significant *hútòng* have red enamel street signs, sporting the alley name (in Chinese and Pinyin) in white. If you can't find the *hútòng* street sign, the *hútòng* name in Chinese also appears on a small metal plaque above doorways strung out along each alley.

Hire a bike and explore this historic world on two wheels (p212), or if you want to join a tour, the Chinese Culture Club (see p219) operates a rewarding *hútòng* and courtyard houses tour (Y160); phone for more details or check their website. Any number of other pedicab touts infest the roads around the Shichahai lakes – they will circle you like hyenas, baying, 'Hútòng, hútòng'. Such tours typically cost around Y180. You can also ask about tours at your hotel.

HÚTÒNG LIFE Damian Harper

A few years ago, my wife, my baby son and I hit upon a small, tidy two-bedroom maisonette in a Qing dynasty courtyard house just off Chaoyangmen Nanxiaojie to rent for Y2500 per month. A white plaque outside trumpeted it as the former residence of a high-ranking official called Zhu Qiqian. At first glance, the cheap rent didn't bode well for modern amenities. The owner, however, gaily spun open hot water taps, zapped the air-con with a remote and flung open a curtain to reveal a fully equipped shower room. Capping all of this was a finely crafted traditional Qing roof with upturned eaves, along which slunk a lethargic cat. We were right in the heart of Běijīng, but all we could hear was a dry rustling of leaves in the wind and the click of chess pieces at the gate. Bet your bottom dollar we signed and sealed on the spot.

Our neighbour Mr Ma, a cheerful *yùchú* (imperial chef), gave us a warm welcome that quickly developed into a feast attended by many of the courtyard's residents. Our host regaled us with anecdotes about the domicile. Mr Ma insisted the same pair of hands that fashioned the celebrated Long Corridor at the Summer Palace designed the corridor that linked our courtyards (much nodding from the old-timers). Waving a contemptuous hand at the high-rises beyond, Mr Ma pledged that his courtyard house was sturdy enough to ride out an earthquake.

After a few glasses of Erguotou (white spirit), Mr Ma was even hinting at an ancient, carved stone tablet in the *sihéyuàn* (courtyard house), surely worth a bob or two. He never actually pointed it out; perhaps he thought I would take advantage of a moonless night to crowbar it from the wall and get it under Sotheby's gavel in Hong Kong.

Two huge red doors, each around seven inches thick, fronted the *sihéyuàn*. There were nine courtyards in all, strung out along a bicycle-lined wooden corridor. At night the men of the courtyard would gather by the ancient drumstones in the doorway, with beer, cigarettes, stories or a chess set. Come 10.30pm, they would slip indoors and the gates would be shut by a family paid around Y150 a month to act as *chuándáshì* (gatekeeper) and lookout. If you wandered out for a beer (Y1.50 per bottle from the local) after 10.30pm, you had to take a key and rummage through a sliding hatch on the door for the huge bolt fastening it from the inside.

All of this made us feel very secure. So secure that we would leave our front door open all day; in London that would have been unforgivable stupidity, but here in Běijīng it is the norm. My 18-month-old son could usually be found playing with Mr Ma's young daughter, Xiao Yue (Little Moon), or enveloped in a Chinese world at the home of Mr Ma's parents opposite.

Night-time was magical, with the Qing rooftops silhouetted against the evening sky and the courtyard deep in a nocturnal reverie. Most residents would have returned from work, but the corridor would give the occasional squeak as a straggler returning late wheeled their bicycle home. A gorgeous hush would then invariably settle over the courtyard. At moments like this, we were no longer in Běijīng but had been transported back to Peking.

I returned recently to look at the courtyard home once more, only to find it cruelly overlooked by a newly-built apartment block flung up right next door. Much of the west part of the *hútòng* – Zhao Tangzi Hutong – had been demolished to widen Chaoyangmen Nanxiaojie and erect uniform blocks of flats.

Traditional courtyard of the Lao She Museum (p93)

Walking & Cycling Tours

Walking & Cycling Tours

Běijīng is thankfully flat as a chessboard, but walking around town can be an Olympic challenge, as unrelenting miles of pavement, shocking traffic manoeuvres, vehicle fumes and the stifling heat of summer or bone-chilling cold of winter drain the wind from your sails. So the following walks are short and easy to manage, lassoing in some of Běijīng's most fascinating and charming areas.

TIANANMEN SQUARE & FOREIGN LEGATION QUARTER WALK

From the dignified **Gate of Heavenly Peace 1** (p76), take the underground tunnel beneath Dongchang'an Jie to Tiananmen Square (p81), pompously framed to the west and east by the colossal **Great Hall of the People 2** (p77) and the **China National Museum 3** (p75). Sunrise and sunset are greeted by crowds at the daily flag-raising and flag-lowering ceremony (p82), punctiliously performed at the northern tip of the square. Beyond the **Monument to the People's Heroes 4** (p78) sits the squat **Chairman Mao Memorial Hall 5** (p75) and to the south rises Zhengyang Gate and the Arrow Tower, together known as **Front Gate 6** (p76). Walk to the east side of the square and, if you wish, fortify yourself with a meal of Peking duck at the branch of **Quanjude Roast Duck Restaurant** (7; ☎ 6512 2265; 44 Dongjiaomin Xiang; lunch & dinner) just south of the entrance to Dongjiaomin Xiang (东交民巷; Dongjiaomin Alley). Climb the 16 steps into Dongjiaomin Xiang (formerly known as Legation St due to the area's 19th-century status as the diplomatic-mission quarter): the red brick building next to the Tian'an Hotel at No 39 was the former **French Hospital 8**; the green-roofed, orange brick building on the other side of the road at No 40 was the site of the former **Dutch Legation 9**. Further along on your right stands a building with huge pillars, the erstwhile address of the First National City Bank of New York (花旗银行; Huāqí Yínháng), now the riveting **Beijing Police Museum 10** (p74). Roughly 20m

WALK FACTS

Start Gate of Heavenly Peace
End Raffles Beijing Hotel; Wangfujing Dajie
Distance 2.5km
Time Two hours
Fuel Stop Quanjude Roast Duck Restaurant (above)

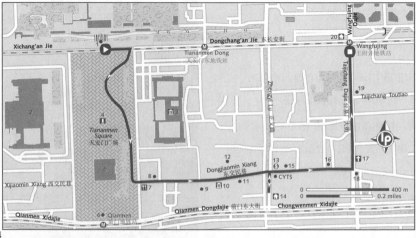

up the road at No 34 (on your right) rises an imposing, red brick building with pillars, the former address of the **Banque de L'Indo-Chine 11** (东方汇理银行; Dōngfāng Huìlǐ Yínháng). Look carefully under the window on the right, and you can discern ghostly, faded Chinese characters that proclaim 'Long live the mighty leader Chairman Mao'. Under the window on the left are the faint characters 'Love live the mighty Chinese Communist Party'. The intimidating **Supreme Court 12** (最高人民法院; Zuìgāo Rénmín Fǎyuàn) is positioned on the other side of the road. Keep walking east to the domed building at 4a Zhengyi Lu on the corner of Zhengyi Lu (正义路) and Dongjiaomin Xiang, in former times the **Yokohama Specie Bank 13**. If the building is open, pop in and examine the period features adorning the interior, especially the ceiling. North on the right-hand side of Zhengyi Lu was the former Japanese Legation, opposite the British Legation to the west, now occupied by the Ministry of State Security and the Ministry of Public Security. South down Zhengyi Lu and beyond the branch of the China Youth Travel Service (CYTS; 30 Zhengyi Lu) is the **Huafeng Hotel 14**, sitting on the site of the former Grand Hotel des Wagon-Lits (六国饭店; Liùguó Fàndiàn). Backtrack and continue along Dongjiaomin Xiang to the low, grey building at No 19 which is the former **French post office 15**, now the Jingyuan Sichuan Restaurant, before reaching the former **French Legation 16**. The main gate stands at No 15, a large red entrance guarded by a pair of stone lions and impassive security guards. The Capital Hotel on the other side of the road is built on the grounds of what was the former German Legation. Backing onto a small school courtyard, the twin spires of the Gothic **St Michael's Church 17** (东交民巷天主教堂; Dongjiaominxiang Catholic Church) rise ahead at No 11, facing the green roofs and ornate red brickwork of the former **Belgian Legation 18**. Walk south down Taijichang Dajie (台基厂大街) – formerly Rue Marco Polo – to Chongwenmen Xidajie and you can gaze all the way to the Temple of Heaven's Hall of Prayer for Good Harvests (p81) at the end of Qinian Dajie (祈年大街). Backtrack north along Taijichang Dajie and hunt down the brick street sign embedded in the northern wall of Taijichang Toutiao (台基厂头条), carved with the old name of the road, **Rue Hart 19**. Located along the north side of Rue Hart was the Austro-Hungarian Legation, south of which stood the Peking Club, entered through a gate on Taijichang Dajie. At the north end of Taijichang Dajie and across busy Dongchang'an Jie is the **Raffles Beijing Hotel 20** (p181), elements of which date back to 1900.

WANGFUJING DAJIE TO THE FORBIDDEN CITY WALK

This walk takes you along Běijīng's signature shopping street before reaching the Forbidden City via historic backstreets, alleys and historic ruins. You can continue from the conclusion of the Tiananmen Square and Foreign Legation Quarter Walk, or simply take the subway to Wangfujing station where this expedition commences.

Facing north up Wangfujing Dajie, on your left is the Raffles Beijing Hotel (p181), while dazzling **Oriental Plaza 1** (p163) sparkles to your east, a gargantuan shopping mall spanning the entire block to Dongdan Beidajie.

Just north of Oriental Plaza is the **Wangfujing Bookstore 2**, one of Běijīng's largest Chinese-language bookstores (good for maps). Beyond the large 24-hour McDonald's (where the pedestrianised part of Wangfujing Dajie begins), the **Beijing Arts & Crafts Central Store 3** (p162) is a large tourist outlet (the sign outside says 'Artistic Mansions') with several floors of arts and crafts, jade, jewellery, snuff bottles, lacquer, silk, embroideries and ceramics. You may see small tourist buses assembling here for quick tours of the area, but they are banal and best avoided.

Next along on the same side of the road is **Chenggu Zhai 4**, a jade and jadeite outlet over two floors, opposite a colourful *páilou* (decorative archway) that leads to **Wangfujing Snack Street 5** (p124), a bustling melee of open-air food stalls, take-away snack vendors, restaurants and thronging diners. Delve further along the snack street to scoop up souvenirs, collectables and odds and ends from alleyside vendors. If more souvenir shopping is in order, the Yunhong Chopstick Shop (277 Wangfujing Dajie) on the corner on Wangfujing Dajie just north of Wangfujing Snack Street has a colourful range of chopsticks.

Walking north along Wangfujing Dajie, take the first left immediately after the huge Haoyou Emporium (好友世界商场; Hǎoyǒu Shìjiè Shāngchǎng) topped with the vast, green Fujifilm advertising hoarding. This is Datianshuijing Hutong (大甜水井胡同) – the name literally means 'Big Sweet Water Well Alley' – and it's typical of the narrow alleyways that fragment much of central Běijīng into its delightful waffle-grid. Wander along the lane for a few hundred metres before returning to Wangfujing Dajie.

Buried along Shuaifuyuan Hutong (帅府园胡同), just beyond the Zhongguo Zhaoxiang photographic shop on the east side of Wangfujing Dajie, is a popular branch of the celebrated **Quanjude Roast Duck Restaurant** 6 (p131). Continuing along Shuaifuyuan Hutong brings you to the small **Central Academy of Fine Arts Gallery** 7 (p74); ahead of you is the Chinese-style Beijing Union Hospital. Backtrack to Wangfujing Dajie and keep walking north, passing the Xin Zhongguo Kid's Stuff (p165), a hectic shop sprawling wildly with children's games and beeping gadgets. Further ahead on the east side of Wangfujing Dajie stretches the long shopping mass of **Dong An Plaza** 8 and **Sundongan Plaza** 9, all the way to Jinyu Hutong (Goldfish Alley; 金鱼胡同), where handy bicycle hire can be found (p213) if you want to continue the journey on two wheels.

A short foray north along Wangfujing Dajie is rewarded by the abrupt appearance of **St Joseph's Church** 10 (p93), with lovingly tended rose bushes along its flank. Further bike rental can be found on the other side of the road.

Backtrack south and walk west along Donganmen Dajie (东安门大街) past the vocal stallholders of **Donghuamen Night Market** 11 (p128) plying their snacks and culinary exotica from the four corners of China (from mid-afternoon onwards).

At the junction of Donganmen Dajie and Donhuangchenggen Nanjie runs the thin strip of the **Imperial Wall Foundation Ruins Park** 12 (皇城根遗址公园; Huáng Chéng Gēn Yízhǐ Gōngyuán), following the course of the Imperial City Wall all the way north to Dianmen Dongdajie. Cross the road and examine the pitiful remains of **Dongan Men** 13 (p86) – the razed east gate of the Imperial City.

Traverse the road and continue west along Donghuamen Dajie, past several traditional-style teahouses and cafés that have opened in

WALK FACTS

Start Oriental Plaza
End Forbidden City
Distance 3.2km
Time Two to three hours
Fuel Stop Megabite (p124)

Walking & Cycling Tours

WANGFUJING DAJIE TO THE FORBIDDEN CITY WALK

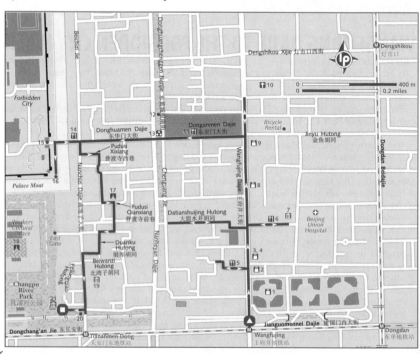

recent years. Cross Beichizi Dajie and pop into **Courtyard 14** (p131), a restaurant hidden behind bamboo fronds, where you can enjoy a fine meal. Just west over the bridge that straddles the Forbidden City moat rises the twin-eaved **Donghua Men 15**, the east gate of the Forbidden City (p87). It's tempting to follow the delightful moat-side road to the Meridian Gate of the palace; on the way you'll pass one of the intricate **decorative corner towers 16** of the Forbidden City wall. The lethargic can take one of the buggies (Y1) that run from here to the Meridian Gate and back.

Alternatively, head south down Nanchizi Dajie and take the first left turn into Pudusi Xixiang (普渡寺西巷; Pudu Temple West Alley), a restored *hútòng* (alleyway) with exclusive, red-painted *sìhéyuàn* (courtyard homes) doors, many topped with *méndāng* (wooden ornaments) and flanked by pairs of *méndūn* (door stones). Follow the alley as it turns south till you reach Pudusi Qianxiang (普渡寺前巷), which heads east to **Pudu Temple 17** (普度寺; Pǔdù Sì), a charmingly-restored temple, its two halls tranquilly sitting atop a terrace. Continue due south from here along Pudusi Qianxiang for about 130m, then turn right when you can go no further, bringing you onto Duanku Hutong (缎库胡同) – 'Satin Storehouse Alley' – where satins for use in the Imperial household were kept. Passing a small, attractive Běijīng courtyard residence at No 18, follow the *hútòng* to its end and find yourself once more on Nanchizi Dajie, a few metres north of another *hútòng* opening, Beiwanzi Hutong (北湾子胡同).

With its attractive historic rooftops and brickwork, regularly spaced trees and narrow *hútòng* openings, Nanchizi Dajie is thick with the flavours of traditional Běijīng. The halls of the **Supreme Temple 18** lie splendidly just to the east in the Workers Cultural Palace (p82), which can be reached through the east gate on the other side of the road.

Further down the road are the **Imperial Archives 19** (p77) and the Wan Fung Art Gallery, both well worth a visit. The small *hútòng* opening just opposite the south gate of the Imperial Archives opens onto the splendidly named Feilongqiao Hutong (飞龙桥胡同; Flying Dragon Bridge Alley). Running east and west along Dongchang'an Jie are pleasant walks along **Changpu River Park 20** (菖莆河公园; Chāngpú Hé Gōngyuán). If you head west, visit the **Imperial City Exhibition 21** (p77), before proceeding to the **Gate of Heavenly Peace** (p76), **Tiananmen Square** (p81) and the **Forbidden City** (p87).

LAKESIDE WALK

This short walk is best undertaken after visiting **Beihai Park 1** (p84). Exit the park from the north gate and cross Dianmen Xidajie (地安门西大街) to **Lotus Lane 2** (天荷坊; Tiānhé Fāng), which runs along a section of Qianhai Xiyan (前海西沿) skirting the western shore of Qianhai Lake. Take your pick from one of the waterfront restaurants or cafés – many offering alfresco seating. Keep walking north and exit Lotus Lane onto Qianhai Beiyan (前海北沿). An optional diversion west leads to **Prince Gong's Residence** (p99) on the east side of Liuyin Jie (柳荫街), a broad and dignified willow-lined alley that continues north from Qianhai Xijie (前海西街).

Continue along Qianhai Beiyan and you will soon reach an undignified profusion of **bars and cafés 3** – at the last count almost 50 setups made up the crowd – that wraps its way around Houhai Lake's southern shore to the north. A shorter strip of bars faces you along Houhai Beiyan (后海北沿) while further bars and cafés cluster in pockets elsewhere around the lake. Boats can also be hired at several spots for trips around the lake.

WALK FACTS

Start Beihai Park
End Beihai Park
Distance 2.5km
Time One to two hours
Fuel Stop Drum & Bell Bar (p142)

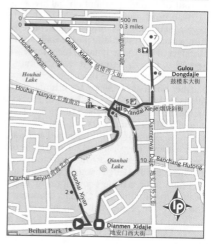

Cross **Silver Ingot Bridge 4**, and hang a right onto Yandai Xiejie (烟袋斜街) – a narrow jumble of shops, bars and cafés which have quickly dislodged the dilapidated businesses that once operated here. The ancient and diminutive **Guangfuguan Taoist Temple 5** functions as the Guangfuguan Greenhouse (p142), a popular café. It's on your left as you walk east along Yandai Xijie – look out for the rounded archway. The road is a snapshot of the new Běijīng economy with Tibetan and ethnic jewellery shops and cafés cheek by jowl with dazed-looking local residents.

Exit onto bustling Dianmenwai Dajie to find the **Drum Tower 6** (p86) rising massively northwards, obscuring the **Bell Tower 7** (p85) behind; both worth a visit. For a breather and premier views, the rooftop terrace of the **Drum & Bell Bar 8** (p142) is romantically slung out between the namesake towers.

Return to Silver Ingot Bridge and walk south along the east bank of Qianhai Lake, past the famous Muslim restaurant **Kaorouji 9** and the Yuan dynasty **Wanning Bridge 10** to your left, with its original stonework dating from 1285. The weather-beaten stone beasts that lie prone on either side of the bank appear to be water dragons. Continuing south brings you back to Dianmen Xidajie.

BĚIJĪNG BIKE RIDE

Běijīng's sprawling distances and scattered sights can make for blistering sightseeing on foot, but voyaging the city's streets and alleyways by bike allows you to take it all in at just the right velocity. Hop on a pair of wheels (p213), get that bell jangling and tour past some of the city's finest monuments and rarely visited spots off the beaten track. Many of Běijīng's *hútòng* have red-painted signs in Pinyin and Chinese characters, so following the route should not be too difficult, but *hútòng* names have been added in Chinese characters below to aid navigation.

Start at **Donghua Men 1** (东华门), the east gate of the Forbidden City, and cycle south between the moat and the red walls of the palace, observing in particular the **southeast corner tower 2** of the Forbidden City wall. The walls around the palace, 10m high and containing 12 million bricks, are adorned with a tower (角楼; *jiǎolóu*) at each corner, each one a highly elaborate construction with exceptional roof arrangements, supporting three eaves.

The trip around the moat is a spectacular route with unique views of historic Běijīng. At the large gate of **Quezuo Men 3** (阙左门) you may have to dismount, but you can push your bike through and past **Meridian Gate 4** (午门; Wǔ Mén; p88), the grand portal to the Forbidden City. Tour guides may pounce, so push on unless you want to tour the palace (without your bike). Traversing the courtyard, take your bike through the gate of **Queyou Men 5** (阙右门) to continue along the moat. Reaching **Xihua Men 6** (西华门; no admission), the palace's west gate, look directly west along Xihuamen Dajie (西华门大街) and all the way to the eastern gates of **Zhōngnánhǎi 7**, the out-of-bounds (without official invite) nerve centre of Běijīng's political power.

Head north onto Beichang Jie (北长街) past the bright red doors and brass knockers of several *sìhéyuàn* and on your right, **Fuyou Temple 8** (福佑寺; Fúyòu Sì), sadly locked away behind closed gates and the palace wall (although you can catch a glimpse of its roofs). Built at the start of the Qing dynasty, the temple was once a study for the Kangxi emperor and later served as a Lama temple. It was also known as the Rain God Temple (Yǔshén Miào).

On your left at No 45 Beichang Jie is a small shop selling Peking Opera face-painting masks. Further north at No 39 are the crumbling remains of the **Wanshouxinglong Temple 9** (万寿兴隆寺; Wànshòuxīnglóng Sì) – its band of monks are long gone and it's now occupied by Běijīng residents. Dating to the reign of the Kangxi emperor (1661–1722), the temple was built on the site of a Ming dynasty arsenal and after 1949 served as the residence for surviving imperial eunuchs. Look for its white-painted archway, graced with full-form Chinese characters on the plaque above. Pop in and take a look at the old temple roof ornaments and original paint on the crossbeams (but take care not to disturb residents). Other temples of the Imperial City existed on this road; at 81 Beichang Jie was the Ming dynasty Jingmo Temple, which is no more.

When you reach the T-junction with Jingshan Qianjie (景山前街) and Wenjin Jie (文津街), bear right onto Jingshan Qianjie, dismount your bike and push it across the zebra crossing to the other side of the road. Push your wheels a short distance east to No 23 Jingshan Xijie (景山西街) and peer through the gates to the remains of the vast Taoist **Dagaoxuan Temple 10** (大高玄殿). Dating to 1542, it was once fronted by a fabulous *páifāng* (memorial archway), but you won't be allowed into the temple as it's now a restricted military zone.

Backtrack west to the narrow *hútòng* opening to **Dashizuo Hutong 11** (大石作胡同; Big Stonemason's Alley) which heads north. The alley – where the stone for the Forbidden City was carved – bends to the right, then left. Follow the *hútòng* to the end and as you exit, look to your right and you will see the rear hall of the Dagaoxuan Temple on the other side of the compound wall. A lovely cylindrical building capped with a blue-tiled umbrella roof topped with a gold knob, the **hall 12** is clearly visible through the gate around the corner at No 21 Jingshan Xijie (again remember that you are not allowed to enter). Looking back down to the junction with Jingshan Qianjie will give you an idea of the colossal size of the temple in its entirety! If you head west along Zhishanmen Jie (陟山门街) you will find the east gate to **Beihai Park 13** (p84), while to your east is the west gate of **Jingshan Park 14** (p91). Park your bike if you want and clamber up the hill for unparalleled views over the Forbidden City.

Cycle north along Jingshan Xijie and at the northern tip of the street head up Gongjian Hutong (恭俭胡同); its entrance is virtually straight ahead of you. You will exit the alley on Dianmen Xidajie (地安门西大街). Beihai Park can also be accessed here through the north gate, a short distance to your west.

Push your bike over the zebra crossing and cycle north along Qianhai Nanyan (前海南沿) on the east shore of Qianhai Lake. Pass quaint **Yinding Bridge 15** (银锭桥) to your west and continue up along Houhai Beiyan (后海北沿) past a strip of bars until you reach the small **Dazanglonghua Temple 16** (大藏龙华寺) at No 23, a modest temple dating from 1719 and now a kindergarten. The lakes here are called Shichahai – literally 'Ten Buddhist Temple Seas' – after the many temples in the area. A number survive, including this one, but others have vanished. If you reach the rebuilt Sea-Overlooking Pavilion (望海楼; Wànghǎi Lóu) further along, you have overshot.

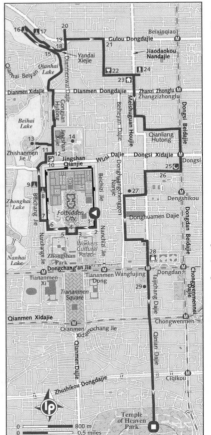

BIKE RIDE FACTS

Start Donghua Men
End Temple of Heaven Park
Distance 14km
Time Three to four hours
Fuel Stop Passby Bar (p143)

Take the first right about 10m after the Dazanglonghua Temple and work your way through this minute, five-foot-wide alley which leads to Ya'er Hutong (鸦儿胡同). Turn right onto Ya'er Hutong and cycle back in the direction of Silver Ingot Bridge, passing the Buddhist **Guanghua Temple 17** (广化寺) on the way.

At the end of Ya'er Hutong you will meet **Yandai Xiejie 18** (烟袋斜街; Pipe Cross-Street), with Silver Ingot Bridge to your right. Cycle along Yandai Xiejie – stuffed with name chop vendors, Tibetan silver trinket sellers, bars and cafés and exit onto Dianmenwai Dajie (地安门外大街). Head north towards the **Drum Tower 19** (p86) and the **Bell Tower 20** (p85) before heading east along Gulou Dongdajie (鼓楼东大街).

After cycling about 700m along Gulou Dongdajie, turn right and immediately duck into **Nanluogu Xiang** 21 (南锣鼓巷), a splendid north-south running alley in a constant state of renovation and replete with wi-fi bars, cafés and trinket shops and sporting a healthy crop of fully-restored *sìhéyuàn*. If you want to rest your feet, take in a coffee in relaxed, snug surrounds by popping into the **Passby Bar** 22 (p143), delightfully installed in an old courtyard home. Also look out for hole-in-the-wall kebab sellers that cook sizzling lamb kebab skewers along the alley – an economical and tasty way to stave off hunger.

Take the first turning on your left just beyond the Passby Bar at the street sign that says 'Police Station'. You are now cycling along Banchang Hutong (板厂胡同), a charming stretch of old *sìhéyuàn,* some adorned with plaques attesting to their historic significance. You'll pass the old **Lusongyuan Hotel** 23 (p183) at No 22, an old courtyard house now serving as a hotel.

As Banchang Hutong meets Jiaodaokou Nandajie (交道口南大街), it's worth taking a small detour north and into the first *hútòng* entrance on your right – Fuxue Hutong (府学胡同). A very short way along the alley on the left-hand side is the **Wen Tianxiang Temple** 24 (文天祥祠; 63 Fuxue Hutong; adult Y10; 9am-5pm Tuesday to Sunday), a shrine fronted by a huge *páilou*.

Head south along Jiaodaokou Nandajie, cross the junction with Dianmen Dongdajie (地安门东大街) and continue south down Meishuguan Houjie (美术馆后街). Take the fourth street on your left and follow the promisingly named Dafosi Dongjie (大佛寺东大街; Big Buddha Temple East St). Spot the residence on your left at No 6 – now part of a hospital – with a spirit wall (*yǐngbì*) facing the gate and a pair of stepping-on stones (*shàngmǎ shí*) by the door that the owner would have once used for clambering onto his horse.

Follow the road as it turns the corner and heads south. The Big Buddha Temple in question was actually located ahead at No 76 Meishuguan Houjie. Nothing remains today except a modern, white neo-classical confection built on its footprint, but elderly locals recall the original temple buildings before they were torn down during the Cultural Revolution.

Take the turning to the east just before Dafosi Dongjie opens onto Meishuguan Houjie and cycle along the courtyard-studded alley of Qianliang Hutong (钱粮胡同), where a few Western bars are making an appearance. Exiting Qianliang Hutong, hang a right onto Dongsi Beidajie (东四北大街), a lively stretch of shops and restaurants. Heading south, cross the intersection with Dongsi Xidajie (东四南大街) and continue along Dongsi Nandajie (东四南大街), past the **Dongsi Mosque** 25 on your right. One of Běijīng's few historic mosques, the guardians at the door may be fickle about admitting non-Muslims. Take the first right past the mosque into **Baofang Hutong** 26 (报房胡同), strung out like many of Běijīng's alleys with lamb-kebab sellers, restaurants and courtyard houses, and illuminated with lanterns at night. At the end of Baofang Hutong, turn left onto Wangfujing Dajie (王府井大街) and cycle past the Capital Theatre on your left. At the first main intersection turn right onto Dengshikou Xijie (灯市口西街) – but if you haven't yet seen St Joseph's Church continue south along Wangfujing Dajie and then double back – and look out for the second *hútòng* turning on your right which leads into Fengfu Hutong (丰富胡同), home of the small **Lao She Museum** 27 (p93) at No 19. This old courtyard residence is worth examining as it is typical of small-style Běijīng courtyard houses.

Continuing west, turn left onto Donghuangchenggen Nanjie (东黄城根南街) and pounce onto the bicycle lane immediately to your left, and journey south along this road that follows the original line of the Imperial City wall. After about 700m and beyond the intersection with Donghuamen Dajie (东华门大街), you will see a big sign ahead of you for the Donglaishun Muslim Restaurant – turn left onto the charming Datianshuijing Hutong (大甜水井胡同), which threads back to Wangfujing Dajie. You may have to dismount your bike as you approach Wangfujing Dajie as the eastern end of Datianshuijing Hutong can get busy with shoppers, but you will have to get off your bike anyway when you reach Wangfujing Dajie as this section of the road is pedestrianised.

Push your bike down to **Oriental Plaza** 28 (p163), cross Dongchang'an Jie and cycle south down pleasant Taijichang Dajie (台基厂大街) into the former **Foreign Legation Quarter** 29 (p76). See the Tiananmen Square & Foreign Legation Quarter Walk (p114) for a rundown of this district.

At the end of Taijichang Dajie, level your eyes straight ahead and you will see the distant form of the Hall of Prayer for Good Harvests at the **Temple of Heaven Park** 30 (p79), lying due south at the end of Qinian Dajie (祈年大街). Keep cycling and you will reach the north gate to Temple of Heaven Park, where your bike ride concludes.

Eating

Eating

Two pointed sticks of ivory or ebony, do the office of knife and fork; their meats are cut into small square pieces, and served up in bowls; their soups are excellent, but they use no spoons; so that after sipping the thin, the grosser parts of it are directed to mouth by their chopsticks.

An Historical Account of the Embassy to the Emperor of China, Sir George Staunton (1797).

It's hard to overstate the pleasure the Chinese take in eating. Meal times in China are unrestrained, raucous affairs, where voices are raised along with glasses and no one stands on ceremony. The dishes arrive in waves and as soon as they hit the table, everyone starts digging in with a gusto that will startle those who aren't aware of China's not-too-distant history of famines and food shortages. Běijīng's restaurants can seem like organised chaos, as the *fúwùyuán* (waiters) weave around packed tables, the decibel level goes through the roof and stray debris from the meal ends up on the floor.

In the past, food, or the lack of it, was an absolute obsession for the Chinese. The older generation still greet each other with the phrase '*nǐ chī fàn le ma?*' (literally, 'have you eaten rice yet?') Now, dining out is the main social activity for the Chinese. It's over meals that the Chinese hold family reunions, hang out with friends, romance each other or do business.

Restaurants are where you'll find the Chinese at their most relaxed and convivial. Big groups of people are seated around circular tables, dishes are communal, diners fill up other people's glasses before their own, toast each other liberally and there's always a competition to pay the bill.

Běijīng's restaurant scene has changed dramatically in recent years, as rising incomes and the influx of foreigners have transformed the city into a haven of fine dining. Běijīng

STREET FOOD BĚIJĪNG STYLE

Off the main roads and in Běijīng's alleys is a world teeming with steaming food stalls and eateries buzzing with activity. Be adventurous and eat this way, and you will be dining as most Běijīngers do.

Breakfast can be easily catered for with a *yóutiáo* (油条; deep-fried dough stick), a sip of *dòuzhī* (豆汁; bean curd drink) or a bowl of *zhōu* (粥; rice porridge). Other snacks include the crunchy, pancake-like and filling *jiānbǐng* (煎饼); *jiānbǐng* vendors are easily spotted as they cook from tricycle-mounted white painted wooden stalls where pancakes are fried on a large circular griddle. The heavy meat-filled *ròubǐng* (肉饼; cooked bread filled with finely chopped pork) are lifesavers and very cheap. A handy vegetarian option is *jiǔcài bǐng* (韭菜饼; bread stuffed with cabbage, chives, leek or fennel and egg). *Dàbǐng* (大饼; a chunk of round, unleavened bread sprinkled with sesame seeds) can be found everywhere and of course there's *mántou* (馒头; steamed bread). *Málà tàng* (麻辣烫) is a spicy noodle soup (very warming in winter) with chunks of *dòufu* (豆腐; tofu), cabbage and other veggies – choose your own ingredients from the trays. Also look out for *ròu jiāmó* (肉夹馍), a scrumptious open-your-mouth-wide bun filled with diced lamb, chilli and garlic shoots. Another must are *kǎo yángròu chuàn* (烤羊肉串; lamb kebabs), without a doubt Běijīng's favourite cheap snack. You can find kebab chefs all over town; try the more expensive **Donghuamen Night Market** (p128), **Wangfujing Snack Street** (p124) or cheaper options that are hidden away down Běijīng's alleyways (look for the billowing plumes of smoke), where you can pick up a skewer for between Y0.50 and Y1. If you want your kebabs spicy ask for *là* (辣); if you don't, ask for *búlà* (不辣). Vendors usually belong to either the Muslim Huí or Uyghur minority.

Hóngshǔ (红薯; baked sweet potatoes) are cheap, filling snacks (Y2) sold at street stalls throughout the city during winter. Vendors attach oil drums to their bikes which have been converted into mobile ovens. Choose a nice soft sweet potato and the vendor will weigh it and tell you how much it costs.

cuisine (京菜; *jīngcài*) is one of the four major Chinese styles of cooking (p40), so there's no shortage of local specialities for visitors to enjoy, but you can find food from every region of China here. Then there is the ever-increasing number of restaurants that take their inspiration from all the world's continents. If you think that eating out in Běijīng just means the obligatory visit to a Peking duck restaurant, then you're in for a pleasant surprise.

The finest Chinese chefs gravitate to Běijīng, making the capital the best place in the country to sample the huge variety of China's cuisines. Foreign chefs too, have descended on the city in droves. With all the new money sloshing around town, restaurants are opening every week to cater for the demand. And you don't have to travel very far to find them – most can be found within the Second Ring Rd and reaching even the most far-flung does not involve a major expedition. The main restaurant neighbourhoods are Dōngchéng, Cháoyáng and Chóngwén and South Chaoyang.

Even the most picky or jaded diner will find something to satisfy them here, so do as the locals do and pick up those chopsticks and dive in. Some of your most memorable Běijīng experiences will be when you're sitting around the dining table.

Opening Hours

Běijīng restaurants are generally open from around 10am to 11pm. Some establishments shut after lunch and reopen at 5pm or 6pm. Generally, the Chinese eat much earlier than Westerners, lunching at around midday and having dinner about 6pm. Cafés open, and sometimes, shut earlier. All the cafés in this chapter have wireless access.

How Much?

Despite the rich aromas around town, you won't pay through the nose for it all. One of the joys of Běijīng is that eating out is an inexpensive experience. But if you want to splash out, then there are plenty of upmarket places which will be happy to take your cash.

The restaurants listed below cater to all budgets. At cheap eateries, meals (for one) will cost less than Y50, midrange dining options will cost between Y50 to Y100 and top-end choices more than Y100.

Credit cards are still only accepted at most midrange hotel restaurants and the most expensive eateries. If you're dining anywhere else, make sure you have enough money on you.

Be warned that some (but by no means all) restaurants in tourist areas still fob off foreigners with an English menu (英文菜单; *yīngwén càidān*) with prices in excess of the Chinese menu. Unfortunately, deciphering the Chinese menu (中文菜单; *zhōngwén càidān*) will require either assistance or Chinese reading skills. But more and more places have picture and/or English menus now. All restaurants serving foreign food have English menus. Generally, very few waiting staff will be able to speak any English, no matter how expensive the restaurant is. Service too, can be erratic and/or lackadaisical.

If your preferred tipple is wine, then restaurants in Běijīng can be a financial challenge. The Chinese tend to drink beer or *báijiǔ*, which is a super-strong white spirit,

PRICE GUIDE FOR RESTAURANTS

The following guide is for one person

Y	up to Y50
YY	Y50-100
YYY	Y100-200
YYYY	over Y200

with their meals. Some restaurants will stock domestic wines, like Great Wall, but many won't. In places that do have foreign wines, you can expect to pay well over the odds for a bottle.

A good option is to visit one of the supermarkets or Western delis listed later in this chapter and choose your own wine before going out to eat. Most places are happy for you to bring your own bottle and many won't charge a corkage fee.

CHÓNGWÉN & SOUTH CHAOYANG
崇文、朝阳南

Busy with shoppers and tourists alike, these districts are packed with dining options and have places to suit all budgets. You can dine in style at any of the top-end hotels that gather along Chang'an Jie or delve into the areas around the embassy district of Jianguomen for reliably good food. Some of Běijīng's most well known Peking duck restaurants can be found around the bustling Qianmen district and there are some excellent restaurants located in the catchment area of the Forbidden City and Wangfujing Dajie.

WANGFUJING SNACK STREET

Map pp268-9   Chinese Mixed Y
王府井小吃街
West off Wangfujing Dajie; kebabs from Y3, dishes from Y5; ⏰ **lunch & dinner;** Ⓜ **Wangfujing**
Fronted by an ornate archway, this quadrant has bright and cheery restaurants and stalls overhung with colourful banners and bursting with character and flavour. This is a good place to pick up Xīnjiāng or Muslim Uyghur cuisine such as lamb kebabs and flat bread. Also on offer are other dishes from all over China, including *málà tàng* (a spicy soup from Sìchuān), *zhájiàngmiàn* (noodles in fried bean sauce) and noodles in peppery sauce. Also being scoffed by the bowl here are Lánzhōu *lāmiàn* (Lánzhōu noodles), Shāndōng *jiānbǐng* (Shāndōng pancake), Yúnnán *guòqiáo mìxiàn* (Yúnnán across-the-bridge noodles) and oodles of Sìchuān food. At most outlets you have to sit outside elbow-to-elbow with other diners.

MEGABITE

Map pp268-9   Chinese Mixed Y
Dáshídài 大食代
Basement, Oriental Plaza, 1 Dongchang'an Jie; dishes from Y10; Ⓜ **Wangfujing**
This hygienic fast food emporium puts Cantonese, Yúnnán, Sìchuān, teppanyaki, clay pot, Korean and porridge (粥; *zhōu*) outlets all under one roof. Look out for outlets like Hokkien Delights, Lanzhou Noodles, Hotplate Specials, Indian Roti Prata, Shànghǎi and Chinese Dumplings –

the latter puts together some great dumplings (饺子; *jiǎozi*) of pork, lamb and other fillings, and buns (包子; *bāozi*). Sichuan Delights serves up a fine chilli-oil red *dàndanmiàn* (担担面; Sìchuān noodles in peppery sauce; Y9). The layout is both intelligent and spacious, and the food generous and good value – you can eat very well for around Y20. Don't pay in cash for your dish – buy a card (Y5 deposit; cards come in denominations of Y30, 50, 100, 200, 500 and 1000 units) at the kiosk at the entrance. Credits are deducted with each dish ordered so you can pick and mix your plates from different outlets (check the expiry date of your card). Don't get timid at the sight of half of Běijīng eating here, it's very easy to order. Food is either cooked in front of you canteen-style or arrayed uncooked on plates – it's simply a case of pointing at what you want.

NIÚGĒ JIǍOZI

Map pp268-9   Chinese Dumplings Y
牛哥饺子
☎ **6525 7472; Nanheyan Dajie; meals Y15;** ⏰ **breakfast, lunch & dinner;** Ⓜ **Tiananmen Dong**
East of the Forbidden City, this pocket-sized and homely restaurant dishes up dozens of varieties of Chinese dumplings. All the *jiǎozi* are listed on red plaques on the four walls but there's no English menu. Here's a sample of what you can order (*liǎng* means 'portion' here): lamb (羊肉; *yángròu*; Y5 per *liǎng*), pork (猪肉; *zhūròu*; Y3 per *liǎng*), beef (牛肉; *niúròu*; Y4 per *liǎng*), donkey (驴肉; *lǘròu*; Y8 per *liǎng*) and mushroom and cabbage (香菇白菜; *xiāngsū báicài*; Y4); but there are many other fillings, from pork and aubergine, to chicken and garlic, celery and chicken and shrimp. There are only around 10 tables draped in simple, embroidered tablecloths, busied over by the restaurant's unfussy and polite owners. The restaurant is opposite the building with the sign on the roof saying 'Hualong St'.

MAKYE AME

Map pp268-9   Tibetan YY
Mǎjí Āmǐ 玛吉阿米
☎ **6506 9616; 2nd fl, 11a Xiushui Nanjie; dishes from Y20;** ⏰ **lunch & dinner;** Ⓜ **Yonganli or Jianguomen**
Tucked behind the Friendship Store, this is one of Běijīng's few Tibetan restaurants.

The homely, upstairs room has a great atmosphere. The walls are lined with Tibetan art and ornaments, there are sofas to sink into and a prayer wheel to spin. Some might say that the floor show, which consists of Tibetan dancers and singers in traditional costume, is a little over-the-top, but we like it. The menu is extensive, if pricey. Go all out for the lamb ribs (Y58), boiled yak with chilli (Y40), *tsampa* (roasted barley meal) and yoghurt (Y28), butter tea and cooling salads (from Y20). It's advisable to book.

SEQUOIA BAKERY AND CAFE

Map p264   Café Y

美洲杉咖啡屋

☎ 6501 5503; 44 Guanghua Lu; coffee Y18, sandwiches Y25; ⏰ breakfast & lunch; ⓔ Jianguomen
Deservedly popular with diplomats from the neighbouring embassies, this friendly café is a good place to pick up a caffeine fix if you're chasing visas in the area. Decent pastries and deli-style sandwiches too. There's another branch in **Sanlitun** (☎ 6415 6512; Bldg 15, North Sanlitun Beijie; ⏰ 8am-8pm).

SCHINDLER'S TANKSTELLE

Map p264   German YY

申德勒加油站

☎ 8562 6439; 15a Guanghua Lu; dishes from Y35; ⏰ lunch & dinner; ⓔ Jianguomen
Foaming steins of beer and lots of sausages and sauerkraut make this reliable place a good option for anyone seeking a taste of central Europe in Běijīng. Beer drinkers will enjoy the wide selection of German brews available. There's an outside terrace at the back in summer. You can walk off the meal afterwards in nearby Ritan Park.

STEAK AND EGGS

Map pp268-9   Western YY

喜来中北美西餐甜点吧

☎ 8470 1550/1559; 5 Xiushui Nanjie; breakfast specials from Y45; ⏰ breakfast, lunch & dinner; ⓔ Yonganli or Jianguomen
A home away from home for Americans pining for blueberry pie and grits in Běijīng, Steak and Eggs' diner format hits the spot with early risers and families at weekends, as well as revellers looking for late-night sustenance. The American-sized portions

SELF-CATERING

Eating outside of restaurants in Běijīng is getting easier all the time, although, given the low cost of dining out many people abandon cooking for the duration of their stay. Those people staying in apartments may also find themselves stumped by the lack of an oven in their kitchens; Chinese cooking doesn't call for them.

There are now numerous supermarkets in Běijīng. The best is the French hypermarket chain **Carrefour**, which moved into China early on and continues to expand at pace. There are currently six branches in Běijīng and they stock just about everything you need, as well as providing ATMs and taking credit cards. They're open every day and are always crowded. You can find them in the following districts: **Cháoyáng** (☎ 8460 1043; 6B Beisanhuan Donglu) and (☎ 5190 9500; 31 Guangqumenwai Dajie); **Xuānwǔ** (☎ 6332 2155; 11 Malian Dao); **Fēngtái** (☎ 6790 9911; 15, Zone 2 Fangchengyuan Fangzhuang); **Hǎidiàn** (☎ 8836 2729; 56a Zhongguancun Dajie) and (☎ 5172 1516/17; Zhongguancun Plaza).

Other reliable supermarkets include **Olé**, which have a number of branches around town. The most convenient are the ones at the China World Shopping Mall in Guomao (basement of Oriental Plaza, Jianguomenwai Dajie; ⏰ 9.30am-9.30pm; ⓔ Guomao) and the Oriental Plaza Mall in Wangfujing (1 Dongchang'an Jie; ⏰ 8.30am-10.30pm; ⓔ Wangfujing). Then there's the two branches of the redoubtable **Friendship Supermarket** (☎ 6500 3311; 17 Jianguomenwai Dajie; ⏰ 9.30am-8.30pm; ⓔ Jianguomen) and (☎ 6532 1871; 7 Sanlitun Lu; ⏰ 8.30am-8.30pm; ⓔ Dongzhimen), once the only place in Běijīng to go for a taste of home. Just north of the Great Wall Sheraton is the enormous Lufthansa Center, home to the **Lufthansa Center Youyi Shopping City** (p166), a multistorey shopping mall. The **Yansha Supermarket** (⏰ 9am-10pm) is in the basement, chock-a-block with imported goods.

Despite being an acquired taste for the Chinese palate, coffee has become a cherished commodity in Běijīng's flourishing café culture. Western cafés such as Starbucks have become hugely popular with middle-class Běijīngers, despite the Western-style prices, and are always busy. Otherwise, there are an ever-increasing number of Chinese cafés that can rustle up a decent cup of coffee. Nearly all have wireless internet access too.

Many restaurants will also deliver food or do take-aways, but Běijīng now has **I-mart** (www.i-martgroup.com), an English-language 24 hour online supermarket that enables you to order groceries for home delivery. It's not cheap, but there's a wide selection of imported food and wine available for when you're feeling lazy. There's free delivery for orders over Y100.

will satisfy all but the most ravenous. The breakfast specials are particularly good, but so are the sandwiches (from Y25) and the burgers (from Y35). Pasta, pizza and salads are all available too.

FENGZEYUAN Map pp268-9　　Shandong YY
丰泽园

☎ 6318 6688, ext 125; 83 Zhushikou Xidajie; meals Y60; ☺ lunch & dinner; ◉ Qianmen

This Běijīng institution attracts crowds of locals who toast each other with rounds of snake wine and devour Fengzeyuan's Shāndōng specialities (鲁菜; lǔcài), such as sea cucumber with scallion or sautéed fish slices.

XIAO WANG'S HOME RESTAURANT
Map p264　　Chinese Běijīng YY
Xiǎowáng Fǔ 小王府

☎ 6594 3602/6591 3255; 2 Guanghua Dongli; meals Y70; ☺ lunch & dinner; ◉ Guomao or Yonganli

Treat yourself to home-style Běijīng cuisine from this excellent, bustling restaurant and go for one of Xiao Wang's specials. The deep-fried spareribs with pepper salt (piāoxiāng páigǔ; Y48) are simply delectable. Xiao Wang's fried hot and spicy Xīnjiāng-style chicken wings (zīrán jīchì; Y35) are deservedly famous, as is the crispy and lean Peking duck (Y88 per duck, Y5 for sauce, scallions and pancakes). Also try the deep-fried crispy bean curd with mild chilli sauce (Y18) or the barbecue mutton slices with coriander (zīrán yángròu; Y28). Xiao Wang – the cordial entrepreneurial owner – has devised a formula that goes down well with both expats and local Chinese. There's a swankier, more expensive branch inside Ritan Park (☎ 8561 7859; Inside North Gate of Ritan Park, Ritan Beilu).

BIANYIFANG Map pp268-9　　Peking Duck YYY
便宜坊烤鸭店

☎ 6712 0505; 2a Chongwenmenwai Dajie; economy/standard half duck Y69/84; ☺ lunch & dinner; ◉ Chongwenmen

Dating back to the reign of the Qing emperor Xianfeng, Bianyifang offers midrange comfort reminiscent of a faded Chinese three-star hotel with sparse decoration. Roasted in the menlu style, the cheaper half ducks cost Y69 (plus Y5 for pancakes,

scallions and sauce), while ducks prepared in the more expensive Huaxiangsu style are Y84 (half) or Y168 (whole). Ducks find their way into numerous other preparations, including boiled duck blood in hot soup (Y22) and duck hearts in chilli (Y28). A bottle of Maotai will set you back Y430, but if you simply require the effect of the alcohol, why not settle for the rougher, locally distilled Erguotou (Y12). Otherwise, jasmine tea will cost you Y10. Be warned that waiting staff will steer you towards the special (read: pricier) duck, so be vigilant.

LIQUN ROAST DUCK RESTAURANT
Map pp268-9　　Peking Duck YYY
Lìqún Kǎoyādiàn 利群烤鸭店

☎ 6702 5681; 11 Beixiangfeng Hutong; roast duck Y98; ☺ lunch & dinner; ◉ Qianmen

This tiny eatery is buried away in east Qianmen in a maze of hútòng (alleyway) that are disappearing by the minute. It's well known and very busy – chefs scamper about as waiters scurry by with sacks of garlic and crates of Erguotou; no medals for service. Troll past the flaming ovens (fruit-tree wood is exclusively used, piled up outside) to reach your table, which may be next to a frame of ducks hanging from hooks. Waiting staff insist you phone first to reserve a table; otherwise turn up off-peak (eg 2.30pm) when most punters have moved on. You will have to wait about an hour for your duck. The duck is superb and there are other dishes on the menu.

QIANMEN QUANJUDE ROAST DUCK RESTAURANT
Map pp268-9　　Peking Duck YYY
Qiánmén Quànjùdé Kǎoyādiàn
前门全聚德烤鸭店

☎ 6511 2418; 32 Qianmen Dajie; half duck Y84, scallions, sauce Y5; ☺ lunch & dinner; ◉ Qianmen

As fundamental to a Běijīng trip as a visit to the Great Wall, the sampling of Peking duck is an absolute must – to miss out you'd have to be completely quackers. Despite the restaurant's name and pedigree (dating back to 1864), service at this branch is pretty lousy (staff sling you sachets of sauce as though they're dealing cards) and it's geared mainly to the tourist hordes (both domestic and foreign). Enter to photos of George Bush poking a duck with his finger and Fidel Castro sizing up

STORY OF THE DUCK

Without argument, most people would agree that Peking (or Běijīng) duck is the capital's most famous dish. Once imperial cuisine, now the legendary duck dish is served at restaurants around the world.

The culinary history of Peking duck goes as far back as the Yuan dynasty, where it was listed in royal cookbooks as an imperial food. The Qing poet Yuan Mei once wrote in a cookbook, 'roast duck is prepared by revolving a young duckling on a spit in an oven. The chief inspector Fang's family excel in preparing this dish'. When the Qing dynasty fell in 1911, former palace chefs set up restaurants around Běijīng and brought the dish to the public.

To prepare the duck, chefs go through a lengthy process. First the ducks are inflated by blowing air between the skin and body. The skin is then pricked and boiling water poured all over the duck. Sometimes the skin is rubbed with malt sugar to give it an amber colour and then is hung up to air dry before being roasted in the oven. When roasted, the flesh becomes crispy on the outside and juicy on the inside. The bird is meticulously cut into 120 slices and served with fermented bean paste, light pancakes, sliced cucumbers and green onions.

Perhaps the best Peking duck restaurant is **Liqun Roast Duck Restaurant** (opposite). The duck here is so popular that you need to call in advance to order one. The restaurant itself is a little ramshackle, but the sublime duck makes it a culinary experience to savour. The most famous restaurants in Běijīng that serve Peking duck though, are the **Quanjude Restaurant** (opposite) chain, which first opened in 1864. There are six branches around town, but the flagship of the empire is at Qianmen Dajie. Ducks here are roasted with fruit-tree wood, giving the dish a special fragrance.

Another famous roast duck restaurant is **Bianyifang** (opposite), founded in 1855. Instead of fruit-tree wood, the ducks here are cooked in an oven with straw as fuel. Prior to being put in the oven the duck is filled with soup.

---

an imaginary duck with his hands (perhaps they were dining here at the same time), plus other luminaries doing something or other at Quanjude. There is another branch nearby (☎ 6301 8833; 14 Qianmen Xidajie) and a superior branch just off Wangfujing Dajie (p131). There is an English menu and you can get your duck to go at the booth outside (vacuum packed duck Y68; vacuum packed pancakes Y5; vacuum packed duck sausage Y9.80).

DANIELI'S   Map pp268-9   Italian YYYY
丹尼艾丽意大利餐厅

☎ 6460 6688, ext 2440/2441; 2nd fl, St Regis, 21 Jianguomenwai Dajie; meal Y300; ☺ lunch & dinner; ⊚ Jianguomen

Ensconced in the St Regis hotel, this gorgeous and classy restaurant is Běijīng's finest Italian dining choice, boasting a generous menu and wine list. Glide up the sumptuous marble staircase, past the crackled glass doors to a splendid alcove interior and sit down to a meal served upon marvellously decorated plates.

TIĀNDÌ YĪJIĀ

Map pp268-9   Chinese Mixed YYYY
天地一家

☎ 8511 5556; 140 Nanchizi Dajie; meals Y300 ☺ lunch & dinner; ⊚ Tiananmen Dong

Doing business from a restored building alongside Changpu River Park (p77), this civilised and refined traditional Chinese courtyard-style restaurant is decked out with traditional furniture, water features and side rooms for snug hotpot dinners come winter. Further rooms upstairs include a banquet room and a balcony overlooking the Imperial Archives (p77). The expensive dishes – from Běijīng, Shāndōng, Zhèjiāng and beyond – include shark's fin and abalone. Cantonese dim sum (11am-2pm & 5-9.30pm) is also served. The elegantly presented menus (manufactured from traditional Chinese paper; English version available) may be delivered to your table by snobbish waiting staff – a fly in the ointment. Master-Card, Visa and American Express are all accepted.

DŌNGCHÉNG 东城

This historic part of Běijīng is ideal for atmospheric and traditional dining options. Snackers can pick up tasty bite-sized morsels at the **Donghuamen Night Market** (p128) or at hole-in-the-wall outlets scattered through the local *hútòng*, but there are plenty of fine dining options too. Dōngchéng has its own restaurant strip, known as Gui Jie (鬼街; Ghost St), which runs between Dongzhimennei Dajie and Jiaodaokou Dongdajie and is hugely popular with locals. You'll find hotpot restaurants galore here, as well as speciality seafood joints.

DONGHUAMEN NIGHT MARKET

Map p262   Snacks Y

Dōnghuámén Yèshì 东华门夜市
Donganmen Dajie; ☼ **lunch & dinner, closed**
Chinese New Year; ⊕ **Wangfujing**

A sight in itself, the bustling night market near Wangfujing Dajie is a veritable food zoo: lamb kebabs, beef and chicken skewers, corn on the cob, smelly *dòufu* (tofu), cicadas, grasshoppers, kidneys, quail's eggs, squid, fruit, porridge, fried pancakes, strawberry kebabs, bananas, Inner Mongolian cheese, stuffed aubergines, chicken hearts, pitta bread stuffed with meat, shrimps – and that's just the start. Expect to pay around Y5 for a lamb kebab, far more than you would pay for the same snack from a *hútòng* vendor.

CHUĀN BÀN Map p262   Chinese Sìchuān Y
川办餐厅

☎ 6512 2277 ext 6101; 5 Gongyuan Toutiao, Jianguomennei Dajie; dishes from Y8; ☼ breakfast, lunch & dinner; ⊕ Jianguomen

Every Chinese province has its own official building in Běijīng, complete with a restaurant for cadres and locals working in the capital who are pining for a taste of home. Often, they're the most authentic places in town for regional cuisines. This restaurant in the Sìchuān Government Offices is always crowded and serves up just about every variety of Sìchuān food you could want. As you'd expect, most of the dishes are spicy. The Sìchuān cool noodles (Y10) won't singe your tongue, but the Bashu Boiled Fish (Y45), a Sìchuān classic in which a fish floats in a sea of oil and chilis, will. But there's an English menu and the staff, who are surprisingly helpful given that this is a government-run restaurant, can help you avoid choosing anything too fiery.

JĪN DǏNG XUĀN

Map p262   Chinese Cantonese Y
金鼎轩

☎ 6429 6888; 77 Hepingli Xijie (by south gate of Ditan Park); dim sum from Y8; ☼ 24hr; ⊕ Yonghegong

A giant, busy restaurant on three floors which serves up reliable and cheap dim sum, as well as standard Chinese dishes and good cakes around the clock. There's another branch in Cháoyáng (☎ 8596 8881, 15 Tuanjiehu Nanlu).

TRAKTIRR PUSHKIN

Map p262   Russian YY
彼得堡西餐厅

☎ 8407 8158; 5-15 Dongzhimennei Dajie; dishes from Y16; ☼ lunch & dinner; ⊕ Dongzhimen

Russian restaurants were the first foreign eateries to appear in Běijīng. This is the newest and best of them, perhaps because the chef is from Moscow. Fans of Russian food will be in seventh heaven here, as you can tuck into hearty portions of borscht (Y16) and cold herring (Y24), or classics like chicken Kiev (Y30) and trout roll stuffed with mushrooms (Y42). There's also a good, all-day breakfast. Being a Russian restaurant, there's a sterling selection of alcohol to choose from. If you need a change from weak Chinese beer, go for the Russian variety (Y25), or wash down your meal with one of the many vodkas available (from Y10 a glass). At lunchtime, this is a popular spot for diplomats from the nearby Russian embassy. In the evening, there's a Russian singer in the downstairs section and the place becomes a little more louche as it stays open for late-night drinkers until 4am. But they stop serving food at midnight. Around the corner, there's a cheaper and more basic sister establishment, **Traktirr** (☎ 6403 1896; Dongzhimennei Dajie, Beizhong Jie, 1a Xiyangguan Hutong).

CRESCENT MOON MUSLIM RESTAURANT

Map p262   Chinese Xīnjiāng Y
新疆弯弯月亮维吾尔穆斯林餐厅

☎ 6400 5281; 16 Dongsi Liutiao (off Chaoyangmen Beixiaojie); dishes from Y18; ☼ lunch & dinner; ⊕ Dongsishitiao

You can find a Chinese Muslim restaurant on almost every street in Běijīng. Most though, are run by Hui Muslims, who are Han Chinese, rather than ethnic minority Uighurs from the remote western province of Xīnjiāng. The Crescent Moon, which is tucked away down a *hútòng*, is the real deal, owned and staffed by Uighurs, and it's possibly the best Xīnjiāng joint in town. The *yáng'ròu chuàn* (lamb skewers; Y5) are meaty and succulent, or try the *dàpánjī*, a dish of chicken, potato, peppers and vegetables served over thick, pasta-like noodles. Towards the end of the night, the staff often dance Xīnjiāng style. Picture menu. Alcohol is served here.

Eating

DŌNGCHÉNG

FISH NATION Map p262
鱼邦

Western Y

☎ 6401 3249; 31 Nanluogu Xiang; dishes from Y18; ⏰ breakfast, lunch & dinner; Ⓜ Andingmen

A home from home for those who miss eating fish and chips, whether standing on a street corner in the rain in England, or sitting on the beach at Bondi. There's no sand at Fish Nation, nor does it rain very often in Běijīng, but there is a pleasant roof terrace that offers a view over the surrounding *hútòng*. Apart from obvious choices such as cod in batter (Y18), calamari in beer batter (Y20) and the chunky chips (Y12), they do decent salads here and serve their Big British Breakfast (Y50) until 4pm. There's a good range of foreign beers. It's very kid friendly too. There's a more basic branch that caters for the late-night drinking crowd in **Sanlitun** (☎ 6415 0119, Sanlitun Beijie).

WAITING FOR GODOT Map p262
等待戈多

Café Y

☎ 6407 3093; 24 Jiaodaokou Dongdajie; coffee from Y20; ⏰ lunch & dinner; Ⓜ Yonghegong

Bizarre but charming café that takes it name from Samuel Beckett's most acclaimed play. It maintains the literary theme by housing a Chinese language–only bookshop. During the day, it's a coffee house. At night, it's a quiet place for a drink.

HUĀ JIĀ YÍ YUÁN Map p262
花家怡园

Chinese Mixed YY

☎ 6405 1908; 235 Dongzhimennei Dajie (Gui Jie); dishes from Y20; ⏰ 24hr; Ⓜ Yonghegong

The food at this landmark Běijīng restaurant takes in various Chinese styles, from Cantonese to Běijīng cuisine via Shāndōng. The seafood is particularly good, especially the fish with bean curd (Y48) and the spicy and hot crab (Y88). That might be because the fish and various crustaceans get to await their death in nice, clean tanks, unlike some Běijīng restaurants where the fish float in murky water in distinctly dubious receptacles. Otherwise, you can take your pick from hotpot, dumplings, ribs – whatever you want really. The desserts are justly popular. With its atmospheric setting in a restored courtyard house, topped by a greenhouse-like glass roof, and a house

band that plays traditional Chinese music, this place gets busy at peak times. But it never closes, so it's particularly useful for night birds. English/picture menu.

CAFÉ DE LA POSTE Map p262
云游驿

French YY

☎ 6402 7047; 58 Yonghegong Dajie; dishes from Y25; ⏰ breakfast, lunch & dinner (closed Monday); Ⓜ Yonghegong

Just down the street from the Lama Temple, this is the closest Běijīng gets to an authentic French bistro. With its relaxed vibe and friendly service, it's popular with both French expats and locals. A small bar area where you can sip a glass of wine or a pastis opens into an intimate, nicely-lit dining area. The food is unpretentious and hearty. Try the chef's steak (Y78) and the chicken livers flambéed with cognac (Y65). But there are salads and a decent dessert menu too. The wine list starts from Y78 for a bottle of house red.

BĀ GUÓ BÙ YĪ Map p262
巴国布衣

Sìchuān YY

☎ 6400 8888; 89-3 Dianmen Dongdajie; dishes from Y30; ⏰ lunch & dinner; Ⓜ Andingmen or Gulou

This celebrated and award-winning Chéngdū restaurant chain delivers fine Sìchuān dishes from a marvellous Chinese inn-style setting with balconies, a central stairway and dolled up waiting staff. Enter through huge red doors to a traditional-style building just off Dianmen Dongdajie. There's music, occasional operatic events and a range of good value dishes including *Chóngqìng làzi jī* (重庆辣子鸡; Chongqing hot pepper chicken Y38) and *xiānjiāo yúpiàn* (鲜椒鱼片; chilli fish slices). The food is first rate and the ambience bursts with both character and theatre. There's a branch in **Xīchéng** (☎ 6615 2230; 68 Xizhimen Nanxiaojie).

PATISSERIE Map pp268-9
Sūyuán 酥园

Chocolatier YY

☎ 8518 1234, ext 6362; Grand Hyatt Beijing, 1 Dongchang'an Jie; Ⓜ Wangfujing

This small outlet is a fine choice if you have to get your hands on quality chocolate – either as a present or to satisfy an admittedly costly (if you shop here) craving.

PURPLE VINE TEAHOUSE

Map p262   Chinese Teahouse YY

Zǐténglú Cháyúguǎn 紫藤庐

☎ 6606 6614; 2 Nanchang Jie; tea from Y40;
🕐 lunch & dinner; Ⓜ Dongsishitiao or Dongzhimen
Experience a traditional tea ceremony at
the Purple Vine Teahouse, where you'll be
greeted with the gentle sounds of *gǔzhēng*
(Chinese zither) music and the smell of
incense. Traditional Chinese furniture
and century-old Shānxī wooden screens
decorate this tiny oasis just outside the
west gate of the Forbidden City. Choose
from the menu of jasmine, black, green
or oolong teas; a pot ranges in price from
Y40 up to Y250 for oolong. There's another
branch in **Sanlitun** (Map p264). The teahouse
accepts all major credit cards.

VINEYARD CAFÉ Map p262   Western YY

葡萄院儿

☎ 6402 7961; 31 Wudaoying Hutong; set lunch
Y45; 🕐 lunch & dinner; Ⓜ Yonghegong
A few minutes walk from the Lama Temple,
this hip café/restaurant is an ideal spot for
brunch or lunch. The British owner does
an excellent full English breakfast, while
the set lunch, a salad and pizza or quiche,
is terrific value. There's a small outside
area and lots of sofas to sink into. In the
evening, it's a restaurant as well as a laid-
back spot for a drink.

SICHUAN RESTAURANT

Map p262   Sìchuān YY

四川饭店

☎ 6513 7591/7593; 37a Donganmen Dajie; meals
Y70; 🕐 lunch & dinner; Ⓜ Wangfujing
This spacious restaurant decorated with
traditional Chinese eaves is rather worn in
its old age and the manager's office is still
forlornly decorated with a portrait of Mao,
but the dishes are well worth your time
and portions are generous. Try the filling
crispy tinfoil-wrapped mutton (纸包羊肉;
zhǐbāo yángròu; Y22), while the deep fried
eggplant with garlic and chilli sauce (鱼
香茄子; *yúxiāng qiézi*; Y26) is tender and
swimming in a sea of hot red chilli oil. The
menu extends to shark's fin and abalone,
and other seafood such as the hot, sweet
and spicy crab (香辣蟹; *xiānglà xiè*; Y58).
You can sweat over a *yuānyāng huǒguō*
(鸳鸯火锅; literally Mandarin duck hotpot) –
the celebrated Sìchuān hotpot that is

divided into hot (辣; *là*) and not-hot (不辣;
búlà) sections. Note the countertop array of
home fermented wines infused with various flora and fauna (for around Y20 a shot).
The restaurant takes Visa.

RED CAPITAL CLUB Map p262   Běijīng YYY

Xīnhóngzī Jùlèbù 新红资俱乐部

☎ 6402 7150 day, 8401 8886 night & weekend;
9 Dongsi Liutiao; dishes from Y60; 🕐 dinner;
Ⓜ Dongsishitiao then 🚌 113
Hidden away down a quiet *hútòng* is this
meticulously restored Qing-styled courtyard house, offset by props from a 1950s
Politburo meeting room and cuisine from
Zhōngnánhǎi. It's pricey, leans heavily on
the nostalgia pedal and the prolix menu requires dedication and patience (every dish
has an accompanying myth), but the food
hits the mark. Look for the big red doors
with no sign. Reservations required. The
restaurant is next door to the Red Capital
Residence (p184).

DALI COURTYARD

Map p262   Chinese Yúnnán YYY

大理

☎ 8404 1430; 67 Xiaojingchang Hutong, Gulou
Dongdajie; set menu from Y100; 🕐 lunch & dinner;
Ⓜ Andingmen
Specialising in the subtle flavours of the
cuisine of southwestern Yúnnán province,
the beautiful setting in a restored courtyard house in a *hútòng* makes it one of
Běijīng's more romantic places to eat. It's
also one of the more eccentric. You have
to book in advance and there's no menu.
Instead, you pay Y100 a head (drinks are
extra) and the chef decides what to give
you, depending on what inspires him and
what ingredients are fresh. Normally, that
means five or six dishes, with an emphasis
on fish and pork flavoured with Yúnnán
herbs. Specify your dietary requirements
when booking.

DǏNG DǏNG XIĀNG

Map p264   Chinese Hotpot YYY

鼎鼎香

☎ 6417 9289; 2f Yuanjia International Apt,
Dongzhimenwai, Dongzhong Jie; dishes from Y25;
🕐 lunch & dinner; Ⓜ Dongsishitiao
Hotpot restaurants are a favourite with
Běijīngers. You sit around a bowl of boil-

ing water (the hotpot) flavoured to your specifications and cook the raw ingredients yourself. It's a fun, sociable way of dining and the staff are always on hand to help you out. Dǐng Dǐng Xiāng is at the posh end of hotpot dining and it's notorious for its offhand service and for charging for everything, including napkins. But the food makes up for it. Try the fish dumplings with vegetable flavour (Y26) and the superior assorted beef and mutton (Y68). Throw in some white king oyster mushrooms (Y18), the three kinds of beancurd (Y15) and a few veggies and you're away. Don't forget to order the excellent dipping sauces; the *xiāng xiāng* double-flavour sauce (Y9) and *dǐng dǐng xiāng* special sauce (Y3) are particularly good. Picture menu. There's another branch just down the road (☎ 6417 2546; 1f/14 Dongzhong Jie, Dongzhimenwai).

QUANJUDE ROAST DUCK RESTAURANT

Map p262   Peking Duck YYY

Quànjùdé Kǎoyādiàn   全聚德烤鸭店

☎ 6525 3310; 9 Shuaifuyuan Hutong; whole duck Y168; ☽ lunch & dinner; ◉ Wangfujing

This huge and well-presented restaurant is less famous than its Qianmen sibling (p126), but more convenient if you're shopping along Wangfujing Dajie and less touristy. The prices are the same as the Qianmen branch though.

FANGSHAN RESTAURANT

Map p262   Imperial Chinese YYYY

Fángshàn Fànzhuāng 仿膳饭庄

☎ 6401 1889; Jade Islet, Beihai Park; set menus Y200-500; ☽ lunch & dinner

Běijīng's most elaborate imperial cuisine is served up in this restaurant in a pavilion overlooking the lake in Beihai Park (enter through either the west or south gate). All dishes are elaborately prepared, and range from delicately filled pastries to sea cucumber with deer tendon, peppery inkfish-egg soup and camel paw with scallion (no, it's not a real camel paw). The Y500 menu will get you a selection of rare delicacies. Reservations here are a must. Another less expensive **branch** (Map p262; ☎ 6523 3555; 12 Dongzongbu Hutong) can be found to the east of Chaoyangmen Nanxiaojie.

HUANG TING

Map p262   Chinese Cantonese YYYY

凰庭

☎ 8516 2888, ext 6707; Peninsula Palace Hotel, 8 Jinyu Hutong; meals Y300; ☽ lunch & dinner; ◉ Dongdan

Faux Old Peking is taken to an extreme in the courtyard setting of Huang Ting. Enter though a *sìhéyuàn* (courtyard house) entrance with carved lintels and a wooden portal to an interior fashioned from grey bricks with stone lions, water features, bird cages, stone floor flagging, decorated lanterns and Ming and Qing dynasty-style mahogany and sandalwood furniture – it's like a Fifth Generation film set.

Despite its artificiality and location (in the bowels of a five star hotel), the setting is impressive, caressed by the sounds of *zhēng*, *pípa* and other traditional Chinese instruments. With so many of Běijīng's *hútòng* falling to the sledgehammers of property developers, diners can toast their demise from the comfort of this simulacrum. Even the loos have their own wooden door and brass courtyard-style handles. Despite the Běijīng setting there are also Cantonese dishes (including dim sum). Dishes include whole Peking duck (Y220), roast suckling pig (Y100), braised spareribs in tangy brown sauce (Y70) and braised 'Běijīng style' meatball with cabbage (Y40).

COURTYARD

Map p262   Fusion YYYY

Sìhéyuàn 四合院

☎ 6526 8882; 95 Donghuamen Dajie; meal Y400; ☽ dinner; ◉ Tiananmen Dong

The Courtyard enjoys a peerless location overlooking the Forbidden City. You may have to forage to find the entrance (up the steps curtained by fronds of bamboo), but once inside you will be guided to a table and through a fine menu. Among the dishes on the menu are black cod in fennel marmalade (Y185), braised prime beef (Y225) and grilled veal tenderloin (Y245). The superb starters include paradise prawns from New Caledonia (Y120) and salmon and tuna sashimi tartare in miso cream sauce (Y95). The wine list starts at Y200 and goes up to Y28000 for really big spenders. There's a 15% service charge here too.

Eating

DŌNGCHÉNG

CHÁOYÁNG 朝阳

While restaurants can be found throughout the district, the dining action focuses on the Sanlitun bar and embassy area and the district around the Workers' Stadium. If you are on the hunt for non-Chinese dishes, this is a good place to start and there are plenty of bar and entertainment options for after the meal. The booming 798 Art District (p103) in Dashanzi (大山子) in the north of Cháoyáng (朝阳) is now home to an increasing selection of cafés and restaurants.

APRIL GOURMET Map p264   Deli
Lǜyèzi Shípǐndiàn 绿叶子食品店

☎ 8460 1030; Sanlitun Beixiaojie (next to Jenny Lou's); ☯ 8am-9pm; ◉ Dongzhimen, then 🚌 416
A rival with Jenny Lou's for the affections of home cooking–starved Westerners, April Gourmet operates three stores in Běijīng. The selection isn't as extensive as Jenny Lou's, but the prices are similar. Cheese, fresh bread, butter, wine, sauces, Western soups, coffee, milk, meats and frozen food are all available. Another branch (☎ 6417 7970; 1f Jiezuo Mansion, Xingfucun Zhonglu), stays open till midnight.

JENNY LOU'S Map p264   Deli
婕妮璐食品店

☎ 6461 6928; 6 Sanlitun Beixiaojie; ☯ 8am-10pm; ◉ Dongzhimen, then 🚌 416
The most popular deli for expats and locals in the area alike, thanks to the fresh meat and the array of cheeses, as well as an impressive selection of wine. It stocks all the usual staples as well. Not cheap but they cater to a captive market. There are six branches. The most convenient are this one and the one by Chaoyang Park (Map p264; ☯ 6501 6249; west gate of Chaoyang Park; ☯ 8am-10pm).

KEMPINSKI DELI Map p264   Deli
超市

☎ 6465 3388, ext 5741; Kempinski Hotel, Lufthansa Center, 50 Liangmaqiao Lu; ☯ 7am-10pm; ◉ Dongsishitiao, then 🚌 701 heading east
Just off the shuddering Third Ring Rd, the deli in the Kempinski Hotel (p186) is well liked for its desserts, breads and cakes (discounted after 8pm). Tables are available for patrons to park themselves for coffee and a chat in a smart environment.

MANCHURIAN SPECIAL FLAVOUR JIĂVOZI RESTAURANT
Map p264   Chinese Dongbei Y
Dōngběirén 东北人

☎ 6415 2855; 1 Xinzhong Jie; jiǎozi Y6; ☯ lunch & dinner; ◉ Dongzhimen
With its singing waitress in their colourful qípǎo and a menu that proclaims, 'We all love you', this is a friendly, noisy place. As the name suggests, it specialises in the cuisine of northeastern China, a region of icy winds and biting cold. That means lots of hearty meat dishes such as Harbin sausage (Y15), stir-fried mutton (Y25) and shredded pork with wild vegetables (Y25). But the real deal here is the delicious and cheap dumplings, or jiǎozi. There's a whole range to pick from, but the green pepper and pork, Chinese cabbage and pork and pumpkin and egg are particularly addictive. If you're very brave you can try the minced donkey meat jiǎozi. Wash the meal down with a few bottles of Hapi, Harbin's very own beer (Y12). English menu.

MIDDLE 8TH Map p264   Chinese Yúnnán Y
中捌楼餐厅

☎ 6413 0629; Sanlitun Zhongjie, Zhongba Lu; dishes from Y12; ☯ lunch & dinner; ◉ Dongsishitiao, then 🚌 701 heading east
The pace of Sanlitun's reconstruction has forced this sophisticated Yúnnán restaurant to shift locations along and off Zhongba Lu (Middle 8th St) a number of times. Here's hoping its latest home will prove to be more lasting, because it's a comfortable place with an authentic, wide-ranging menu. The deep-fried bamboo worms with spiced pepper and salt (Y22) make for an interesting starter. The mains include such signature Yúnnán dishes as drunken shrimps (Y22), pan-fried whole fish with dried pepper and vegetables (Y39) and braised rice with pineapple in a bamboo shoot (Y12). If you're feeling less adventurous, there's always the scrambled eggs topped with jasmine buds. A glass of rice wine (Y6) is recommended. English menu.

AT CAFÉ Map pp258-9   Café Y
爱特咖啡

☎ 6438 7264; 4 Jiuxianqiao Lu; coffee Y15; ☯ lunch & dinner; ◉ Dongzhimen, then 🚌 909 heading east

As befits a café in the 798 Art District, this is a cleverly designed place – check out the holes in the interior walls – that serves the local artists and poseurs. Good coffee and juices, as well as pasta dishes (from Y28), salads (from Y25) and sandwiches (from Y20). There also a small outside terrace.

VINCENT CAFÉ/CREPERIE

Map pp258-9   Café Creperie Y
北京季节咖啡店
☎ 8456 4823; 2 Jiuxianqiao Lu; crepes from Y15; ◷ lunch & dinner; ◉ Dongzhimen, then 🚍 909 heading east
A cornucopia of crepes is available at this French-run café in the 798 Art District (p103). The 'fisherman': shrimps, leeks and white wine (Y35), goes down a treat. Salads, pizzas, French onion soup, coffee and juices are also on the menu. Good chips and there is an outside area in the summer.

KOSMO Map p262   Café Y

天荷坊
☎ 8400 1567; 225 Chaoyangmennei Dajie; coffee Y18; ◷ breakfast, lunch & dinner; ◉ Chaoyangmen
A trendy and relaxing café, Kosmo serves up ultra-health conscious organic herbal teas, fruit juices and smoothies, as well as a range of coffees. Smokers are segregated here. You can also purchase a variety of organically grown coffee from all around the world.

CAFÉ PAUSE

Map pp258-9   Café Y
闲着也是闲着
☎ 6431 6214; 2 Jiuxianqiao Lu; coffee Y18, tapas from Y18; ◷ breakfast, lunch & dinner; ◉ Dongzhimen, then 🚍 909 heading east
Artfully designed, hip café in the heart of the 798 Art District which attracts a mixed bag of trendy locals and passing tourists. Housed in a converted warehouse, it has comfy sofas, intriguing light fittings and a small outside area. The central European-inspired menu features Vienna schnitzel (Y32) and Hungarian goulash (Y32), as well as an all-day breakfast (Y50). In the evening, it's a pleasant spot for a glass of wine. They mix decent cocktails (from Y35) here too.

KIOSK Map p264   Western Y

南斯拉夫烤肉屋
☎ 6413 2461, Sanlitun Beijie; hamburgers/sandwiches from Y22; ◷ lunch & dinner (closed Monday); ◉ Dongsishitiao, then 🚍 701 heading east
The perfect place for a quick lunchtime snack, or for early evening, pre-drinking sustenance, Kiosk serves up burgers, chips and sandwiches from a tiny hut just off Sanlitun's bar street. The big bite burger (Y29) is a classic, as is the grilled sausage sandwich (Y23). You can get a salad and a beer here too. There's a little outside area to eat at.

BOCATA Map p264   Café Y

☎ 6417 5291; 3 Sanlitun Beijie; sandwiches from Y23, coffee Y18; ◷ breakfast, lunch & dinner; ◉ Dongsishitiao, then 🚍 701 heading east
Great spot for lunch, especially in the summer, located slap-bang in the middle of Sanlitun's bar street. There's a vague Mediterranean/Middle-Eastern theme to the food, as the name suggests, with decent hummus, but the sandwiches on ciabatta and top-class chips (Y12) are decidedly Western in flavour. The juices and smoothies (from Y30) go down a treat too. The large outside terrace gets busy if the weather's nice.

PURPLE HAZE Map p264   Thai Y

紫苏庭
☎ 6413 0899; down a small alley opposite the north gate of the Workers' Stadium (first alley east of Xinjiang Red Rose Restaurant); dishes from Y24; ◷ lunch & dinner; ◉ Dongsishitiao
Congenial Thai restaurant that serves up dependable food in a purple-coloured environment. The small café-like area at the front, which has a selection of dog-eared paperbacks, is a mellow place for a coffee during the day.

XINJIANG RED ROSE RESTAURANT

Map p264   Chinese Xīnjiāng Y
新疆红玫瑰餐厅
☎ 6415 5741; opposite Workers' Stadium north gate, 5 Xingfuyicun; meals Y40; ◷ lunch & dinner; ◉ Dongsishitiao
This is a touristy, but fun restaurant with good value and tasty dishes from Xīnjiāng province. There's live Uighur music and dancers from 7.30pm every night and you

may find yourself dragged up on stage to perform with them. It gets very loud, so avoid sitting next to the speakers and prepare to shout. You can pass on the whole roast lamb (Y800) unless you're a crowd, but the roast leg of lamb, Y30 per *jīn* (0.6kg), is filling and chunky lamb kebabs (Y5 each) good value.

SOUK Map p264 — Middle Eastern YY
Sūkè Huìguǎn 苏克

☎ 6506 7309; by the west gate of Chaoyang Park; kebabs from Y8; ☽ dinner; ◉ Dongsishitiao, then 🚍 431 heading east

Hip hangout in a strip of bars and restaurants on the west side of Chaoyang Park. If you get there early enough, you can kick off your shoes and eat in style in one of the curtained corner booths. As much a place for a drink as it is to eat, the Y100 jugs of sangria seem to disappear quickly here. The menu is standard Middle Eastern fare: kebabs, falafel, pitta bread and hummus. The couscous is good value at Y40. There's a big outside terrace in the summer.

GL CAFÉ Map p264 — Cantonese YY
金湖茶餐厅

☎ 6588 9963; 20 Chaowai Dajie (just behind the Full Link Plaza); dishes from Y15; ☽ 24 hr; ◉ Chaoyangmen

Busy Hong Kong–style eatery that serves up a wide variety of rice and noodle dishes with a southern Chinese flavour, as well as Western fare like omelettes, salads and sandwiches. There's a good range of coffee, shakes and tea, wi-fi access, and you can peruse the latest editions of the *South China Morning Post* while you're eating. It's the perfect place for late night/early morning munchies. There are other branches in the China World Shopping Mall (p162) and at 21 Jianguomenwai Dajie (next to the St Regis Hotel).

LOTUS IN MOONLIGHT
Map p264 — Vegetarian YY
Hétángyuèsè Sùshí 荷塘月色

☎ 6465 3299; 12 Liufang Nanli (inside a housing complex, just off Zuojiazhuang Jie); dishes from Y15; ☽ lunch & dinner; ◉ Liufang

Běijīng isn't the best place in the world for vegetarian dining. Vegetarianism is a puzzle to most Chinese (with the exception of Buddhist monks). This smart place though,

will satiate those in search of meat and fish-free dishes. There's a wide variety of tofu-dominated options.

BELLAGIO Map p264 — Taiwanese YY
鹿港小镇

☎ 6551 3533; 6 Gongrentiyuchang Xilu; dishes from Y23; ☽ lunch & dinner; ◉ Dongsishitiao, then 🚍 701 heading east

Despite the Italian name, this is a slick, late-opening Taiwanese restaurant conveniently located next to the strip of nightclubs on Gongrentiyuchang Xilu (Gongti Xilu). During the day and the evening, it attracts cashed-up locals and foreigners. After midnight, the hipster club crowd move in. There's a seemingly endless menu, which includes Taiwanese favourites like cold noodles (Y28), stir-fried squid and celery (Y37) and hot and spicy boiling fish (Y63). But the real reason to come here is for the wonderful puddings. The shaved ice cream desserts are rightly renowned. Try the red bean ice cream (Y26) or the fresh mango cubes on shaved ice (Y32). The coffee is top-notch too. English menu. There's another branch in East Chaoyang (☎ 8451 9988; 35 Xiaoyun Lu).

CHINA LOUNGE Map p264 — Chinese YY
唐廊

☎ 6501 1166; south gate of the Workers' Stadium; dishes from Y28; ☽ lunch & dinner; ◉ Dongsishitiaon, then 🚍 701 heading east

Chinese cuisine from all over the country gets served up at this elegant restaurant next to the Blue Zoo inside the Workers' Stadium. The thoughtful design means you're not elbow-to-elbow with other diners, even if that makes the place seem a little cold when it's not busy.

THREE GUIZHOU MEN
Map p264 — Chinese Guìzhōu YY
Sāngè Guìzhōu Rén 三个贵州人

☎ 6551 8517; inside the west gate of the Workers' Stadium (around the cnr from Bellagio), Gongrentiyuchang Xilu; dishes from Y35; ☽ lunch & dinner; ◉ Dongsishitiao

Hip but relaxed restaurant specialising in the spicy cuisine of southwestern Guìzhōu province. The food here is delicious, some of the best in Běijīng. The fried pork ribs (Y58) are a must, but almost everything on the menu is good. Try the stir-fried grass roots with Guìzhōu bacon (Y35), or any of the superb salads. The Guìzhōu smashed potato (Y25), a regional version of mashed potato, is sublime. The spacious dining room is decorated with Chinese contemporary art and the only drawback is that they don't do wine by the glass. There's another branch in **Jianwai Soho** (☎ 5869 0598; Jianwai Soho, Bldg 7, Dongsanhuan).

SERVE THE PEOPLE Map p264   Thai YY
Wèi Rénmín Fùwù 为人民服务
☎ 8454 4580; 1 Sanlitun Xiwujie; meals Y50; ⏰ lunch & dinner; ⓜ Dongzhimen, then 🚌 416 heading east

It has been around a while, but Serve the People is still Běijīng's best Thai restaurant. You'll find all the classics here, red chicken curry (Y35), *tom yum goong* (Y48), as well as superb fish cakes with plum and chilli sauce (Y40). It's the warm atmosphere and central location that attracts the crowds though.

HAITANGHUA PYONGYANG COLD NOODLE RESTAURANT
Map p264   Korean YY
平壤海棠花冷面馆
☎ 6461 6295/6298; 8 Xinyuanxili Zhongjie (on the cnr of Xin Donglu); cold noodles Y50; ⏰ lunch & dinner; ⓜ Dongzhimen

There aren't many North Korean restaurants around the world, but then there aren't that many in the DPRK itself. A night at this kitsch hangover from the Cold War is rather more fun than an evening out in Pyongyang though, thanks to the accomplished singing waitresses who take it in turns to serenade the diners with a selection of classic Korean tunes. There's not much difference between North Korean and South Korean cuisine; apart from the cold noodles, it's *kimchi* and barbecue all the way.

LE BISTROT PARISIEN Map p264   French YY
巴黎乐事多餐厅
☎ 6417 8188; 1f Tongli Bldg, Sanlitun Houjie; daytime set menu Y60; ⏰ lunch & dinner; ⓜ Dongsishitiao, then 🚌 701 heading east

Upmarket French eatery in one of Sanlitun's busiest areas. The French chef certainly knows what he's doing and this is a good place for Francophones to enjoy such

delights as marbled foie gras with port and red wine preserve (Y108), or the excellent cheese plate (Y58). The two-course set menu, available between 11am and 6pm, is decent value. Good, if pricey, wine list. But you can get a glass of the house vino for Y25.

BOOKWORM Map p264   Western YY
Shūchóng 书虫
☎ 6586 9507; Bldg 4, Nan Sanlitun Lu; lunch set menu Y78, dinner set menu Y108; ⏰ 9am-1am; ⓜ Dongsishitiao, then 🚌 701 heading east

A combination of a bar, café, restaurant and library, the Bookworm is a Běijīng institution and a comfortable, friendly place to while away an afternoon or an evening. Perhaps it's the 14,000 books you can browse while sipping your coffee, or working your way through the extensive wine list, but some people spend whole days in here. The food ranges from sandwiches (Y35) to pasta dishes (from Y45), but the set menus offer more substantial fare. The Bookworm though, is much more than just an upmarket café. It's one of the epicentres of Běijīng expat life and hosts lectures, a classical music club and a poetry reading night, amongst many other things. Any author of note passing through town gives a talk here. The local listings mags will tell you what events are coming up. There's a Y300 annual fee to join the library, but you can also buy new books here, including Lonely Planet guides, and magazines. There's a roof terrace in the summer and it's one of the few places in Běijīng to have a non-smoking section.

MOREL'S Map p264   Belgian YYY
莫劳龙玺西餐厅
☎ 6416 8802; Gongrentiyuchang Beilu, opposite north gate of Workers' Gymnasium; dishes from Y35; ⏰ lunch & dinner (closed Monday); ⓜ Dongsishitiao

Top-notch steaks and fine fresh fish are the trademark of this homely Belgian eatery. The food is pricey, but you get a lot of it. The Brussels pepper steak (Y118), Flemish beer beef stew (Y68) and the pot of mussels (Y98) are deservedly popular. Good desserts and a vast selection of Belgian beers. It's advisable to book in the evenings. Near the Lufthansa Centre, you'll find another **branch** (☎ 6437 3939; 27 Liangmaqiao Lu).

ALAMEDA Map p264 — Western YYY

☎ 6417 8084/6413 1939; Sanlitun Beijie; set lunch menu Y60, set dinner menu Y128; ☾ lunch & dinner; ◉ Dongsishitiao, then 🚌 701 heading east

Consistently high-class fusion cuisine with a Brazilian twist in a light and spacious environment makes this Běijīng's finest Western restaurant. The Brazilian chef changes the menu daily, but regular dishes include filet mignon in a rosemary and red wine sauce with roasted potatoes and pan-fried whole tiger prawns. There is an à là carté menu but the two-course set lunch and dinner menus will satisfy most people's appetites. Dessert costs extra though, while the extensive wine list is not cheap (from Y200 a bottle). Sophisticated without being snobbish, it's a place to splash out. It's essential to book.

MARE Map p264 — Spanish YYY
Gǔlǎohǎi Xīcāntīng 古老海西餐厅

☎ 6417 1459; 14 Xindong Rd; set lunch Y75, tapas from Y15; ☾ lunch & dinner; ◉ Dongsishitiao, then 🚌 701

Don't be fooled by the view through the front windows of Běijīng's best Spanish restaurant. The seemingly cramped space opens out into a big, tastefully decorated dining area. The tapas are authentic and include sizzling garlic prawns, stir-fried chorizo with potato and *patatas bravas*, while the Sunday paella (Y90 per person) is justly popular. Extensive, but expensive wine list (from Y240 a bottle). The set lunch doesn't include dessert.

BEIJING DADONG ROAST DUCK
RESTAURANT Map p264 — Peking Duck YYY
Běijīng Dàdǒng Kǎoyā Diàn 北京大董烤鸭店

☎ 6582 2892/4003; 3 Tuanjiehu Beikou; duck Y98; ☾ lunch & dinner; ◉ Dongsishitiao, then 🚌 431 heading east

A long-term favourite of the Peking duck scene, this restaurant has a tempting variety of fowl. The hallmark bird is a crispy, lean duck without the usual high fat content (trimmed down from 42.38% to 15.22% for its 'superneat' roast duck, the brochure says), plus plum (or garlic) sauce, scallions and pancakes. Also carved up is the skin of the duck with sugar, an old imperial predilection. Fork out an extra Y20 and get the duck of your choice. The menu also dishes up some fine local non-duck dishes.

PURE LOTUS VEGETARIAN
Map p264 — Vegetarian YYY
Jìngxīnlián 净心莲

☎ 6592 3627; Zhongguo Wenlianyuan, 10 Nongzhanguan Nanlu; meals from Y100; ☾ breakfast, lunch & dinner; ◉ Dongsishitiao, then 🚌 431 heading east

The monks who run this place serve up some of the tastiest and most creative vegetarian food in the city, but they charge a lot for it. The spicy chopped vegetable chicken (Y108) is good, as is the boiled vegetable fish (Y88) and the Wutaishan mushroom (Y188).

1001 NIGHTS
Map p264 — Middle Eastern YYY
Yīqiānlíngyī Yè 一千零一夜

☎ 6532 4050; opposite Zhaolong International Youth Hostel, Gongtrentiyuchang Beilu; meals Y100; ☾ lunch & dinner; ◉ Dongsishitiao, then 🚌 701 heading east

Helped by its location just off the Sanlitun bar strip, the large outside dining area and nightly belly dancing, this is still the most popular Middle Eastern restaurant in Běijīng. The food is pretty good too; they throw together an excellent concoction of kebabs, falafel, hummus, pitta bread. No credit cards.

SORABOL
Map p264 — Korean YYY
萨拉伯尔

☎ 6465 3388, ext 5720; basement, Lufthansa Centre, 50 Liangmaqiao Lu; meals Y150; ☾ lunch & dinner; ◉ Dongsishitiao, then 🚌 701 heading east

This dependably good Korean chain restaurant is the place to come for barbecue and *banfan* (rice, egg, meat, vegetables and hot pepper sauce), as well as *paigu* (roast spareribs). Another branch can be found at Landmark Towers (☎ 6590 6688, ext 5119; 2/F Landmark Towers, 8 Dongsanhuan Beilu) in Cháoyáng.

HǍIDIÀN 海淀

SCULPTING IN TIME Map p271 — Café Y
Diāokè Shíguāng 雕刻时光

☎ 8259 8296; Bldg 12, 1 Huaqing Jiayuan, Chengfu Lu; coffee Y20; ☾ breakfast, lunch & dinner; ◉ Wudaokou

An easy place to while away an afternoon, Sculpting in Time offers books and magazines to browse through, as well as sandwiches and pasta for when you get peckish. There are other branches in Hǎidiàn and also **Cháoyáng** (☎ 5135 8108; 2b Jiangtai Lu, Hairun International Apt, Shop 3a, near the Lido Hotel).

MIMA Map p271   Café Y
☎ 8268 8003; east gate of Old Summer Palace; coffee Y25; ☪ breakfast, lunch & dinner; ⊖ Xizhimen, then minibus 375

If you're visiting the Old Summer Palace (Yuánmíng Yuán), then be sure to check out this great, eccentric café. From the bar made up of books, to the most memorable toilet in Běijīng, this place is all about creative design. It's particularly nice in the summer, when you can sit outside surrounded by a small army of cats.

ISSHIN JAPANESE RESTAURANT
Map p271   Japanese YY
日本料理一心
☎ 8261 0136; 35 Chengfu Lu; set meal Y35; ☪ lunch & dinner; ⊖ Wudaokou

Just off an unpromising looking road, about 50 metres north of the traffic lights at the intersection of Chengfu Lu and Wudaokou subway station, Isshin is well worth tracking down if you're in the area. With its thoughtful design, laid-back atmosphere and reasonable prices, it's a place where business types, expat Japanese and students can all feel at home. The sushi starts from Y20, or you can just a order a plate of Isshin sushi or sashimi (Y68). The menu includes hotpots, Udon noodles and teriyaki dishes. The set meals (from Y38) are good value.

XĪCHÉNG 西城
The main cluster of restaurants worth visiting in Xīchéng is located around Houhai and Qianhai Lakes and in the surrounding *hútòng*. Some offer views over the lakes, which are swamped with pedalos in the summer. The boats give way to ice-skaters in the winter, when the lakes freeze over. The west side of Qianhai is home to a touristy, mostly over-priced and over-rated strip of bars and restaurants known as Lotus Lane.

HÀN CĀNG Map p262   Chinese Hakka Y
汉仓
☎ 6404 2259; by north gate of Beihai Park (just off Dianmen Xidajie); dishes from Y12; ☪ lunch & dinner; ⊖ Gulou

In the summer, when the large outside terrace comes into its own, this is one of Běijīng's hot restaurant destinations. It's still good in winter too, especially if you get one of the upstairs rooms that have a great view over the frozen lake. Hakka (客家; *kèjiā*) cuisine uses a lot of fresh fish. Go for the baked crab with ginger and onion (Y48) and the whole fried fish with pine nut (Y38). But there's also plenty here for meat-lovers. The roast beef fillet with garlic and wrapped in a lotus leaf (Y28) and the baked *san huang* chicken with salt (Y28 for a half chicken) are both worth trying. It gets loud here and it's always crowded, so book, or be prepared for a wait, if you want an outside table in the evenings. English and picture menu.

SOUTH SILK ROAD Map p262   Yúnnán YY
南秀水街
☎ 6615 5515; 12-13, 19A Qianhai Xiyan Rd; dishes from Y18; ☪ lunch & dinner; ⊖ Gulou

Another addition to the growing army of stylish Yúnnán restaurants in Běijīng, this spacious, hip and busy restaurant is spread over two floors and offers a bird's-eye view over Qianhai Lake. The dishes are authentic Yúnnán, from the baked beef in Yúnnán tea (Y58) to the pot-roasted frog (Y58). There's a range of spicy barbecued fish dishes from Y38, a reasonable wine list and the beers start at Y25. There are two other branches, one in **Soho** (☎ 8580 4286; 3/F, Bldg D, Soho New Town, 88 Jianguo Lu, Cháoyáng) and another in **Chaoyang** (☎ 6481 3261; 2-3F, North Bldg 4, Area 2, Anhuili, Cháoyáng).

RAJ Map p262   Indian YY
拉兹印度音乐餐厅
☎ 6401 1675; 31 Gulou Xidajie; dishes from Y28; ☪ lunch & dinner; ⊖ Gulou

With soothing sitar music on the stereo, comfy cushions, red drapes and an extensive menu of north Indian cuisine classics, such as chicken tikka masala (Y42), rogan josh (Y42) and assorted vindaloos and kormas, the Raj satisfies curry fanatics looking for a taste of the subcontinent in Běijīng. They deliver and take credit cards too.

CAFÉ SAMBAL Map p262 Malaysian YY

☎ 6400 4875; 43 Doufuchi Hutong (off Jiugulou Dajie); set lunch Y50, dishes from Y35; ☻ lunch & dinner; ◉ Gulou

Cool Malaysian restaurant located in a cleverly-converted courtyard house at the entrance to Doufuchi Hutong. The minimalist bar opens into a narrow dining area that has a temporary roof during the winter, but is open in the summer so you can dine under the stars and satellites. The food is classic Malaysian. Try the beef rendang (Y48), or the various sambals (from Y50). The wine list is decent and gets updated every six months, while the barman here mixes what many claim to be the best mojito (Y35) in town.

HUTONG PIZZA Map p262 Pizza YY
胡同比萨

☎ 6617 5916; 9 Yindingqiao Hutong; pizzas from Y52; ☻ lunch & dinner; ◉ Gulou

Nestling in a *hútòng* that was one of the locations for the movie *Beijing Bicycle*, Hutong Pizza is hard to find but worth the effort because they offer the best pizza in town. There's a wide selection to choose from, including veggie options, or you can build your own, and they're big: the large pizzas (Y85) will easily satisfy two hungry people. There are salads, burgers and pasta options, as well local and foreign beers. It gets busy, so it's advisable to book at peak times. They do deliver though. Watch out for the mini-pond just inside the entrance; put one step wrong and you'll be swimming with the fish.

YUELU SHANWU Map p262 Chinese Hunan YY
岳麓山屋

☎ 6617 2696; 10-11 Tianhe Fang (Lotus Lane); meals from Y80; ☻ lunch & dinner; ◉ Gulou

With a marvellous view over the lake of Qianhai, this pretty, neat and civilised Húnán restaurant and bar – the name means 'house at the foot of the mountain' – serves a range of hot and mild dishes from the province renowned for its searing flavours. If you're feeling flush, the spicy snake is a snip at Y320. English menu.

Entertainment

Entertainment

Deng Xiaoping's maxim, 'When you open the window for fresh air, expect some flies to blow in', gauged the tolerable risks of China's open-door policy. But even the prescient Deng can't have imagined that opening up China to Western influences would lead to a nightlife revolution that shows no sign of stopping. On the contrary, Běijīng's strait-laced past seems ever more distant as new bars and clubs open every week. Běijīng might not be as sophisticated as Shànghǎi, or as glam as Hong Kong, but it has a distinct nightlife identity that reflects its residents desire to play as hard as they work.

Traditionally, Běijīng's bars are more laidback and a little grungier than the ones you'll find further south, something that reflects Běijīngers disdain for Shànghǎi's surface flash. That's changing and there are an increasing number of places that wouldn't look out of place in London or New York. The city's clubs are catching up too, thanks to enthusiastic promoters who fly in top-name DJs from around the world to spread the dance music gospel. The live-music scene is more parochial but you can find everything from jazz to punk and, with recording contracts hard to come by in China, Běijīng's best bands are always playing live.

Where Běijīng does lord it over Shànghǎi is in the sheer variety of entertainment options available. This is the cultural capital of China as well as the political one and the place to be if you're interested in seeing contemporary art exhibitions, modern theatre, ballet or classical music concerts. Běijīng is also the movie capital of China, which means you'll find more films showing here than anywhere else. Then there are the traditional pastimes, such as Beijing opera (*jīngjù*) or acrobatics, which are fixtures on the tourist circuit and draw regular crowds.

Thanks to the monthly expat magazines (p227) circulating in town, events listings can easily be found.

PUBS & BARS

Necessity being the mother of invention in Běijīng, as everywhere else, first came *píjiǔ* (beer, c 1903), which gradually dislodged *báijiǔ* (white spirits, the strong stuff) as the nation's favourite tipple. Later came the bars (c late 1980s). It wasn't until sometime in the mid-1990s, however, that the gift-wrapping truly came off Běijīng's tavern scene.

Despite the best efforts of the authorities, Sanlitun in Cháoyáng district remains the hub of Běijīng's bar scene. Although Sanlitun's much-loved South Bar Street disappeared under the wrecking ball in late 2005, and rumours continue to abound as to the future of the area, Sanlitun is still where you'll find many of the most popular expat bars. Sanlitun Lu, known to taxi drivers as Sanlitun Jiǔbā, which runs between Gongrentiyuchang Beilu and Dongzhimenwai Dajie is one long strip of bars. Most are firmly aimed at the tourist trade and should be avoided, but there are some good places in the surrounding streets.

Sanlitun's stranglehold on Běijīng's bar scene is loosening though, as enterprising locals and Westerners look elsewhere for cheaper rents and more innovative locations. Further west in Dōngchéng district, you'll find cool little *hútòng* (alleyway) bars in renovated courtyard houses. Nanluogu Xiang, a *hútòng* which runs between Gulou Dongdajie and Dianmen Dongdajie, is home to a thriving bar scene. Just east of that, the lakes of Qianhai and Houhai (north of Beihai Park) have become a magnet for bars in recent years. Especially popular in the summer, they attract more locals than foreigners these days. There are also an increasing number of bars in Wǔdàokǒu in Hǎidiàn district (Běijīng's student heartland), the 798 Art District (p103) and around the Holiday Inn Lido Beijing (p188) in northeast Chaoyang.

Remember this is China, where change is constant, so bars open and close with a bewildering frequency. Above all, don't judge Běijīng's bars by their exterior appearances. There are plenty of swish-looking places that are dire, while many of the finest establishments look less than enticing from the outside.

SOUTH CHAOYANG 朝阳南

LAN Map pp268-9
兰会所

☎ 5109 6012; 4th fl, Twintowers Shopping Mall B-12, Jianguomenwai Dajie; cocktails from Y60; ⏰ 10-3am; Ⓜ Yonganli

Despite the incongruous location in an anonymous shopping mall opposite the Silk Market, this Philippe Starck–designed bar and restaurant is far from ordinary. On the contrary, the eccentric, eye-catching look of the place, which spreads through a number of rooms, is its main attraction. Paintings dangle from the ceilings, giant mirrors are everywhere and the private dining rooms are done in the style of Mongolian Yurts. The toilets are the most extravagant in Běijīng. None of it comes cheap though. There's live jazz and DJs and a big wine list.

MAGGIES Map p264
美琪

☎ 8562 8142/8143; just by the south gate of Ritan Park; beers Y30; ⏰ 7.30pm-4.30am Sun-Wed, 7.30pm-5am Thu-Sat; Ⓜ Jianguomen

A Běijīng legend and (in)famous enough for the odd, visiting Hollywood type to pop in, Maggies is not the place for everyone. A somewhat older crowd gathers here, as do many Mongolian ladies. But it is open late and has pool tables, while the spacious bar is a fine spot for people-watching. They serve excellent hotdogs as well.

PALACE VIEW BAR Map pp268-9
观景酒吧

☎ 6513 7788; 10th fl, Grand Hotel Beijing, 35 Dongchang'an Jie; cocktails from Y60; May-September 5-9pm; Ⓜ Tiananmen Dong or Wangfujing

For liquid refreshment with a top-notch panorama, the Palace View is in a league of its own. Outdoor tables graced by a string of palm trees make this a wonderful place to escape the city and size up the view overlooking Dongchang'an Jie, the Forbidden City and Tiananmen Square.

PRESS CLUB Map pp268-9
记者俱乐部酒吧

☎ 6460 6688; St Regis, 21 Jianguomenwai Dajie; beer Y35; ⏰ 4.30pm-1am; Ⓜ Jianguomen

If Sanlitun is just too sordid for you, seek out the dignified repose of the wood-panelled Press Club in the top-drawer St Regis, off Ritan Lu. Its five-star bar has five-star prices, a large-screen sports TV and a lounge with a library-like ambience.

RED MOON BAR Map pp268-9
Dōngfāng Liàng 东方亮

☎ 8518 1234, ext 6366; Grand Hyatt Beijing, 1 Dongchang'an Jie; beer Y60, cocktails from Y75; ⏰ 11.30am-2.30pm & 5pm-1am; Ⓜ Wangfujing

Arriving at the Red Moon, customers are met by a svelte female attendant and ushered through a looking-glass door to a gorgeous lounge bar blessed with a huge selection of wines. The lighting is subdued, soporific jazz wafts over the chilled-out clientele, and the evening's live music goes down well with those who are not in a rush to go anywhere else. The overall effect is particularly seductive and the perfect antidote to some of Běijīng's rawer bar spots. Japanese snacks are nearby, and a private function room at the rear is available for more intimate gatherings. There's also a cigar bar.

STONE BOAT BAR/CAFÉ Map p264
Shífǎng 石舫酒吧

☎ 6501 9986; inside Ritan Park, southwestern cnr; beers from Y20, cocktails from Y30; ⏰ 10am-late; Ⓜ Jianguomen

A lovely bar on a summer evening, this is a place to come to escape the traffic and noise of Sanlitun. There's mellow live music, an outside area where you can sit beneath the trees of Ritan Park and a refreshing ambience that comes with the shock of being so close to nature in Běijīng. During the day, it functions as an equally pleasant café. To get there after Ritan Park closes, go to the south gate on Guanghua Lu and tell the gate-people you're going to the jiǔbā (bar) and they'll let you in.

DŌNGCHÉNG & XĪCHÉNG
东城、西城

Bars and cafés have overrun the area around the Shichahai lakes in recent years, especially along Houhai Nanyan, running south of Houhai Lake. Yandai Xijie (Chinese Pipe Cross St) has also been ambushed by a mob of recently opened bars, cafés, arts and crafts shops, and purveyors of trinkets. Both the economics and character of the area have been redefined and there's little to differentiate the competition. But after a turn around the lakes, you can duck into nearby *hútòng* and find some of Běijīng's best watering holes. Alternatively, you can head straight for the humming *hútòng* that is Nanluogu Xiang, where you'll find a nice range of homely bars with roof terraces and views over the surrounding area.

BED BAR Map p262
Chuángbā 床吧
☎ 8400 1554; 17 Zhangwang Hutong, Jiugulou Dajie; beers from Y20, cocktails from Y35; ☺ 4pm-late Mon-Tue, noon-late Wed-Sun; ⊕ Gulou Dajie
One *hútòng* north of Café Sambal (p138) is this gem of a bar, sited in a cleverly converted courtyard house. The bar area leads onto a succession of inner rooms, some with beds, and the overall effect is of a place that's both intimate and spacious. Bed can often be crowded, but there's always a spot where you can hide away. There's a DJ and small dance floor and they do finger food too.

BUDDHA BAR Map p262
Búda Jiŭba 不大酒吧
☎ 6617 9488; 2 Yinding Qiao; beer Y15; ☺ 2pm-2am; ⊕ Gulou Dajie, then 🚌 60
Its name in Chinese is a clever play on the word 'not big' or 'small'. This is no longer the reclusive bar it once was, but is still worth visiting for the South American tunes that dominate the house stereo.

DRUM & BELL Map p262
Gŭzhōng Kāfēiguǎn 钟鼓咖啡馆
☎ 8403 3600; 41 Zhonglouwan Hutong; beers Y20, cocktails from Y35; ☺ noon-2am; ⊕ Gulou Dajie
Located in between the Drum and Bell Towers, from which it takes its name, the main attraction of this bar is its splendid roof terrace. It's a great place to catch some rays during the summer. Downstairs, there are comfy sofas to sink into. There are bar snacks too.

EJE BAR Map p262
Zhóuba 轴吧
☎ 8404 4424; 20 Guoxue Hutong; ☺ 2pm-late ⊕ Yonghegong
The self-styled (and probably accurate) 'hardest-to-find bar in Běijīng' is well worth

the effort, but pack a compass. Tucked away behind the rear wall of the Confucius Temple, this cultured courtyard bar is sedately arranged with sofas and set to the chirruping of grasshoppers. Away from even the remotest action, it's well worth a detour. Arriving at night is like reaching the light at the end of a tunnel: from Yonghegong Dajie follow Guanshuyuan Hutong (官书院胡同) round the corner, take the first right and you will see the Confucius Temple ahead on your left. Follow the road round to your right, take the first left and it's opposite the temple's rear wall (check the bar website for a map).

GUANGFUGUAN GREENHOUSE Map p262
Guǎngfúguàn de Wēnshì 广福的观温室
☎ 6400 3234; 36 Yandai Xijie; ☺ 5pm-late; beers from Y20; ⊕ Gulou Dajie, then 🚌 60
This laid-back place on the bar-cluttered Yandai Xijie gets full marks for novelty. Formerly the Guangfuguan Taoist Temple (according to the characters carved on the lintel above the arched doorway), the shrine has been requisitioned for the city's exploding bar scene and simply decked out with art posters. The temple's roof guardians are still intact and the presence of religious statues reminds visitors that they drink on sacred turf.

HOUHAI ZOO Map p262
后海卒
☎ 6403 6690; Bldg 2, Qianhai (just off Dianmenwai Dajie); beers Y10, cocktails Y15; ☺ 10-3am; ⊕ Gulou Dajie
An offshoot of a growing Běijīng bar empire that specialises in serving up super-cheap drinks in friendly, if rowdy, surroundings, this is much the nicest of the chain, thanks to its prime location on the east side of Qianhai Lake. It's loud and gets crowded as the night wears on, but you can't beat the prices.

NO NAME BAR Map p262
Bái Fēng 白枫
☎ 6401 8541; 3 Qianhai Dongyan; beers Y20, cocktails Y40; ☺ noon-2am; ⊕ Gulou Dajie
Perched beside Qianhai Lake, this was the first bar to open in the area and was so successful that it spawned countless imitators around the lake. Thankfully, the No

Name has resisted going down the neon sign route beloved by its competitors. Nor are there any aggressive bar touts standing outside vying for your custom. Instead, it's a laid-back joint with pleasant staff where you can sit in a rattan chair and watch the world go by through the large windows.

PASSBY BAR Map p262
Guòkè 过客

☎ 8403 8004; www.gk01.com; 108 Nanluogu Xiang; beer Y20, meals from Y40; ⏰ 9-2am; ⊕ Andingmen

Something of an institution, the Passby attracts a diverse crowd of expats, locals and travellers. The bar operates from a courtyard house which has polished beams, a low ceiling, a mezzanine floor (up the ladder) and a useful and growing library of books that are available for loan; you need to donate three books to join the library. There's also a small outside area that's normally over-subscribed in the summer. The menu offers Italian, Chinese and Western dishes and there's a fair selection of wines to choose from. It's not cheap, but it's a welcoming place where you're likely to bump into other travellers, and they do sell Lonely Planet guides.

REEF BAR Map p262
触礁

☎ 6403 2736; 14-1 Nanluogu Xiang; beers from Y10, cocktails from Y15; ⏰ 11-2am; ⊕ Andingmen

A refugee from the old Sanlitun South Bar Street, the Reef Bar has the comforting feel of your local back home. Located in a tiny *hútòng* house, there's a small bar area, a few sofas and armchairs and a wide selection of foreign beers. Run by a cheerful husband-and-wife team, the place attracts their (many) friends, as well as foreigners who live in the area.

RUÌ FǓ Map p262
瑞府

☎ 6404 2711; 3 Zhang Zizhong Lu; cocktails Y50; ⏰ 7pm-late; ⊕ Yonghegong or Dongsishitiao, then 🚌 106 heading west

Housed in a historic building that's been home to Qing dynasty royalty, warlords and the occupying Japanese army in the 1930s, this is reputedly one of the most haunted spots in all Běijīng. You could probably hear the ghosts screaming, if it wasn't for the resident DJ (on weekends) and the

throng of upmarket locals and expats who flock here to enjoy properly mixed cocktails around the marble bar or to recline on the fancy sofas. There's a VIP cigar lounge and an outside terrace in the summer.

CHÁOYÁNG 朝阳

The days when Sanlitun Lu was the be-all and end-all of Běijīng nightlife are long gone. These days, the increasingly tacky bars on the main drag attract mostly local drinkers, naive tourists and expat teenagers. It's rather depressing in the evenings, with beggars, DVD hawkers and touts for massage parlours and hookers crowding the pavement. But Nan Sanlitun Lu, the road running south from Sanlitun Lu on the other side of Gongti, is picking up some of the slack with a number of promising places opening up. Otherwise, there's a cluster of good, lively bars in the streets behind the 3.3 Shopping Centre (p166) on the western side of Sanlitun Beijie.

If you've spent the day exploring the galleries in the 798 Art District (p103), there are a few cafés that turn into pleasant spots for a drink in the evening. Or you can head to the nearby Lido area, where there are a few bars worth visiting.

ALFA Map p264
Āěrfǎ 阿尔法

☎ 6413 0086; 5 Xingfu Yicun, opposite north gate of the Workers' Stadium; cocktails from Y35; ⏰ 11am-late; ⊕ Dongsishitiao

With a great outside terrace, complete with cushion-strewn booths to lounge in and a water feature to fall into, as well as an in-house Asian-French restaurant to satisfy late-night hunger pangs, decent cocktails and DJs, this is a deservedly popular spot. The 80s night every other Friday packs them in. Just down from the Xinjiang Red Rose Restaurant (p133).

APERITIVO Map p264
意式餐吧

☎ 6417 7793; 43 Sanlitun Beijie; wine & cocktails from Y35; ⏰ 10-2am; ⊕ Dongsishitiao, then 🚌 701 heading east

A popular bar with the Euro-crowd thanks to the continental café–like vibe, lengthy wine list and small terrace shielded from the street by some artfully-placed shrubs. Inside, it's less appealing but they do bar food as well.

BAR BLU Map p264

蓝吧

☎ 6417 4124; 4th fl, Tongli Studio, Sanlitun Beijie; beers from Y20, cocktails from Y35; ☯ 4pm-2am Sun-Thu, 4pm-4am Fri & Sat; ⊕ Dongsishitiao, then ⌨ 701 heading east

This is one of Běijīng's hotspots, thanks to the roomy layout, its roster of DJs, Western food, Běijīng's most popular pub quiz (Wednesdays at 9pm) and, above all, one of the best roof terraces in the city. It's packed at weekends and pretty busy during the rest of the week.

BEER MANIA Map p264

Màiní Píjiǔbā 麦霓啤酒吧

☎ 6585 0786; 1st fl, Taiyue Fang, Nan Sanlitun Lu; beers from Y45; ☯ 2pm-late; ⊕ Dongsishitiao, then ⌨ 701 heading east

A shrine to Belgian brews, this is a small, simple establishment where the beer comes before everything. It's guaranteed that you won't have heard of some of the 75 different ales on offer. There's a happy hour from 4pm to 8pm, which is just as well as this place isn't cheap. Belgian-style snacks, waffles and chips are available as well.

BROWNS Map p264

红磨坊

☎ 6591 2717; just off Nan Sanlitun Lu; beers from Y30, cocktails from Y35; ☯ 11-2am Mon, Tue, Thu, Sun, 11-4am Wed, Fri & Sat; ⊕ Dongsishitiao, then ⌨ 701 heading east

A huge, cavernous space that fills up on weekends and Wednesdays, when it's ladies night from 10pm, Browns is the sort of place where it's perfectly acceptable, indeed it's encouraged, to dance on the bar. At busy times, it is industrial drinking UK style, with the punters elbow-to-elbow with each other and conversation near impossible. That doesn't seem to worry the younger crowd who come here.

CENTRO Map p264

Xuànkù 炫酷

☎ 6561 8833, ext 6388; Kerry Center Hotel, 1 Guanghua Lu; cocktails Y75; ☯ 24hr; ⊕ Guomao

A favourite with visiting foreign businessmen, older expats and younger ones out to impress, Centro is a swish lounge bar with a black glossy bar, sofas and an eccentric carpet pattern. The service is impressive and there's live jazz during the week and a DJ on the weekends. The cocktails are good, but they should be for the prices they charge.

CLUB FOOTBALL CENTER

Map p264

万国群星足球俱乐部

☎ 6417 0497; www.wanguoqunxing.com; Red House Hotel, 10b Chunxiu Jie; beer from Y10; ☯ 11-2am (weekends until football matches finish); ⊕ Dongzhimen or Dongsishitiao

With its wall-to-wall football memorabilia, live English premiership action, big screens and yelping punters at the bar, this is the most genuine British pub in town. A must for anyone obsessed with the beautiful game and/or beer (Y10 for a bottle of Tsingdao) and/or pool and darts. There's a solid menu of pub food favourites. This is the focal point of Běijīng's amateur football scene and the place to come if you're looking for a team to join. If you sign up for the free membership, you'll get emails of forthcoming matches and events. It's an adjunct of the Red House Hotel (p186) and reception will direct you there. Or you can enter directly by going up the alley to the side of the Red House.

FACE BAR Map p264

妃思

☎ 6551 6738; 26 Dongcaoyuan, Gongrentiyuchang Nanlu; wine from Y50, cocktails from Y70; ☯ 6pm-late; ⊕ Dongsishitiao, then any ⌨ heading east

Stylish and expensive, Face is the Běijīng branch of a successful Shànghǎi bar. Spacious, tastefully decorated and comfortable, it attracts moneyed locals and the expat business crew.

FRANK'S PLACE Map pp258–9

翠欧

☎ 6437 8399; Jiangtai Xilu, west of the Rosedale Hotel; beers from Y20, cocktails from Y40; ☯ 11-2am

Reputedly the oldest bar in Běijīng, Frank's has shifted locations many times in the course of its life. Its latest incarnation is in the Lido area in northeast Chaoyang, an area popular with older expats and visiting business types staying in the nearby four-star hotels. Frank's caters to their needs by providing live sport on many TVs, pints of Guinness and German beer (Y50), English-speaking staff and average pub food. The place has a chameleon-like feel; if the NFL is on then it could be an American bar, if the footie is on you could be in England. There's pool and darts, occasional live music and an outside terrace in the summer.

GOOSE & DUCK PUB
Map p264
É Hé Yā 鹅和鸭
☎ 6538 1691; 1 Bihuju Nanlu; beer Y15; ☽ 24hr; ⊕ Dongsishitiao, then 🚌 431 heading east
Despite the British name, this is a sports bar that gets busy when big games are on. There are also pool tables and darts and a pub food–style menu. Located opposite the west gate of Chaoyang Park, it offers two drinks for the price of one between 4pm and 8pm.

Q BAR Map p264
Q 吧
☎ 6595 9239; top fl Eastern Inn Hotel, Nan Sanlitun Lu; cocktails from Y35; ☽ 6pm-2am; ⊕ Dongsishitiao, then 🚌 701 heading east
Possibly the most amenable cocktail lounge in the city, Q Bar benefits from a laid-back atmosphere, a solid music selection and some of the best-mixed drinks available in Běijīng. There's a long bar to perch at, sofas to sink into, or you can head to the large roof terrace when the weather's right.

There's a big 'Q' hanging off the side of the Eastern Inn Hotel to guide you there.

TREE Map p264
隐藏的树
☎ 6415 1954; 43 Sanlitun Beijie; beers from Y20; ☽ 11am-late Mon-Sat, 1pm-late Sun; ⊕ Dongsishitiao, then 🚌 701 heading east
Another refugee from the old Sanlitun South Bar Street, where it was known as the Hidden Tree, the Tree is a long-term favourite of expats, locals and tourists alike. There's a fine selection of Belgian beers (from Y40), decent pizzas cooked in a wood-fired oven (from Y45) and low-key live music from a Filipino band. It gets busy, but has a far less manic vibe than some of the surrounding bars. It's off the courtyard of the You Yi Youth Hostel (p185).

HǍIDIÀN 海淀

LUSH Map p271
LUSH 酒吧
☎ 8286 3566; 2nd fl, Bldg 1, Huaqing Jiayuan, Chengfu Lu; beers from Y15, cocktails from Y25; ☽ 24hr; ⊕ Wudaokou
For the hordes of students in Wǔdàokǒu, both foreign and local, all roads lead to Lush. During the day, it functions as a café with a Western menu, including filling sandwiches (from Y25). After dark, it becomes the epicentre of nightlife in the area. Every evening offers something different, whether it's movie screenings,

---

KARAOKE CRAZY

Western-style bars and clubs might be proliferating in China's big cities but karaoke remains the number one leisure pastime on the mainland. Known by the acronym 'KTV', there are over 100,000 karaoke joints in China and they range from seedy hole-in-the-wall operations that are often fronts for prostitution, to giant chains where the prices are as high as some of the notes you'll hit while singing.

For the Chinese, karaoke is where you go to hang out with your friends, or to unwind with your workmates after a hard week in the office. Westerners who aren't used to singing in public can find the experience nerve-wracking. But forget your inhibitions (alcohol comes in handy for that) and do as the locals do and you'll be surprised how quickly karaoke becomes addictive.

Although true karaoke fans will want to try crooning the latest mando-pop hits, most places have a selection of English-language songs. Some of the tunes might be a bit ancient, but you'll always find something you can sing. At the places listed below, drinks and snacks are available and the staff will happily help you out if you need backing vocals to add a semblance of credibility to your singing. It's always advisable to book ahead at weekends.

Melody (Map p264; ☎ 6551 0808; A-77 Chaoyangmenwai Dajie, Cháoyáng; small room before 8pm per hr Y35, after 8pm per hr Y109; ☽ 8-2am)

Partyworld (Map p264; ☎ 6588 3333; Fanli Building, 22 Chaowaishichang Jie, Cháoyáng; rooms from Y49; ☽ 7-2am)

live music, a pub quiz, DJs and an open-mic night for aspiring poets and singers. There's a daily happy hour, where it's two drinks for the price of one, from 8pm to 10pm.

CLUBBING

Běijīng's clubs might not be cutting edge in comparison to Berlin or London, but they're increasingly busy as more and more locals tune into the dance music lifestyle. Popularity though, has brought a cookie-cutter approach with many places, especially those in the Sanlitun area, resembling each other. But thanks to the international DJs who fly in and out of Běijīng on an almost weekly basis, there's a fair variety in the sounds you can hear. The capital's clubs are also a good place to observe the cultural divide between East and West. Many Chinese, especially the thirtysomething businessman crowd, visit nightclubs to knock back expensive whisky with green tea (it tastes better than it sounds) and to play dice games, while refusing to set foot on the dance floor. Consequently, most dancing areas in Běijīng clubs are smaller than the ones you'll find in the West. Bear in mind that if a top foreign DJ is playing, you'll need to get tickets in advance and the entrance fee will be far higher than normal.

BANANA Map pp268-9
Bānànà 吧那那
☎ 6526 3939; SciTech Hotel, 22 Jianguomenwai Dajie; Y20-30; ☽ 8.30pm-4am Sun-Thu, 8.30pm-5am Fri & Sat; ◎ Jianguomen or Yonganli
It's been around a while but Banana continues to pack them in, thanks to its no-nonsense mix of happy house and other attractions, like dancers in cages, fire-eaters and bongo players. The upstairs Spicy Lounge offers a more eclectic mix of sounds, depending who is on the decks.

CARGO Map p264
咖钩
☎ 6551 6898/78; 6 Gongrentiyuchang Xilu; Y40; ☽ 8pm-late; ◎ Dongsishitiao, then any 🚌 heading east
The best of the cluster of clubs located in the strip just south of the west gate of the Workers' Stadium, Cargo consistently flies

in some of the biggest names in dance music to play to a more music-savvy crowd than you get in most of Běijīng's clubs.

DESTINATION Map p264
Mùdìdì 目的地
☎ 6551 5138; 7 Gongrentiyuchang Xilu; Y30; ☽ 6pm-late; ◎ Dongsishitiao, then any 🚌 heading east
Běijīng's premier gay and lesbian club is a little more spartan in design than most of the city's other clubs, but that doesn't seem to worry its many fans who flock there at the weekends.

LATINOS Map p264
拉提诺
☎ 6409 6997; A12 Historical Complex, Nanxincang; ☽ 9pm-late; ◎ Dongsishitiao
Salsa has taken off in a big way in Běijīng in the last couple of years and this is one of the busiest clubs in the city. There's a big dance floor to show off your moves, the house band is from South America and guest DJs spin the latest Latin sounds.

MIX Map p264
Mìkèsī 梅克斯俱乐部
☎ 6530 2889; inside the Workers' Stadium north gate; Y40; ☽ 7.30pm-5am; ◎ Dongsishitiao
Hip-hop and R&B is what draws the crowd who come here and they're some of the most enthusiastic dancers in the city. Opposite Vics (below).

PROPAGANDA Map p271
五星
☎ 8286 3679; east gate, Huaqing Jiayuan; ☽ 8pm-4am; ◎ Wudaokou
Wǔdàokǒu's student crew are drawn like moths to this unpretentious club, thanks to cheap drinks, party hip-hop sounds and suitably grungy surroundings.

VICS Map p264
Wēikèsī 威克斯
☎ 6593 6215; inside the Workers' Stadium north gate; Y40 Fri, Y50 Sat; ☽ 7pm-late; ◎ Dongsishitiao
Vics is not the most sophisticated nightclub in the world but it remains a favourite with the younger crowd. The music is mostly standard R&B and hip-hop, but the

sounds are not the only reason people come here. There's an infamous ladies night on Wednesdays (Y30 and free drinks for women before midnight) and weekends see it rammed with the footloose and fancy free. If you can't score here, you never will.

WORLD OF SUZIE WONG
Map p264
Sūxī Huáng 苏西黄
☎ 6593 6049; 1a Nongzhanguan Lu, west gate Chaoyang Park; Y50; ☼ 7pm-3.30am; ⓔ Dongsishitiao, then ⌂ 431 heading east
Opium-den chic with a 21st-century twist, which means traditional wooden beds to recline on while sipping fancy cocktails, decent DJs and models galore, Suzie Wong's is a Běijīng institution. While it's not as hip or exclusive as it once was, it's still pretty glamorous for Běijīng and it's always busy. You have to get there early if you want to claim a bed or a space on the small roof terrace (during the summer), or even just to get in sometimes.

BEIJING OPERA & TRADITIONAL CHINESE MUSIC

Beijing opera, or Peking opera as it is still sometimes referred to, is one of those aspects of Chinese cultural life that can seem impenetrable to foreigners. Everything about it, from the costumes to the singing style and, of course, the language, conspires to maintain its mystique. But if you've only ever seen it televised, then taking in a live performance will help you understand it far better. Bear in mind that the plot lines are simple and not dissimilar to Shakespearean tragedy, including elements of low comic relief, while the long performances aren't meant to be viewed in stunned silence. The operas have natural highs and lows, which you'll be able to gauge from the reaction of your fellow audience members. Let them be your guide. Above all, remember Beijing opera is as much a visual experience as it a musical one (for more details on Beijing opera, see p35). You can also tune into CCTV 11, which is solely devoted to traditional opera.

CHANG'AN GRAND THEATRE
Map pp268-9
Chángān Dàjùchǎng 长安大剧场
☎ 6510 1309; Chang'an Bldg, 7 Jianguomennei Dajie; tickets Y50-380; ☼ performances 7.30pm; ⓔ Jianguomen
This theatre offers a genuine experience, and the erudite audience chatters knowledgably among themselves during weekend matinee classics and evening performances.

HUGUANG GUILD HALL Map pp266-7
Húguǎng Huìguǎn 湖广会馆
☎ 6351 8284; 3 Hufangqiao Lu; tickets Y150-580; ☼ performances 7.30pm; ⓔ Hepingmen, then ⌂ 25
Similarly decorated to the Zhengyici Theatre (p148), with balconies surrounding the canopied stage, this theatre dates back to 1807. It is the site where the Kuomintang, led by Dr Sun Yat-sen, was established in 1912. The interior is magnificent, coloured in red, green and gold, and decked out with tables and a stone floor. There's also a very small opera museum (Y10) opposite the theatre displaying operatic scores, old catalogues and other paraphernalia. There are also colour illustrations of the *liǎnpǔ* (types of Beijing opera facial makeup) – examples include the *hóu liǎnpǔ* (monkey face) and the *chǒujué liǎnpǔ* (clown face). Sadly, there are few English captions.

LAO SHE TEAHOUSE Map pp268-9
Lǎo Shě Cháguǎn 老舍茶馆
☎ 6303 6830, 6304 6334; www.laosheteahouse .com; 3rd fl, 3 Qianmen Xidajie; evening tickets Y40-280; ☼ 7.30pm; ⓔ Hepingmen or Qianmen
Lao She Teahouse (west of the large KFC on Qianmen Xidajie) has nightly shows, mostly in Chinese. The performances here are a combination of Beijing opera, cross-talk and acrobatics. Prices depend on the type of show and where you sit. Enter the teahouse past statues of Weituo, Sakyamuni and Guanyin on your left and an effigy of President Bush on your right. There are several halls: in the small hall there is folk music (2.30pm to 5pm Monday to Friday), and in the large hall there are folk music and tea ceremony performances (3pm to 4.30pm Friday), theatrical performances (2pm to 4.30pm Wednesday and Friday),

and matinee Beijing opera performances (3pm to 4.30pm Sunday). Evening performances of Beijing opera, folk art and music, acrobatics and magic (7.50pm to 9.20pm) are the most popular. Phone ahead or check online for the schedule. The teahouse is named after the celebrated Běijīng writer Lao She, who has a museum dedicated to him (p93). Major credit cards accepted.

LIYUAN THEATRE Map pp266-7

Líyuán Jùchǎng 梨园剧场

☎ 6301 6688, ext 8860; Qianmen Jianguo Hotel, 175 Yong'an Lu; tickets Y40-280; ⊙ martial arts 12.30pm, opera 7.30pm; ◉ Hepingmen, then ⊟ 25
This touristy theatre, across the lobby of the Qianmen Jianguo Hotel (p187) and past the mannequins outside, has regular performances for Beijing opera greenhorns, performed over servings of Peking duck and other local delicacies. The setting isn't traditional and it resembles a cinema auditorium (the stage façade is the only authentic touch), but there are also matinee shows of gōngfu (kung fu) performed by Shaolin monks (see p152).

SANWEI BOOKSTORE Map pp266-7

Sānwèi Shūwū 三味书屋

☎ 6601 3204; 60 Fuxingmennei Dajie; cover charge Y30; ⊙ performances 8pm; ◉ Xidan
Opposite the Minzu Hotel, this place has a small bookshop on the ground floor and a teahouse on the second. It features music with traditional Chinese instruments on Saturday night. On other evenings, you can hear live jazz here.

ZHENGYICI THEATRE Map pp266-7

Zhèngyìcí Jùchǎng 正乙祠剧场

☎ 8315 1649; 220 Xiheyan Dajie; Y380-680; ⊙ performances 7.30pm Thu, Fri & Sat; ◉ Hepingmen
Originally an ancient temple, this ornately decorated building is the oldest wooden theatre in the country and the best place in the city to experience Beijing opera and other operatic disciplines like Kunqu. The theatre was restored by a private businessman with an interest in reviving the dying art, and it was reopened in 1995 after a long period of disrepair. Opera can be appreciated over a dinner of Peking duck (Y200 for a full meal).

LIVE MUSIC
ROCK, POP, JAZZ, BLUES & COUNTRY

There might be an instinctive Chinese fondness for the manufactured, syrupy sound of Canto pop or Taiwanese boy bands, but some of Běijīng's residents have grittier tastes that require music with more bite and imagination. Having discovered Western rock music in the early '80s via the cassette tapes of foreign students, Běijīngers have always been at the forefront of the Chinese rock scene. Now there are all sorts of acts plugging away on an admittedly limited circuit. The best bands land record contracts with Japanese or Taiwanese labels, or obscure US ones, but most survive by endless gigging. Běijīng though, is still a backwater when it comes to international pop and rock acts, few of whom make it here.

You can find musical events of varying quality lifting Běijīng's roofs every night of the week, and there should be something up your street, whether it be rock, indie, metal, punk, folk or jazz. Check the expat mags (p227) for full listings of who's playing.

2 KOLEGAS Map pp258-9

两个好朋友

☎ 8196 4820; 21 Liangmaqiao Lu (inside the drive-in movie park); Y20 or sometimes free; ⊙ 8pm-2am Mon-Sat, 10am-9pm Sun; ◉ Dongzhimen, then ⊟ 909; or ◉ Dongsishitiao, then ⊟ 701
Tucked away to the side of Běijīng's drive-in cinema, this is a great little venue that hosts ska and reggae DJs, as well as local punkers and a fair proportion of out-of-town acts. In the summer, you can take a break from the aural assault by sitting outside with a beer, while munching yángròu chuàn (skewers of lamb).

CD JAZZ CAFÉ Map p264

Sēndì Juéshì Jùlèbù 森帝爵士

☎ 6506 8288; south of the main gate of the Agricultural Exhibition Centre, Dongsanhuan Beilu; ⊙ 4pm-2am; ◉ Dongsishitiao, then ⊟ 701 heading east
A mainstay on the Běijīng jazz scene, this place has regular live performances on Fridays and Saturdays. No cover charge, but the drinks are expensive.

D-22

Map p271

D-22 酒吧

☎ 6265 3177; 13 Chengfu Lu; entrance from Y20; ☻ 6pm-2am Tue-Sun; ⓜ Wudaokou

A new addition to Běijīng's live music venues, D-22 is a friendly, intimate place dedicated to showcasing the more experimental Běijīng bands and the odd, visiting foreign act. It also shows films on Tuesdays and Wednesdays.

EAST SHORE JAZZ CAFÉ

Map p262

Dōngàn Kāfēi 东岸咖啡

☎ 8403 2131; 2nd fl, 2 Qianhai Nanyanlu, just off Dianmenwai Dajie; ☻ 11-2am; ⓜ Gulou Dajie

Cui Jian's saxophonist, whose quartet play here, opened this chilled venue by Qianhai Lake. It's a place to hear the best local jazz bands, with live performances from Thursdays to Sundays, in a more authentic atmosphere than the CD Jazz Café. Expect lengthy jam sessions in the wee hours of the morning. There's no cover charge and the drinks are reasonably priced.

JIANGJINJIU

Map p262

Jiāngjìn Jiǔbā 疆进酒吧

☎ 8405 0124; 2 Zhongku Hutong; ☻ 11-2am; ⓜ Gulou Dajie

Situated between the Drum and Bell Towers, this is a friendly café/bar that puts on lots of folk and ethnic minority, particularly Uighur, bands. No cover charge.

MAO LIVEHOUSE

Map p262

猫

☎ 6402 5080; 111 Gulou Dongdajie; from Y30; ☻ 8pm-late; ⓜ Andingmen

Běijīng's newest live venue is quickly establishing itself as the unofficial HQ of the local music scene. Moody muso types can be found boasting or bemoaning their luck over their Yanjing beers (Y10) in the separate bar, while the actual concert area is big enough to give the gigs a sense of occasion, but still small enough to feel intimate. The décor is functional and the sound tight. All sorts of bands, including some from overseas, play here. At the time of writing, the venue was only open for concerts.

NAMELESS HIGHLAND Map pp258-9

Wúmíng Gāodì Jiǔbā 无名高地酒吧

☎ 6489 1613; Bldg 14, Anhuili Area 1, Yayuncun; Y30 or sometimes free; ☻ 7pm-2am; ⓜ Datun Line 5, under construction

All sorts of groups, from folk to death metal via Brit-pop clones and punk acts, take to the stage here. It's a rare night when they don't have a band on. It's one of Běijīng's larger, better-organised venues. You'll need to take a taxi to get here.

STAR LIVE Map p262

Xīngguāng Xiànchǎng 星光现场

☎ 6425 5166; 79 Heping Xijie (inside 3rd fl, Tango nightclub); from Y40; ☻ 6.30pm-late; ⓜ Yonghegong

It's a great space but eccentric management make this place a bit hit and miss. But it's the only venue in Běijīng where you'll see visiting international bands who aren't big enough to play the stadium circuit.

WHAT? BAR Map p262

Shénme? Jiǔbā 什么酒吧

☎ 133 4112 2757; 72 Beichang Jie; Y25 (includes free beer); ☻ 2pm-late; ⓜ Tiananmen Xi, then ☒ 5 heading north

If you like to get up close and personal with the bands you go and see, then this is the place for you. That doesn't mean it's groupie heaven here; rather it's just that this venue is so small that the audience might as well be on stage with the musicians. It's a good place to hear up-and-coming local talent. Just north of the west gate of the Forbidden City.

CLASSICAL MUSIC

As the nation's cultural centre, Běijīng has several venues around town where the city's increasingly cosmopolitan residents can satisfy their highbrow needs. The annual 30-day Beijing Music Festival takes place between October and November, and is an excellent time to catch international and homegrown classical music. By the time you read this the new National Grand Theater (Map pp268–9) to the west of Tiananmen Square, which will also host classical music, should be completed. Again, refer to the expat listings mags (p227) for details of what's on and what's coming up.

BEIJING CONCERT HALL

Map pp266-7

Běijīng Yīnyuè Tīng 北京音乐厅

☎ 6605 7006/5812; 1 Beixinhua Jie; Y60-580; ⓦ performances 7.30pm; ◎ Tiananmen Xi or Xidan

The 2000-seat Beijing Concert Hall showcases performances of classical Chinese music as well as international repertoires of Western classical music.

CENTURY THEATRE Map p264

世纪剧院

☎ 6466 4805; 40 Liangmaqiao Lu; Y80-880; ⓦ 7.30pm; ◎ Dongsishitiao, then 🚌 701

Musical presentations here are perhaps smaller in scale than those at other venues – they feature smaller orchestras and solo performances where the violin, cello and flute get centre stage. Ballet performances are also presented.

FORBIDDEN CITY CONCERT HALL

Map pp268-9

Zhōngshān Gōngyuán Yīnyuè Táng
中山公园音乐堂

☎ 6559 8285; Zhongshan Park; Y50-680; ⓦ performances 7.30pm; ◎ Tiananmen Xi

Located on the eastern side of Zhongshan Park, this is the most central venue for performances of classical and traditional Chinese music. Tickets can be purchased at the concert hall box office inside the Friendship Store (p162).

POLY PLAZA INTERNATIONAL THEATRE Map p264

Bǎolì Dàshà Guójì Jùyuàn 保利大厦国际剧院

☎ 6500 1188, ext 5126; 14 Dongzhimen Nandajie; Y180-880; ⓦ performances 7.30pm; ◎ Dongsishitiao

Located in the Poly Plaza right by Dongsishitiao subway station, this venue hosts a wide range of performances including ballet, classical music, opera and traditional Chinese folk music.

THEATRE

Gong Li and Zhang Ziyi, big names of the big screen, might have learned their art at the **Central Academy of Drama** (Zhōngyāng Xìjù Xuéyuàn), but theatre (*huàjù*) never commanded much of a following in China.

Spoken drama appeared in China only in the 20th century, but never won the hearts of the masses. The great 20th-century playwright Cao Yu penned tragic family tableaux, such as the stifling *Thunderstorm* and *Daybreak*. Lao She is also famed for his ironic social commentary and observations of Běijīng life, with *Teahouse* being his most famous play.

Much of the last century saw drama stubbing its toe on unexpected political corners, such as the Cultural Revolution. As a literary art, creative drama is still unable to express itself fully and remains sadly sidelined. Plays do, however, make it to the stage, so if you want to know what's waiting in the wings in Běijīng, try some of the venues below. The expat listings mags (p227) have up-to-date details of what's playing.

CAPITAL THEATRE Map p262

Shǒudū Jùyuàn 首都剧场

☎ 6524 9847/6512; 22 Wangfujing Dajie; Y80-600; ⓦ performances 7.30pm Tue-Sun; ◎ Wangfujing

Located in the heart of the city on Wangfujing Dajie, this central theatre has regular performances of contemporary Chinese productions and is home to a number of theatre companies, including the People's Art Experimental Theatre. Classic plays in the Chinese language often feature.

CENTRAL ACADEMY OF DRAMA THEATRE Map p262

Zhōngyāng Xìjù Xuéyuàn Jùchǎng
中央戏剧学院剧场

☎ 8404 6174; Y60-280; ⓦ 7.30pm; 39 Dongmianhua Hutong; ◎ Andingmen

Situated just off Nanluogu Xiang, China's future movie stars train at this academy and can be seen here in regular performances of Chinese-language plays. Bear in mind the actors, and sometimes the directors, are students, so the productions can be hit-or-miss.

CHINA PUPPET THEATRE

Map pp258-9

Zhōngguó Mùòu Jùyuàn 中国木偶剧院

☎ 6425 4847; 1A Anhua Xili, Beisanhuan Zhonglu; Y50-100; ⓦ performances 10.30am & 2pm; ◎ Andingmen or Gulou Dajie

This popular theatre has regular events, including shadow play, puppetry, music and dance. A good place to take kids if they're rebelling over the prospect of more sightseeing.

CINEMAS

Movies, both domestic and foreign, are hugely popular in China, as you'd expect from the country with the third-largest film industry in the world. However, a severe shortage of cinemas (*diànyǐngyuàn*), just 1300 or so for a population of 1.3 billion, stringent censorship and a strict quota on the number of foreign films that can be shown each year means the country has never had a big cinema-going culture. In Běijīng, the combination of high ticket prices and rampant DVD piracy ensures that going to the movies is a middle-class pursuit.

Chinese-language films almost never have subtitles when shown in cinemas. Before you go and see a Western movie, be sure to check whether it is screened with subtitles (*zìmù*) or has been dubbed (*pèiyin*) into Chinese. There are a number of alternative venues in Běijīng that show Chinese movies with English subtitles, as well as Western arthouse and classic movies. They're often the best places to see films. Various foreign cultural centres and embassies also have screenings of their native cinema. See the expat mags (p227) for schedules.

Apart from that, you can offer up futile prayers for a good movie to be shown on CCTV, or you can tune into your hotel film channels. But if you have a laptop with you, or a DVD player in your hotel room, then you won't have to travel far to find someone willing to sell you something to play on it.

CHERRY LANE THEATRE
Map pp258-9
北京电影发行公司
☎ 139 0113 4745; www.cherrylanemovies.com.cn; inside Kent Centre, 29 Liangmaqiao Lu, Anjialou; Y50; ⊙ Dongzhimen, then 🚌 909 or ⊙ Dongsishitiao, then 🚌 701
Located in a Peking opera photo studio, Cherry Lane provides a valuable service in screening contemporary Chinese films with English subtitles, many of which were never shown in domestic cinemas because

the censors didn't like them. However, the screen here has seen better days and sometimes they put on a DVD of the movie rather than showing a 35mm print. Screenings take place every Friday and Saturday at 8pm.

EAST GATE CINEMA
Map p264
东环影城
☎ 6418 5931; Bldg B, basement East Gate Plaza, Dongzhong Jie; from Y60 (half price before noon); ⊙ Dongsishitiao
Shows the latest big releases, both domestic and foreign, and is the only cinema in town that offers double seats (from Y140).

STAR CITY
Map pp268-9
新世纪影城
☎ 8518 5399; www.xfilmcity.com; shop BB65, basement, Oriental Plaza, 1 Dongchang'an Jie; Y60-80; ⊙ Wangfujing
This six-screen cinema is the best place to go and see Western movies that get released in China because they always have one screening a day with the original, un-dubbed print (but that doesn't mean it hasn't been cut by the scissor-happy Chinese censors). It's a plush multiplex that feels no different from its equivalents in the West.

SUNDONGAN CINEMA CITY
Map p262
新东安影城
☎ 6528 1988; 5th fl, Sundongan Plaza, Wangfujing Dajie; Y30 for Chinese movies, Y40-50 for foreign films (half price on Tuesdays); ⊙ Wangfujing
Don't expect a huge selection, but this is one of Běijīng's most conveniently located cinemas and there's usually a Hollywood feature showing.

Other cinemas around town worth trying your luck at include the **Dahua Cinema** (Dàhuá Diànyǐngyuàn; Map p262; ☎ 6525 0343; 82 Dongdan Beidajie, Dōngchéng); **Drive-in Cinema** (Map pp258–9; ☎ 6431 9595; 100 Daliangmaqiao; only open May to September); **UME International Cineplex** (Map p271; ☎ 8211 5566; 44 Kexueyuan Nanlu, Hǎidiàn) and **Xinjiekou Cinema** (Map pp260–1; ☎ 6225 2767; 69 Xizhimennei Dajie, Xīchéng).

ACROBATICS & MARTIAL ARTS

Two thousand years old, Chinese acrobatics is one of the best deals in town. Most of today's acrobatic repertoire originates from the works of Zhang Heng (AD 25–120), who is credited with creating acts including balancing on a high pole, jumping through hoops, swallowing knives and spitting fire. Wuqiao County in Héběi is said to be the original bastion of Chinese acrobatics. As well as the following listings, acrobatic performances are also held at the Dongyue Temple (p94).

The monks of Shaolin from Songshan in Hénán province have gained an international reputation for their legendary fighting skills honed from a recipe of physical deprivation, spiritual illumination, patience and ironclad willpower. They can be seen in action at the Liyuan Theatre (p148).

See p154 for details on participating in martial arts classes.

CHAOYANG THEATRE Map p264

Cháoyáng Jùchǎng 朝阳剧场

☎ 6507 2421; 36 Dongsanhuan Beilu; Y180-380; ⊗ performances 5.15pm, 7.30pm; ⊕ Chaoyangmen
Probably the most accessible place for foreign visitors and often bookable through your hotel, this theatre is the venue for visiting acrobatic troupes filling the stage with plate-spinning and hoop-jumping.

TIANQIAO ACROBATICS THEATRE

Map pp268-9
万圣剧场

☎ 6303 7449; 95 Tianqiao Shichang Lu; Y100-200; ⊗ performances 7.15pm; ⊕ Qianmen, then ⊜ 819
West of the Temple of Heaven Park, this 100-year-old theatre offers one of Běijīng's best acrobatic displays performed by the Beijing Acrobatic Troupe. Less touristy than the other venues, the high-wire display here is awesome. The entrance is down the eastern side of the building.

UNIVERSAL THEATRE (HEAVEN & EARTH THEATRE) Map p264

Tiāndì Jùchǎng 天地剧场

☎ 6416 0757, 6416 9893; 10 Dongzhimen Nandajie; Y100-300; ⊗ performances 7.15pm; ⊕ Dongsishitiao

Around 100m north of Poly Plaza, young performers from the China National Acrobatic Troupe perform their mind-bending, joint-popping contortions. This is a favourite with tour groups, so book ahead. Tickets are pricier the further from the stage you sit. Look for the awful white tower that looks like it should be in an airport – that's where you buy your tickets (credit cards not accepted).

SPORTS, HEALTH & FITNESS

It's worth getting in touch with your embassy's cultural section, which should have useful information about teams, sports clubs, health centres and other health-and-fitness-related questions you might have.

WATCHING SPORT

The impressive National Stadium, known locally as the 'Bird's Nest', thanks to its intricate design of interlocking steel girders, will be the main venue for all future national and international athletics championships. The Workers' Stadium (Gōngrén Tǐyùguǎn; Map p264) in the Sanlitun area, is another venue, while athletics events are also held at the Asian Games Village, just within the Fourth Ring Rd in the north of town. With China determined to top the medals table at the 2008 Olympics, more and more emphasis is being put on athletics.

The Chinese are avid football (zúqiú) fans, but most prefer to watch foreign leagues like the English Premiership, Italy's Serie A and Spain's La Liga, rather than their own China Super League. A succession of match-fixing scandals, dubious refereeing and the generally poor quality of the football means that only a few thousand diehard fans turn out to watch Běijīng Guo'an, the capital's team, play their home matches at the Workers' Stadium. The national team has failed to impress in recent years too, failing to qualify for the 2006 World Cup.

Basketball is more and more popular, with China's leading player, the giant Yao Ming, who plays for the Houston Rockets in the NBA, a massive star. The Chinese league, the CBA, is televised and a number of rising young players are being tipped for future success in the NBA. The local team, the Beijing Ducks, play in the far western suburbs at the **Shougang Basketball Centre** (☎ 8829 6158, 159 Fushi Lu, Shijingshan District).

HEALTH & FITNESS
Ballet
The **Western Ballet School** (Map p264; ☎ 6507 1426; 1st fl, Kempinski Hotel, 50 Liangmaqiao Lu) in Cháoyáng is a popular ballet school offering three-month courses (Y900) for children aged between four and 14.

Fencing
Swashbucklers can find a place in Běijīng to practise their epee, sabre and foil strokes. The **Fenxing Fencing Club** (Map pp258–9; ☎ 6492 9041; Olympic Sports Center, inside the Asian Games Complex, 1 Anding Lu, Yayuncun, Cháoyáng) provides equipment and tuition at a range of levels. Classes are held seven days a week from 10am.

Fitness Clubs
CHINA WORLD FITNESS CENTRE
Map pp268–9
中国大饭店健身中心
☎ 6505 2266, ext 33; 1 Jianguomenwai Dajie; per day Y200; ⏰ 6am-11pm; ⓜ Guomao
A 20m pool and squash courts, as well as a steam-bath, Jacuzzi and the usual classes are on offer here. It's in the same complex as the China World Hotel (p182).

EVOLUTION FITNESS CENTRE
Map pp268-9
进步健身中心
☎ 6567 0266; Jianguomenwai Dajie & Dongsanhuan Zhonglu; ⏰ 6.30am-10.30pm Mon-Fri, 8am-9pm Sat & Sun; per day Y100; ⓜ Guomao
Exercise on your own or join a class for aerobics, *tàijíquán* (taichi), hip-hop dancing, kickboxing, Latin dancing, yoga or aquaerobics. Personal training programs, fitness consultation and sports therapy are also available, and there's a 25m five-lane pool.

Football
An ever-increasing number of expat 11-a-side and 5-a-side teams play in Běijīng in a variety of leagues. If you are inter-ested in joining a team or watching a team play, get in touch with the **Club Football Center** (p144), where you can meet like-minded folk over a pint of beer who should be able to steer you in the right direction. Games are played all over the city.

It is also possible to catch the big foreign domestic leagues from Europe on either CCTV 5 or BTV 6 on your hotel TV. Alternatively, try Běijīng sports bars like the **Club Football Center** (p144), **Goose & Duck Pub** (p145) or **Frank's Place** (p144) for live matches on ESPN or Star Sports. Phone ahead to find out what's on.

Golf
The game of golf (*gāoěrfūqiú*) enjoys high prestige in China and is becoming such a part of business life that some universities are making golf lessons compulsory for their business students. Běijīng's freezing winters though, don't lend themselves to a life on the links. Nor is it cheap to get on a course. In fact, you can pick up a basic set of clubs in one of Běijīng's many golfing stores for not much more than a day's green fees. Such is the sport's growing popularity that it's advisable to book ahead.

BEIJING GOLF CLUB
Map pp258-9
Běijīng Gāoěrfūqiú Jùlèbù
北京高尔夫球俱乐部
☎ 8947 0245; Shunyi; green fees Mon-Fri Y800, Sat & Sun Y1200 ⏰ 7.30am-dusk
The Beijing Golf Club's 36-hole golf course is northeast of town on the eastern bank of Chaobai River (Chaobai He).

BEIJING INTERNATIONAL GOLF CLUB
Map pp258-9
Běijīng Guójì Gāoěrfūqiú Jùlèbù
北京国际高尔夫球俱乐部
☎ 6076 2288; Changping; green fees Mon-Fri Y800, Sat & Sun & public holidays Y1400; ⏰ 7am-7pm
This Japanese-designed 18-hole course is 35km north of town, close to the **Ming Tombs** (p197) and north of Shisanling Reservoir. Hitting that little ball around is not cheap, but the course is in top condition and the scenery is spectacular. You can rent a set of golf clubs and shoes for an additional fee. You will also have to pay the compulsory caddy fee of Y200.

Hiking & Biking

Several groups in Běijīng organise hiking and biking expeditions to villages and temples outside town. Needless to say, this can be an excellent way for visitors to get out and see sights that are more remote and difficult to reach. **Beijing Hikers** (☎ 139 1002 5516; www.bjhikers.com) organises regular hikes (Y200 per person) and is open to everyone, including children (Y150 for under 12s). The price includes round-trip transport, snacks and drinks. **Mountain Bikers of Beijing** (themob@404.com.au) coordinate one-day, 40km to 120km weekend mountain bike rides at locations outside town.

Ice Skating

Běijīng's winter chill clamps the city's lakes in sheets of ice – but the usual warnings apply about safety and ice thickness for those who want to skate (liū bīng). Popular outdoor venues include the lake in Beihai Park and the Shichahai lakes southwest of the Drum Tower, where local entrepreneurs will rent you skates, as well as the lakes on the campuses of Peking and Tsinghua Universities. Do not try skating on the moat around the Forbidden City.

LE COOL ICE RINK Map pp268-9
国贸溜冰场

☎ 6505 5776; basement 2, China World Shopping Mall, 1 Jianguomenwai Dajie; per 90 min Y30-50;
🕙 10am-10pm; Ⓜ Guomao
This is the most accessible indoor ice rink in town. Located in the basement of the China World Shopping Mall, it's easy to reach and perfect for kids. The cost varies depending on the time of day you skate; skate hire is included.

Martial Arts

Běijīng is an excellent place to stretch a leg. Legions of elderly folk start the day with a bout of tàijíquán, and you'll get used to seeing octogenarians doing the splits without grimacing. Certainly, if you have any interest in China's martial arts heritage, you won't want to miss out on this opportunity to learn from the experts.

Many visitors will probably settle for a dose of tàijíquán and some qìgōng (exercise that channels qì or energy) to limber up, learn some breathing techniques and get the blood

circulating. More adventurous visitors can dig a bit deeper into China's exciting fighting arts; you never know what you'll unearth.

Visiting Běijīng's parks early in the morning and approaching practitioners is possible, if you speak Chinese. You might encounter that grand master of Eight Trigram Palm (Bāguàzhǎng), willing to instruct you in some deadly device. Or you might catch an early morning glimpse of a White Eyebrow Boxing (Báiméiquán) expert going through clandestine moves. Unfortunately, it's easy to get out of one's depth. Chinese martial arts can be bewilderingly enigmatic and some are deeply esoteric; on top of which you might find yourself learning tae kwon do (a Korean martial art), kickboxing or some jazzy health system. Another problem is that some teachers insist that students prove their loyalty by making them wait for long periods before they're admitted to a class. Also, you will probably encounter communication problems if you don't speak Chinese.

Martial arts lessons in English are held daily at the **Jinghua Wushu Association** (Map p264; ☎ 6465 3388; Kempinski Hotel, Liangmaqiao Lu). The teachers are all trained in the traditional Shaolin forms and charge Y90 a lesson. The **Evolution Fitness Centre** (p153) also has classes in English. Otherwise, check the classified pages of the expat mags (p227), as English-speaking gōngfu teachers occasionally advertise here. Be aware that some martial artists exploit the gullible, while a great number of teachers are decidedly substandard. Try to get a personal recommendation from other enthusiasts if possible.

See p152 for details on watching martial arts performances in Běijīng.

Massage

Walking around Běijīng's vast distances can put serious stresses on both ligaments and musculature. Thankfully, there are several places in town where you can have your feet and body massaged and reinvigorated.

BODHI Map p264
菩提会所

☎ 6417 9595; 17 Gongrentiyuchang Beilu;
🕙 11.30-12.30am; Ⓜ Dongsishitiao
The serene setting just moments away from the madness of Běijīng's traffic helps you shift gears straightaway, and that's before the many masseurs here get to work in one

THE SECRETS OF TAICHI

Characterised by its lithe and graceful movements, *tàijíquán* (太极拳; literally 'Fist of the Supreme Ultimate'), also known as taichi, is an ancient Chinese physical discipline practised by legions of Chinese the land over.

Considerable confusion exists about taichi – is it a martial art, a form of meditation, a *qìgōng* (气功) style or an exercise? In fact, taichi can be each and all of these, depending on what you seek from the art and how deep you dig into its mysteries.

As a straightforward health regimen, taichi strengthens the leg muscles, exercises the joints, gives the cardiovascular system a good work out and promotes flexibility. It also relaxes the body, dissolving stress, loosening the joints and generating a feel of well-being.

It may look undemanding, but the 108-movement, 20-minute Yang-style long form is tiring, while the low postures of the Chen style of taichi – closest in essence of all the taichi styles to Shaolin boxing – can be excruciatingly strenuous to perform and will have your legs shaking with the strain.

Taichi is indeed a superlative system of *qìgōng*, and despite being a moving sequence of *qìgōng* moves in itself, the art is also taught with stationary exercises to circulate *qì*. All of the benefits associated with *qìgōng* come with the practice of taichi.

As a system of meditation, taichi promotes relaxation and makes practitioners feel both centred and focused. Taichi will also introduce you to the meditation techniques of the Taoists, as the art is closely allied to the philosophy of Taoism.

Taichi can be undertaken as martial arts training as all the movements can ultimately be traced to Shaolin, although to be used effectively for this purpose requires a huge investment of time and patience, compared to other more direct martial arts. In order to use taichi effectively, the student has to learn how to relax the body during confrontation, and this requires suppressing one's instincts to tense up when threatened. Martial arts practice commences with 'push hands', a two-person routine where one student tries to unbalance the other. 'Push hands' develops sensitivity in the hands and teaches the student to relax the body in all situations. If adept at taichi, it is far easier to learn other martial arts, as the student will have learned a way of moving that is common to all of the fighting arts.

Taichi students outdo each other with fables of super-human exploits by legendary taichi masters, with anecdotes becoming more implausible at each retelling. Stories abound of masters who can crush pieces of ceramic between their fingers, fling their opponents 30ft across the room with a shrug or return hardened karate practitioners to square one. Such anecdotes dangle tempting carrots in front of students on their gruelling and elusive path to mastery of their art.

If taking up taichi, a few useful pointers will help you progress in your practice:

- When executing a movement, bodily motion and power is directed by the waist before moving to the hands (observe a skilled practitioner and see how the motion reaches the hands last). The hands never lead the movement.
- When performing a form (as the moving sets are called), keep your head on a level, neither rising nor dipping.
- Practise taichi as if suspended by an invisible thread from a point at the top of your head.
- Don't lean forward or backwards and keep your torso vertical.
- Relax your shoulders and let your weight sink downwards.

of their comfy private rooms. Bodhi offers excellent foot and full-body massages, both Y138 for an hour (Y78 before 5pm, Monday to Thursday), as well as facials, aromatherapy and other treatments. You get free snacks and drinks here, and with TVs in all the rooms you can lie back and watch a DVD while being pummelled into shape. It's opposite the north gate of the Workers' Stadium, just a few metres from the Xinjiang Red Rose Restaurant (p133).

DRAGONFLY THERAPEUTIC RETREAT
Map p264
悠庭保健会所

☎ 6593 6066; 1st fl, Eastern Inn Hotel, Nan Sanlitun Lu; ☽ 11-1am; ⊚ Dongsishitiao, then 🚍 701

This Shànghǎi chain has recently arrived in Běijīng. The surroundings aren't as pleasant as Bodhi, but the staff know what they're doing. An hour-long full body massage is Y120.

Running

Běijīng's toxic atmosphere might deter you from sampling extra lungfuls of air, but some groups organise runs in, around and outside town. **Hash House Harriers** (www.hash.cn) – the eccentric expat organisation ('drinkers with a running problem') that originated with the British in Malaysia – organises 8km to 10km runs most Sundays at 2pm. It costs Y50 and that buys you all the beer you can drink afterwards, as well as some food.

Skiing

Several ski resorts within reach of Běijīng lure skiers and snowboarders during the winter months. Bear in mind that the Chinese ski like they drive, so exercise caution. Nor will the slopes challenge advanced skiers and boarders.

BEIJING SNOW WORLD SKI PARK

Map pp258-9
北京雪世界滑雪场
☎ 8976 1886; Xiǎogōngmén, Shísānlíng, Chāngpíng; entrance Y20, skiing per day Mon-Fri Y200, Sat & Sun Y340; 🚌 345 from Deshengmen, get off at Zhengfa Daxue, then minibus 3 to ski park

Not far from the Ming Tombs (p197) and the closest ski resort to town, this resort features lodging, equipment hire and two modest ski runs. Snowboarders have to pay more than skiers here: Y320 for a full day.

JUNDUSHAN SKI RESORT

Map pp258-9
军都山滑雪场
☎ 6072 5888; Cuicunzhen 588 Zhenshuncun, Changping; skiing per day Mon-Fri Y240, Sat & Sun Y380

Just 34km from Běijīng, Jundushan advertises that skiing can help people 'relieve psychic tension and return themselves to nature for intimacy with God'. Skiing charges vary according to the day of the week and how long you want to ski (1 hr Mon-Fri Y60, Sat & Sun Y80; 2 hr Mon-Fri Y100, Sat & Sun Y140; one day Mon-Fri Y220, Sat & Sun Y340). The resort also offers discounts for regular users and has a team of 'more than 30 professional skimeisters'. The resort provides ski clothing hire (Y30), sledge hire (Y20), lessons (in Chinese only), a cable car (one way/return Y15/20) and accommodation in wooden villas.

NANSHAN SKI VILLAGE

Map pp258-9
南山滑雪度假村
☎ 6445 0990/91/92; www.nanshanski.com; Shengshuitou Village, Henanzhai Town, Miyun County; entrance Y20, skiing per day Mon-Fri Y220; Sat & Sun Y360

This popular resort in Miyun County has 10 trails for skiers of all abilities, a snowboard park and a toboggan run. It's 90 minutes from Běijīng. Packages are available (including transport, meals, equipment and use of slopes). The resort also has villas and cabins, restaurants, a car park and equipment hire.

SHIJINGLONG SKI RESORT

Map pp258-9
石京龙滑雪场
☎ 6919 1617; Zhongyangfang Village, Zhangshanying Town, Yanqing County; entrance Y20, skiing per day Mon-Fri Y200; Sat & Sun Y340

The longest trails around town and a snowboard park pack them in at this resort in Yanqing County. There are also hot springs (Y50) to warm up in. Snowboarders pay more here (Y320).

Snooker, Billiards & Pool

Snooker and pool are both very popular with the Chinese. Many tip China's teenage snooker prodigy Ding Junhui as a future world champion. You can find pool tables in many bars around town, including Bar Blu (p144), the Club Football Center (p144), Frank's Place (p144) and the Goose & Duck Pub (p145). For snooker and billiards, you can try the Xuanlong Pool Hall (Map p262; ☎ 8425 5566; 79B Hepingli Xijie, Cháoyáng; table per hr Y28; 🕐 24hr) or the Baizhifang Amusement Club (☎ 6351 4490; 13 Baizhifang Beili, Xuānwǔ; table per hr Y25; 🕐 10-2am).

Squash

Some five-star hotels have squash courts but most are for guests only, or require you to take out lengthy and pricy memberships. The best option is the Pulse Club (Map p264; ☎ 6465 3388, ext 5722; Kempinski Hotel, Lufthansa Center, 50 Liangmaqiao Lu; nonmembers per 45 min Y85).

Swimming

You can find pools at some four-star and all five-star hotels, but although access is free for guests, as a non-guest you will have to pay a fee. The China World Hotel (p182) charges Y150, but you get to use the sauna and gym as well. The venerable Friendship Hotel (☎ 6849 8888, ext 32; 1 Zhongguancun

Nandajie) in Hǎidiàn has a great Olympic-sized pool, costing Y100 for two hours plus a Y500 deposit. Outside hotels, the pool at the **Dongdan Sports Center** (☎ 6523 1241; 2a Dahua Lu, Dōngchéng; Y30; ✆ 9am-10pm Sat & Sun) is popular. You can also try the **Ditan Swimming Pool** (Map p262; ☎ 6426 4483; 18 Anwai Hepingli Zhongjie, Dōngchéng; Y30; ✆ 8.30am-3.30pm Mon-Fri, 8.30am-10pm Sat & Sun).

Tennis

Tennis *(wǎng qiú)* is a popular sport in Běijīng that draws enthusiastic crowds, so phone well in advance to make reservations for tennis events or for playing on a court. Many top-end hotels have tennis courts which can be used for free by guests and by non-guests for a fee. The **Kerry Center Hotel** (p186) charges Y400 an hour for non-members. Alternatively, try the **Chaoyang Tennis Club** (Map pp258–9; ☎ 6501 0959/0953; 1a Nongzhanguan Nanlu; non-members per hr Mon-Fri Y200, Sat & Sun Y240; ✆ 8am-noon) by the south gate of Chaoyang Park, or the **International Tennis Center** (Map pp268–9; ☎ 6711 3872, 50 Tiantan Lu; non-members per hr Y300; ✆ 10am-10pm), which has indoor and outdoor courts and is southeast of the Temple of Heaven Park. There are also tennis courts inside the Workers Cultural Palace right next to the Forbidden City, at **Huangjiatingyuan Tennis Club** (Huángjiāti'ngyuàn Wǎngqiú Jùlèbù; ☎ 6512 2856; non-members per hr before 5pm Mon-Fri Y40, per hr after 5pm Mon-Fri Y60, per hr before 5pm Sat & Sun Y60, per hr after 5pm Sat & Sun Y80; ✆ 6am-midnight).

Yoga

Older Chinese might choose the more homegrown methods of *qìgōng* and *tàijíquán* over the imported variant of yoga, but the disciplines have much in common. Both focus on the circulation of energy, called *qì* by Chinese and *prana* by Indians. **Yoga Yard** (Map p264; ☎ 136 1126 6962; www.yogayard.com; 6th fl, 17 Gongrentiyuchang Beilu) charges Y90 for a 90-minute lesson, or Y700 for an unlimited one-month pass. Class instruction is largely in English. A good place for a weekend yoga retreat is **Mountain Yoga** (Map pp258–9; ☎ 6259 6702; www.mountainyoga.cn; 6 Gongzhufen Cun, Fragrant Hills, Hǎidiàn). Located in a homely wooden house with a fine view of the nearby Fragrant Hills, there are lungfuls of fresh air to breathe in and visiting teachers to instruct you. It's Y800 for two days, which includes accommodation and tasty, all-vegetarian, MSG-free meals. A single day costs Y300.

Shopping

Shopping

Although not exactly a dictum of the late Mao Zedong, 'shop till you drop' has become a mantra of the Communist Party's popular reform drive. Building a strong consumer economy is one of the government's main goals. But persuading the Chinese to spend, spend, spend is easier said than done. China is a nation of savers, even more so now with the rising cost of education and healthcare, and in any case much of the population lacks the disposable income needed to splash out on fancy consumer items.

Běijīng though, is the exception to this. With much of the nation's wealth concentrated in the capital, there is a diverse and ever-growing selection of shops to choose from. They range from vast malls, which are still too expensive for most Běijīngers and so are great places to escape the crowds on weekdays, and department stores to roadside markets, street-side vendors and itinerant hawkers. Běijīng is a good place to find sought-after curios and souvenirs. It's worth spending a bit of time getting to know where the markets are and trawling through them with a careful eye and the bargaining gloves off.

There are several notable shopping districts offering abundant goods and reasonable prices, including Wangfujing Dajie, Xidan Beidajie and Qianmen (including Dashilar). More luxurious shopping areas can be found around the embassy areas of Jianguomenwai and Sanlitun; also check out five-star hotel shopping malls. Shopping at open air markets is an experience not to be missed. Běijīng's most popular markets are the Silk Street (p164), Panjiayuan (p163), Hongqiao Market (p162) and Sanlitun Yashow Clothing Market (p167). There are also specialised shopping districts such as Liulichang and the area around Panjiayuan for antiques.

Those on the hunt for silks, jade, Mao memorabilia, pearls, chops (carved name seals), brushes, inks, scrolls, handicrafts and antiques won't leave Běijīng empty-handed. Small or light items to buy are silk scarves, embroidered purses, paper cuttings, wooden and bronze Buddhas, paper lanterns and kites. Fashionistas can peruse the latest creations from the increasing number of homegrown designers.

You'll also be tripping over fakes by the bundle-load. The latest DVDs and CDs come smoking off the pirate's press seven days a week, to be hawked from roadsides and shops across the city. Pirate DVDs retail for between Y7 and Y10, but can be of dodgy quality. Generally, the newer the movie, the worse the copy will be. In shops, you can ask to see a clip before buying to see what you're getting. Top brand names – including Dunhill, Burberry and North Face – are faked wholesale. Unless you're buying from a shopping mall or a reputable outlet, assume it's counterfeit. For pharmacies, see p228.

Shopping Tips

Shops in Běijīng open earlier than in the West, between 8am and 8.30am, and close later, generally between 8pm and 9pm. The opening hours of all the shops listed below are included in the individual listing. Open-air markets are generally open from dawn to around sunset, but might open later and close earlier.

Always remember that foreigners are very likely to be quoted an inflated price for

TOP FIVE SHOPPING HAUNTS

- Wangfujing Dajie (opposite) Běijīng's foremost shopping drag can be found in the Dōngchéng area, east of the Forbidden City.
- Liulichang (p167) Curios and souvenirs amid flavours of old Běijīng in Xuānwǔ district.
- Dashilar (opposite) Bustling street of historic Qing dynasty shops not far from Tiananmen Square.
- Hongqiao Market (p162) Pearls and pirated labels.
- Panjiayuan (p163) Antiques and collectibles in a market atmosphere; only at weekends.

goods and services in Běijīng . Prices at department stores are generally fixed (although a 10% discount might be possible if you ask), but bargaining is very much standard practice everywhere else and vendors expect it. In markets such as the Silk Street, Hongqiao and Yashow, haggling is essential. It's best to bargain with a smile on your face. Remember, the point of the process is to achieve a mutually acceptable price; no market vendor is going to lose money

BEST BUYS IN BĚIJĪNG

Arts and crafts and antiques are all tempting buys in Běijīng, but it takes an expert eye to sort the wheat from the chaff, and even connoisseurs end up getting fleeced. Don't forget it's not just DVDs that are pirated; ceramics, oils and carvings regularly get the facsimile treatment. Those after real treasures will be looking for special certificates to take genuine antiques out of China (see Customs p220) and checking for the red wax seal that allows the owner to export it. Technically, items dating from before 1795 cannot be exported from China, but it is unlikely you will find anything genuinely that old. If buying a convincing reproduction or fake, ask the vendor to provide paperwork proving it does not infringe export regulations. Don't expect to unearth anything of real value; China has largely been sieved of nuggets.

Silk (sīchóu) is an important commodity in Běijīng, and excellent prices for both silk fabrics and clothing can be found. The top places for silk in Běijīng include the **Silk Street** (p164), **Beijing Silk Store** (p162) and **Ruifuxiang** (p163).

Carpets (dìtǎn) can be found at several stores, and Běijīng is an excellent place to shop for rugs, both antique and new, from all over China – from Xīnjiāng and Níngxià to Gānsù and Tibet. Antique carpets are often preferred for their richness in colour, attained through the use of natural dyes, and because they are handmade. As well as specialist stores, carpet vendors can be found at **Panjiayuan Market** (p163), **Beijing Curio City** (p162), **Zhaojia Chaowai Market** (p164) and some five-star hotels, including the **Kempinski Hotel** (p186). It pays to know that some rugs advertised as Tibetan are actually made in factories in mainland China, so try to visit a reputable dealer rather than hunting out the cheapest item. Other carpets are woven from imported Australian wool, the fibres of which are not particularly suitable for rugs. A carpet should be woven from a durable rather than a soft wool. The quality of the dye is something else to ask about.

Tailor-made clothes can be an excellent idea if you have the time, and made-to-measure clothing, including traditional Chinese gowns (qípáo, or cheongsam in Cantonese) and Mao suits, can be a bargain in Běijīng. Most tailors supply material, or you can bring your own. Cashmere (yángróngshān) from Inner Mongolia is another good buy in Běijīng . The 2nd floor of the Silk Street is a good place to hunt for cashmere bargains; however, as with other things here, eye it up carefully as synthetics sometimes pose as the real thing.

When looking for bookstores, don't expect to find a wide range of decent modern literature. Although things are improving, the selection in town remains sadly limited by Western standards. Our advice is to bring your own reading material. But if you like coffee table books about China, or classic 19th century literature, you'll do fine here.

just to get a sale. Unless you really want the item in question and can't find it anywhere else, simply walking away from the vendor's stall often results in a price reduction.

Most large department stores take credit cards, but always check that your card type is accepted. Smaller stores might take only Chinese credit cards and markets deal in cash, so come with plenty of it. Large department stores and hotels have ATMs with international access.

It's worth noting that in many shops, you can't just pay for your goods and walk out in one movement. The salesperson will give you a ticket for your goods. You then go to a till, hand over your ticket and pay for your goods; the stamped ticket is then returned to you. You then return to the salesperson who takes the stamped ticket and hands you your purchase. It's a tiresome, time-consuming process, so be prepared.

Many tourist shops can arrange shipping overseas, but you should go into the details of the costs and charges with the vendor before proceeding.

CHÓNGWÉN & SOUTH CHAOYANG

崇文、朝阳南

A prestigious, partly pedestrianised shopping street heading north just west of Oriental Plaza, Wangfujing Dajie boasts a solid strip of stores and is a favourite commercial haunt of locals, out-of-towners and tourists. Also called Gold St (Jin Jie) by Běijīng locals, in pre-liberation days Westerners knew it as Morrison St. The present name of Wangfujing Dajie remembers a 15th-century well.

If Wangfujing Dajie is too organised for you, the place to go and rub shoulders with the proletariat is Dashilar, a hútòng (alleyway) running west from the top end of Qianmen Dajie. Imperial Běijīng's shops and theatres were not permitted near the city centre and the Qianmen-Dashilar District was outside the gates. Many of the city's oldest shops, including Ruifuxiang (p163) and Tóngréntáng (p164), can be found along or near this crowded hútòng. It's a heady jumble of silk shops, tea shops, department stores, theatres, herbal medicine stores, food and clothing specialists and some unusual architecture.

A medieval flavour hangs over Dashilar, an echo of the days when bustling markets plying specialised products thronged each *hútòng* – lace in one *hútòng*, lanterns in the other, jade in the next. Dashilar was Silk St, but its official name referred to a wicket gate that was closed at night to keep prowlers out. At the time of writing, the area was undergoing an extensive pre-Olympics facelift, so expect some changes by the time you get there. In this area beware of scam artists who offer to guide you around, or to take you to see a traditional tea ceremony. Some visitors have been stung for a lot of money here.

BEIJING ARTS & CRAFTS CENTRAL STORE Map p262
Arts & Crafts/Jade

Gōngyè Dàshà 工艺美术服务部

☎ 6523 8747; 200 Wangfujing Dajie; ☺ 9am-8pm Mon-Fri, 9.30am-8pm Sat-Sun; ◉ **Wangfujing**

This centrally located store (with a sign outside saying Artistic Mansion) is well known for its good selection of jade (with certificates of authenticity), jadeite, cloisonné vases, carpets and other Chinese arts and crafts. Jewellery (gold, silver, jade and pearl) is on the ground floor, with glass, paintings, calligraphy and fans on the 2nd floor. You can find woodcarvings, cloisonné, lacquerware and silks on the 3rd floor and jade carvings on the 4th floor.

BEIJING CURIO CITY
Map pp268-9
Arts & Crafts/Antiques

Běijīng Gǔwán Chéng 北京古玩城

☎ 6774 7711; 21 Dongsanhuan Nanlu; ☺ 9.30am-6.30pm; ◉ **Guomao**, then 🚌 28

South of Panjiayuan (opposite) and next to the Antique City Hotel, Curio City is four floors of antiques, scrolls, ceramics, carpets and furniture. The ground floor is jade and pearls, the 2nd and 3rd floors are antiques and carpets and the 4th has antique clocks and watches. Popular with tour groups, this is a good place to find knick-knacks and souvenirs, but don't assume all antiques are the real deal.

BEIJING SILK STORE
Map pp268-9
Silk

Běijīng Sīchóu Shāngdiàn 北京丝绸商店

☎ 6301 6658; 50 Dazhalan Jie; ☺ 8.30am-7.30pm; ◉ **Qianmen**

This big store has been supplying silk since 1840. The silk costs from Y40 a metre, or

you can visit the 2nd floor and pick up ready-to-wear pyjamas and shirts.

CHINA WORLD SHOPPING MALL
Map pp268-9
Shopping Mall

Guómào Shāngchéng 国贸商城

☎ 6505 2288; 1 Jianguomenwai Dajie; ☺ 9.30am-10pm; ◉ **Guomao**

Adjacent to the first-rate China World Hotel (p182), this is a soulless mall packed with top-name brands, including Burberry, Moschino, Prada, as well as boutiques, jewellery stores such as Cartier (☎ 6505 6660; shop L104) and fast food restaurants. The Le Cool (p154) ice rink is in the basement.

FRIENDSHIP STORE
Map pp268-9
Department Store

Yǒuyì Shāngdiàn 友谊商店

☎ 6500 3311; 17 Jianguomenwai Dajie; ☺ 9.30am-8.30pm; ◉ **Jianguomen** or **Yonganli**

The Friendship Store is badly over-priced, but the books and magazines section is worth a look (you can pick up overseas newspapers here) and the supermarket is OK.

HAOYUAN MARKET
Map pp268-9
Souvenirs

Háoyuán Shìchǎng 豪园市场

West off Wangfujing Dajie; ◉ **Wangfujing**

Branching off from Wangfujing Snack Street (p124) is this small, bustling souvenir market. There's lots of Mao memorabilia and other tacky tourist tat, but if you're pushed for time and need a last-minute present you might find something. Haggling is imperative.

HONGQIAO (PEARL) MARKET
Map pp268-9
Market

Hóngqiáo Shìchǎng 红桥市场

☎ 6711 7429; Tiantan Donglu; ☺ 8.30am-7pm; ◉ **Chongwenmen**, then 🚌 610

Besides a cosmos of clutter (shoes, clothing, electronics and much more) and an impressive (and smelly) fish market in the basement, Hongqiao is home to more pearls than the South Seas. A huge range of them are available – freshwater and seawater, white pearls and black pearls – on the 3rd floor and prices vary incredibly depending on the quality. Hongqiao is a well-established spot on the Běijīng tourist trail and so prices for all goods are generally high, while the vendors, who often speak some English, are canny bargainers. There's a decent view of the Temple of Heaven from the 5th floor, and if you have kids in tow, don't miss the **Kids Toys market** (Hóngqiáo Tiānlè Wánjù Shìchǎng; ☻ 8.30am-7pm) in the building behind, stuffed to the gills with soft toys, cars, kits, electronic games, film tie-ins, models and more.

JINGDEZHEN CERAMIC CITY

Map pp268-9   Ceramics

Jíngdézhèn Táocí Chéng 景德镇陶瓷城
☎ 6512 4925/4867; www.jdtcc.com.cn; 277 Wangfujing Dajie; ☻ 10am-9pm; ◉ Wangfujing
Just off Wangfujing Dajie, this huge emporium is spread over several floors with displays of well-lit ceramics from the Jingdezhen kilns. Pieces are modern, but many works on view employ traditional decorative styles and glazes, such as *doucai* (blue and white and coloured), *fencai* (*famille rose*) and *qinghua* (blue and white).

NEILIANSHENG SHOE SHOP

Map pp268-9   Shoes

Nèiliánshēng Xiédiàn 内联升鞋店
☎ 6301 4863; 34 Dazhalan Jie; ☻ 9am-8.30pm; ◉ Qianmen
They say this is the oldest existing cloth shoe shop in China (it opened in 1853), and it has a factory that still employs more than 100 workers. Mao Zedong and other luminaries had their footgear made here and you too can pick up ornately embroidered shoes, or simply styled cloth slippers.

ORIENTAL PLAZA

Map pp268-9   Shopping Mall

Dōngfāng Guǎngchǎng 东方广场
☎ 8518 6363; 1 Dongchang'an Jie; ☻ 9.30am-10pm; ◉ Wangfujing
You could spend a day in this staggeringly large shopping mega-complex at the foot of Wangfujing Dajie. Prices might not be cheap, but window shoppers will be overjoyed. There's a great range of shops and restaurants, the Star City Cinema (p151) and **Megabite** (p124) in the basement is a good place to grab a cheap meal when you're in the area. Many top names are here, including Max Mara, Paul Smith, and Valentino. Also in the basement, more affordable but still stylish clothes can be found at MNG (☎ 8518 6918), where prices start from Y300 for trousers and

Y900 for leather coats. The **Olé** supermarket nearby (p125) is one of Běijīng's best.

PANJIAYUAN MARKET

Map pp268-9   Antiques/Crafts/Collectibles

Pānjiāyuán Gǔwán Shìchǎng 潘家园市场
☎ 6775 2405; Panjiayuan Qiao; ☻ 4.30am-6.30pm Sat & Sun; ☻ Guomao, then 🚌 28
Hands down the best place to shop for arts (*yìshù*), crafts (*gōngyì*) and antiques (*gǔwán*) in Běijīng is Panjiayuan (aka the Dirt or Sunday Market). The market takes place only at weekends and has everything from calligraphy, Cultural Revolution memorabilia and cigarette ad posters to Buddha heads, ceramics and Tibetan carpets.

The market hosts up to 50,000 visitors a day scoping for treasures. Serious collectors are the early birds, swooping here at dawn to snare those precious relics. If you want to join them, early Sunday morning is the best time. You might not find that rare Qianlong *doucai* stem cup or late Yuan dynasty *qinghua* vase, but what's on view is no less than a compendium of Chinese curios and an A to Z of Middle Kingdom knick-knacks. Bear in mind that this market is chaos – especially if you find crowds or hard bargaining intimidating. Also, ignore the 'don't pay more than half' rule here – some vendors might start at 10 times the real price. Make a few rounds to compare prices and weigh it all up before forking out for anything. Off Dongsanhuan Nanlu (Third Ring Rd).

RUIFUXIANG Map pp268-9   Silk

Ruìfúxiáng Sīchóudiàn 瑞蚨祥丝绸店
☎ 6303 5313; 5 Dazhalan Jie; ☻ 9am-7.30pm; ◉ Qianmen
Housed in a historic building on Dashilar, this is one of the best places in town to browse for silk. There's an incredible selection of Shāndōng silk, brocade and satin-silk. Ruifuxiang also has an outlet at **Wangfujing Dajie** (☎ 6525 0764; 190 Wangfujing Dajie).

TEN FU'S TEA Map p262   Tea

Tiānfú Míngchá 天福茗茶
☎ 6524 0958; www.tenfu.com; 88 Wangfujing Dajie; ☻ 9am-11pm; ◉ Wangfujing
With 26 branches across Běijīng, this Taiwanese chain has all the tea in China. They stock top-quality loose tea (prices start at Y10 for a bag) from all over the country. The staff can line you up with a free tea tasting.

TÓNGRÉNTÁNG

Map pp268-9   Chinese Medicine

同仁堂

☎ 6303 1155; 24 Dazhalan Jie; ⏱ 8am-7.30pm;
Ⓜ Qianmen

This famous, now international, herbal medicine shop has been peddling pills and potions since 1669. It was a royal dispensary in the Qing dynasty and its medicines are based on secret prescriptions used by royalty. You can be cured of anything from fright to encephalitis, or so the shop claims. Traditional doctors are available on the spot for consultations. You can find the three-storey shop just west of the Zhang Yiyuan Teastore, with a pair of *qilin* (statues of mythical Chinese creatures) standing outside.

SILK STREET Map pp268-9   Silk/Clothing

Xiùshuǐ Shìchǎng 秀水市场

☎ 6501 8811; 14 Dongdaqiao Lu; ⏱ 10am-8.30pm; Ⓜ Yonganli

Relocated into a four-storey building on the corner of Jianguomenwai and Dongdaqiao Lu, the Silk Street continues to thrive despite some vendors being hit by lawsuits from top name brands tired of being counterfeited on such a huge scale. Not that the legal action has stopped the coachloads of tourists who descend on this place every day. Their presence makes effective bargaining difficult. But this is a good place for cashmere, T-shirts, jeans, sneakers and the odd, chic dress.

ZHAOJIA CHAOWAI MARKET

Map pp268-9   Furniture

Zhàojiā Cháowài Shìchǎng 朝外市场

☎ 6770 6410; 43 Huawei Beili; ⏱ 10am-5.30pm Mon-Fri, 9am-5.30pm Sat & Sun; Ⓜ Guomao, then 🚌 28

This huge four-storey warehouse is packed to the gills with traditional Chinese furniture –

TOP FIVE CLOTHING STOPS

- Sanlitun Yashow Clothing Market (p167) Běijīng's best multi-floor clothing emporium.
- China World Shopping Mall (p162) Top names and top prices.
- Oriental Plaza (p163) Upscale brands mingle with the trendy here.
- Silk Street (above) Haggle, haggle, haggle.
- Beijing Silk Store (p162) Well-priced, huge range of silk material.

---

from opium beds to barrel stools to ornately carved side tables and carpets. Prices are reasonable, but remember to factor in shipping costs (which vendors can arrange). Many stallholders say their wares are genuine Ming or Qing items, but take it all with a pinch of *yán* (salt). The stalls get fancier the higher the floor, and prices rise accordingly. The 4th floor contains ceramics and other antiques. The market is on the southern part of Dongsanhuan Nanlu at Panjiaqiao, a short distance north of **Beijing Curio City** (p162).

DŌNGCHÉNG 东城

FIVE COLOURS EARTH

Map p264   Clothing

Wǔsètǔ 五色土

☎ 6415 3839; www.fivecoloursearth.com; 10 Dongzhimen Nandajie (just north of the Old Poly Plaza); ⏱ 9am-6pm; Ⓜ Dongsishitiao

Stylish clothing with a traditional Chinese twist from a local designer can be found at this store. The sexy tops incorporate embroidery made by the Miao minority in Guìzhōu province. It's good for jackets and coats too. Much of Five Colours Earth's stock is sold overseas, in the US and Italy, but you can pick it up far cheaper here.

FOREIGN LANGUAGES BOOKSTORE

Map p262   Books

Wàiwén Shūdiàn 外文书店

☎ 6512 6911; 235 Wangfujing Dajie; ⏱ 9am-10pm; Ⓜ Wangfujing

This bookshop has a reasonable selection of English-language novels, a range which seems to be improving all the time, as well as lots of nonfiction and a selection of art, architecture and design books. There's a good kids section and they stock a limited number of Lonely Planet guides. English-language books and those in other languages are located on the 3rd floor.

LU PENG TRENDSETTERS

Map p262   Clothing

Běijīng Xīndélù Huáyī Shānghǎng
北京鑫德路华衣商行

☎ 6402 6769; 198 Gulou Dongdajie; ⏱ 9am-7pm; Ⓜ Andingmen or Gulou

Exquisite, hand-tailored *qípáo* (traditional Chinese dresses) are the order of the day

ART CLASS

With the boom in contemporary Chinese art showing no signs of slowing down, more and more visitors to Běijīng are searching for artwork to take home with them. Buying a piece that is going to be of lasting value though, as opposed to something that is useful only for covering up that damp patch on your living room wall, is not as simple as it sounds. But there are a few guidelines you can follow which will increase your chances of walking off with a future masterpiece. Spending some time researching the art scene before you arrive is a good way to get started. Visit galleries in your hometown and check out magazines like *Art Forum* (artforum.com), *Art News* (www.artnews.com) and *Flash Art* (www.flashartonline .com) to find out about current trends and artists attracting attention. Once you're in Běijīng visit as many galleries as you can (p28). By seeing a lot of art, you'll develop a sense of what is good or bad and, more importantly, what appeals to you. The staff in reputable galleries will help you too. Galleries depend on word of mouth for their reputations and the established ones won't just try and sell you any old piece, they'll try to find something that fits with what you want. Rely on your gut instinct when dealing with the galleries; if you think you're being taken for a ride, walk away. Once you do find something you want to buy, you should be able to bargain a little. Unless the gallery is under strict instructions from the artist not to negotiate, or they feel the artist is truly exceptional, they will be flexible over the price. Ultimately, how much you're prepared to spend will depend on your bank balance and how much you like the piece you're interested in. But the days when Chinese artists let their work go for knockdown prices are long gone. Realistically, you'll need to spend at least US$1000 for something from an up-and-coming artist that will subsequently increase in value.

at this tiny shop. They're not cheap but the quality is superb and Lu Peng is one of the few Chinese designers who specialises in making them these days.

XIN ZHONGGUO KID'S STUFF

Map p262   Toys
Xīn Zhōngguó Értóng Yòngpin Shāngdiàn
新中国儿童用品商店
☎ 6528 1774; 168 Wangfujing Dajie; ☉ 9am-9pm; ◉ Wangfujing
If you need to find somewhere to occupy kids, bring them to this maze of toys, model cars and trains, gadgets, puzzles, flashing lights and electronic noises, overseen by helpful staff. On the 2nd floor, you can find nappies (diapers) and other essentials.

PLASTERED T-SHIRTS

Map p262   T-shirts
Chuàngkětiē Tìxù 创可贴T-恤
☎ 139 102 05721; www.plastered.com.cn; 61 Nanluogu Xiang; ☉ 1-10pm Mon-Fri, 10am-10pm Sat & Sun; ◉ Andingmen
Purveyors of ironic T-shirts, this is a shop for people with a sense of humour. The T-shirts, from Y80, incorporate iconic Běijīng logos: Yanjing beer, old taxi rate stickers, the Běijīng subway map, or you can go for the ones that portray the capital as a Hawaii-like haven of palm trees and sunsets. For brave foreigners resident in Běijīng there's the 'expat prick' T-shirt, as well as one with the characters for *gong bao ji ding* (every Chinese-challenged foreigners' favourite chicken dish) on it.

SHOPPING ARCADE, PENINSULA BEIJING HOTEL Map p262   Shopping Mall
Wángfǔ Fàndiàn
☎ 6559 2888; 8 Jinyu Hutong; ☉ 11am-9.30pm; ◉ Wangfujing or Dongdan
The big boys of fashion: Chanel, Dior, Gaultier, Gucci, Hermès, Louis Vuitton, Prada and Versace, can be found in this exclusive and very hushed basement-level shopping haunt beneath the Peninsula Beijing hotel (p185). There are also Cartier and Tiffany outlets, so you can pick up the diamonds you'll need to go with your new outfit.

VINTAGE STORE Map p262   Clothing
Chāinà 拆那
☎ 130 010 90247; 6 Yandai Xiejie; ☉ 4pm-9pm Wed-Sun; ◉ Gulou
Can't leave Běijīng without a retro Bruce Lee T-shirt? Desperate to replace your vintage Levis? Then this is the place for you. With posters of Steve McQueen on the wall, a solid selection of old-school T-shirts (Y100), jackets and jeans (Y800), entering this funky little store is like stepping back in time to the '70s.

ZHAOYUANGE Map p262   Kites
Zhāoyuángé 昭元阁
☎ 6512 1937; 41 Nanheyan Dajie; ☉ 9am-8.30pm; ◉ Tiananmen Dong
If you're into Chinese kites, you will love this minute shop on the west side of Nanheyan Dajie. There's a range of traditional Chinese paper kites here, starting at Y5 for a simple kite, up to around Y300 for a dragon. You

can also pick up Běijīng opera masks. The owner does not speak much English, but you can browse and make a selection.

CHÁOYÁNG 朝阳

The vast Cháoyáng district, home to the Sanlitun embassy area with its numerous bars and restaurants and the cluster of top-end hotels around the Lufthansa Center, is also one of Běijīng's foremost shopping areas.

3.3 SHOPPING CENTRE

Map p264   Shopping Mall
Fúshì Dàshà 服饰大厦
☎ 6417 3333; 33 Sanlitun Beijie; ☽ noon-midnight; ◉ Dongsishitiao, then ⛟ 701 heading east
With its collection of trendy boutiques and accessories stores, this brand new mall in the heart of Sanlitun caters for Běijīng's bright young things. The 5th floor has a selection of tailors who promise a 24-hour turnaround.

3501 PLA SURPLUS STORE

Map p264   Clothing/Hiking
3501 Jūnyòngpǐn Diàn 军用品店
☎ 6585 9312; 23 Dongsanhuan Beilu (just south of intersection with Chaoyangmenwai Dajie); ☽ 9am-5pm; ◉ Guomao, then ⛟ 421 or 701 heading north
The Chinese armed forces, the PLA, are the largest in the world and this is where you can pick up some of their kit. Staffed by a cheery crew of middle-aged ladies, it's a good place to find cheap but hard-wearing boots, heavy greatcoats (Y125) – ubiquitous in the Chinese winter, fur hats (Y42), long johns and waterproofs. Sturdy binoculars, compasses, knives and watches are also available, but at the time of writing Long March rockets were not in stock. Located just south of the intersection with Chaoyangmenwai Dajie.

ALIEN'S STREET MARKET

Map p264   Clothing Market
Lǎo Fān Jiē Shìchǎng 老番街市场
Chaowaishichang Jie; ☽ 9.30am-7pm; ◉ Chaoyangmen
This market just northwest of Ritan Park is packed with a huge variety of clothing, as well as tons of accessories. You can find most things here. It's popular with visiting Russian traders, which means the clothes come in bigger sizes than usual and the vendors will greet you in Russian. Haggling is essential.

BAINAOHUI COMPUTER SHOPPING

MALL Map p264   Computers/Electronics
Bǎinǎohuì Diànnǎo Shìchǎng 百脑汇电脑市场
☎ 6599 5912; 10 Chaoyangmenwai Dajie; ☽ 9am-8pm; ◉ Chaoyangmen, then ⛟ 112 heading east
Four floors of gadgetry, including computers, Ipods, MP3s, blank CDs and DVDs, gaming gear, software and other accessories. The prices are fairly competitive and you can bargain here, but don't expect too much of a reduction. Next to this mall there are a number of shops – good places to pick up mobile phones and local SIM cards.

BOOKWORM Map p264   Books

Shūchóng 书虫
☎ 6586 9507; Bldg 4, Nan Sanlitun Lu; ☽ 9am-1am; ◉ Dongsishitiao, then ⛟ 701 heading east
Apart from its lending library of 14,000 books, the 'worm (see p135) has a small but interesting selection of new English-language fiction and nonfiction tomes available for sale. You can find Lonely Planet guides here, as well as UK and US magazines.

DARA Map p264   Furniture/Household Items

Sānlǐtún Shēnghuó Fāngshì Diàn
三里屯生活方式店
☎ 6417 9365; 17 Gongrentiyuchang Beilu;
☽ 9.30am-8pm, to 9pm in summer; ◉ Dongsishitiao
Trendy destination for stylish household accessories: ceramics, cushions, lamps, mirrors, and antique and repro furniture. Swish and expensive, they design to order too. Opposite the north gate of the Workers' Stadium.

EXTREME BEYOND Map p264   Hiking

Zhōngshuāng Tànxiǎn Yěyíng Dēngshān Zhuāngbè Izhuānmàidiàn
中双探险野营登山装备专卖店
☎ 6506 5121; 6 Gongrentiyuchang Donglu; ☽ 10am-7.30pm; ◉ Dongsishitiao, then ⛟ 701 heading east
This small shop has a good selection of real brand-name hiking boots, waterproof jackets, backpacks and sleeping bags. Prices aren't cheap (eg Y650 for hiking boots), but goods are the genuine article. Only JCB cards.

LUFTHANSA CENTER YOUYI

SHOPPING CITY Map p264   Shopping Mall
Yànshā Yǒuyì Shāngchǎng 燕莎友谊商场
☎ 6465 1188; 50 Liangmaqiao Lu; ☽ 9am-10pm; ◉ Dongsishitiao, then ⛟ 701 heading east

The gigantic Lufthansa Center was the first Western-style mall to appear in Běijīng. It's looking its age a bit now, but is still a reliable, if pricey, source of upmarket Western clothing and cosmetics and is especially good for sports gear. The Yansha Supermarket (p125) in the basement is one of Běijīng's best, while the Yansha (☎ 6465 1188) bookstore on the 4th floor is worth a browse. There are restaurants and ATMs here too.

PACIFIC CENTURY PLACE

Map p264   Department Store
Tàipíngyáng Bǎihuò 太平洋百货
☎ 6539 3888; 2 Gongrentiyuchang Beilu;
🕙 10am-10pm; 🚇 Dongsishitiao, then 🚌 701 heading east

This upmarket store has clothing for all, as well as electronics and cosmetics, a pharmacy, laundry and a supermarket. The basement is particularly useful for those with kids; you can find extra-large nappies (diapers) and sterilising equipment here.

SANLITUN YASHOW CLOTHING MARKET Map p264   Clothing
Sānlǐtún Yǎxiù Fúzhuāng Shìchǎng
三里屯雅秀服装市场
☎ 6416 8945; 58 Gongrentiyuchang Beilu;
🕙 9.30am-9pm; 🚇 Dongsishitiao, then 🚌 701 heading east

Five floors of virtually anything you might need and a favourite with expats and visitors. Basement: shoes, handbags and suitcases. Big Shoes (☎ 137 0113 9838) is useful for anyone struggling to find suitably sized footwear. First floor: coats and jackets. Second floor: hiking gear, suits, ladies wear. Third floor: silk, clothes, carpets, fabrics and tailors to fashion your raw material into something wearable. Fourth floor: jewellery, souvenirs, toys and a beauty salon. Bargain hard here.

TORANA GALLERY Map p264   Carpets
图兰纳西藏手工地毯店
☎ 6465 3388 ext 5542; Shop 8, 1st fl, Kempinski Hotel; 🕙 10am-10pm; 🚇 Dongsishitiao, then 🚌 701 heading east

The owner of this popular store, Chris Buckley, wrote the first editions of the Lonely Planet China guide back in the '80s. But nepotism isn't why his shop features here. Instead, it's the range of rugs exclusively made of wool from Tibetan highland sheep

and decorated with traditional emblems. Prices start at Y2200 and you can also custom design your own carpet.

FĒNGTÁI & XUĀNWǓ
丰台、宣武

Not far west of Dashilar is Liulichang, Běijīng's premier antique street. Worth delving into for its quaint, albeit dressed-up, village-like atmosphere, the shops on Liulichang (meaning 'glazed-tile factory') trade in (largely fake) antiques. Alongside ersatz Qing monochrome bowls and Cultural Revolution kitsch, you can also rummage through old Chinese books, paintings, brushes, ink and paper. Prepare yourself for pushy sales staff and stratospheric prices – wander round and compare price tags. If you want a chop made, you can do it here.

At the western end of Liulichang Xijie, a collection of ramshackle stalls flog bric-a-brac, Buddhist statuary, Cultural Revolution pamphlets and posters, fake Tang dynasty three-colour porcelain (sāncǎi), shoes for bound feet, silks, handicrafts, kites, swords, walking sticks, door knockers and so on.

Elsewhere in the Xuānwǔ area, you can find Sogo (see p168), perhaps Běijīng's best mall, and the giant Xidan Bookshop (p168).

CATHAY BOOKSHOP

Map pp266-7   Books/Chinese Artwork
Zhōngguó Shūdiàn 中国书店
☎ 6303 2104; 34 Liulichang Xijie; 🕙 9am-6pm;
🚇 Hepingmen

There are several branches of the Cathay Bookshop on Liulichang. This branch (Gǔjí Shūdiàn), on the south side of Liulichang Xijie opposite Róngbǎozhāi, is worth checking out for its wide variety of colour art books on Chinese painting, ceramics and furniture, and its books on religion (most books are in Chinese). Upstairs has more art books, stone rubbings and antiquarian books. The store takes MasterCard and Visa. There's another branch at 18 Liulichang Xijie that has a paper cuts exhibition. It also sells an interesting set of bookmarks (Y10) – photographs of the old Qing imperial household, including snapshots of Reginald Johnson (Last Emperor Henry Puyi's English tutor), Puyi practising shadow boxing, eunuchs and Cixi dressed as Avalokiteshvara (Guanyin). Another branch is at Liulichang Dongjie (106 Liulichang Dongjie).

LOST IN TRANSLATION *Damian Harper*

Běijīng may be a minefield of shoddy English, but nothing is more adept at mangling the language than Chinese–English computer-translating. This run-of-the-mill offering from a Běijīng DVD hawker-stall offers a glimpse into the mesmerising chaos of machine translations. The film is *Hollow Man 2* and the blurb says:

'Christian the history is especially, annoyed detective method gram of Seattle, member living creature learn a of a read, an employ the soldier, they have what contact? Originally the history was especially seduce into wrong doing by a of the, taking the research to manufacture a kind of and can chase the person. The body becomes the transparent syrup liquid.'

At first glance this impenetrable chunk of text – designed to convince you to part with your hard-earned *qián* and actually buy *Hollow Man 2* – resembles some kind of psychedelic gibberish or the ravings of a lunatic. With careful study and patience, however, readers of Chinese and English may identify *'Christian the history is especially'* as none other than Christian Slater, whose Chinese name is 克里斯蒂安 史莱特. Slater's Chinese surname – 史莱特 – is meaningless and is used for sound value alone, as it approximates the pronunciation of the name Slater – *Shiläite*. The machine translator has committed an impressive error by translating Slater's Chinese surname literally into English. So 史 is translated as 'history', and 特 is translated as 'especially', obliterating the actor's name in the process and generating nonsense English.

Compounding this, the machine translator has retranslated Slater's first name – Christian – back into the Chinese as 基督徒 – literally a 'Christian believer' – so neither the English nor the Chinese affirm that Christian Slater is in the film. *'Annoyed detective method gram of Seattle'* may have you scratching your bonce, but let me assist. The Chinese is as follows: 烦闷的西雅图侦探法兰克, which literally means 'Annoyed Seattle detective Frank'. Again, a name in Chinese has caused confusion; the name Frank (法兰克) has gone through the machine, emerging as *'method gram'*, a literal rendering of the characters 法 (method) and 克 (gram).

Please bear with me. *'Member living creature learn a of a read'* is a crazy rendering of '分子生物学家玛姬道尔读顿' which actually means 'molecular biologist Maggie Dalton', one of the film's principal characters. The characters for molecular biologist (分子生物学家) have come up as *'member'* (分子) and *'living creature'* (生物), while *'learn a of a read'* is a tangled translation of '学家' (part of the word 'biologist') and the name Maggie Dalton (玛姬道尔读顿), all of which plays havoc with the translation machine's low IQ.

If you're getting the hang of it, you won't be fazed by: *'Originally the history was especially seduce into wrong doing by a of the...'* which naturally means 'What happened was that Christian Slater was tempted by Maggie Dalton', while *'The body becomes the transparent syrup liquid'* is a feeble stab at selling the film's sci-fi gimmick, a gel that can render you invisible.

RÓNGBǍOZHĀI Map pp266-7   Chinese Artwork
荣宝斋

☎ 6303 6090; 19 Liulichang Xijie; ⌚ 9am-5.30pm;
⊕ Hepingmen

Spread over two floors and sprawling down quite a length of the road, this store has a selection of scroll paintings, woodblock prints, paper, ink and brushes. As it's state-run, the effect is rather uninspiring and the collection somewhat flat. Prices are generally fixed, although you can usually get 10% off. The shop accepts JCB credit cards.

SOGO Map pp266-7   Shopping Mall
Chóngguāng Bǎihuòshāngchǎng 崇光百货

☎ 6310 3388; 8 Xuanwumenwai Dajie; ⌚ 9.30am-10pm; ⊕ Xuanwumen

Sogo is probably Běijīng's most pleasant mall experience. The mix of hip Japanese (Sogo is a Japanese company) and European boutiques, the convenient layout and an excellent and cheap food court on the 6th floor make a trip around here far more fun than you'd expect from a shopping centre. Add espresso bars on each floor, the impressive basement supermarket, with pharmacy, and the 6th-floor games arcade, where you can deposit kids (and boyfriends and husbands) while shopping, and you're in mall heaven.

XIDAN BOOKSHOP Map pp266-7   Books
Xīdān Túshū Dàshà 西单图书大厦

☎ 6607 8477; 17 Xichang'an Jie; ⌚ 8.30am-9pm;
⊕ Xidan

The titles at this absolutely vast bookshop (Běijīng's largest) are largely Chinese, but the basement is home to what might be the city's best selection of English-language titles. There are all the classics, Austen, Dickens, Hemingway, Twain et al, but there are also books on China you wouldn't expect to have passed the beady eye of the censor, as well as an expanding range of new fiction. You can pick up Lonely Planet guides and maps of Běijīng here too.

1 *Imperial Vault of Heaven in the Temple of Heaven Park (p79)* **2** *Small house shrine at the Lama Temple (p91)* **3** *Waving the Chinese national flag, Tiananmen Square (p81)*

1 *Hall of Supreme Harmony (p89), Forbidden City* **2** *Sunset at the Great Wall of China (p191)* **3** *Decorated ceiling, Summer Palace (p102)* **4** *Buddhist Fragrance Pavilion (p104), Summer Palace*

1 Red Gate Gallery (p79)
2 Billboard advertisement for a Chinese film (p34) 3 Wares for sale, Panjiayuan Market (p163)
4 Water feature, Peninsula Beijing hotel (p185)

1 Evening shopping along Wangfujing Dajie (p161) 2 Fashion show, Wangfujing Dajie (p161) 3 Statues in the White Cloud Temple (p97) 4 Sculpted column in front of the Gate of Heavenly Peace (p76)

173

1 *Practising taichi (p155) at Temple of Heaven Park*
2 *Streetside tea (p46) for sale*
3 *Stopping for a meal in a hútòng (p106)*

1 *Market shopping*
2 *Wangfujing Snack Street (p124)* **3** *Donghuamen Night Market (p128)*

1 *Palace Moat, Forbidden City (p87)* **2** *Statue at the entrance to Beihai Park (p84)* **3** *Water calligraphy, Temple of Heaven Park (p79)*

Sleeping ■

Sleeping

Hotels in Běijīng have undergone a rapid evolution over the past 20 years, but the manufactured and formulaic feel of many establishments persists. Few hotels in the capital have any pedigree, character or strong historic associations that make stays memorable or unique. Nonetheless, comfort and luxury are easy to find as long as you are willing to pay for it and accommodation options in all budget brackets exist.

Midrange Chinese-run hotels – three to four star – are frequently uniform and indistinguishable from each other. Overall midrange standards are acceptable, although English-speaking skills and comprehension of foreign traveller needs are often superior in the budget youth hostel bracket. Unlike Shànghǎi, Hong Kong and Macau, which all have distinguished hotels dating to colonial and foreign concession days, Běijīng has precious few. Instead, if you want history, courtyard hotels (sìhéyuàn bīnguǎn) allow you the chance to eke out Běijīng's inimitable courtyard and hútòng (alleyway) ambience, and many travellers opt for this. The downside of courtyard hotels is the smallish size of the rooms and a frugal range of amenities, but the atmosphere is uniquely Běijīng.

Běijīng's growing band of stylish four- and five-star hotels means the top-end bracket is crammed with options in most parts of town. The best five-star hotels offer a standard equivalent to international hotels abroad, but be warned that Chinese-managed hotels may be ranked as five stars, but this may only be because an establishment has a swimming pool – other aspects of the hotel may be wanting. Four-star hotels can similarly be a star lower when measured objectively. This is particularly important when travelling to destinations outside Běijīng.

Běijīng's budget hotel sector belatedly responded to the hordes of travellers seeking cheap rooms and dorm beds and a healthy crop of youth hostels can now be found. Youth hostels are typically centrally located, offer doubles as well as dorms and are staffed by young English-speakers tuned-in to the needs of foreigners. Some ultra-cheap guesthouses (called zhāodàisuǒ 招待所; lǚdiàn 旅店; or lǚguǎn 旅馆 in Chinese) still refuse to take foreigners.

English-language skills can be frustratingly poor, even at five-star hotels, so be prepared. Hotels that deal mainly with Chinese and overseas Chinese guests may have no English-speaking staff.

When you check into a hotel, you will have to complete a registration form, a copy of which will be sent to the local Public Security Bureau (PSB; Gōngānjú).

Price Ranges & Reservations

It often pays to reserve a hotel room through the hotel's website, where discounts are regularly offered. Also visit travel agencies and browse for the best deals online; try **CTrip** (☎ 800-820 6666; www.english.ctrip.com) or **Beijing Hotels Travel Guide** (www.beijing-hotels.net).

If you are arriving in Běijīng without a reservation and are planning to stay in midrange or top-end accommodation, stop one of the airport hotel reservations counters, which could secure you a discount of up to 50% off the rack rates. Counters are located just outside the arrivals area, after you pass through customs.

Rackrates for room prices are listed in hotel reviews below, but discounting is the norm, so it is imperative to ask what the discount (dǎzhé; 打折) is. Outside peak times (during the Chinese New Year and the first weeks of May and October), discounts of 30% to 40% are common, but make sure you check whether the discounted price includes the service charge, as this will eat up 10% to 15% of the discount. Also ask about special promotional packages at top-end hotels, especially newly opened ventures. If staying long-term, you should be able to get good deals, especially at top-end hotels.

Top-end hotels may list their room rates in US dollars, but you will have to pay in local currency. Practically all hotels will change money for guests, and most midrange and top-end hotels accept credit cards. All hotel rooms are subject to a 10% or 15% service charge, but many cheaper hotels don't bother to charge it.

Longer-Term Rentals

If you are planning to live in a hotel, you should be able to negotiate a discount for a long-term stay.

Fully-furnished serviced apartments are expensive, but offer security, maid service and hotel facilities. For information on rents and availability of serviced and other apartments in Běijīng, consult www.moveandstay.com/beijing.

Housing developments for the Chinese moneyed class and those on expat packages are generally first-rate, with expensive management fees, 24-hour security, guards, sports facilities, swimming pools, kindergartens and shops selling imported goods and delicacies. While you can find a smart three-bedroom flat for as little as Y11,500 per month, prices can top Y75,000 per month for ultra-luxurious apartments.

Modern Chinese housing (eg apartment blocks), however, offers substantially lower rents (from Y4000 per month for a three bedroom flat), and although standards are lower than typical foreign housing, they're much higher than average Chinese housing (there will be tiles on the floor, decent plumbing, guards at the gate, parking etc). Further down the scale is older housing, where rents can be as low as Y1500 per month for a basic two-bedroom flat.

Some long-term residents prefer to live in courtyard houses (see the 'Hútòng Life' boxed text, p112), as they have more personality and charm than sterile modern high-rises and expat housing developments and are located within the Second Ring Rd. What you gain in history and character, however, you might sacrifice in amenities: there is usually nowhere to park the car, the toilet might be outside, heating might be wanting and chances are there won't be any satellite TV. But many courtyard homes on the rental market now have air-con, shower rooms, lavatories and fully equipped kitchens, and have been recently redecorated. Prices for courtyard houses start at around Y4000 per month, rising to over Y75,000 for the most luxurious. Using an expat-oriented estate agent is convenient, but far more expensive; if you manage to find a courtyard residence through a Chinese estate agent, it could be much, much cheaper. Look around and compare prices.

Housing laws stipulate that foreigners can live in Chinese housing as long as the owners of the apartment register the foreign resident with the local PSB. Failure to do so could well incur foreigners a fine of around Y3000 (per person).

If you're coming to study, your school will probably have a dormitory. It's possible to move in with a Chinese family and simply pay rent, but make sure you are officially registered. Families typically charge Y1000 per month for a room. If you teach or work for the government, your housing will likely be provided free or at the local Chinese price.

Homestays can be a fun and educational way to live for long periods in Běijīng. Take a look at www.chinahomestay.org for details of rent-free homestays.

Foreigners expecting to make Běijīng their permanent home can buy property, and by doing so also gain a residence permit. In most cases, buying actually means leasing the property for 75 years, after which it reverts to state ownership. Over recent years, property prices in Běijīng have gone through the roof, averaging around Y8000 per sq metre, although expect to pay much more than that in a desirable part of the city.

Besides word of mouth, the best way to find housing in Běijīng is through a real estate agent or by checking housing ads in the expat mags. *That's Beijing* (www.thatsmagazines.com) is a useful source of rental information and advertisements.

BOOK ACCOMMODATION ONLINE

For more accommodation reviews and recommendations by Lonely Planet authors, check out the online booking service at www.lonelyplanet.com. You'll find the true, insider lowdown on the best places to stay. Reviews are thorough and independent. Best of all, you can book online.

PRICE GUIDE

YYYY	Over Y2000 a night
YYY	Y1000-2000 a night
YY	Y600-Y1000 a night
Y	Under Y600 a night

CHÓNGWÉN & SOUTH CHAOYANG
崇文、朝阳南

This area is probably Běijīng's most popular hotel district, at least for midrange and top-end accommodation. Local hotels all offer either proximity or simple transport access to Tiananmen Square, Temple of Heaven Park, Wangfujing Dajie and Běijīng's commercial and business district in the east. Some of Běijīng's best top-notch and midrange hotels are found here, as well as a handful of decent budget alternatives.

EASTERN MORNING SUN YOUTH HOSTEL Map pp268-9 Y
Běijīng Dōngfāng Chénguāng Qīngnián Lǚguǎn
北京东方晨光青年旅馆

☎ 6528 4347; www.hostelsbeijing.com; fl B4, East Bldg, Oriental Plaza, 8-16 Dongdan Santiao 东单三条8-16号; east side d/tr/5-bed Y120-140/180/300, west side d/tr/q Y140/180/240; ☻ Dongdan; ▣

The windowless, cramped rooms, deficient daylight and bunker-style effect is claustrophobic, but many travellers consider these worthwhile sacrifices when weighed against the ultra-central location off Wangfujing Dajie, 2pm check-out and budget tariff. Make a mental note of the fire escape location,

nonetheless. All loos and showers are communal (clean); centralised air-con. Internet café (from 7.30am to midnight), tourist info office, noticeboards, slightly harried staff.

LEO YOUTH HOSTEL Map pp268-9 Y
Guǎngjùyuán Fàndiàn 广聚元饭店

☎ 6303 1595; 52 Dazhalan Xijie 大栅栏西街 52号; 12-bed/4-bed dm Y45/70; d without toilet/shower Y140-160, d with toilet/bath Y200-240; ☻ Qianmen; ▣

Popular and busy, it's advisable to phone ahead and make reservations at this bargain hostel tucked away down Dazhalan Xijie where staff make solid efforts at wooing international backpackers. There's an attractive interior courtyard decked out with plastic plants, OK dorm rooms (pricier dorms with toilet), simple but passable doubles, a small but lively bar, and a location that knocks the spots off lesser competitors.

BEIJING CITY CENTRAL YOUTH HOSTEL Map pp268-9 Y
Běijīng Chéngshì Guójì Qīngnián Lǚshè
北京城市国际青年旅社

☎ 6525 8866/8511 5050; www.centralhostel.com; 1 Beijingzhan Jie 北京站街1号; 4-8 bed dm Y60, s with\without shower Y160/120, d Y298; ☻ Beijingzhan; ▣

Across the road from Beijing Train Station and right next to the underground, this recently opened hostel compensates for

HOTEL PRIMER

Single room	单人间	dānrénjiān
Double room	双人间	shuāngrénjiān
Triple room	三人间	sānrénjiān
Quad	四人间	sìrénjiān
Suite	套房	tàofáng
Reception	总台	zǒngtái
Bathroom	卫生间	wèishēngjiān
Passport	护照	hùzhào
Hotel	饭店/酒店/大酒店	fàndiàn/jiǔdiàn/dàjiǔdiàn
Youth hostel	青年旅馆	qīngnián lǚguǎn
Toilet paper	卫生纸	wèishēngzhǐ
TV	电视	diànshì
Telephone	电话	diànhuà
Air-con	空调	kōngtiáo
Taxi	出租车	chūzūchē
Check-out	退房	tuìfáng
Discount	折扣	zhékòu

lack of character with a definitively handy location. A natural target for backpack-laden travellers closing in on the capital by train, rooms go fast, so phone ahead. Notice board, info desk, TV and video room, kitchen plus a handy internet café on the 2nd floor.

HOME INN Map pp268-9   Y
Rújiā Kuàijié Jiǔdiàn 如家快捷酒店
☎ 6317 3366; www.homeinns.com; 61 Liangshidian Jie, Dashilar 大栅栏粮食店街61号; d Y178-218; ◉ Qianmen; 💻

Most branches of this budget/midrange chain are unhelpfully scattered around in marginal parts of town, but earmark this one located a short trot south of Tiananmen Square. Double rooms are small, but clean, with modern fittings and bright soft furnishings. Parallel to Qianmen Dajie, Liangshidian Jie (Grain Shop St) is gritty and repellent, but that's OK if you only want somewhere to hit the sack. Internet access (per hour Y10); small restaurant.

TIÁNSHUǏ LǙGUǍN Map p262   Y
甜水旅馆
☎ 6527 9284; 45 Datianshuijing Hutong 大甜水井胡同 45号; s/d Y180; ◉ Wangfujing/ Tiananmen Dong

Good slow season rates (rooms down to Y130) make this handy place – tucked away down a *hútòng* with loads of authentic Běijīng personality – a pleasant choice. Rooms have air-con, TV and shower, but no phone. There's no English sign, but it's on the north side of the alleyway, around 50m west of Chenguang Jie, adjacent to a restaurant. Spoken English could be problematic, so refer to the Hotel Primer (opposite).

GUANQI HOTEL Map pp268-9   Y
Guānqí Bīnguǎn 观旗宾馆
☎ 6303 8490; No 1 Building, Zhengyang Market, off Qianmen Dajie 正阳市场一号楼; r Y238-300; ◉ Qianmen

Its mediocrity only matched by its stupendous outlook onto the Arrow Tower (p76) of Qianmen, this place is worth contemplating if being at the bull's-eye of Běijīng on a budget tops your priorities. The name means 'See the Flag Hotel' – indicating the views of Tiananmen Square – and even though some of its small and grubby rooms (all with TV, air-con and shower) face the

wrong way or are viewless, the location is exceptional. This is the cheaper of two hotels of the same name; the slightly pricier namesake (☎ 6705 8230/6702 7988; fax 6303 5630; 18 Qianmen Dongdajie 前门东大街18号; r Y280 & Y380) is across the road.

JIANGUO HOTEL
Map pp268-9   YYY
Jiànguó Fàndiàn 建国饭店
☎ 6500 2233; www.hoteljianguo.com; 5 Jianguomenwai Dajie 建国门外大街5号; d Y1350; ◉ Yonganli; 💻 ♿

It had to happen sooner or later – this popular old-timer has undergone restyling. Old touches persist amid the modern rehash, with Charlie's Bar (a mainstay for boozy embassy staff and dyed-in-the-wool expats) surviving unscathed. Rooms in the four-storey building 'A' are nicely fitted out, and the ground floor patio decking and greenery is tempting, but rooms opposite the bar can be noisy at night. Rooms in the less attractive nine-storey building 'B' were being renovated at the time of writing. Wi-fi available.

RAFFLES BEIJING HOTEL
Map pp268-9   YYY
Běijīng Fàndiàn Láifóshì Jiǔdiàn 北京饭店莱佛士酒店
☎ 6526 3388; www.beijing.raffles.com; 33 Dongchang'an Jie; d incl breakfast Y1688; ◉ Wangfujing; 💻 📶

With a history dating to 1900 (when it was called the Grand Hotel de Pekin), a winning location on the cusp of Wangfujing Dajie and elegant rooms, the Raffles Beijing is an attractive choice. Service is cordial and the overall presentation impressive, with a good selection of Chinese and international dining options, including **East 33** (☎ 6526 3388 ext 5172), for a smart modern Chinese ambience.

NOVOTEL XINQIAO Map pp268-9   YYY
Běijīng Xīnqiáo Nuòfùtè Fàndiàn 北京新桥诺富特饭店
☎ 6513 3366; www.accorhotels.com/asia; 2 Dongjiaomin Xiang 东交民巷2号; d Y1750; ◉ Chongwenmen; 💻 ♿

A dated '90s effect reigns supreme in the foyer with soft colours, ageing wood design and undulating oval curves, but the tariff offers reasonable value and the location, conveniently out of the action while plugged directly into the metro system, is a bonus. Rooms are modern, if unremarkable, and thin on home comforts. A big choice of restaurants and bars and there's a handy post office (open from 8am to 6pm) on the ground floor and an outdoor tennis court.

GRAND HYATT BEIJING

Map pp268-9   YYYY

Běijīng Dōngfāng Jūnyuè Dàjiǔdiàn
北京东方君悦大酒店
☎ 8518 1234; www.beijing.grand.hyatt.com;
1 Dongchang'an Jie 东长安街1号; d Y2150;
Ⓜ Wangfujing; 🖥 ✕ 🛒 ♿

It may be five years old, but a freshness still reigns at this elegant creation lording it over Oriental Plaza – from the grand sweep of its foyer to the whirl of (largely empty) whizz brand name stores (Shanghai Tang, Zenith, Taghauer) downstairs, syphoning off stray shoppers from the attached Oriental Plaza. Standard rooms are not that spacious, but are attractively designed with glass work tables and modern furnishings. Located only 10 minutes walk from the Forbidden City and Tiananmen Square, the hotel boasts several excellent restaurants, cafés and bars – including the smart Made in China and the luxuriant Red Moon Bar. Has Wi-fi access.

CHINA WORLD HOTEL

Map pp268-9   YYYY

Zhōngguó Dàfàndiàn 中国大饭店
☎ 6505 2266; www.shangri-la.com; 1 Jianguomenwai Dajie 建国门外大街1号; d Y3200,
ste Y5000-Y31000; Ⓜ Guomao; 🖥 ✕ 🛒 ♿

TOP FIVE PLACES TO STAY

- St Regis (right) The pinnacle of elegance in Běijīng, lavish and sumptuous with full-on pampering.
- Peninsula Beijing (p185) Faultless presentation, outstanding service, great location.
- Haoyuan Hotel (p184) Delightful and charming courtyard hotel with oodles of history and character.
- Far East International Youth Hostel (p187) Loads of personality, good-value rooms and the thumbs up from enthusiastic travellers.
- Peking Downtown Backpackers Accommodation (opposite) Winning location in the heart of the old town on traveller-friendly Nanluogu Xiang.

Extensively renovated in 2003, the gorgeous five-star China World Hotel delivers an outstanding level of service to its well-dressed complement of largely executive travellers. The sumptuous foyer is a masterpiece of Chinese motifs, glittering chandeliers, robust columns and smooth acres of marble, an effect complemented by thoroughly modern and comfortable rooms. The amenities are extensive, dining options are first-rate and shopping needs meet their match at the upscale China World Trade Center. Wi-fi access is available.

ST REGIS

Map pp268-9   YYYY

Běijīng Guójì Jùlèbù Fàndiàn
北京国际俱乐部饭店
☎ 6460 6688; www.stregis.com/beijing;
21 Jianguomenwai Dajie 建国门外大街21号;
d/ste Y3150/3980; Ⓜ Jianguomen; 🖥 ✕ 🛒 ♿

Its extravagant foyer augmented by thorough professionalism and a tip-top location, the St Regis is a marvellous, albeit costly, five-star choice. Sumptuous and soothing rooms ooze comfort, 24-hour butlers are at hand to fine tune your stay and a gorgeous assortment of restaurants, including Danieli's, steers you into one of Běijīng's finest dining zones.

GRAND HOTEL BEIJING

Map pp268-9   YYYY

Guìbīnlóu Fàndiàn 贵宾楼饭店
☎ 6513 7788; www.grandhotelbeijing.com.cn;
35 Dongchang'an Jie 东长安街35号; standard
tw/ste incl breakfast Y3450/5175; Ⓜ Tiananmen
Dong or Wangfujing; ♿

With regal views over the Forbidden City, this hotel finds itself on some of Běijīng's most prized real estate, but a failure to capitalise on its assets results in a tired and unexceptional presentation, considering the weighty tariff. Wi-fi access.

DŌNGCHÉNG 东城

Riddled with both *hútòng* and history, you'll find the best courtyard hotels in Dōngchéng, as well as a handful of decent budget options. High-calibre top-end hotels tend to cluster close to the shopping street of Wangfujing Dajie.

BEIJING SAGA INTERNATIONAL YOUTH HOSTEL Map p262   Y

Běijīng Shíjiā Guójì Qīngnián Lǚshè
北京时家国际青年旅社

☎ 6527 2773; sagayangguang@yahoo.com; 9 Shijia Hutong 史家胡同9号; dm Y55, d Y180/198, tr Y210; ⊕ Dengshikou (under construction); 🖳 This modern and very popular hostel is ensconced within a historic *hútòng*, offering a standard array of clean and well-kept rooms, a spacious seating area in the main reception area, rooftop common area, table football, a refectory, bar, internet access (Y10 per hour) and washing machine (Y10 per load). Great Wall trips can be arranged, as well as outings to watch acrobats.

PEKING DOWNTOWN BACKPACKERS ACCOMMODATION Map p262   Y

Dōngtáng Kèzhàn 东堂客栈

☎ 8400 2429; www.backpackingchina.com; 85 Nanluogu Xiang 南锣鼓巷85号; 4/3-bed dm Y65/75, windowless d/d incl breakfast per person Y60/80; ⊕ Andingmen; For backpacker arrivals in town, the central location, helpful staff and lively *hútòng* aspect are hard to beat. Doubles are tidy (no TV), with plastic wood floor and clean shower rooms. Free breakfast and free pickup from Capital Airport (you pay the toll, Y20), plus bike rental (per day Y20, Y300 deposit), internet access (Y6 per hour), adjacent backpacker restaurant, all the nearby bars of Nanluogu Xiang and trips to the Great Wall.

LUSONGYUAN HOTEL Map p262   Y

Lǚsōngyuán Bīnguǎn 侣松园宾馆

☎ 6404 0436; 22 Banchang Hutong 板厂胡同 22号; s/d/ste Y458/780-880/1600; ⊕ Zhangziz-honglu (under construction); 🚌 104 to Bei Bingma Si stop; 🖳 Rooms may be a bit cramped at this *hútòng* hotel, a courtyard house built by a Mongolian general during the Qing dynasty, but the location and setting are big plus points, and guests can sit out quaffing drinks in the courtyard during spring and summer. Pocket-sized singles come with pea-sized baths; dorms have three beds (with TV, no windows, common shower), there is just one suite and a handful of double bedrooms, so book ahead. Rooms facing

onto the courtyard are slightly more expensive. There's also bike rental (half/full day Y15/30) and a pricey email centre (open from 7.30am to 10pm; Y5 for 10 minutes).

XINMINGJI HOTEL Map p262   Y

Xīnmíngjī Bīnguǎn 新明基宾馆

☎ 6407 9911; fax 6401 2337; 140 Jiaodaokou Nandajie 交道口南大街140号; d from Y160; ⊕ Zhangzizhonglu (under construction) Handily located, this modest hotel may not be buried down a *hútòng*, but it's in the old part of town with decent and very competitively priced rooms over a small number of floors and friendly staff.

FANGYUAN HOTEL Map p262   Y

Fāngyuán Bīnguǎn 芳园宾馆

☎ 6525 6331; www.cbw.com/hotel/fangyuan; 36 Dengshikou Xijie 灯市口西街36号; d inc breakfast Y198-280, ste Y422; ⊕ Dengshikou (under construction); 🖳 Without its strategic location just west of Wangfujing Dajie or helpful tourist info centre, this good-value spot – its front door guarded by a pair of stone felines – would swiftly join the ranks of the anonymous two star. A minor refit has occurred and all rooms – downstairs cheapies included – are comfortable enough. Staff is used to dealing with foreign travellers, so blank expressions at reception are mercifully kept to a minimum. Breakfast is free, but it's of the boiled egg and congee variety. Internet access is Y10 per hour, bike rental Y20 per day.

BAMBOO GARDEN HOTEL Map p262   Y

Zhúyuán Bīnguǎn 竹园宾馆

☎ 5852 0088; www.bbgh.com.cn; 24 Xiaoshiqiao Hutong 小石桥胡同24号; s/d/ste Y380/680-880/980; ⊕ Gulou Within roaming distance of the Drum and Bell Towers and Houhai Lake, the cosy, intimate and leafy courtyard aspect is impaired by the jarring modern block opposite and occasionally casual staff, but this place still gets good reviews. The buildings date to the late Qing dynasty, its gardens belonging to a eunuch from Empress Cixi's entourage. The small singles are cheap but ordinary, so upgrading to the more pleasant doubles and suites is recommended. Reception is through the gates on your left.

HAOYUAN HOTEL Map p262 Y

Hǎoyuán Bīnguǎn 好园宾馆

☎ 6512 5557; www.haoyuanhotel.com; 53 Shijia Hutong 史家胡同53号; standard/deluxe d Y585/715, ste Y780-1040; ⊕ Dengshikou (under construction); 🖳

Visitors aiming to get into *hútòng* mode could do worse than hanging their hat in this charming courtyard hotel guarded by a pair of stone lions, where tasteful standard double rooms are delightfully arranged with classical Chinese furniture and the red lantern-hung courtyard feng shui weaves its magical charms. The Qing dynasty buildings were once home to Hua Guofeng (Communist Party chairman after Mao Zedong) but the suites in the rear tree-dotted courtyard boast unexpected mod cons – one has a sauna, the other a Jacuzzi bath. Internet is Y10 per hour. Reception is on the left as you enter; pursue discounts during the slack season.

CUI MING ZHUANG HOTEL

Map p262 YY

Cuìmíng Zhuāng Bīnguǎn 翠明庄宾馆

☎ 6513 6622; www.cuimingzhuanghotel.com .cn; 1 Nanheyan Dajie 南河沿大街1号; d/ste Y600/1200; ⊕ Tiananmen Dong

Fronted by a reproduction Chinese roof with green tiles, this pleasant and quiet three-star hotel dates from the 1930s. During the 1940s, the building was an office of the Chinese Communist Party, which helped agree to the ceasefire between the Kuomintang and the communists. It largely caters to Chinese guests, but is excellently located for the Forbidden City and Wangfujing Dajie. Facilities include a billiard room, ticketing office, Sunshine Café and shuffleboard.

NANJING GREAT HOTEL

Map p262 YY

Běijīng Nánjīng Dàfàndiàn 北京南京大饭店

☎ 6526 2188; 5 Xi Jie 西街5号; d incl breakfast Y998; ⊕ Wangfujing; 🖳

This popular, new Chinese-managed mid-range hotel right in the centre of town has competitively priced and comfortable rooms. The location, a ten-minute walk east of the Forbidden City and just by Wangfujing Dajie is a winner, although staff English-language skills can be rudimentary.

REGENT BEIJING Map p262 YYY

Běijīng Lìjīng Dàjiǔdiàn 北京丽晶大酒店

☎ 8522 1888; www.regenthotels.com; 99 Jinbao Lu; d incl breakfast Y1200 (only promotional rate available at time of writing); ⊕ Dengshikou (under construction); 🖳 ✕ 🐾 🕭

Christmas unwrapped 2006, the lavish brand new 500-room Regent has staked out a precious plot of land on the corner of Jinbao Lu and Dongdan Beidajie to the east of Wangfujing Dajie. Guest rooms are luxuriously-styled and up-to-the-minute (complimentary high-speed internet access, flat screen TVs) and a full range of health and leisure facilities and five restaurants round off the impressive picture.

RED CAPITAL RESIDENCE

Map p262 YYY

Xīnhóngzī Kèzhàn 新红资客栈

☎ 6402 7150; www.redcapitalclub.com.cn; 9 Dongsi Liutiao 东四六条9号; r incl breakfast Y1200-1450; ⊕ Dongsishitiao

Dressed up with Liberation-era artefacts and established in a glorious Qing dynasty courtyard, this unusual guesthouse is heady with the nostalgia of a vanished age. Make your choice from five rooms decked out with stuff that wouldn't look out of place in a museum: the Chairman's Residence, the Concubine Suites (each with their own courtyard), or the two author suites named after Edgar Snow and Han Suyin. Also in the spirit of the pastiche is the Bomb Shelter Bar, pampering its guests with wine, cigars and propaganda films from a shelter excavated on the orders of Vice-Chairman Lin Biao. For those who really want to get into the swing, the hotel can also arrange cruises of Běijīng's streets in the Red Flag limousine that belonged to Jiang Qing (Mao's doomed wife and Gang of Four member).

NOVOTEL PEACE HOTEL

Map p262 YYY

Běijīng Nuòfùtè Hépíng Bīnguǎn 北京诺富特和平宾馆

☎ 6512 8833; www.novotelpeace.bj.com; 3 Jinyu Hutong 金鱼胡同3号; West Bldg d Y1826, East Bldg d Y1992; ⊕ Dengshikou (under construction); 🖳 🕭

The centrally located Novotel has more flair and a better location than its Chongwenmen sibling, and is far cheaper than the

TOP FIVE COURTYARD HOTELS

- **Haoyuan Hotel** (opposite) Delightful Qing dynasty courtyard in the centre of Běijīng.
- **Lusongyuan Hotel** (p183) Tucked delightfully away down a historic *hútòng*, with bundles of character.
- **Red Lantern House** (p187) Budget hotel with courtyard-style charm in an authentic Běijīng locale.
- **Red Capital Residence** (opposite) Historic courtyard hotel with a handful of nostalgically styled rooms.
- **Bamboo Garden Hotel** (p183) Quiet and spacious courtyard hotel with pleasant grounds in the vicinity of the Drum and Bell Towers.

gilt-edged tariff of the Peninsula across the street. With a fresh and cosmopolitan feel, a straightforward elegance rules without the ostentatious frills. A popular ground floor buffet restaurant and good facilities round off the picture. The cheaper and older rooms in the more scuffed West Wing were undergoing renovation at the time of writing, so prices could take a hike.

PENINSULA BEIJING Map p262 YYY
Wángfǔ Fàndiàn 王府饭店
☎ 8516 2888; www.peninsula.com; 8 Jinyu Hutong 金鱼胡同8号; d Y1920; ⊕ Dengshikou (under construction); 🖵 🖼 ᬓ
Owned by the Peninsula Group and having been repackaged with a further name change (it was previously the Peninsula Palace), the ever-popular Peninsula Beijing is a cornerstone of ostentatious living in Běijīng. Up front with its exclusivity, the hotel hints at classical Chinese grandeur, from the decorative arch outside to the lobby's white marble bridge arching over the fountain floors below, but this is a purely modern tower hotel. Even if the exclusive basement mall is a ghost town of empty, hyperpriced outlets, this is also where you find Jing – with its profusion of glass beads cascading from the lobby above – and Huang Ting, the Peninsula's two signature restaurants.

CROWNE PLAZA HOTEL Map p262 YYYY
Běijīng Guójì Yìyuàn Huángguàn Jiàrì Jiǔdiàn
北京国际艺苑皇冠假日酒店
☎ 6513 3388; www.crowneplaza.com; 48 Wangfujing Dajie 王府井大街48号; d/ste Y2760/4410; ⊕ Dengshikou (under construction)
Refitted and overhauled in 2005, the five-star Crowne Plaza enjoys an excellent cen-

tral location on Wangfujing Dajie, but has little character or charm with odd-looking sculpture dotted around. Up-to-date rooms have the full range of business comforts and pleasant bathrooms. Wi-fi access.

CHÁOYÁNG 朝阳

Most top-end options in this district can be found near the Sanlitun embassy area and the Lufthansa Center. Midrange options are more limited and a few hotels for those on a budget can be found. This might not be the most historic part of town and only a few of Běijīng's top sights are located here, but travellers will appreciate the proximity to the bar streets of Sanlitun.

ZHAOLONG INTERNATIONAL YOUTH HOSTEL Map p264 Y
Zhàolóng Qīngnián Lǚshè 兆龙青年旅社
☎ 6597 2299; www.zhaolonghotel.com.cn; 2 Gongrentiyuchang Beilu 工人体育场北路2号; 2-/3-/4-/5-/6-bed dm Y70/60/60/50/50, s/deluxe r Y100/380; ⊕ Dongsishitiao; 🖵
A six-floor block tucked away behind the Zhaolong Hotel, this good choice has tidy common areas and clean rooms, laundry (Y10 to Y20), internet (Y10 per hour), kitchen, reading room, air-con, safe, bike rental (Y30 per day), 24-hour hot water (communal showers) and a ground floor café. Non-HI members pay an extra Y10 on all dorms but the mark-up is larger on other rooms. Breakfast is an additional Y15 (from 7am to 10am). Book rooms in youth hostels nationwide for a Y10 deposit.

YOU YI YOUTH HOSTEL Map p264 Y
Yǒuyì Qīngnián Jiǔdiàn 友谊青年酒店
☎ 6417 2632; fax 6415 6866; 43 Beisanlitun Nan 北三里屯南43号; dm/d Y70/180; ⊕ Dongsishitiao or Dongzhimen
Adjacent to Poacher's Inn and readily equipped with popular on-site bar the Tree (p145; ☎ 6415 1954; www.treebeijing.com), this handy hostel lies at the nucleus of the Sanlitun bar and restaurant ghetto. Rooms are clean and comfortable enough: four-bed dorms have dark-wood bunks and air-con, doubles (with phone, TV, air-con and radiator) are bright and spacious with large beds and the free laundry service is a hospitable,

albeit sometimes erratic, gesture. There is internet access (Y10 per hour), and room rates include breakfast (from 7.30am to 9am; toast, coffee, eggs and sausage).

HOME INN Map p264   Y
Rújiā Kuàijié Jiǔdiàn 如家快捷酒店
☎ 5120 3288; fax 5120 3299; www.homeinns .com; 2a Xinzhong Jie 新中街2甲; d from Y279; ⊚ Dongzhimen

A link in the successful and value-for-money lower midrange Home Inn chain (p181), this large branch may not be centrally located, but the position a short distance from Dongzhimen underground station immediately plugs you into the Běijīng subway system. The overall effect is formulaic, but dependably modern and clean. Reserve ahead.

RED HOUSE HOTEL Map p264   Y
Ruìxiù Bīnguǎn 瑞秀宾馆
☎ 6416 7500; www.redhouse.com.cn; 10 Chunxiu Lu; s/tw Y350/400, ste Y600; ⊚ Dongzhimen

Putting you within orbit of the Sanlitun bar scene, rooms are clean and tidy, with wood-strip flooring, traditional-style furniture and good shower rooms. Breakfast is thrown in, there's bike rental (per day Y30), a handy on-site pub with essential English Premier League football action (Club Football Center, p144) and free laundry.

COMFORT INN Map p264   YYY
Kāifù Fàndiàn 凯富饭店
☎ 8523 5522; fax 8523 5577; 6 Gongrentiyu-chang Beilu 工人体育场北路6号; d incl breakfast Y1357; ⊚ Dongsishitiao then bus113; 🖥 ✖ 🏊 ♿

Benefiting from a first rate location near the Sanlitun bar and restaurant district, this modern midrange hotel has rather bland but serviceable rooms, equipped with free internet, cable and satellite TV and a top-floor indoor pool.

KERRY CENTER HOTEL
Map p264   YYY
Jiālǐ Zhōngxīn Fàndiàn 嘉里中心饭店
☎ 6561 8833; www.shangri-la.com; 1 Guanghua Lu 光华路1号; d Y1600; ⊚ Guomao; 🖥 🏊 ♿

Since opening in 1999, the business type-oriented Kerry Center remains modern and eye-catching – from the funky, droopy col-oured glass bowls at reception to the svelte female attendants at Centro, the hotel's signature bar. The 34 sq metre doubles are crisp and comfortable, with sliding doors onto well-designed bathrooms with both shower and (small) bath. The gym is huge and well-equipped, the swimming pool substantial, and the adjacent Kerry Mall answers shopping needs. Wi-fi access.

SWISSÔTEL Map p264   YYYY
Gǎngào Zhōngxīn Ruìshì Jiǔdiàn
港澳中心瑞士酒店
☎ 6553 2288; www.swissotel-beijing.com; 2 Chaoyangmen Beidajie; d/ste Y2755/3675; ⊚ Dongsishitiao; 🏊

Located just outside the Dongsishitiao subway station, this five-star hotel (managed by Raffles International) has decent-sized rooms, an excellent gym and swimming pool and a much-liked buffet breakfast that gets travellers' thumbs up. Guests moan that spoken English is not up to scratch, but staff are helpful and the (expensive) restaurants get positive reviews. Excellent discounts.

KEMPINSKI HOTEL Map p264   YYYY
Kǎibīnsījī Fàndiàn 凯宾斯基饭店
☎ 6465 3388; www.kempinski-beijing.com; Lufthansa Center, 50 Liangmaqiao Lu; d Y3010; ⊚ Dongsishitiao then bus 701

The location next to the Lufthansa Center Youyi Shopping City (p166) might be convenient for shopping sprees, but this corner of Běijīng has precious little history. If you want gleaming shoes, stop off at the shoe-shine man and his marvellous, glittering brass shoe rest in the lobby (he operates from 7am to 10pm). There's also a large range of shops, including carpet shops and art galleries (with insipid artwork). As well, there is a decent gym and a good deli and bakery.

ORIENTAL GARDEN HOTEL
Map p264   YYYY
Dōngfāng Huáyuán Fàndiàn 东方花园饭店
☎ 6416 8866; fax 6415 0638; 6 Dongzhimen Nandajie 东直门南大街6号; d/ste Y2580/3110; 🖥 🏊 ♿

This recently renovated four-star Chinese-run business hotel has comfortable and attractive guest rooms, Cantonese and Shànghǎi restaurants and a coffee shop.

FĒNGTÁI & XUĀNWŬ
丰台、宣武

BEIJING FEIYING INTERNATIONAL YOUTH HOSTEL

Map pp266-7   Y

Běijīng Fēiyīng Qīngnián Lǚshè
北京飞鹰青年旅社

☎ 6315 1165; iyhfy@yahoo.com.cn; Bldg 10; Changchun Jie Hou Jie, Xuanwumen Xidajie 宣武门西大街长椿街后街10号楼; 10-/5-bed dm Y30/50, d Y180; ⓜ Changchunjie; 🖳

On the edge of things as youth hostels go, but easy access to the subway is a plus here. Bicycle hire, washing machine, kitchen, tourist info as well as internet access (Y10 per hour); no lift. Non-HI members pay Y10 extra for five-bed dorms and an additional Y20 for double rooms. Take exit C at Changchunjie subway stop and walk east past the McDonalds for around 200m.

FAR EAST INTERNATIONAL YOUTH HOSTEL

Map pp266-7   Y

Yuǎndōng Guójì Qīngnián Lǚshè;
远东国际青年旅社

☎ 6301 8811, ext 3118; courtyard@elong.com; 113 Tieshu Xiejie 铁树斜街113号; Youth Hostel dm high/low season Y60/45; ⓜ Hepingmen

This hostel is in a pretty old courtyard opposite the hotel of the same name. It is an extremely pleasant and clean place with loads of character, internet (Y10 per hour), bike rental (Y20 per day, Y200 deposit), kitchen, washing facilities and a fine bar-café. There is also a table tennis room, a shop (selling IP cards), a tourist office (open from 7.30am to 11.30pm), pricey VCD rental (Y2 to Y5) and guests can lounge around in the courtyard when the weather's warm. Rooms come without TV, phone or shower. The **Far East Hotel** (Map pp266-7; s/d/tr Y238/398/378, q Y75 per person) opposite is an unremarkable two-star hotel, but the quads downstairs are clean with wood-strip floorings and well-kept bunk beds. The hotel has a decent café-bar with sports TV downstairs (open from noon to midnight), plus a kitchen with two washing machines and a fridge.

QIANMEN JIANGUO HOTEL

Map pp266-7   YYY

Qiánmén Jiànguó Fàndiàn 前门建国饭店
☎ 6301 6688; fax 6301 3883; 175 Yong'an Lu 永安路175号; d/tr/ste incl breakfast Y1078/1298/1430; ⓜ Hepingmen; ♿

Elegant in parts and popular with tour groups (lured by its combination of excellent location and value), this hotel makes brave efforts to ward off that great curse: the generic three-star Chinese hotel effect. Business is brisk so staff is on their toes, even if somewhat reluctant. Rooms are spacious, clean and attractively carpeted and come with satellite TV and phones in bathrooms. You can find the Liyuan Theatre (p148) to the right of the domed atrium at the rear of the hotel.

MARCO POLO BEIJING

Map pp266-7   YYY

Běijīng Mǎgē Bóluó Jiǔdiàn 北京马哥孛罗酒店
☎ 6603 6688; www.marcopolohotels.com; 6 Xuanwumennei Dajie 宣武门内大街6号; d/ste Y1080/1580; ⓜ Xidan or Xuanwumen; 🖳

North of the South Cathedral (p97), this unfussy four-star hotel is the best in this part of town. A length in the hotel pool may only take a few strokes, but the basement Clark Hatch Fitness Centre is well-equipped and handy underground stations are nearby.

HĂIDIÀN & XĪCHÉNG
海淀、西城

RED LANTERN HOUSE

Map pp260-1   Y

Fǎnggǔ Yuán 仿古园
☎ 6611 5771; 5 Zhengjue Hutong 正觉胡同5号; 4-bed dm Y60, 6-bed dm Y55, d Y180-220; ⓜ Jishuitan; 🖳

This great place couples its homely courtyard-style look – hung outside with climbing plants – with a winning *hútòng* location a short stroll from Houhai Lake. The context of its surrounding alleys and local markets transports you to a genuine Běijīng setting. Internet (Y6 per hour), washing (Y10 per kg), restaurant/bar in main lobby area. If it's full, try the equally good Red Lantern House 2 (p188; within walking distance).

RED LANTERN HOUSE 2

Map pp260-1 Y

Hóng Dēnglong 红灯笼

111 Xinjiekou Nandajie 新街口南大街111号;

6-bed dm Y55, s/d Y140-180/220; ▢

Its pretty, open courtyard charms, lazy tempo and helpful staff make this recently opened enclave of peace – just off busy Xinjiekou Nandajie – a relaxing proposition but the absence of phones in double rooms is an inconvenience. Our visit coincided with the construction of a new batch of rooms with adequate heating to fend off Běijīng's cruel winters. Hidden discreetly away off the main drag, take the small alley to the green door and hunt for the door bell. Laundry, bike rental, lockers, internet (Y6 per hour, from 8am to midnight).

SLEEPY INN Map pp260-1 Y

Lìshè Shíchàhǎi Guójì Qīngnián Jiǔdiàn
丽舍什刹海国际青年酒店

☎ 6406 9954; fax 6401 0235; www.sleepyinn .cn; 103 Deshengmennei Dajie 德胜门内大街 103号; 6-bed dm Y60, 4-bed dm Y80, tw/d Y258/258

This newcomer, with a mere 27 rooms and an adorable perch on Houhai Lake, has managed to incorporate one of the halls of the former Taoist Zhenwu Temple into its engaging and peaceful formula. Rooms are in the three-storey block, with clean pine-bed dorms and well-looked after doubles, similarly decked out with pine furnishings, but without phone or TV.

SHANGRI-LA HOTEL

Map pp260-1 YYY

Xiānggé Lǐlā Fàndiàn 香格里拉饭店

☎ 6841 2211; www.shangri-la.com;

29 Zizhuyuan Lu 紫竹园路29号;

d incl breakfast Y1370; ▢ ▣ ♿

The perfumed and air-freshened lobby and muted Chinese motifs may not have the majesty of sibling China World Hotel but rates are far lower, while the overall business and high occupancy rates – coupled with the looming 2008 Olympics – have prompted the construction of a new tower brimful with spacious Horizon rooms, due for unwrapping in 2007. Modest-sized swimming pool.

RITZ-CARLTON BEIJING, FINANCIAL STREET

Map pp260-1 YYYY

Běijīng Jīnróng Jiē Lìjiā Jiǔdiàn
北京金融街丽嘉酒店

☎ 6601 6666; www.ritzcarlton.com;

1 Jinchengfang Dongjie 金城坊东街1号;

d Y4600; wi-fi ▢ ▣

The magnificent Ritz-Carlton (opened 2006) in Běijīng's financial district has further raised the bar in Běijīng's exclusive hotel sector. Spacious rooms are at the apex of luxury, with outrageously comfortable beds, huge 37-inch flat screen TVs and further TVs in the bathroom. Occupying an entire floor, the spa and health club has won praise from pampered guests working off their meals enjoyed at the hotel's excellent restaurants.

FURTHER AFIELD

HOLIDAY INN LIDO BEIJING

Map pp258-9 YYY

Běijīng Lìdū Jiàrì Fàndiàn
北京丽都假日饭店

☎ 6437 6688; www.beijing-lido.holiday-inn.com;

cnr Jichang Lu & Jiangtai Lu; d Y1330;

▢ ✕ ▣ ♿

On the way to the airport, this hotel – the first Holiday Inn built in China – has virtually everything you may need with excellent amenities and a well-resourced shopping mall.

Excursions

Excursions

He who has not climbed the Great Wall is not a true man.

Mao Zedong

Getting out of town can help blow the nitrogen dioxide and construction dust from your hair and lungs, while offering a glimpse of more rugged and exciting terrain. You've already made it to Běijīng, so why not go that extra mile and dig a bit deeper into the China experience.

Some of China's most famous monuments lie within Běijīng Municipality, outside the city proper. The **Great Wall** is an obligatory sight for visitors, and several restored stretches can be visited on day trips outside town. Trips to the Great Wall are often combined with visits to the **Ming Tombs**, the stately burial place of 13 of the Ming emperors. For those interested in dynastic remains and Chinese tomb architecture, further imperial tombs can also be explored at the **Eastern Qing Tombs**.

Several of Běijīng's most famous temples lie within reach of town, including **Tanzhe Temple** and **Jietai Temple**. The remoteness of the ancient hillside village of **Chuāndǐxià** has partially protected its charming streets and buildings from full-scale commercialisation and the community still provides a fascinating snapshot of disappearing China.

Further from Běijīng (300km), the Ming dynasty garrison town of **Shānhǎiguān** is being repackaged from the soles up, but visits allow travellers to skirt the edge of China's mighty northeast while exploring a famous section of the Great Wall north of town.

A one- or two-day trip to the imperial retreat of **Chéngdé**, 255km northeast of Běijīng, should be a high priority for travellers to Běijīng. The scenery is magnificent and beyond the grounds of the imperial estate rises an impressive scattering of hillside temple architecture.

THE GREAT WALL 长城

Also known to the Chinese as the '10,000 Li Wall' (Wànlǐ Chángchéng; 万里长城) – one 'Li' is a Chinese unit of distance equal to around half a kilometre, so this effectively means the '5000km Wall' – and famously ignored by Marco Polo in his travelogue, the piecemeal Great Wall (Chángchéng) meanders across China, snaking from its scattered remnants on the North Korean border through Inner Mongolia and staggering on to its earthen vestiges at Lop Nur in the mighty northwest province of Xīnjiāng.

Standard histories emphasise the unity of the Wall. The 'original' Wall was begun over 2000 years ago during the Qin dynasty (221–207 BC), when China was unified under Emperor Qin Shihuang. Separate walls, constructed by independent kingdoms to keep out marauding nomads, were linked together. The effort required hundreds of thousands of workers, many of them political prisoners, and 10 years of hard labour under General Meng Tian. An estimated 180 million cu metres of rammed earth were used to form the core of the original Wall, and legend has it that one of its more gruesome building materials was the bones of workers.

The Wall never really did perform its function as an impenetrable line of defence. As Genghis Khan supposedly said, 'The strength of a wall depends on the courage of those who defend it'. Sentries could be bribed and loyalties could be swayed. However, it did work very well as a kind of elevated highway, transporting people and equipment across mountainous terrain. Its beacon tower system, using smoke signals generated by burning wolves' dung, transmitted news of enemy movements quickly back to the capital. To the west in Gānsù province was the fort at Jiāyùguān, a strategic link on the Silk Rd, where unwanted mortals were ejected through the gates to face the terrifying wild west.

Prior to the Ming era, the Wall was largely constructed of tamped earth, without an outer brick cladding. During the Ming dynasty a valiant effort was made to fortify the bastion, this time facing it with bricks and stone slabs – some 60 million cu metres worth. The project took over 100 years, and the costs in human effort and resources were phenomenal.

INJURIES ON THE GREAT WALL

Never in his most vivid nightmares could the Great Wall's first architect Emperor Qin Shihuang picture barbarians wobbling around his bastion in 'I climbed the Great Wall' T-shirts. His edifice occasionally retaliates, however, against ill-prepared or over-adventurous tourists.

Despite being a generally hazard-free outing for most day-trippers, more elderly or unfit travellers can drag a twisted ankle or even a broken leg back with them through customs. Certain parts of the rampart, especially the steeper reaches, can exhaust the unfit and the steps are often uneven.

Sīmǎtái can be precarious and Huánghuā, with its wilder sections, can be quite treacherous. Solo travel along the Great Wall can be perilous: walkers have fallen from the Wall, while there have been reports of travellers being assaulted on more remote parts of the Wall. In 2002, a British tourist was murdered on the Wall.

Avoid climbing the Great Wall during thunderstorms. A Greek tourist was killed by lightning in 2005; reports suggest she was using a mobile phone when struck, although it is uncertain whether there is any causal connection between lightning strikes and mobile phone use. Take bottled water and shoes with a good grip. If going on a long hike, be well-prepared for changeable weather.

Perhaps because they breached the bastion with little fuss at Shānhǎiguān (p200) to install the Qing dynasty (1644–1911), China's Manchu overlords had little time for the Wall, which fell into further disrepair during the republic (1911–1949). The war with Japan and the civil war further compounded the damage, a decline that was exacerbated by the communists under Mao Zedong, who encouraged the pillaging of the Wall for building materials. According to locals, the reservoir dam at Huánghuā (p196) was assembled with bricks from the neighbouring Wall.

Classic postcard images of the Wall – flawlessly clad in bricks and stoutly undulating over hills into the distance – stretch the truth of the bastion today. Much of the Wall has been either neglected or plundered for its raw materials (farmers have pillaged its earthen core for use on the fields and the Wall has generated a useful and free supply of stone, stripped from its rampart for use on road and building construction) leaving it either in a state of ruin or reduced to dust by the erosion of time. According to some estimates, two thirds of the Wall has now been lost.

In recent years the Great Wall has had to contend with a growing popularity as a venue for summer parties ('wild orgies' according to the *China Daily*). Attended by thousands of drunken revellers, the festivities at Jīnshānlǐng sparked concern at the perceived desecration of a national monument. A company was recently fined US$50,000 for driving a road through a section of the Wall in Inner Mongolia.

Popular sections of the Wall outside Běijīng have been restored and dolled up for tourist consumption and so arrive heavily packaged, replete with souvenir shops, raucous hawkers, restaurants, amusement park rides and guard rails. Seeking communion with the Wall *au naturel*, unimpressed travellers have increasingly ferreted out unrestored sections of the Wall where local communities charge far less than the official sites. Huánghuā (p196) is the most well-known example of such undeveloped chunks of the Great Wall. The authorities discourage such visits with threats of fines. They argue that they are seeking to prevent damage to unrestored sections of the Wall by traipsing visitors, but they are also keen to keep the tourist revenue flowing to designated parts of the Wall.

The myth that the Great Wall is visible with the naked eye from the moon was finally laid to rest in 2003, when China's first astronaut Yang Liwei failed to see the barrier from space. The Great Wall is certainly not visible from the moon, where even individual continents are barely perceptible. The Great Wall is not wide enough to be visible from space; motorways, which are far wider, would certainly be more visible at altitude. The myth is to be edited from Chinese textbooks, where it has cast its spell over generations of Chinese.

The most touristed area of the Wall is Bādálǐng. Also renovated but less touristy are Sīmǎtái and Jīnshānlǐng. The Jiǎo Shān section at Shānhǎiguān (p201) is also worth seeing.

When choosing a tour, it is essential to check that it visits the places you want to see. Tours to the Great Wall are often combined with trips to the Ming Tombs, so ask beforehand and if you don't want to visit the Ming Tombs, choose another tour. Far more worryingly, less reputable tours make painful (and sometimes expensive) diversions to gem exhibition halls and Chinese medicine centres. At the latter, tourists are herded off the bus and analysed by white-coated doctors, who diagnose ailments that can only be cured with high-priced Chinese remedies (supplied there and then). The tour organisers receive a commission from the gem showroom/medicine centre for every person they manage to funnel through, so you are simply lining other people's pockets. See Organised Tours in the Sights for a selection of outfits that can arrange tours to the Great Wall, but ensure you know what the tour entails. The handiest tours to the Great Wall depart from the Beijing Sightseeing Bus Centre (Běijīng Lǚyóu Jísàn Zhōngxīn; ☎ 8353 1111) east and west of Front Gate (p76) at Qianmen alongside Tiananmen Square but your hotel may run an equally convenient tour; many of the youth hostel tours to the Great Wall come recommended. As with other popular destinations in China, avoid visiting the Great Wall at weekends and during the big national holiday periods in the first week of May and October.

If trudging along the Wall fails to get your heart pumping, consider turning your legs to stone tackling the 3700 steps and brutal inclines of the Great Wall Marathon (www.great-wall-marathon.com).

BĀDÁLǏNG 八达岭

This is a Great Wall and only a great people with a great past could have a great wall and such a great people with such a great wall will surely have a great future.

President Richard Nixon

At an elevation of 1000m, the Great Wall's most high-profile and most-photographed vista is 70km northwest of Běijīng at Bādálǐng. Most visitors to the Great Wall take in Bādálǐng, including US President Richard Nixon, on his 1972 visit to China.

The masonry here was first erected during the enterprising Ming dynasty (1368–1644), with subsequent heavy restoration work in the 1950s and 1980s. Punctuated with watchtowers (dílóu), the 6m wide wall is clad in brick, typical of the neat stonework so characteristic of the Ming.

Amid raw and striking scenery, this is the place to see the Wall snaking off in classic fashion into the hills. Also come here for guardrails, souvenir stalls, a fairground feel and the companionship of squads of tourists surging over the ramparts. If your visit coincides

TRANSPORT

Distance from Běijīng 70km
Direction Northwest
Tours All the operators under Organised Tours in the Sights chapter (p71) run tours to Bādálǐng. Some hotels charge astronomical prices for tours, but they can be convenient and you can depart from your hotel. Youth hostels run popular and value-for-money tours.
Local Bus The cheapest route to Bādálǐng is on bus 919 from just north of the Deshengmen gate tower, about 500m east of the Jishuitan subway stop. Buses leave regularly from 6.30am; ordinary buses take two hours and cost Y5, while faster, nonstop buses take one hour and cost Y12. The last bus leaves Bādálǐng for Beijing at 6.30pm.
Tour Bus Tour buses to Bādálǐng depart from the twin depots of the Beijing Sightseeing Bus Centre (Běijīng Lǚyóu Jísàn Zhōngxīn; ☎ 8353 1111) east and west of Front Gate (p76) at Qianmen alongside Tiananmen Square. The main depot is the western station. Line C (Y90 return; price includes entry to Great Wall; departures 8am-11.30am) runs to Bādálǐng; Line A runs to Bādálǐng and Dìng Líng at the Ming Tombs (Y160; includes entrance tickets and lunch; departures 6.30am-10.30am). Plan about nine hours for the whole trip. Touts for inexpensive Chinese tour buses patrol the Beijing Train Station forecourt, but they may detour to scam destinations and are best avoided.
Taxi A taxi to Bādálǐng and back will cost a minimum of Y400 for an eight-hour hire with a maximum of four passengers.

with a summer weekend crush, you won't be able to move, so aim to visit during the week. Winter trips are also possible, but you will need to seriously wrap up and be prepared for stinging cold and sharp winds – Bādálǐng can be much colder than urban Běijīng.

Two magnificent sections of wall trail off to the left and right of the main entrance. The restored sections crawl for quite a distance before nobly disintegrating into ruins; unfortunately you cannot realistically explore these more authentic fragments. Cable cars exist for the weary (Y50 round trip).

Apart from the pristine battlements, you can be conveyed back into history via 15-minute films about the Great Wall at the **Great Wall Circle Vision Theatre**, a 360-degree amphitheatre. The admission fee also gets you into the **China Great Wall Museum**. The **Badaling Safari World** (Bādálǐng Yěshēng Dòngwùyuán; admission Y70; 🕗 8am-5pm) is hardly what coming to the Wall is all about and children could be traumatised by watching live sheep being fed to the lions.

MÙTIÁNYÙ 慕田峪

The 2250m-long granite section of the Great Wall at Mùtiányù, in Huáiróu County, dates from Ming dynasty remains built upon an earlier Northern Qi-dynasty conception. Originally developed as an alternative to Bādálǐng, this stretch of the Wall is, in the balance, a less commercial experience. Despite some motivated hawking and tourist paraphernalia, Mùtiányù is notable for its numerous Ming dynasty guard towers and stirring views. The Wall is also equipped with a **cable car** (Y50 round trip; 🕗 8.30am to 4.30pm). October is the best month to visit, for the autumn colours of the trees that envelop the surrounding countryside.

TRANSPORT

Distance from Běijīng 90km
Direction Northeast
Local Bus From Dongzhimen long-distance bus station (Dōngzhímén Chángtú Qìchēzhàn; ☎ 6467 4995) take either bus 916 or 980 (both Y8, one hour 40 minutes) to Huáiróu (怀柔) then change for a minibus to Mùtiányù (Y25). Note: There is a possibility that buses from the Dongzhimen long-distance bus station could move to the nearby Dongzhimen Transport Hub (still under construction at the time of writing).
Tour Bus The Line A bus to Mùtiányù and Hongluo Temple (Hóngluó Sì) runs on Sundays and public holidays (Y110; price includes entrance ticket and return fare) between 6.30am and 8.30am from the Beijing Sightseeing Bus Centre (Běijīng Lǚyóu Jísàn Zhōngxīn; ☎ 8353 1111) east and west of Front Gate (p76) at Qianmen alongside Tiananmen Square and also from outside the South Cathedral at Xuanwumen.

JŪYŌNGGUĀN 居庸关

Originally constructed in the 5th century and rebuilt by the Ming, Jūyōngguān (Juyong Pass) was considered one of the most strategically significant parts of the Wall. Even though this section in Chāngpíng County feels as though all authenticity has been renovated out of it, it's the closest section of the Wall to Běijīng, it's usually reasonably quiet and the steep and somewhat strenuous circuit can be done in under two hours.

TRANSPORT

Distance from Běijīng 50km
Direction Northwest
Local Bus Jūyōngguān is on the road to Bādálǐng, so the public buses for Bādálǐng listed earlier will get you there.
Tour Bus From the Beijing Sightseeing Bus Centre (Běijīng Lǚyóu Jísàn Zhōngxīn; ☎ 8353 1111) east and west of Front Gate (p76) at Qianmen alongside Tiananmen Square, Line B buses travel to Jūyōngguān and Dìng Líng at the Ming Tombs (Y125; includes entrance tickets and lunch) with departures between 6.30am and 10am.

SĪMǍTÁI 司马台

In Mìyún County near the town of Gǔběikǒu, the stirring remains at Sīmǎtái make for an exhilarating Great Wall experience. Built during the reign of Ming dynasty emperor Hongwu, the 19km stretch is characterised by watchtowers, steep plunges and scrambling ascents.

This rugged section of wall can be heart-thumpingly steep and the scenery is dramatic, although the masonry was due for a makeover, which could pacify its wilder moments. The eastern section of wall at Sīmǎtái is the most treacherous, sporting 16 watchtowers and dizzyingly steep ascents. From around the 12th watchtower, the climb gets very precarious. A few slopes have 70-degree inclines and you need both hands free, so bring a day-pack to hold your camera and other essentials. One narrow section of footpath has a 500m drop, so it's no place for acrophobics. The cable car (Y50 round trip) saves time and could be an alternative to a sprained ankle. Take strong shoes with a good grip.

Sīmǎtái has some unusual features, such as 'obstacle-walls' – walls-within-walls used for defending against enemies who'd already scaled the Great Wall. Small cannon have been discovered in this area, as well as evidence of rocket-type weapons, such as flying knives and flying swords.

TRANSPORT

Distance from Běijīng 110km
Direction Northeast
Local Bus Take a minibus (Y10; 1¼ hours) to Mìyún (密云) or bus 980 (Y10) from Dongzhimen long-distance bus station and change to a minibus to Sīmǎtái or a taxi (round trip Y120). Note: There is a possibility that buses from the Dongzhimen long-distance bus station could move to the nearby Dongzhimen Transport Hub (still under construction at the time of writing).
Tour Bus The weekend Line D tour bus (Y95; price includes entrance ticket) runs to Sīmǎtái from the Beijing Sightseeing Bus Centre (Běijīng Lǚyóu Jísàn Zhōngxīn; ☎ 8353 1111) east and west of Front Gate (p76) at Qianmen alongside Tiananmen Square and also from outside the South Cathedral at Xuanwumen. Buses depart on Fridays and Saturdays and public holidays between 6.30am and 8.30am.
Hotel Tours Backpacker hotels often run morning trips by minibus (Y60 to Y80, not including ticket).
Taxi Hiring a taxi from Běijīng for the day costs about Y400.

JĪNSHĀNLǏNG 金山岭

Though neither as steep nor as impressive as Sīmǎtái, the Great Wall at Jīnshānlǐng (Jīnshānlǐng Chángchéng; admission Y40) has 24 watchtowers and is relatively less developed, despite restoration work.

Jīnshānlǐng is also the starting point for a popular hike to Sīmǎtái. The distance between Jīnshānlǐng and Sīmǎtái is only about 10km, but it takes nearly four hours as the trail is steep and stony. Parts of the Wall between Jīnshānlǐng and Sīmǎtái have collapsed and much is in a state of ruin, but it can be traversed without too much difficulty even if you occasionally have to navigate around more precarious sections. Reaching Sīmǎtái, however, you will have to cross a suspension bridge (Y5), and you may be stung for another ticket to enter the Sīmǎtái section.

You can do the trek in the opposite direction, but getting a ride back to Běijīng from Sīmǎtái is easier than from Jīnshānlǐng. Of course, this won't be a problem if you've made arrangements with your driver to pick you up (and didn't pay him in advance).

TRANSPORT

Distance from Běijīng 110km
Direction Northeast
Local Bus From Dongzhimen long-distance bus station (☎ 6467 4995) take a minibus (Y10; 1¼ hours) or bus 980 (Y10) to Mìyún (密云), change to a minibus to Gǔběikǒu (古北口) and get off at Bākèshíyíng (巴克什营; Y7). If you are heading to Chéngdé (p203) you will pass Jīnshānlǐng en route. Note: There is a possibility that buses from the Dongzhimen long-distance bus station could move to the nearby Dongzhimen Transport Hub (still under construction at the time of writing).
Hotel Tours Běijīng youth hostels typically run day tours to Jīnshānlǐng, picking up hikers at Sīmǎtái.

HUÁNGHUĀ 黄花

The ever popular sections of the Great Wall at Huánghuā have breathtaking panoramas of partially unrestored brickwork and watchtowers snaking off in two directions. There is also a refreshing absence of amusement park rides, exasperating tourist trappings and the full-on commercial mania of Bādálǐng and other tourist bottlenecks.

Clinging to the hillside on either side of a reservoir, Huánghuā is a classic and well-preserved example of Ming defence with high and wide ramparts, intact parapets and sturdy beacon towers. Periodic but incomplete restoration work on the Wall has left its crumbling nobility and striking authenticity largely intact, with the ramparts occasionally dissolving into rubble. The Wall was much more impressive before parts of the Wall were knocked down to provide stones for the construction of the dam.

It is said that Lord Cai masterminded this section, employing meticulous quality control. Each *cùn* (inch) of the masonry represented one labourer's whole day's work. When the Ministry of War got wind of the extravagance, Cai was beheaded for his efforts. In spite of the trauma, his decapitated body stood erect for three days before toppling. Years later a general judged Lord Cai's Wall to be exemplary and he was posthumously rehabilitated.

Despite its lucrative tourist potential, authorities have failed to wrest Huánghuā from local villagers, who have so far resisted incentives to relinquish their prized chunks of heritage.

Official on-site signs declare that it's illegal to climb here, but locals pooh-pooh the warnings and encourage travellers to visit and clamber on the Wall. Fines are rarely enforced, although a theoretical risk exists.

From the road, you can go either way along the battlements. On the east side of the reservoir dam past the ticket collector (Y2; stick to the main entrance, other access points may charge Y4), the Wall climbs abruptly uphill from a solitary watchtower through an initial series of further watchtowers before going over and dipping down the hill to continue meandering on. Be warned that it's both steep and crumbling – there are no guardrails here and the Wall has not been restored. There may be further tickets ahead, depending on how far you venture. It's possible to make it all the way to the Mùtiányù section of the Wall (see p194), but it'll take you a few days and some hard clambering (pack a sleeping bag). Local hawkers have got wind of foreigners in the vicinity, but they won't follow you up the Wall.

In the other direction to the west, climb the steps past the ticket collector (Y2) to the Wall, from where an exhilarating walk can be made along the parapet. At the time of writing the path beyond the second watchtower was being restored, but should be finished by the time you read this. Things get a bit hairier beyond the third watchtower as there's a steep gradient and the wall is fragile here, but the view of the overgrown bastion winding off into hills is magnificent.

Shoes with good grip are important for climbing Huánghuā as some sections are either slippery (eg parts of the Wall south of the reservoir are simply smooth slopes at a considerable incline) or uneven and crumbling.

There are several simple outfits here if you want to spend the night at Huánghuā, with rooms ranging in price from Y10 to around Y100. At the entrance to the western part of

TRANSPORT

Distance from Běijīng 60km
Direction North

Local Bus From Dongzhimen long-distance bus station, take bus 916 or 980 to Huáiróu (怀柔; Y8; one hour 40 minutes; frequently from 5.30am-6.30pm) and get off at Míngzhū Guǎngchǎng (明珠广场), then cross the road and take a minibus and ask for Huánghuāchéng (黄花城; Y5; 40 minutes) – don't get off at the smaller Huánghuāzhèn by mistake. *Miàndi* (taxi van) drivers charge around Y30 to Y40 one way to reach Huánghuāchéng from Huáiróu. Note: There is a possibility that buses from the Dongzhimen long-distance bus station could move to the nearby Dongzhimen Transport Hub (still under construction at the time of writing).

Tour Bus The weekend Line G tour bus (Y75; includes entrance ticket) runs on Sunday and public holidays to the Huanghuacheng Great Wall Lakeside Reserve (opposite) from where you can take a taxi van to Huánghuā (Y10) or walk. Buses depart between 6.30am and 8.30am from the Beijing Sightseeing Bus Centre (Běijīng Lǚyóu Jísàn Zhōngxīn; ☎ 8353 1111) east and west of Front Gate (p76) at Qianmen alongside Tiananmen Square, and from outside the South Cathedral at Xuanwumen.

the wall, the **Ténglóng Fàndiàn** (腾龙饭店; ☎ 6165 1929; summer/winter d Y60/30) has clean and simple rooms (no fan, common toilet), with winter heating and a restaurant. The **Fúwàng Fàndiàn** (福旺饭店; ☎ 6165 2224) has clean Y100 doubles with toilet, shower and TV. Many of the restaurants at Huánghuā also offer rooms so ask around.

About 3km from Huánghuā (Y15 by taxi van) is the **Huanghuacheng Great Wall Lakeside Reserve** (Huánghuāchéng Shuǐchángchéng Lǚyóuqū; 黄花城水长城旅游区; ☎ 6165 1111; admission Y25) which has undeniably splendid views of the Wall clambering downhill above a reservoir. You cannot actually get on the Wall here so it is ultimately disappointing, although you can walk around the reservoir, and speedboats (Y15) can whisk you across the water. Also look out for old local women selling charming handmade embroidered children's shoes decorated with tiger faces, butterflies and flowers (Y25 a pair).

MING TOMBS 十三陵

Shísān Líng

The Ming Tombs (Shísān Líng) are the final resting place of 13 of the 16 Ming emperors. The Confucian layout and design may intoxicate erudite visitors, but some find the necropolis lifeless and ho-hum. Confucian shrines lack the vibrancy and colour of Buddhist or Taoist temples, and their motifs can be bewilderingly inscrutable.

The first Ming emperor, Hongwu, is buried not here but in Nánjīng, the first capital of the Ming dynasty. Three tombs have been opened up to the public – Cháng Líng, Dìng Líng and Zhāo Líng.

The Ming Tombs follow a standard layout for imperial tomb design. The plan typically consists of a main gate (Líng Mén), leading to the first of a series of courtyards and the main hall, the Hall of Eminent Favours (Língēn Diàn). Beyond lie further gates or archways, leading to the Soul Tower (Míng Lóu), behind which rises the burial mound (tumulus).

Cháng Líng, burial place of the Emperor Yongle, is the most impressive, with its series of magnificent halls lying beyond its yellow-tiled gate. Seated upon a three-tiered marble terrace, the most notable structure is the Hall of Eminent Favours, containing a recent statue of Yongle and a breathtaking interior with vast *nanmu* (cedar wood) columns. The pine-covered burial mound at the rear of the complex is yet to be excavated and is not open to the public.

Dìng Líng is the burial place of the emperor Wanli, and contains a series of subterranean interlocking vaults and the remains of the various gates and halls of the complex. Excavated in the late 1950s, some visitors find this tomb of more interest, as you are allowed to descend into

TRANSPORT

Distance from Běijīng 50km
Direction Northwest
Local Bus Take bus 345 (branch line, *zhīxiàn* 支线) from Deshengmen (德胜门), 500m east of Jishuitan subway station, to the Chāngpíng Dōngguān stop (昌平东关; Y6; one hour) and change to bus 314 for the tombs. Alternatively, take the standard bus 345 to Chāngpíng (昌平) and then a taxi to the tombs (Y20). You can also reach the Chāngpíng Dōngguān stop on bus 845 (Y10) from Xizhimen long-distance bus station, just outside the Xizhimen subway stop. It's about a 10-minute ride from Chāngpíng to the entrance to the tombs.

Tour Bus The easiest way to reach the tombs is by tour bus. Most tour buses usually combine a visit to the Ming Tombs with a visit to the Great Wall at Bādálǐng. The Line A bus (Y160; includes entrance tickets and lunch; departures 6.30am-10.30am) runs to Bādálǐng and Dìng Líng at the Ming Tombs from the Beijing Sightseeing Bus Centre (Běijīng Lǚyóu Jísàn Zhōngxīn; ☎ 8353 1111) east and west of Front Gate (p76) at Qianmen alongside Tiananmen Square. The Line B bus travels from the Beijing Sightseeing Bus Centre to Jūyōngguān and Dìng Líng at the Ming Tombs (Y125; includes entrance tickets and lunch) with departures between 6.30am and 10am.

the underground vault. Accessing the vault down the steps, visitors are confronted by the simply vast marble self-locking doors that sealed the chamber after it was vacated. Note the depression in the floor where the stone prop clicked into place once the door was finally closed.

Zhāo Líng, the resting-place of the 13th Ming emperor Longqing, follows an orthodox layout and is a tranquil alternative if you find the other tombs too busy. The rest of the tombs are in various stages of dilapidation and are sealed off by locked gates.

The road leading up to the tombs is a 7km stretch called the **Spirit Way** (Shén Dào; 神道). Commencing with a triumphal arch, the path enters the Great Palace Gate, where officials once had to dismount, and passes a giant *bìxì* (a mythical tortoise–dragon like animal), which bears the largest stele in China. A guard of 12 sets of stone animals and officials follows this. Your tour-bus driver may well speed past them, so insist if you want to see them.

EASTERN QING TOMBS 清东陵

Qīng Dōng Líng

The area of the Eastern Qing Tombs (Qīng Dōng Líng) could be called Death Valley, serving as the resting place for five emperors, 14 empresses and 136 imperial consorts. In the mountains ringing the valley are buried princes, dukes, imperial nurses and others.

As at the Ming Tombs, a spirit way (Shén Dào; 神道) is a principle design feature. Five emperors are interred here: Qianlong (Yù Líng), Kangxi (Jǐng Líng), Shunzhi (Xiào Líng), Xianfeng (Dìng Líng) and Tongzhi (Huì Líng). Emperor Qianlong (1711–99) started preparations when he was 30 and by the time he was 88 he had used up 90 tonnes of his silver. His resting place covers half a square kilometre. Some of the beamless stone chambers are decorated with Tibetan and Sanskrit sutras, and the doors bear bas-relief Bodhisattvas. Apart from Huì Líng, all of the tombs listed above are open to visitors.

Empress Dowager Cixi also got a head start. Her tomb, **Dìng Dōng Líng**, was completed some three decades before her death and also underwent considerable restoration before she was finally laid to rest. Her

TRANSPORT

Distance from Běijīng 125km
Direction East
Tour Bus The easiest way to reach the Eastern Qing Tombs is on the Line E tour bus (Y145; price includes entrance ticket) which runs on Saturday and public holidays between 6.30am and 8.30am from the Beijing Sightseeing Bus Centre (Běijīng Lǚyóu Jísàn Zhōngxīn; ☎ 8353 1111) east and west of Front Gate (p76) at Qianmen alongside Tiananmen Square and also from outside the South Cathedral at Xuanwumen. Pedicabs are available at the tombs (Y15).
Taxi A taxi from Běijīng should cost around Y400 for a day trip to the tombs.

tomb lies alongside the tomb of Empress Cian. The phoenix (the symbol of the empress) appears above that of the dragon (the symbol of the emperor) in the artwork at the front of the tomb – not side by side as on other tombs. Both tombs were plundered in the 1920s.

Located in Zūnhuā County, Héběi province, the Eastern Qing Tombs are blessed with a more dramatic setting than the Ming Tombs, although getting there is an expedition and getting around is difficult without a vehicle.

TANZHE TEMPLE & JIETAI TEMPLE

潭柘寺、戒台寺

Tánzhè Sì & Jiètái Sì

The largest of all Běijīng's temples, Tanzhe Temple (Tánzhè Sì) dates as far back as the 3rd century, with considerable later modifications.

The Buddhist temple is attractively placed amid trees in the mountains, its ascending temple grounds overlooked by towering cypress and pine trees – many of which are so old that their gangly limbs are supported by metal props. Don't miss the small **Talin Temple** (Tǎlín Sì; 塔林寺), by the forecourt where you disembark the bus, with its assembly of stupas. Visits to Tanzhe Temple around mid-April are recommended, as the magnolias are in bloom.

About 10km southeast of Tanzhe Temple, the smaller Jietai Temple (Jiètái Sì) was originally built in the 7th century. The main complex is dotted with ancient pine trees. One of these, **Nine Dragon Pine**, is claimed to be over 1300 years old, while the **Embracing Pagoda Pine** does just what it says.

MARCO POLO BRIDGE 卢沟桥

Lúgōu Qiáo

Described by the great traveller himself, the 266m-long grey marble bridge (Lúgōu Qiáo) is host to 485 carved stone lions. Each animal is different (the smallest is only a few centimetres high), and folklore attests that they move around at night.

Spanning the Yongding River near the little walled town of Wǎnpíng, the stone bridge dates from 1189, but is a composite of different eras (it was widened in 1969).

The bridge would have rated as a mere footnote in the history of China were it not for the historic Marco Polo Bridge Incident, which ignited a full-scale war with Japan. On 7 July 1937 Japanese troops illegally occupied a railway junction outside Wǎnpíng. Japanese and Chinese soldiers started shooting, giving Japan an excuse to attack and occupy Běijīng.

The **Memorial Hall of the War of Resistance Against Japan** is a gory look back at Japan's occupation of China, but there are no captions in English. Also on the site are the Wanping Castle, Daiwang Temple and a hotel.

TRANSPORT

Tanzhe Temple & Jietai Temple It's easiest to take the Line L tour bus (Y115) which runs on Saturday and public holidays between 6.30am and 8.30am from the Beijing Sightseeing Bus Centre (Běijīng Lǚyóu Jísàn Zhōngxīn; ☎ 8353 1111) east and west of Front Gate (p76) at Qianmen alongside Tiananmen Square and also from outside the South Cathedral at Xuanwumen. Alternatively, take the subway to the Pingguoyuan stop and take bus 931 (Y3) to the last stop for Tanzhe Temple (don't take the bus 931 branch line, zhīxiàn 支线, however). This bus also stops near Jietai Temple, where it's a 10-minute walk uphill from the bus stop.

Marco Polo Bridge Take bus 6 from the north gate of Temple of Heaven Park to the last stop at Liùlǐ Qiáo (六里桥), and then either bus 339 or 309 to Lúgōu Xīnqiáo (卢沟新桥); the bridge is just ahead.

CHUĀNDĬXIÀ 川底下

Nestled in a valley 90km west of Běijīng and overlooked by towering peaks is Chuandixia Village (Chuāndǐxià), a gorgeous cluster of historic courtyard homes and old-world charm. The backdrop is lovely: terraced orchards and fields, with ancient houses and alleyways rising up the hillside.

Chuāndǐxià is also a museum of Maoist graffiti and slogans, especially up the incline among the better-preserved houses. Despite their impressive revolutionary credentials, Chuāndǐxià's residents have sensed the unmistakable whiff of the tourist dollar on the north-China breeze, and T-shirt vendors have appeared.

Two hours is more than enough to wander around the village as it's not big. A number of houses also sell local produce, including *fēngmì* (honey) and *hétao* (walnuts).

Sights

Badaling Great Wall (☎ 6912 1338/1423/1520; admission adult/student Y45/25; ☾ summer 6am-10pm, winter 7am-6pm)

China Great Wall Museum (☾ 9am-4pm)

Chuāndǐxià (admission Y20)

Eastern Qing Tombs (Ten tomb admission adult/student Y90/45; ☾ 8am-5pm)

Great Wall Circle Vision Theatre (☾ 9am-9.45pm)

Jietai Temple (admission adult/student Y35/20; ☾ 8am-6pm)

Jinshanling Great Wall (admission Y40)

Juyongguan Great Wall (☎ 6977 1665; admission Y40; ☾ 6am-4pm)

Marco Polo Bridge (☎ 8389 3919; 88 Lugouqiao-chengnei Xijie; admission adult/student Y10/5; ☾ 8am-5pm)

Ming Tombs (☎ 6076 1424; admission Cháng Líng Y45, Dìng Líng Y60, Zhāo Líng Y30; ☾ 8am-5.30pm)

Mutianyu Great Wall (☎ 6162 6873/6022; admission adult/student Y35/17.5; ☾ 6.30am-5.30pm)

Simatai Great Wall (☎ 6903 5025/5030; admission adult/student Y30/15; ☾ 8am-5pm)

Tanzhe Temple (admission adult/student Y35/17; ☾ 8.30am-6pm)

TRANSPORT

Distance from Běijīng 90km
Direction West
Local Bus Take bus 929 (make sure it's the branch line, or *zhīxiàn* 支线, not the regular bus) from the bus stop to the right of Pingguoyuan subway station to Zhāitáng (斋堂; Y7; two hours), then take a taxi van (Y10). If going off season, arrange with the taxi van to return to pick you up. The last bus returns from Zhāitáng to Pingguoyuan at 4.20pm. If you miss the last bus, a taxi will cost upwards of Y80 to Pingguoyuan. It's not easy to get to Chuāndǐxià Village and if taking public transport bank on taking well over three hours from central Běijīng.

SHĀNHǍIGUĀN 山海关

The Great Wall meets the sea at Shānhǎiguān in Héběi province, where a strategic pass leads to northeast China. The area was originally part of the state of Guzhu during the Shang and Zhou dynasties but came into its own in 1381, when it was developed under General Xuda, who converted it into a fortified garrison town with four gates at the compass points and two major avenues running between them.

Until recently, considerable charm survived within the old walled enclosure, although colossal swathes have been levelled in an attempt to rebuild and repackage the historic town; Shānhǎiguān consequently – at the time of writing – resembled Grozny on a bad day. The obliteration is extensive (and unpardonable some might say), but at least some temple reconstruction has accompanied the devastation and the town now sports a newly built drum tower. The Great Wall here has been extensively rebuilt and is a major, and dramatic, tourist drawcard.

First Pass Under Heaven (Tiānxià Dìyī Guān) is also known as East Gate (Dōng Mén; 东门; also called Dōng Guān; 东关). Long views of factories stretch off to the east as decayed sections of battlements trail off into the hills. The Wall here is 12m high and the principal watchtower – a two-storey structure with double eaves and 68 arrow slit windows – is a towering 13.7m high.

Several other watchtowers can also be seen and there's a *wèngchéng* (enceinte) extending east from the Wall. The Manchus stormed the gate in 1644 before enslaving China for 250 years.

Admission includes entry to the **Great Wall Museum** (Chángchéng Bówùguǎn), housed in a pleasant, one-storey traditional Chinese building with upturned eaves, with photographs and memorabilia relating to the Wall. Sadly, there is a lack of captions in English. The nearby **Wang Family Courtyard House** (Wángjiā Dàyuán; 3 Dongsantiao Hutong; ☺ 7.30am-6pm) is a large, historic *hútòng*-style residence faced with a spirit wall.

Old Dragon Head (Lǎolóngtóu; 老龙头) was the serpentine conclusion of the Great Wall. The name derives from the legendary carved dragon head that once faced the waves (this is no more). Avoid buying the pricey ticket and instead take the left-hand road to the sea (under the arched gate) where you can walk along the sandy beach to Old Dragon Head or ride a horse (Y20).

The views here are spectacular and you can also join the winkle-pickers and cockle-hunters along the rocks. To get here take bus 25 (Y1) from Shānhǎiguān's South Gate.

Among temples and historic structures undergoing reconstruction as part of Shānhǎiguān's full-on metamorphosis are the four (originally Ming-built) halls of the **Dabei Pavilion** (Dàbēi Gé) in the northwest of town, and the Taoist **Sanqing Temple** (Sānqīng Guàn 三清观; Beihou Jie), outside the walls.

Shānhǎiguān's **Drum Tower** (Gǔlóu) has been similarly rebuilt with a liberal scattering of newly constructed **páilou** (decorative arches) running off east and west along Xi Dajie and Dong Dajie.

Although the unrestored **North Gate** (Běi Mén) stands in a state of dreary neglect, you can climb up onto the overgrown sections of the city wall attached to it if you head up the brick steps to the east of the gate (go through the compound). Like the East Gate, the city gates once had circular enceintes attached to them – the excavated outlines of the enceinte outside the **West Gate** (Xī Mén) are discernible as well as slabs of the original Ming dynasty road, lying around 1m below the current level of the ground.

A half-hour walk (taxi Y10; motor tricycle Y5) beyond the North Gate is **Jiǎo Shān** (角山), where the Great Wall mounts its first high peak. It's a trying 20-minute clamber from the base, but a cable car can

yank you up for Y20 (return trip). The views are spectacular on a clear day. Continue along the Wall or hike over to **Qixian Monastery** (Qixián Sì; 栖贤寺).

Mengjiangnü Temple (Mèngjiāngnǚ Miào; 孟姜女庙) is a famous and historic temple 6km east of Shānhǎiguān. A taxi should cost around Y12.

Information

Bike Rental (Giant Bikes; Jiédantè Zìxíngchē; 115 Nan Dajie; Half/full day Y20/30)

Bank of China (Zhōngguó Yínháng; Diyiguan Lu; 8.30am-noon & 1.30-5.30pm) No international ATM.

Lüdao Kongjian Internet Cafe (Lǜdǎo Kōngjiān Wǎngbā; per hr Y2; 24hr) In between Friendly Cooperate Hotel and post office.

Kodak Express (Kēdá; south of First Pass Under Heaven; CD burning per disc Y15)

Post office (Yóujú; eastern side of Nan Dajie; 8am-5.30pm); further branch on Nanhai Xilu.

Public Security Bureau (PSB, Gōngānjú; ☎ 0335 505 1163) Opposite entrance to First Pass Under Heaven on corner of small alleyway slightly to the south.

Sights

First Pass Under Heaven (cnr Dong Dajie & Diyiguan Lu; admission Y40; 7.30am-5.30pm) Open longer hours in summer.

Great Wall Museum (Diyiguan Lu; admission incl in First Pass Under Heaven ticket, Y10; 8am-6pm)

Jiǎo Shān (admission Y15; 5am-sunset) 3km north of Shānhǎiguān.

Mengjiangnü Temple (admission Y40; 7am-5.30pm) 6km east of town.

Old Dragon Head (4km south of Shānhǎiguān; admission Y50; 7.30am-5.30pm)

Qixian Monastery (Qīxián Sì; admission Y5)

Wang Family Courtyard House (29-31 Dong Santiao; admission Y25, joint ticket with First Pass Under Heaven Y50)

Eating

At the time of writing the walled part of town was being bulldozed, but restaurants may have resurfaced by the time you read this. Restaurants concentrate in the area south of the city wall in the direction of the train station.

Mike Hamn Fast Food (Màikè Hànmǔ; Guancheng Nanlu) The Héběi fast-food experience (chicken meals, chips, 'Hotel California' on the stereo etc). One of the few places where you can find a coffee.

Sleeping

Jiguan Guesthouse (Jīguān Zhāodàisuǒ; ☎ 0335 505 1938; 17 Dongsitiao 东四条17号; d Y100-180, ste Y320) This pleasant hotel has rooms off two courtyards. The simple doubles come without bathrooms, but have clean, tiled floors and TVs. The Y180 doubles have showers.

Longhua Hotel (Lónghuá Dàjiǔdiàn; ☎ 0335 507 7698; 1 Nanhai Dajie 南海大街1号; s/d/large d Y168/188/288) This hotel has spacious, so-so rooms with 20% discounts the norm.

Friendly Cooperate Hotel (Yìhé Jiǔdiàn; ☎ 0335 593 9069; fax 0335 507 0351; 4 Nanhai Xilu 南海西路 4号; d/tr Y288/388) Large two-star hotel large, clean-ish double rooms, with water coolers, TVs, phones and bathrooms. Staff are pleasant and there's a restaurant next door.

Jingshan Hotel (Jìngshān Bīnguǎn; ☎ 0335 505 1130; 1 Dong Dajie 东大街1号; s/d/tr Y580/580/680) OK but rather musty rooms; pleasant surroundings. Healthy discounts, so ask.

TRANSPORT

Distance from Běijīng 300km
Direction East
Train Shānhǎiguān is accessible directly by train from Běijīng. As more trains stop at nearby Qínhuángdǎo, it is often more convenient to go there first. Express trains from Běijīng to Qínhuángdǎo (soft seat Y75, 3 hours) leave at 7.30am, 8.30am, 2pm and 7.47pm; from Qínhuángdǎo take bus 33 to Shānhǎiguān (Y2, 30 minutes). An alternative is the night sleeper to Shānhǎiguān from Běijīng (Y70; seven hours).
Long-Distance Buses depart for Běijīng's Bawangfen bus station (p214) from Qínhuángdǎo (Y62 to Y66, 3½ hours) between 7am and 7pm. Direct buses also run from Qínhuángdǎo to Chéngdé (Y61, 5½ hours), departing hourly from 7am to 11am, and at 5pm.
Air There's a small airport between Shānhǎiguān and Qínhuángdǎo, with flights to several cities.

CHÉNGDÉ 承德

Once known as Jehol, Chéngdé is an 18th-century imperial resort area boasting the remnants of the largest regal gardens in China.

Chéngdé was an obscure town until 1703 when Emperor Kangxi began building a summer palace with all the court trappings, including a throne room. More than a home away from home, Chéngdé became a seat of government, since wherever the emperor went his seat went too. Kangxi called his summer creation the **Imperial Summer Villa** or **Fleeing-the-Heat Mountain Villa** (Bìshǔ Shānzhuāng).

By 1790, during the reign of Kangxi's grandson Qianlong, it had grown to the size of both Běijīng's Summer Palace and the Forbidden City combined. Qianlong extended an idea started by Kangxi, to build replicas of minority architecture in order to make envoys feel comfortable. In particular he was keen on promoting Tibetan and Mongolian Lamaism. This explains the Tibetan and Mongolian features of the monasteries north of the Imperial Summer Villa, one of them a replica of the Potala Palace in Lhasa. Emperor Xianfeng died in Chéngdé in 1861, an event that initiated the gradual demise of the imperial retreat: Chéngdé was never used again by the emperors, who associated it with misfortune.

Today Chéngdé has slipped back into being the provincial town it once was, its grandeur long decayed and its emperors long gone. Chéngdé is on Unesco's World Heritage list, but sadly this does not guarantee a programme of full restoration and some features are gone for good.

Visiting Chéngdé in autumn is an option as tourists choke the place in summer. Autumn adds its own rich colours to the landscape and sees far less visitors in town, while remaining warm enough to be comfortable. The train from Běijīng to Chéngdé passes level fields, dark mountains, factories, terraced slopes, occasional pagoda-capped hills and crumbling lengths of the Great Wall.

Imperial Summer Villa
Bìshǔ Shānzhuāng

The Imperial Summer Villa is a park covering a vast 590 hectares and bounded by a splendid 10km wall. About 90% of the Imperial Summer Villa is composed of lakes, hills, mini-forests and plains. Passing through the **Main Gate** (Lìzhèng Mén) you reach the **Front Palace** (Zhèng Gōng), containing the main throne hall. The refreshingly cool **Hall of Simplicity and Sincerity** is built of an aromatic hardwood called *nánmù;* on display is a carved throne. There are also the emperor's fully-furnished bedrooms, as well as displays of ceramics, drum stones and calligraphy.

The double storey **Misty Rain Tower** (Yǔ Lóu), on the northern side of the main lake, was an imperial study. While here, you can also take boats out for trips around the lake (Y10 per hour). Further north is the **Wenjin Chamber** (Wénjīn Gé) built in 1773 to house a copy of the *Sìkùquánshū*, a major anthology of classics, history, philosophy and literature commissioned by Qianlong.

In the east, the tall green and yellow **Yongyousi Pagoda** (Yǒngyòusì Tǎ) soars above the fragments of its vanished temple and dominates the area.

Guandi Temple
Guāndì Miào

Also called the Wumiao, the Guandi Temple is a Taoist temple first built in 1732 and located outside the Imperial Summer Villa to the southwest of the Main Gate. In the courtyard at the rear are two **steles**, supported on the backs of a pair of disintegrating and distressed-looking *bìxì* (mythical tortoise-dragon like creatures).

The **Hall of the Three Clear Ones** stands at the rear to the left. The temple is home to a band of Taoist monks, garbed in distinctive jackets and trousers, their long hair twisted into topknots.

CHÉNGDÉ 承德

0 _____ 2 km
0 _____ 1 mile

A **B** **C** **D**

1
Arhat Hall Ruins
(Luohan Táng)
罗汉堂
Guangan Temple
广安寺
Shuxiang Temple
殊像寺
7
6 8
Guangyuan
Temple
广缘寺

Huancheng Beilu 环城北路
Xibei Gate
西北门
Shizi Gouche
9

2
Beizhen
Twin Peaks
北枕双峰
Wulie
River
1

Imperial Summer Villa
Huidiji Gate
惠迪吉门
11
To Club Rock;
Toad Rock
(1.5km)
20
5

3
Wulie River
Shanzhuang Donglu 山庄东路
10
4
Puren
Temple
普仁寺

4
Bifeng Gate
碧峰门
Bifengmen Donglu 碧峰门东路
Fragrant
Garden House
(Fangyuanju)
芳园居
Main Gate
(Lizheng Mén)
丽正门
Dehui Gate
德汇门
17
12
3
24
28
16
2
13
30
Nanxinlong
Xiaochi Jie
Chaichang
Hutong
柴厂胡同
Dutongfu Dajie
都统府大街
25
27
29

5
31
Shankyjing Jie
Qunglong Donglie 群龙东街
Nanying Jie
Shidongzi Gou 石洞子沟
27
18
Xinhua Lu
Luoshan
Mountain
罗汉山

6
19
23
26
Chezhan Lu 车站路
Train Station
火车站
15
To East Bus
Station (8km)

Eight Outer Temples & Other Sights
Wàibā Miào

Some fine examples of religious architecture can be found in the foothills outside the northern and northeastern walls of the Imperial Summer Villa. Some of the Eight Outer Temples remain closed, but there are enough to keep you occupied. The temples and monasteries were all built between 1750 and 1780 and are 3km to 5km from the garden's front gate; bus 6 taken to the northeastern corner will drop you in the vicinity – going by bike is an excellent idea.

Puning Temple (Pǔníng Sì) – the Temple of Universal Tranquillity – is a Chinese-style (*hànshì*) temple with more Tibetan-style (*zàngshì*) features at the rear. Enter the temple grounds to a stele pavilion with inscriptions by the Qianlong emperor in Chinese, Manchu, Mongol and Tibetan. Behind are halls arranged in a typical Buddhist temple layout, featuring the **Hall of Heavenly Kings** and the **Mahavira Hall** (Dàxióngbǎo Diàn) beyond. Behind lie steep steps (the temple is arranged on a mountainside) leading to a gate tower, a terrace and the **Mahayana Hall**. The highlight of the temple is the heart-arresting golden statue of the Buddhist **Goddess of Mercy** (Guanyin) in the Mahayana Hall. The effigy is astounding: it's over 22m high (the highest of its kind in the world) and radiates a powerful sense of divinity. Hewn from five kinds of wood (pine, cypress, fir, elm and linden), Guanyin has 42 arms, with each palm bearing an eye, and each hand holds instruments, skulls, lotuses and other Buddhist devices. On Guanyin's head sits the **Teacher Longevity Buddha**. To her right stands **Shancai**, a male guardian and disciple, opposite his female equivalent, **Longnü** (Dragon Girl).

You can clamber up to the first gallery (Y10) for a closer inspection of Guanyin; torches (flashlights) are provided to cut through the gloom so you can pick out the uneven stairs (take care). Sadly, the higher galleries are often out of bounds, so an eye-to-eye with the goddess may be impossible. If you want to climb the gallery, try and come in the morning, as it is often impossible to get a ticket in the afternoon (especially outside of summer).

Puning Temple has a number of friendly lamas who manage their domain, so be quiet and respectful at all times. You can catch bus 6 from in front of the Mountain Villa Hotel to Puning Temple.

The largest of the Chéngdé temples, **Putuozongcheng Temple** (Pǔtuózōngchéng Zhī Miào) – also called the Little Potala Palace (Xiǎo Bùdálā Gōng; 小布达拉宫) – is a mini facsimile of Lhasa's Potala Palace. The temple is a marvellous sight on a clear day, its vast red walls standing out against its mountain backdrop.

Excursions

CHÉNGDÉ

Fronted by **prayer wheels** and flags, the **Red Palace** (also called the Great Red Terrace) contains most of the main shrines and halls. Continue up and past an exhibition of Thangka (Tibetan sacred art) in a restored courtyard and look out for the marvellous sandalwood pagodas further up. Both are 19m tall and contain 2160 effigies of the Amitabha Buddha. Among the many exhibits on view are displays of Tibetan Buddhist objects and instruments, including a *kapala* bowl, made from the skull of a young girl (all captions are in Chinese). The main hall is housed at the very top, surrounded by several small pavilions; the climb to the top is worth it for the views.

The **Temple of Sumeru, Happiness and Longevity** (Xūmífúshòu Zhī Miào) is a further huge temple, around 1km to the southeast of the Putuozongcheng Temple. It was built in honour of the sixth Panchen Lama, who stayed here in 1781; and being an imitation of a temple in Shigatse, Tibet, it incorporates elements of Tibetan and Han architecture. Note the eight, huge, glinting dragons (each said to weigh over 1000kg) that adorn the roof of the main hall.

Pule Temple (Pǔlè Sì) was built in 1776 for the visits of minority envoys (Kazakhs among them). At the rear of the temple is the unusual Round Pavilion, reminiscent of the Hall of Prayer for Good Harvests at the Temple of Heaven in Běijīng. It's a 30-minute hike to **Club Rock** (Bàngchuí Fēng) from the Temple of Universal Happiness – the rock is said to resemble a club used for beating laundry dry. Nearby is **Toad Rock** (Hámá Shí). There is pleasant hiking, good scenery and commanding views of the area. You can save yourself a steep climb to the base of Club Rock (Y20) and Toad Rock by taking the chairlift (Y40 return), but it's more fun to walk if you're reasonably fit. Bus 10 will take you to Pule Temple. East of Puning Temple is **Puyou Temple** (Pǔyòu Sì). While it is in a somewhat sad state, there is a plentiful contingent of merry gilded *luóhàn* (*arhat*, or a Buddhist monk who has attained enlightenment and passes to nirvana at death) in the side wings.

Anyuan Temple (Ānyuǎn Miào) is a copy of the Gurza Temple in Xīnjiāng. Only the main hall remains and it contains deteriorating Buddhist frescoes. Further south, **Puren Temple** (Pǔrén Sì) is not open to the public. Located to the northwest of the Imperial Villa and surrounded by a low red wall, **Shuxiang Temple** (Shūxiàng Sì) is sometimes closed, although it may open in the summer months (unless it is being restored). Just to the west of Shuxiang Temple is a sensitive military zone where foreigners are not allowed access, so don't go wandering around.

Information

Bank of China (Zhōngguó Yínháng; 4 Dutongfu Dajie & east of the Mountain Villa Hotel) ATM access

Chaosu Internet Café (Cháosù Wǎngbā; Chezhan Lu; per hr Y2; ☻ 24hr) Northwest of the train station.

China International Travel Service (CITS, Zhōngguó Guójì Lǚxíngshè; ☎ 0314 202 4816; 3 Wulie Lu, 2nd fl) It's the building on your right in a dishevelled courtyard on the western side of Wulie Lu; not much use. Further small branch on Bifengmen Donglu.

Kodak Express (Kēdá; 5-7 Lizhengmen Dajie, opposite the Guandi Temple) CD burning (Y15 per disc)

Luggage Storage East Bus Station ticket hall and train station ticket hall.

No 5 Hospital (Diwǔ Yīyuàn; Chezhan Lu)

Post office (Yóujú; Nanyingzi Dajie; ☻ 8am-6pm) The main post office is on Nanyingzi Dajie and there's a smaller branch on Lizhengmen Dajie just east of the Main Gate (Lizhèng Mén) of the Imperial Summer Villa.

PSB (Gōngānjú; ☎ 0314 202 2352; Wulie Lu)

Tiancheng Internet Cafe (Tiānchéng Wǎngbā; Chaichang Hútòng; per hr Y2; ☻ 8am-midnight)

Xiandai Internet Café (Xiàndài Wǎngbā; Chezhan Lu; per hr Y2; ☻ 24hr) Northwest of train station.

Sights

Anyuan Temple (admission Y10; ☻ 8am-5.30pm)

Guandi Temple (Lizhengmen Dajie; admission Y20; ☻ 8am-5pm),

Imperial Summer Villa (admission Y90, winter Y60, guide Y50; ☻ park 5.30am- 6.30pm, palace 7am-5pm)

Pule Temple (admission Y30, winter Y20; ☻ 8am-6pm)

Puning Temple (Puningsi Lu; admission Y50, winter Y40; ☻ summer 7.30am-6pm, winter 8am-5pm)

Putuozongcheng Temple (Shizigou Lu; admission Y40, winter Y30; ☻ 8am-6pm)

Puyou Temple (admission Y20; ☻ 8am-6pm)

Temple of Sumeru, Happiness and Longevity (Shizigou Lu; admission Y30, winter Y20; ☻ 8am-5.30pm)

Eating

For street food, try the restaurants on **Shaanxi-ying Jie** (at the northern end of Nanyingzi Lu), with its barbecue (shāokǎo) restaurants (and dog meat outlets). **Qingfeng Dongjie** just north of the railway line and south of Dong Dajie has a colourful choice of restaurants. Also try **Nanxinglong Xiaochi Jie** (across from Lizhèng Mén, the main gate of the Imperial Summer Villa), for local dishes, including pheasant, dog meat (gǒuròu; 狗肉) and many Chinese staples. Chéngdé's local speciality is wild game – deer (lùròu; 鹿肉) and pheasant (shānjīshānjī; 山鸡), which you can find all over town.

Dongpo Restaurant (Dōngpō Fànzhuāng; ☎ 0314 210 6315; Shanzhuang Donglu; meals Y30) With red lanterns outside, steaming shāguō (clay pot) at the door and a large aquarium, this lively and popular restaurant has no English menu but a large choice of Sìchuān dishes.

Máojiā Xiāngcàiguǎn (☎ 0314 296 5511; Lizhengmen Dajie; meal Y30) Small, handy and unassuming Húnán restaurant serving up staples from the fiery province; go for the máoshì hóngshāoròu (毛氏红烧肉; chunky nuggets of pork in sauce; Y18) or the hot, sour and tasty suāncài dòufutāng (酸菜豆腐汤; sour cabbage and tofu soup; Y8).

Beijing Roast Duck Restaurant (Běijīng Kǎoyādiàn; ☎ 0314 202 2979; 5-12 Lizhengmen Dajie; duck Y50) Central restaurant with tasty duck roasted over fruit-tree wood. It's opposite Guandi Temple.

Sleeping

Touts around the train station could well find you a room in a family hotel near the train station for around Y80.

Jingcheng Hotel (Jīngchéng Fàndiàn; ☎ 0314 208 2027; next to train station; d/tw/tr/quad Y260/260/240/240) Convenient location by the train station but rather tatty with plain rooms.

Mountain Villa Hotel (Shānzhuāng Bīnguǎn; ☎ 0314 202 3501; fax 202 2457; 11 Lizhengmen Lu 丽正门路 11号; d Y280-480, tr Y210) This recently renovated hotel has clean, cheap rooms and pole positioning for trips inside the Imperial Summer Villa. Take bus 7 from the train station and from there it's a short walk.

Qiwanglou Hotel (Qǐwànglóu Bīnguǎn; ☎ 0314 202 2196; 1 Bifengmen Donglu 碧峰门东路1号; tw Y500-800) With peacocks strolling around the green grounds, the attractive and secluded setting of this hotel next to the summer villa is alluring, but cheaper rooms are worn and you will have to strain for views of the villa grounds over the treetops.

Shenghua Hotel (Shènghuá Dàjiǔdiàn; ☎ 0314 227 1000; www.shenghuahotel.com; 23 Wulie Lu 武烈路 23号; s/d Y700/780) Decent four-star hotel with a modern exterior of glass and steel and a voluminous marble foyer.

Yunshan Hotel (Yúnshān Dàjiǔdiàn; ☎ 0314 205 5888; fax 0314 205 5885; 2 Banbishan Lu 半壁山路2号; d/ste Y780/1600) Despite the ghastly exterior (white tiles, office-block style), rooms at this four-star hotel are clean, elegant and spacious.

TRANSPORT

Distance from Běijīng 255km
Direction Northeast
Long-Distance Bus Buses (Y46; four hours) to Chéngdé depart hourly from the Liuliqiao and Sihui long-distance bus stations (p214). Minibuses for Běijīng (Y45) leave every 20 minutes from outside the Chengde Train Station. Buses for Běijīng (Y45) also leave every 20 minutes from outside the Yunshan Hotel. The Jingcheng Expressway (Běijīng–Chéngdé) should be completed by 2007, which will shorten the voyage to 2½ hours. For Shānghǎiguān, first take a bus to Qínhuángdǎo from the East Bus Station (Dōngzhàn 东站; Y80; four hours; five to six per day), 8km south of Chengde Train Station, reachable by bus 1 or taxi (Y10).
Train Regular trains run between Běijīng and Chéngdé, with the first and most convenient departing Běijīng at 7.16am, and returning at 2.40pm. The fastest trains take four hours (Y41 hard seat, Y61 soft seat); slower trains take around seven hours.
Local Transport Taxis are Y5 at flag fall, which should get you to most destinations in town, but be warned most drivers don't use meters. There are half-a-dozen bus lines (Y1), including bus 5 and 15 from the train station to the Imperial Summer Villa, bus 1 from the train station to the East Bus Station and bus 6 to the Eight Outer Temples (Wàibā Miào). Hiring a bike is an excellent way to get around, but at the time of writing the only place renting out bicycles was the Mountain Villa Hotel (Y50 per day).
Tours The only practical way to see all the sights in one day is to take a hotel tour by minibus, most of which start out at 8am. The cheapest bus tours cost around Y30 (check at the Mountain Villa Hotel), but are Chinese-speaking only; a personal tour costs about Y100, excluding admission prices.

Directory ▪

Directory

TRANSPORT

As it's the national capital, getting to Běijīng is straightforward. Rail and air connections link the capital to virtually every point in China, and fleets of buses head to abundant destinations. Using Běijīng as a starting point to explore the rest of the land makes perfect sense.

Central Běijīng's roads may be of orderly design, but getting around town can be gruelling as the huge distances and overburdened transport options make navigation exhausting. The city is undergoing rapid development to haul its transport infrastructure into the modern age, but until the new lines of the subway are up and running, getting around Běijīng will remain an effort. Road construction and widening has eased vehicular flows, but progress has been reversed by the rapidly multiplying number of cars (approaching three million) in the capital, which consequently slows down the city's buses and taxis. Běijīng's mushrooming population over the past decade has only added to the burden on the creaking transport infrastructure.

For the moment, taking the subway is the surest way of reaching your destination on time. If you have to take to the road, jump in a taxi. They are cheap and efficient, but avoid the rush hour and prepare for incessant traffic jams. Alternatively, combine the underground with taxi rides. Riding the extensive bus network is very cheap and buses are plentiful, but traffic can slow things to a crawl.

Tackling Běijīng by bicycle is a fascinating and effective way of getting about. Walking about on foot is only realistic in the centre of town and over short distances – some of Běijīng's roads seemingly go on to the ends of the earth.

Flights, tours and rail tickets can be booked online at www.lonelyplanet.com /travel_services.

AIR

Tickets for Chinese carriers flying from Běijīng can be booked through most midrange and top-end hotels, at any one of the ubiquitous ticket offices (航空售票处;

GETTING INTO TOWN

Běijīng's **Capital Airport** is 27km from the centre of town; about 45 minutes to one hour by car, depending on traffic.

A rail link from Capital Airport to Dongzhimen in Běijīng is under construction, and due for completion in time for the 2008 Olympic Games. Passengers will be able to transfer to the subway system from Dongzhimen station.

Several express bus routes (☎ 6459 4375, 6459 4376) run regularly to Běijīng every 10 to 15 minutes during operating hours. Tickets on all lines are Y16. Line 3 (first bus 7.30am, last bus meets arrival of last flight) is the most popular with travellers, running to the Beijing International Hotel and Beijing Train Station via Chaoyangmen. Line 2 (first bus 7am, last bus meets arrival of last flight) runs to the Aviation Building (opposite) in Xidan, via Dongzhimen. Line 1 (first/last bus 7.30am/10.30pm) runs to Fangzhuang, via Dabeiyao, where you can get onto the subway Line 1 at Guomao.

Public bus 359 (Y3) runs to Dongzhimen from the airport, from where you can get on the subway.

From the city to the airport, the most useful place to catch the bus is at the west door of the Beijing International Hotel (Map pp268–9), where buses leave every half-hour between 6am and 7.30pm (Y16). You can also take a bus (☎ 6459 4375/4376; Y16; one hour) from the eastern end of the Aviation Building (the CAAC ticket office) on Xichang'an Jie in Xidan district; departures are every 30 minutes between 5.45am and 7.30pm.

Many top-end hotels runs shuttle buses from the airport to their hotels. Check at the hotel desks at the airport upon arrival or check with the hotel beforehand. You do not necessarily have to be a guest of the hotel to use these, but you do have to pay for the service. The price for the minibuses is higher than that for the regular airport buses.

A taxi (using its meter) should cost between Y80 and Y100 from the airport to the centre of town, including the Y15 airport expressway toll; make sure the driver uses the meter. Queue for your taxi outside and never take a taxi from touts inside the arrivals halls, where a well-established illegal taxi operation at the airport attempts to lure weary travellers into a Y300-plus ride to the city (one man acts as a taxi pimp for a squad of drivers).

Don't expect to be able to rent a car at the airport, unless you have a residence permit and a Chinese driving licence.

---

hángkōng shòupiào chù) around town (one can be found to the left of the entrance to Beijing Train Station) or from the **Aviation Building** (Mínháng Yíngyè Dàshà; Map pp266–7; ☎ 6656 9118; ☎ domestic 6601 3336, international 6456 3604; 15 Xichang'an Jie; ☒ 7am-midnight). A downtown check-in service desk is situated just inside the door, available for passengers with carry-on luggage only (☒ 8am-5pm; domestic flights only); you must check in at least three hours prior to departure.

Make inquiries for all airlines at Běijīng's **Capital Airport** (☎ 6512 8931, or 962580 from Běijīng only). Call ☎ 6459 9567 for information on international arrivals and departures and ☎ 1689 6969 for information on domestic flights, or click on www.bcia .com.cn/en/index.jsp or the websites of individual airlines listed below.

Airlines

Chinese carriers in Běijīng include:

Air China (Map pp266–7; ☎ 6601 7755; www.airchina .com.cn; Aviation Building, 15 Xichang'an Jie)

China Eastern Airlines (☎ 6464 1166; www.ce-air.com)

China Southern Airlines (☎ 950 333; www.cs-air.com; 2 Dongsanhuan Nanlu)

Shanghai Airlines (☎ 6456 9019; www.shanghai-air .com in Chinese; Bldg 3, Capital Airport)

International airlines in Běijīng include:

Air Canada (Map p264; ☎ 6468 2001; www.aircanada .com; Room C201, Lufthansa Center, 50 Liangmaqiao Lu)

Air France (Map p264; ☎ 4008 808 808; www.airfrance .com.cn; Room 1606-1611, Bldg 1, Kuntai International Mansion, 12A Chaoyangmenwai Dajie)

British Airways (Map pp268–9; ☎ 8511 5599; www .british-airways.com; Room 210, 2nd fl, SciTech Tower, 22 Jianguomenwai Dajie)

Dragon Air (Map pp268–9; ☎ 6518 2533; www .dragonair.com; Room 1710, Office Tower 1, Henderson Center, 18 Jianguomennei Dajie)

Japan Airlines (Map pp268–9; ☎ 6513 0888; www .jal.com; 1st fl, Changfugong Office Bldg, Hotel New Otani, 26a Jianguomenwai Dajie)

KLM (Map pp268–9; ☎ 6505 3505; www.klm.com; W501, West Wing, China World Trade Center, 1 Jian- guomenwai Dajie)

Lufthansa Airlines (Map p264; ☎ 6468 8838; www .lufthansa.com; Room 101, Lufthansa Center, 50 Liang- maqiao Lu)

Qantas Airways (Map p264; ☎ 6467 3337; www.qantas .com.au; Room 120, Lufthansa Center, 50 Liangmaqiao Lu)

Singapore Airlines (Map pp268–9; ☎ 6505 2233; www .singaporeair.com; Room L109, China World Trade Center, 1 Jianguomenwai Dajie)

Thai Airways International (Map pp268–9; ☎ 8515 0088; www.thaiairways.com; Units 303, Level 3, Office Tower 3, Oriental Plaza, 1 Dongchang'an Jie)

United Airlines (Map p264; ☎ 800 810 8282, 6463 1111; www.united.com; Lufthansa Center, 50 Liangmaqiao Lu)

Airports

Běijīng's Capital Airport is 27km northeast of the city centre. The arrivals hall is on the first floor, the departure hall is on the second floor. For currency exchange, several banks can be found in the arrivals hall. They're open 24 hours and offer a similar exchange rate to banks in the city and probably a better rate than your hotel. There are also several ATMs with international access, where you can draw local currency. A small post office is in the departure hall as you enter the airport, where you can buy a Běijīng map. Phones are at each end of the arrivals hall. Left-luggage facilities (from Y5) are on the first floor, where luggage can be stored for a maximum of seven days. Trolleys are available for free. A small Airport Clinic is on the first floor.

There is a branch of the **Beijing Tourist Information Center** (see p231) in the arrivals hall, where you can pick up a map, literature on Běijīng or book a hotel room. Other desks in the arrivals hall also provide hotel bookings, and you can often obtain substantial discounts on accommodation.

Airport restaurants and shops are generally overpriced. If you're doing last-minute souvenir shopping, try to do it in town.

International/domestic departure tax is Y90/50 and is included in the price of your air ticket.

A colossal new third terminal building is being constructed alongside Capital Airport. A monumental building project designed by Norman Foster and due to be completed in 2007, the new terminal is essential to the airport's ambitions to deal with 60 million arrivals by 2015 and is the world's largest-ever airport expansion project. Construction on a second airport is also planned to commence before 2010, although the location of the new airport is still up in the air.

Directory

TRANSPORT

CLIMATE CHANGE & TRAVEL

Climate change is a serious threat to the ecosystems that humans rely upon, and air travel is the fastest-growing contributor to the problem. Lonely Planet regards travel, overall, as a global benefit, but believes we all have a responsibility to limit our personal impact on global warming.

Flying & Climate Change

Pretty much every form of motor transport generates CO_2 (the main cause of human-induced climate change) but planes are far and away the worst offenders, not just because of the sheer distances they allow us to travel, but because they release greenhouse gases high into the atmosphere. The statistics are frightening: two people taking a return flight between Europe and the US will contribute as much to climate change as an average household's gas and electricity consumption over a whole year.

Carbon Offset Schemes

Climatecare.org and other websites use 'carbon calculators' that allow travellers to offset the greenhouse gases they are responsible for with contributions to energy-saving projects and other climate-friendly initiatives in the developing world – including projects in India, Honduras, Kazakhstan and Uganda.

Lonely Planet, together with Rough Guides and other concerned partners in the travel industry, supports the carbon offset scheme run by climatecare.org. Lonely Planet offsets all of its staff and author travel.

For more information check out our website: www.lonelyplanet.com.

To the Rest of China

Daily flights connect Běijīng to every major city in China. There might not be daily flights to smaller cities throughout the country, but there should be at least one flight a week. You can buy tickets from the Aviation Building (p211), one of the numerous airline offices in Běijīng or through your hotel. Discounts for domestic flights are generally available (full fare may be effective at weekends and public holidays, however). The domestic airfares listed here are approximate only and represent the non-discounted air fare from Běijīng.

Destination	One-way fare (Y)
Chéngdū	1560
Dàlián	710
Guǎngzhōu	1700
Guìlín	1790
Hángzhōu	1150
Hong Kong	2860
Kūnmíng	1810
Lhasa	2430
Nánjīng	1010
Qīngdǎo	710
Shànghǎi	1130
Ūrümqi	2410
Wǔhàn	1080
Xī'ān	1050

BICYCLE

Flat as a mah jong table, widely supplied with bicycle lanes and riddled with alleys, central Běijīng is ideally suited to cyclists. You will need to keep your wits about you on the main thoroughfares, however, as the exponential increase in vehicle numbers has made cycling potentially hazardous. Cycling through Běijīng's often car-free *hútòng* (alleyways) is far safer and it's an experience not to be missed (see p118), although pollution may have you gagging (join the locals donning surgical masks; 面罩; *miànzhào*) and the spring dust storms can be simply stupendous.

Take care when you're on your bike. Hazards include unpredictable vehicle movements, pedestrians crossing the road impulsively and with little warning, icy roads in winter and fierce sand storms in spring. Nighttime brings its own risks, as few Chinese bikes have lights and both pedestrians and cyclists tend to wear dark clothes. Pedestrians are furthermore regularly ejected onto the road by clutter on the pavement. Remember you will be on the lowliest transportation device in town and buses, lorries, taxis, cars and scooters will all honk at you, in that pecking order (just ignore them).

Parking your bike in one of the more secure pavement bike parking lots found all over town is around Y0.50. Very cheap roadside repairs can be found down Běijīng's numerous alleyways.

Purchase is straightforward and you can pick up a mountain bike for as little as Y250 at super/hypermarkets such as Carrefour. Bikes need to be taxed, with a disc displayed (the bike shop will usually arrange this, and hypermarkets have a counter for this).

Hire

Budget hotels are good places to rent bicycles, which cost around Y20 to Y30 per day (plus deposit); rental at upmarket hotels is far more expensive. Tourist-oriented rental outfits can also be found.

A handy **bike rental outfit** (Map p262) in the centre of town is on the pavement along Jinyu Hutong, just west of the Novotel Peace Hotel; a similar **bike rental outfit** with similar prices can be found opposite St Joseph's Church (p93). Further bike rental can be found at **Bird of Freedom Bicycle Rental** (Map pp268–9; Zìxíngchē Chūzū Fúwùzhàn; ☎ 6313 1010; 47 Qianmen Dajie; per hour/day Y15-20/50-60, deposit Y300-600; ⏰ 7am-8pm), opposite the Quanjude Roast Duck Restaurant, and from the shop at 77 Tieshu Xiejie (Map pp266–7; Y20 from 7am-11pm; deposit Y200). The expensive **Universal Bicycle Rental Outlet** (Map p262), has outlets in the vicinity of Qianhai Lake. Tandems (shuāngrén zìxíngchē) are Y20 per hour, single bikes Y10 per hour (Y500 deposit). When renting a bike it's safest to use your own lock(s) in order to prevent bicycle theft, a common problem in Běijīng.

BUS

Relying on buses (公共汽车; gōnggòng qìchē) to get swiftly from A to B can be frustrating unless it's a short hop. Getting a seat can also be impossible, especially during rush hour. Fares are typically Y1 depending on the distance, although air-conditioned buses are slightly more expensive (Y2). You generally pay the conductor, rather than the driver, once aboard the bus. Běijīng's fleet of aged leviathans is busily being replaced with modern low-pollution green buses running on compressed natural gas (CNG).

Buses run from 5.30am to 11pm daily or thereabouts, and stops are few and far between. Routes on bus signs are all in Chinese, with no English. It's important to

work out how many stops you need to go before boarding. If you can read Chinese, a useful publication (Y5) is available from kiosks listing all the Běijīng bus lines; alternatively, tourist maps of Běijīng illustrate some of the bus routes.

One- and two-digit bus numbers are city-core; 100-series buses are trolleys; 200-series are night buses (yèbān gōnggòng qìchē); 300-series are suburban lines and 900-series are long distance buses. Minibuses (xiǎobā) follow some routes and cost from around Y2. If you work out how to combine bus and subway connections you'll find the subway will speed up much of the trip.

Special double-decker buses run in a circle around the city centre and are slightly more expensive, but spare you the traumas of normal public buses and you should be able to get a seat.

The following double-decker routes are useful:

1 Beijing West Train Station, heading east on Fuxingmen Dajie, Xichang'an Jie, Dongchang'an Jie, Jianguomennei Dajie, Jianguomenwai Dajie, Jianguo Lu, Bawang fen (intersection of Jianguo Lu and Xidawang Lu)

2 Shangxing Qianmen, north on Dongdan Beidajie, Dongsi Nandajie, Dongsi Beidajie, Lama Temple, Zhonghua Minzu Yuan (Ethnic Minorities Park), Asian Games Village

3 Jijia Miao (the southwest extremity of the Third Ring Rd), Grand View Garden, Leyou Hotel, Jingguang New World Hotel, Tuanjiehu Park, Agricultural Exhibition Center, Lufthansa Center

4 Beijing Zoo, Exhibition Center, Second Ring Rd, Holiday Inn Downtown, Yuetan Park, Fuxingmen Dajie flyover, Qianmen Xidajie, Qianmen

Useful standard bus routes include:

1 Runs along Chang'an Jie, Jianguomenwai Dajie and Jianguomennei Dajie: Sihuizhan, Bawangfen, Yonganli, Dongdan, Xidan, Muxidi, Junshi Bowuguan, Gongzhufen, Maguanying

4 Runs along Chang'an Jie, Jianguomenwai Dajie and Jianguomennei Dajie: Gongzhufen, Junshi Bowuguan, Muxidi, Xidan, Tiananmen, Dongdan, Yonganli, Bawangfen, Sihuizhan

5 Deshengmen, Dianmen, Beihai Park, Xihuamen, Zhongshan Park, Qianmen

15 Beijing Zoo, Fuxingmen, Xidan, Hepingmen, Liulichang, Tianqiao

20 Beijing South Train Station, Tianqiao, Qianmen, Wangfujing, Dongdan, Beijing Train Station

44 outer ring Xinjiekou, Xizhimen Train Station, Fucheng-men, Fuxingmen, Changchunjie, Xuanwumen, Qianmen, Taijichang, Chongwenmen, Dongbianmen, Chaoyangmen, Dongzhimen, Andingmen, Deshengmen, Xinjiekou

54 Beijing Train Station, Dongbianmen, Chongwenmen, Zhengyi Lu, Qianmen, Dazhalan (Dashilar), Temple of Heaven Park, Yongdingmen, Haihutun

103 Beijing Train Station, Dengshikou, China Art Gallery, Forbidden City (north entrance), Beihai Park, Fuchengmen, Beijing Zoo

332 Beijing Zoo, Weigongcun, Renmin Daxue, Zhongguan-cun, Haidian, Beijing University, Summer Palace

For more information, you can check the Beijing Public Transport website: www .bjbus.com/english/default.htm.

To the Rest of China

No international buses serve Běijīng, but there are plenty of long-distance domestic routes. Although most domestic travel is by train, roads are improving, buses are cheaper and it's easier to book a seat. Sleeper buses are widely available and recommended for overnight journeys.

Běijīng has numerous long-distance bus stations (长途汽车站; *chángtú qìchēzhàn*), positioned roughly on the city perimeter in the direction you want to head. The most useful bus stations for travellers are: **Bawangfen long-distance bus station** (Bāwángfén Chángtú Kèyùnzhàn; Map pp268–9) in the east of town, **Sihui long-distance bus station** (Sìhuì Chángtù Qìchēzhàn; Map pp258–9), **Liuliqiao long-distance bus station** (Liùlíqiáo Chángtúzhàn; Map pp266–7; ☎ 8383 1717) southwest of Beijing West Train station, and **Lianhuachi long-distance bus station** (Liánhuāchí Chángtú Qìchēzhàn; Map pp266–7). Other important stations are at **Zhaogongkou** (Map pp258–9; ☎ 6722 9491/6723 7328) in the south. A huge long-distance bus station and transport hub was under construction at **Dongzhimen Transport Hub Station** (Map p264) at the time of writing.

Buses range in both type and quality, from simple minibuses to luxury air-conditioned buses, equipped with TV sets, toilets, reclining seats and hostesses handing out free mineral water. On long journeys, it is advisable to spend a bit more so that you can travel in comfort.

Sightseeing tourist buses for the Great Wall, Ming Tombs and other sights around Běijīng leave from the twin depots of the

Beijing Sightseeing Bus Centre (北京旅游集散中心; Map pp268–9; Běijīng Lǚyóu Jísàn Zhōngxīn; ☎ 8353 1111) northeast and northwest of Qianmen, alongside Tiananmen Square; certain routes also depart from outside the South Cathedral (p97).

CAR

At the time of writing, only foreigners with residency permits and Chinese driving licences were permitted to drive, effectively excluding tourists from the roads. For the latest update, contact **Hertz** (☎ 800-810 8883 countrywide; www.hertz.net.cn), where car hire is available from around Y320 per day.

Taxis are cheap, however, and even hiring a vehicle plus driver is a good proposition – this can be arranged through Hertz, major hotels, China International Travel Service (CITS) or other travel agencies. Depending on the type of vehicle, a chauffeur-driven car could cost you between Y600 and Y1000 per day, but a cheaper alternative would be to hire a cheap taxi for the day for around Y400 (see below).

TAXI

Taxis (出租车; *chūzūchē*) are everywhere, and finding one is only a problem during rush hour and (infrequent) rainstorms.

Běijīng taxis have red stickers on the side rear window declaring the rate per kilometre. Y2 taxis (Y10 for the first 3km; Y2 per kilometre thereafter) include a new fleet of Hyundai cars which are spacious, have air-con and rear seatbelts; other vehicles include Volkswagen Santanas and Citroëns. Taxis are required to switch on the meter for all journeys (unless you negotiate a fee for a long journey out of town). Between 11pm and 6am there is a 20% surcharge added to the flag fall metered fare. The cheaper *xiali* bone-rattler taxis that infested Běijīng's roads have effectively been phased out.

Běijīng taxi drivers speak little, if any, English, despite encouragement to learn 100 basic phrases in the run up to 2008. If you don't speak Chinese, bring a map or have your destination written down in characters. It helps if you know the way to your destination; sit in the front with a map.

Cabs can be hired by distance, by the hour, or by the day (a minimum of around Y400 per day). Taxis can be hailed in the street, summoned by phone or you can wait at one of the designated taxi zones or outside hotels. Call ☎ 6835 1150 to register a complaint. Remember to collect a receipt (ask the driver to give you a receipt, or *fāpiào*; 发票); if you accidentally leave anything in the taxi, the driver's number appears on the receipt so he or she can be located.

The taxi driver may try to dissuade you from wearing a seatbelt – ignore him/her and prepare yourself for Běijīng's atrocious driving. Watch out for tired drivers – they work long and punishing shifts.

If you're staying for a long time and you meet a taxi driver you like or trust, ask for a name card. Most drivers have home phones or mobile phones and can be hired for the day. Alternatively, **Beijing Beiqi Taxi** (☎ 8661 1062; 28 Xizhimen Nandajie) can hire you a taxi plus driver from around Y400 per day.

SUBWAY & LIGHT RAILWAY

The subway (地铁; *dìtiě*) is probably the best way to travel around. The Underground Dragon can move at up to 70km/h – a jaguar compared with the lumbering buses. The system is modest and trains are showing their age, but five new subway lines are being constructed to take the strain off the roads for the 2008 Olympics. Four lines currently exist: Line 1, Line 2, Line 13 and the Batong Line (the extension of Line 1 which connects Sihui with Tuqiao). Except for the Batong Line (Y2 or Y4 if you transfer from Line 1), the fare is a flat Y3 on all lines, regardless of distance (Y5 if you swap between Line 13 and the rest of the subway system). Only a few platforms have seats, and toilets have only recently begun appearing. Trains, which can get very crowded, run at a frequency of one every few minutes during peak times. The subway runs from 5am to 11pm daily; platform signs are in Chinese characters and Pinyin. Stops are announced in English and Chinese. You'll find a detailed subway map of Běijīng in the colour map section at the back of this book.

To recognise a subway station (地铁站; *dì tiě zhàn)*, look for the subway symbol, which is a blue English capital 'D' with a circle around it. Another way of recognising a subway station is to look for an enormous cluster of bicycles.

Subway lines currently under construction are lines 4, 5, 8, 9, 10 and the Airport Line. Line 5, which will run north–south,

intersecting with Line 2 at Yonghegong and Chongwenmen and intersecting Line 1 at Dongdan, is due to open in mid-2007. Line 4, linking northwest Běijīng with the south of the city, is due to open in 2009. Line 8 (the Olympic Branch Line) will connect with the Olympic Park and is due for completion in 2008. Line 10 will run from Jingsong in the southeast through Guomao and onto Wanliu in the northwest of town and is due for completion in 2008. The Airport Line will connect Capital Airport with Dongzhimen and will be open by 2008.

A non-stop subway line linking Beijing West Train Station and Beijing Train Station is also under construction and is due to start operating in 2007.

Line 1 一号地铁线

With 23 stations, Line 1 runs from Sihuidong to Pingguoyuan, a western suburb of Běijīng. The transfer stations with Line 2 are at Fuxingmen and Jianguomen stations. Passengers for the Batong line transfer at Sihui. Tickets are Y3.

Line 2 二号地铁线

With 18 stations including Beijingzhan (Beijing Train Station), this 16km line intersects with Line 1 at Fuxingmen and Jianguomen. Passengers for Line 13 transfer at Dongzhimen or Xizhimen. Tickets are Y3, unless you are continuing to a station on Line 13 (Y5).

Line 13 十三号地铁线

Classified as part of the subway system but actually a light rail link, Line 13 runs in a northern loop from Xizhimen to Dongzhimen in the north of Běijīng, stopping at 14 stations (approximately three minutes per station) in between (first/last train 6am/9pm). As with the subway, tickets are Y3, but Y5 gets you a ticket to any station on the other lines of the underground system.

Batong Line 八通地铁线

Batong Line stations are Sihui, Sihuidong, Gaobeidian, Guangboxueyuan, Shuangqiao, Guanzhuang, Baliqiao, Tongzhoubeiyuan, Guoyuan, Jiukeshu, Liyuan, Linheli and Tuqiao. Tickets are Y2 unless travelling to or from stations on Line 1 (Y4).

TRAIN

China's extensive passenger rail network covers every province except Hǎinán, and the link to Lhasa was completed in 2006. At any given time it is estimated that over 10 million Chinese are travelling on a train in China, except at the Chinese New Year when everyone appears to be on the railway.

Travelling China by train is an excellent way to voyage, especially by sleeper, as it offers an entertaining ride and brings you together with Chinese travelling the land. Intercity trains are largely air-conditioned, fast and comfortable, and varying classes of travel are often available. The safety record of the train system is also good, but keep an eye on your belongings.

The new fleet of trains that run intercity routes is a vast improvement on the old models – these trains are much cleaner and equipped with air-con. The new 'Z' class express trains (eg from Běijīng to Shànghǎi and Xī'ān) are very plush, with meals thrown in on some routes, mobile-phone charging points and well-designed bunks. Trains nationwide are punctual and depart on the dot.

Buying Tickets

It's cheapest to buy tickets at the train station, but for a small surcharge you can get them at most hotel counters and ticket counters around the city or through travel agents. Avoid buying from the touts who gather outside the train station, unless you are desperate for a ticket. If you do buy from a tout, examine the ticket carefully to check the date of travel and destination before handing over your money.

The queues at the ticket office (售票厅; shòupiàotīng) at Beijing Train Station can be overwhelming. At the time of writing, the ticketing office for foreigners on the first floor had closed, although an English-speaking service was available at ticket window No 26. Information is available at ticket window No 29. A foreigner's ticketing office can be found on the 2nd floor of **Beijing West Train Station** (24hr). Tickets can also be bought online at www.chinatrip advisor.com or www.china-train-ticket .com, but it's cheaper to buy your ticket at the station.

Your chances of getting a sleeper (hard or soft) are good if you book several days ahead. Never just turn up and expect to be able to buy a ticket to a distant destination for same-day travel. Train tickets to and from Běijīng can be booked solid for almost a week around National Day (1 October); the rail network is also totally congested during Chinese New Year. Chinese speakers can call ☎ 962586 to book tickets in advance. Note that tickets can often only be purchased five days in advance at most, which includes the day you buy the ticket and the day you depart; so don't bank on being able to get hold of a ticket a week before you want to travel. In general, tickets are for single (单程; dānchéng) rather than return trips.

Complicated paperback train timetables for the entire country are published every April and October, available in Chinese only (complete/abridged Y5/Y2). The resourceful Duncan Peattie (www.chinatt.org) publishes an English-language Chinese railway timetable. You can also consult www .travelchinaguide.com/china-trains, which allows you to enter your departure point and destination, and gives you the departure times, arrival times and train numbers of trains running that route.

Classes

Trains on longer routes are divided into classes. Hard-seat (硬座; yìng zuò) is actually generally padded, but it can be hard on your sanity, painful on long hauls and typically packed to the gills. Your ticket should have an assigned seat number, but if seats have sold out, ask for a standing ticket (无座; wúzuò or 站票; zhànpiào), which at least gets you on the train, and you can then find a seat or find the conductor and upgrade (补票; bǔpiào) yourself to a hard-sleeper, soft-seat or soft-sleeper if there are any available.

On short express journeys (such as Běijīng to Tiānjīn) some trains have soft-seat (软座; ruǎn zuò) carriages. Seats are two abreast, overcrowding is not permitted and carriages are often double-decker.

Hard-sleeper (硬卧; yìng wò) carriages consist of doorless compartments with half a dozen bunks in three tiers. The lowest bunk (下铺; xiàpù) is the most expensive and the top bunk (上铺; shàngpù) is the cheapest. The middle bunk (中铺; zhōngpù) is preferable, as all and sundry use the lower berth as a seat during the day, whereas the top bunk has little headroom. As with all other classes, smoking is prohibited in hard-sleeper. Lights and speakers go out at around 10pm. Each compartment is equipped with its own hot water flask (热水瓶; rèshuǐpíng), which is filled by an attendant.

Soft sleeper (软卧; ruǎn wò) has four comfortable bunks in a closed compartment with a sliding door. Costing much more than hard sleeper (the upper berth is slightly cheaper than the lower berth), soft sleeper is usually easier to purchase than hard sleeper; however, more and more Chinese are travelling this way.

Services

Travellers arrive and depart by train at **Beijing Train Station** (北京火车站; Běijīng Huǒchē Zhàn; Map pp268–9; ☎ 5101 9999) or **Beijing West Train Station** (北京西站; Běijīng Xī Zhàn; Map pp266–7; ☎ 5182 6273). Beijing Train Station is served by its own underground station, making access simple. International trains to Moscow, Pyongyang and Ulaan Baatar arrive at and leave from Beijing Train Station; trains for Hong Kong and Vietnam leave from Beijing West Train Station. Buses 122 and 721 connect Beijing Train Station with Beijing West Train Station.

Two other stations of significance are **Beijing South Train Station** (Yǒngdìngmén Huǒchē Zhàn; Map pp266–7; ☎ 5183 7262) and **Beijing North Train Station** (Běijīng Běizhàn; Map pp260–1; ☎ 5186 6223) on the Second Ring Rd.

Left luggage counters (寄存处; jìcúnchù) and lockers can be found at most train stations.

Typical train fares and approximate travel times for hard-sleeper tickets to destinations from Beijing Train Station include: Chángchūn (长春; Y239, 9½ hours), Dàlián (大连; Y257, 12 hours), Dàtóng (大同; Y70, 5½ hours), Hāěrbīn (哈尔滨; Y281, 11½ hours), Hángzhōu (杭州; Y363, 15 hours), Jǐ'nán (济南; Y137, 4½ hours), Lhasa (拉萨; Y813, 47½ hours), Nánjīng (南京; Y274, 11 hours), Qīngdǎo (青岛; Y215, 9 hours), Shànghǎi (上海; Y327, 13½ hours, soft-sleeper express 12 hours), Sūzhōu (苏州; Y309, 11 hours) and Tiānjīn (天津; Y30 hard seat, 80 minutes). The fast soft-sleeper Z19 express train departs daily from Beijing West Train Station for Xī'ān (西安; Y417, 11½ hours) at 8.28pm.

PRACTICALITIES

ACCOMMODATION

Běijīng's rapidly growing population of hotels, hostels and guesthouses in the Sleeping chapter are listed by budget within each neighbourhood. Rack rates at midrange and top-end hotels are rarely the rule and discounts are the norm.

Hotel rooms are generally easy to find, although it can be harder during the peak tourist season from June to September and during the 1 May and 1 October holiday periods, so book ahead if visiting during these times. A 15% service charge is levied at midrange and top-end hotels. Checkout time is usually noon, but exceptions are indicated in hotel reviews.

For information on rates and discounts, reservations and other aspects of accommodation in Běijīng, consult the Sleeping chapter (p178).

Before visiting Běijīng, explore online deals. Accommodation websites that can get travellers substantial hotel discounts include **CTrip** (☎ 800-820 6666; www.english .ctrip.com) and **Beijing Hotels Travel Guide** (www .beijing-hotels.net).

BUSINESS

Doing business in China has long been fraught for Westerners since Lord Macartney's turkey of a mission to Chéngdé (p203) in 1793 to develop trade relations.

Things are easing up rapidly, but even simple things can be frustrating. Renting properties, getting licences, hiring employees and paying taxes can generate mind-boggling quantities of red tape. Many foreign businesspeople who have worked in China say that success is usually the result of dogged persistence and finding cooperative officials.

Anyone planning on doing business in China is advised to read *The China Dream: The Elusive Quest for the Greatest Untapped Market on Earth,* written by Joe Studwell (Profile Books Ltd, 2002), which presents a sober and balanced perspective on the Chinese economy and how it all fits together.

Also refer to the City Life chapter (p16) for further information on Chinese etiquette, the Chinese economy and the structure of political power in Běijīng.

If you are considering doing business in China, considerable preliminary research is recommended. In particular, talk to other foreigners who are already doing business in China. Alternatively, approach a firm of business consultants for advice or approach the business associations listed below.

Business Associations

The following organisations can be found in Běijīng:

American Chamber of Commerce (☎ 8519 1920; www.amcham-china.org.cn; Room 1903, 8 Jianguomen Beidajie, China Resources Bldg, Dongcheng)

British Chamber of Commerce (☎ 8525 1111; www.pek.britcham.org; Room 1001, China Life Tower, 16 Chaoyangmenwai Dajie, Chaoyang)

Canada-China Business Council (☎ 6512 6120; www.ccbc.com; Suite 18-2, 18th fl, CITIC Bldg, 19 Jianguomenwai Dajie, Chaoyang)

China-Australia Chamber of Commerce (☎ 6595 9252; admin@austcham.org; Room 314, Great Wall Sheraton Hotel, 8 Dongsanhuan Beilu, Chaoyang)

European Union Chamber of Commerce in China (☎ 6462 2065; www.euccc.com.cn)

French Chamber of Commerce & Industry (☎ 8451 2071; S123, Office Bldg, Lufthansa Center, 50 Liangmaqiao Lu)

US-China Business Council (☎ 8526 3920; www.uschina.org)

Business Cards

The Chinese hand business cards around in place of handshakes, and if you don't have one it can be embarrassing. These are essential items, even if you don't do business. Try to get your name translated into Chinese and have it printed on the reverse. Hotel business centres can print business cards; alternatively, try **Alphagraphics** (Map pp268–9; ☎ 6505 2906; www.alpha graphics.com; L206, 2nd fl, China World Trade Center, 1 Jianguomenwai Dajie).

BUSINESS HOURS

China officially has a five-day working week. Banks, offices and government departments are normally open Monday to Friday, open roughly from 9am (some closing for two hours in the middle of the day) until 5pm or 6pm. Some banks have branches that are open at weekends as well. Saturday and Sunday are both public holidays, but most

Běijīng museums stay open on weekends and make up for this by closing for one day (usually Monday). Museums tend to stop selling tickets half an hour before they close. Bank of China branches are generally open weekdays from 9am to noon and 2pm to 4.30pm Monday to Friday, and 24-hour ATMs (see ATMs, p226) are plentiful. Travel agencies, foreign-exchange counters in the tourist hotels and some of the local branches of the Bank of China have similar opening hours, but are generally open on weekends as well, at least in the morning. Shops are generally open from 10am to 10pm while restaurants tend to run from 10.30am to 11pm, although some shut in the afternoon between the hours of 2pm and 5.30pm. Internet cafés are either open 8am to midnight or are 24-hour. Note that many businesses in Běijīng close for three week–long holidays (p223) or have interruptions in their service.

Parks are generally open from 6am to around 9pm or later, although they can open later and shut earlier in winter. Opening hours for sights are listed under each entry in the Sights chapter.

Běijīng's entertainment sector is working increasingly long hours, and it's possible to find something to eat and somewhere to drink at any hour of the day.

CHILDREN

The Chinese have a deep and uncompli-cated love of children. The treatment you'll receive if you're travelling with a young child or baby can often make life a lot easier (especially if they have blond hair). Don't be surprised if a complete stranger picks up your child or tries to take them from your arms: Chinese people openly display their affection for children.

Baby food and milk powder is widely available in supermarkets, as are basics like nappies, baby wipes, bottles, creams, medicine, clothing, dummies (pacifiers) and other paraphernalia. Few cheap restau-rants, however, have baby chairs, and find-ing baby-changing rooms when you need one can be impossible. Check the Health section for information on recommended vaccinations (p222). If you need a babysit-ter (阿姨; *āyí*), contact **Century Domestic Services** (☎ 6498 8220; from Y10-15 per hour), who can supply an English-speaking *āyí* at an hourly rate.

Admission prices to many sights and museums have children's rates, usually for children under 1.1m to 1.3m in height. Infants under the age of two fly for 10% of the full airfare. Children between the ages of two and 11 need to pay half the full price for domestic flights, and 75% of the adult price for international flights.

Always ensure that your child carries a form of ID and a hotel card, in case they get lost.

International schools where children are educated in the English language are plentiful; among high-profile arrivals is the elite **Harrow International School Beijing** (☎ 6444 8900; www.harrowbeijing.cn).

See the Běijīng For Children boxed text (p96) for recommended diversions and activities for kiddies.

For more information on travelling with children, turn to the following books:

Adventuring with Children Nan Jeffrey; Avalon House Travel Series.

Backpacking with Babies and Small Children Goldie Silverman; Wilderness Press.

Take the Kids Travelling Helen Truszkowski; Take the Kids series.

Travel with Children Maureen Wheeler, Cathy Lanigan; Lonely Planet.

Travelling Abroad with Children Samantha Gore-Lyons; Arrow.

CLIMATE

Autumn (mid-September to early November) is the optimal season to visit Běijīng as the weather is gorgeous and fewer tourists are in town. Local Běijīngers describe this short season as *'tiāngāo qìshuǎng'*, literally 'the sky is high and the air is fresh' – with clear skies and breezy days. Arid spring (March to April) is OK, apart from the sand clouds (see the Dust Devil boxed text, p26) that sweep in from Inner Mongolia and the ubiquitous static electricity that discharges everywhere. Spring also sees the snow-like *liǔxù* (willow catkins) wafting through the Běijīng air. From May onwards the mercury can surge well over 30°C. Běijīng simmers under a scorching sun in summer (May to August), when temperatures can top 40°C, with heavy rainstorms appearing late in the season. Surprisingly, this is also considered the peak season, when hotels typically raise

their rates and the Great Wall nearly collapses under the weight of marching tourists. In winter (early November to February) there are few tourists in town and many hotels offer substantial discounts – but it's glacial outside (dipping as low as -20°C) and the northern winds cut like a knife through bean curd. Heating in public buildings is officially turned on in mid-November every year. Air pollution can be very harsh in both summer and winter (see the Environment, p25).

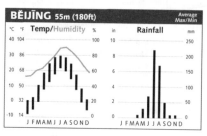

COURSES

With so many *lǎowài* (foreigners) arriving in Běijīng to learn Mandarin in the heartland of the dialect, language schools are burgeoning. You may not have the time to sign up for a whole semester at a university such as the Beijing Language & Culture University or Beijing Normal University (the cheapest and most effective strategy), but there are ample other schools to choose from. It pays to hunt around however, as the rapidly expanding market regularly produces schools of suspect quality. Check out how long the school has been in business and if possible, talk to students attending classes there. For language exchange partners, consult the classified pages of English magazines such as *That's Beijing* (www.thatsbj.com). The following language schools are reputable and either offer tuition in the Chinese language or Chinese culture, and occasionally both:

Berlitz (Map pp268–9; ☎ 6593 0478; www.berlitz.com; Room 801, Sunjoy Bldg, 6 Ritan Lu) Classes in Chinese, including effective immersion lessons for total novices.

Chinese Culture Club (Map p264; ☎ 6432 9341, ext 18; www.chinesecultureclub.org; 29 Liangmaqiao Lu) Offers a range of cultural programmes, taught in English and aimed squarely at foreign visitors and expats. Recommended.

Executive Mandarin (Map p264; ☎ 6561 2486; www
.ecbeijing.com; Hanwei Bldg, 7 Guanghua Lu) Immersion
programs, Mandarin and Cantonese, business Chinese.

FESCO (Map p264; ☎ 8561 6180; www.fesco-training
.com.cn; 1st fl, FESCO Bldg, 14 Chaoyangmen Nandajie)
This long-established institution has courses in Chinese
language, Chinese painting, calligraphy, seal cutting,
music, dance, martial arts, acupuncture, moxibustion
and other traditional crafts and skills. FESCO also holds
regular seminars on subjects relating to Chinese history
and culture.

Global Village (☎ 6253 7737; west side of Wudaokou
light rail station) Popular school with value-for-money
classes in Mandarin. Taster lesson available.

My Chinese (Map p264; ☎ 6417 9553; www.mychinese
classroom.com; Room 8203-8209, Baoliyuan Bldg, 55a
Xingfuyicun) Offers classes in business Chinese, HSK
(Chinese proficiency test) and a range of cultural courses.

CUSTOMS

Chinese customs generally pay tourists
little attention. There are clearly marked
'green channels' and 'red channels' at the
airport. Duty free, you're allowed to import 400 cigarettes or the equivalent in
tobacco products, 1.5L of alcohol and 50g
of gold or silver. Importation of fresh fruit
and cold cuts is prohibited. You can bring
in or take out Y20,000 in Chinese currency without declaring it. There are no
restrictions on foreign currency; however,
you should declare any cash that exceeds
US$5000 (or its equivalent in another
currency).

Objects considered antiques require a
certificate and red seal to clear customs.
To get the proper certificate and seal your
antiques must be inspected by the **Relics
Bureau** (Wénwù Jiàndìng; ☎ 6401 4608),
where no English is spoken. Anything made
before 1949 is considered an antique and
needs a certificate, and if it was made before 1795 it cannot legally be taken out of
the country.

DISCOUNT CARDS

An ISIC card (www.isiccard.com) may be
useful as you could get half-price entry to
some sights. Chinese signs at many sights
clearly indicate that students pay half price –
so push the point. It's worth trying to
get air ticket discounts using your ISIC
card; some travellers report success. If you
are studying in China, your school will

issue you with a student card, which is
more useful for discounts on admission
charges.

Tickets must be purchased for virtually
every sight in Běijīng and beyond, and
there is little that one can do for free (see
the boxed text on p78). The Y80 Beijing
Museum Pass (p74) is an invaluable investment, getting you cut price entrance
to myriad temples, museums and sights
in town.

ELECTRICITY

Electricity is 220 volts, 50 cycles AC. Most
plugs take four designs – three-pronged
angled pins (as in Australia), three-
pronged round pins (as in Hong Kong),
two flat pins (US style but without the
ground wire) or two narrow round pins
(European style). Conversion plugs are
easily purchased in Běijīng. For more information on electricity and adaptors in
China, see www.kropla.com.

EMBASSIES & CONSULATES
Chinese Embassies & Consulates

For a full list of Chinese diplomatic rep-
resentation abroad go to the Ministry of
Foreign affairs website at www.fmprc.gov
.cn/eng.

Australia Canberra (☎ 02-6273 4780, 6273 4781;
http://au.china-embassy.org/eng; 15 Coronation Drive,
Yarralumla, ACT 2600); Melbourne (☎ 03-9822 0604);
Perth (☎ 08-9321 8193); Sydney (☎ 02-9699 2216)

Canada Calgary (☎ 403-264 3322); Ottawa (☎ 613-789
3509; www.chinaembassycanada.org; 515 St Patrick St,
Ottawa, Ontario K1N 5H3); Toronto (☎ 416-964 7260);
Vancouver (☎ 604-736 3910)

Denmark Copenhagen (☎ 039-625 806; Oregards Alle 25,
2900 Hellerup, Copenhagen)

France Paris (☎ 01 47 36 02 58; www.amb-chine.fr;
9 Ave V Cresson, 92130 Issy les Moulineaux, Paris)

Japan Fukuoka (☎ 92-713 1121); Osaka (☎ 06-445 9481);
Sapporo (☎ 11-563 5563); Tokyo (☎ 03-3403 3389, 3403
3065; 3-4-33 Moto-Azabu, Minato-ku, Tokyo 106)

Malaysia Kuala Lumpur (☎ 03-242 8495; 229 Jalan
Ampang, Kuala Lumpur); Kuching (☎ 82-453 344)

Netherlands The Hague (☎ 070-355 1515; Adriaan
Goekooplaan 7, 2517 JX, The Hague)

New Zealand Auckland (☎ 09-525 1589); Wellington (☎ 04-587 0407; 104A Korokoro Rd, Petone, Wellington)

Singapore (☎ 65-734 3361; 70 Dalvey Rd)

Thailand Bangkok (☎ 02-245 7032/49; 57 Th Ratchada-phisek, Bangkok)

UK Edinburgh (☎ 0131-316 4789); London (☎ 020 7636 8845, 24-hr premium-rate visa information 0891 880 808; www.chinese-embassy.org.uk; 31 Portland Place, London, W1N 5AG; Manchester (☎ 0161-224 7480)

USA Chicago (☎ 312-803 0098); Houston (☎ 713-524 4311); Los Angeles (☎ 213-380 2508); New York (☎ 212-330 7410); San Francisco (☎ 415-563 9232); Washington DC (☎ 202-338 6688; www.china-embassy.org; Room 110, 2201 Wisconsin Ave NW, Washington DC, 20007)

Embassies in Běijīng

Embassies in Běijīng are open from 9am to noon and from 1.30pm to 4pm Monday to Friday, but visa departments are often open only in the morning. There are two main embassy areas: Jianguomenwai and Sanlitun.

The following embassies are in the Jianguomenwai area:

India (Map p264; ☎ 6532 1908; www.indianembassy .org.cn/; 1 Ritan Donglu)

Ireland (Map pp268–9; ☎ 6532 2691; fax 6532 2168; 3 Ritan Donglu)

Japan (Map p264; ☎ 6532 2361; fax 6532 4625; 7 Ritan Lu)

Mongolia (Map pp268–9; ☎ 6532 1203; fax 6532 5045; 2 Xiushui Beijie)

New Zealand (Map p264; ☎ 6532 2731; www .nzembassy.com/china; 1 Ritan Dong Erjie)

North Korea (Map p264; ☎ 6532 1186; fax 6532 6056; Ritan Beilu)

Philippines (Map pp268–9; ☎ 6532 1872; fax 6532 3761; 23 Xiushui Beijie)

Singapore (Map pp268–9; ☎ 6532 3926; www.mfa .gov.sg/beijing; 1 Xiushui Beijie)

South Korea (Map pp268–9; ☎ 6505 2608; www .koreaemb.org.cn; 3rd & 4th fl, China World Trade Center, 1 Jianguomenwai Dajie)

Thailand (Map p264; ☎ 6532 1749; www.thaiembassy .org/beijing; 40 Guanghua Lu)

UK (Map p264; ☎ 5192 4000; www.uk.cn; 11 Guanghua Lu)

USA (Map p264; ☎ 6532 3831; http://beijing.usembassy -china.org.cn/; 3 Xiushui Beijie)

Vietnam (Map p264; ☎ 6532 1155; fax 6532 5720; 32 Guanghua Lu)

The Sanlitun area is home to the following embassies:

Australia (Map p264; ☎ 6532 2331; www.austemb.org.cn; 21 Dongzhimenwai Dajie)

Cambodia (Map p264; ☎ 6532 2790; fax 6532 3507; 9 Dongzhimenwai Dajie)

Canada (Map p264; ☎ 6532 3536; www.beijing.gc.ca; 19 Dongzhimenwai Dajie)

France (Map p264; ☎ 8532 8080; www.ambafrance-cn .org; 3 Dongsan Jie)

Germany (Map p264; ☎ 8532 9000; www.deutsche botschaft-china.org; 17 Dongzhimenwai Dajie)

Italy (Map p264; ☎ 6532 2131; www.italianembassy .org.cn; 2 Sanlitun Dong Erjie)

Kazakhstan (Map p264; ☎ 6532 6182; fax 6532 6183; 9 Sanlitun Dong Liujie)

Laos (Map p264; ☎ 6532 1224; 11 Dongsi Jie)

Myanmar (Map p264; ☎ 6532 0359; www.myanmar embassy.com; 6 Dongzhimenwai Dajie)

Nepal (Map p264; ☎ 6532 1795; fax 6532 3251; 1 Sanlitun Xi Liujie)

Netherlands (Map p264; ☎ 6532 0200; fax 6532 4689; 4 Liangmahe Nanlu)

Pakistan (Map p264; ☎ 6532 2504/2558; 1 Dongzhi-menwai Dajie)

Russia (Map p262; ☎ 6532 1381; www.russia.org.cn; 4 Dongzhimen Beizhongjie)

Sweden (Map p264; ☎ 6532 9790; www.swedenabroad .com; 3 Dongzhimenwai Dajie)

EMERGENCY

Important telephone numbers include:

Ambulance	☎ 120
Directory inquiries	☎ 114
Fire	☎ 119
International directory inquiries	☎ 115
Police	☎ 110
Public Security Bureau (foreigners' section)	☎ 8402 0101
Tourist Hotline	☎ 6513 0828
Weather (English & Chinese)	☎ 121

GAY & LESBIAN TRAVELLERS

Even though the Chinese authorities take a dim view of homosexuality, which was officially classified as a mental disorder until 2001, a low-profile gay and lesbian scene exists in Běijīng. For informative and an up-to-date lowdown on the latest gay and lesbian hot spots in Běijīng and the rest of China, have a look at the Utopia website (www.utopia-asia.com/tipschin.htm) or invest in a copy of the *Utopia Guide to China*. The second Beijing International Gay and Lesbian Film Festival was held in 2005.

HEALTH

Except for the thick layer of air pollution that sometimes blankets the city, Běijīng is a reasonably healthy city and you needn't fear tropical bugs like malaria. When weighing up health risks, always bear in mind other, more immediate dangers – the greatest danger you will probably face is crossing the road.

It's a good idea to consult your government's travel health website before departure, if one is available.

Australia (www.dfat.gov.au/travel)

Canada (www.hc-sc.gc.ca)

New Zealand (www.mfat.govt.nz/travel)

UK (www.doh.gov.uk/traveladvice)

USA (www.cdc.gov/travel)

It's worth taking your own medicine kit so that you have remedies at hand. Antibiotics *(kàngjūnsù)*, sleeping pills *(ānmiányào)*, anti-depressants and other medications can be picked up prescription-free from many chemists in Běijīng; but if you require a more specific type of drug, make sure you take an adequate supply. When looking for medications in Běijīng, make sure you take along the brand and the generic name so that pharmacy staff can locate it for you.

By early 2007, there were 22 confirmed human cases of bird flu in China. Of these, 14 died. Currently very close contact with dead or sick birds is the principal source of infection, and bird-to-human transmission does not easily occur. Symptoms include high fever and typical influenza-like symptoms with rapid deterioration, leading to respiratory failure and death in many cases. At this time it is not routinely recommended for travellers to carry anti-viral drugs such as Tamiflu; rather, immediate medical care should be sought if bird flu is suspected.

There is currently no vaccine available to prevent bird flu. For up-to-date information, check the websites www.who.int/en and www.avianinfluenza.com.au.

Required Vaccinations

Yellow Fever Proof of vaccination is required if entering China within six days of visiting an infected country. If you are travelling to China from Africa or South America, check with a travel medicine clinic about whether you need the vaccine.

Recommended Vaccinations

Adult diphtheria/tetanus (ADT) A booster is recommended if it is more than 10 years since your last shot. Side effects include a sore arm and fever.

Hepatitis A One shot provides almost 100% protection for up to a year; a booster after 12 months provides another 20 years' protection. Mild side effects include a sore arm, fever and headaches.

Hepatitis B Now considered a routine vaccination for most travellers. Given as three shots over six months, this vaccine can be combined with Hepatitis A (Twinrix). In most people the course gives lifetime protection. Mild side effects include a sore arm and headaches.

Measles/Mumps/Rubella (MMR) Two lifetime doses of MMR are recommended unless you have had the diseases. Many adults under the age of 35 require a booster. Occasionally a rash and flu-like illness occur about a week after vaccination.

Typhoid Needed if spending more than two weeks in China. A single injection provides around 70% protection for two to three years.

Varicella (chickenpox) If you haven't had chickenpox discuss this vaccine with your doctor. Chickenpox can be a serious disease in adults and has such complications as pneumonia and encephalitis.

Under certain circumstances or for those at special risk the following vaccinations are recommended. Discuss these with a doctor who specialises in travel medicine.

Influenza If you are over 50 years of age or have a chronic medical condition such as diabetes, lung disease or heart disease, you should have an influenza shot annually.

Japanese encephalitis There is risk only in rural areas of China. Recommended if travelling to rural areas for more than a month during summer.

Pneumonia (Pneumococcal) This vaccine is recommended for travellers over 65 or those with chronic lung or heart disease. A single shot is given, with a booster in five years.

Rabies Recommended if spending more than three months in China. Requires three injections given over a one-month period.

If you are pregnant or breast feeding consult a doctor who specialises in travel medicine before having any vaccines.

Diseases

AIDS & SEXUALLY TRANSMITTED DISEASES

The Chinese government is starting to take AIDS seriously as the country is said to be on the brink of a major epidemic. Although most cases so far have occurred in intravenous drug users or from contaminated blood products, the virus is increasingly being spread via heterosexual sex.

Always use condoms if you have sex with a new partner, and never share needles. If you have had unsafe sex while travelling, get a checkup and immediately seek medical advice if you develop pain, a rash or a discharge.

HEPATITIS A

This virus is transmitted through contaminated food and water, and infects the liver, causing jaundice (yellow skin and eyes), nausea and extreme tiredness. There is no specific treatment available; you just need to allow time for the liver to heal, which might take many weeks.

HEPATITIS B

This disease is common in China and is transmitted via infected body fluids, including through sexual contact. The long-term consequences can include liver cancer and cirrhosis.

INFLUENZA

Flu is common in Běijīng in winter. This virus gives you high fevers, body aches and general symptoms, such as a cough, runny nose and sore throat. Antibiotics won't help unless you develop a complication, such as pneumonia. Anyone travelling in winter should think about vaccination, but it is particularly recommended for the elderly or those with underlying medical conditions.

TRAVELLER'S DIARRHOEA

This is the most common problem faced by travellers in Asia. Most traveller's diarrhoea is caused by bacteria and thus responds rapidly to a short course of appropriate antibiotics. How soon you treat your diarrhoea will depend on individual circumstances, but it is a good idea to carry appropriate treatment in your medical kit.

TUBERCULOSIS (TB)

This is a rare disease in travellers and requires prolonged close exposure to a person with active TB infection. Symptoms include a cough, weight loss, night sweats and fevers. Children under the age of five spending more than six months in China should receive BCG vaccination. Adults are rarely immunised.

TYPHOID

This serious bacterial infection is contracted from contaminated food and water. Symptoms include high fever, headache, a cough and lethargy. The diagnosis is made via blood tests, and treatment is with specific antibiotics.

Environmental Hazards

AIR POLLUTION

Běijīng is one of the 10 most polluted cities in the world. Although the government is working to improve the situation before the 2008 Olympics, those with chronic respiratory conditions should ensure they have adequate personal medication with them in case symptoms worsen.

WATER

Don't drink the tap water or eat ice. Bottled water, soft drinks and alcohol are fine.

HOLIDAYS & FESTIVALS

New Year's Day 1 January

Spring Festival (Chinese New Year) Generally held in January or February; 7 February 2008, 26 January 2009, 14 February 2010

International Women's Day 8 March

International Labour Day 1 May

Youth Day 4 May

International Children's Day 1 June

Birthday of the Chinese Communist Party 1 July

Anniversary of the founding of the People's Liberation Army (PLA) 1 August

National Day 1 October

The big holiday periods for the Chinese are the weeks following the 1 May holiday, National Day on 1 October and the Spring Festival. Travelling in China during these periods can be hectic as tourist sights are swamped and bus, train and air tickets are hard to come by (especially during the Spring Festival), although seeing Běijīng during the Spring Festival sees the city at its liveliest and most colourful. See the City Calendar section (p18) for details on annual festivals in Běijīng.

INTERNET ACCESS

Unlike in many small towns dotted around China, public internet access in Běijīng can be elusive, with terminals tucked away down side streets and located inconveniently away from the action. A fire in a Běijīng internet café in 2002 which killed 25 people was used as a pretext to close down scores of operations in town, and the number of licences for internet cafés (网吧, wǎngbā) became strictly controlled. The picture remains hazy, but controls could be eased in the lead up to the 2008 Olympics.

Internet censorship – known as the Great Firewall of China – is draconian, with an army of 30,000 censors working non-stop to stem the tide of undesirable electronic data from corrupting Chinese minds. Pornography is censored, but not as rigorously as politically taboo subjects such as Taiwanese independence, the Tiananmen Square massacre and outlawed groups such as Falun Gong. By some estimates, 10% of websites are inaccessible, including – at the time of writing – the BBC News website and Wikipedia in English. Internet monitors are employed by the state to discreetly usher online chatroom discussions on topical and sensitive issues in authorised directions. Reports suggest that all of this is little more than a minor irritation to Chinese online users who have become inured to constant censorship in all forms of media in China.

Rates should be around Y2 to Y3 per hour for a standard outlet with no frills, but comfier and smarter options often charge more, perhaps with a coffee thrown in. It is increasingly common for bars and cafés (eg along Nanluogu Xiang) to offer free internet access. Be prepared for agonisingly slow connections, especially on congested sites such as Hotmail, and the sudden disappearance of sites for long periods.

Internet cafés in Běijīng are required to see your passport before allowing you to go online, and a record of your visit may be made. Most internet cafés will permit foreigners to use their facilities, but some do not.

Use midrange and top-end hotel business centre computers for going online only if you have no choice, as charges are stratospheric. Many cheaper hotels and youth hostels provide internet access at around Y10 per hour.

To access the internet using a laptop from your hotel room in Běijīng, free dial-up access can be made by hooking up through the phone line and using the local dial-up number (169). In the dial-up connection box enter '169' as your username and password, and in the phone number box again enter '169'. Many midrange and top-end hotels now provide free broadband internet access, so ask.

Many of the cafés and bars along Nanluogu Xiang in Dōngchéng offer free internet access to guests. The following internet cafés are centrally located:

Beijing Huohu Shiji Internet Café (Běijīng Huòhú Shìjì Wǎngbā; Map p264; Chunxiu Lu; per hr Y3; ☺ 8am-midnight) North of Xingfucun Zhonglu on Chunxiu Lu, south of Red House Hotel.

Chengse 520 Internet Café (Chéngsè 520 Wǎngbā; Map pp268–9; 3rd fl, 7 Dashilan Jie; per hr Y4; ☺ 8am-3am) Through clothing market and up the stairs in Dashilar.

Dayusu Internet Café (Dáyǔsù Wǎngbā; Map pp266–7; 2 Hufang Lu; per hr Y3; ☺ 8am-midnight) No English sign, but it's around three shops north of the Bank of China on Hufang Lu.

Hulindao Internet Café (Húlíndào Wǎngbā; Map p262; 2nd fl, cnr Dianmenwai Dajie & Yandai Xiejie; per hr Y3; ☺ 8am-midnight) Look for the characters '上网'.

Internet Café (Wǎngbā; Map pp268–9; Shop No 2601, 2nd fl, Soho New Town, next to exit B Dawanglu subway station; per hr Y3; ☺ 24hr)

Internet Café (Wǎngbā; Map pp268–9; 2nd fl, above the Beijing City Central Youth Hostel; per hr Y5; ☺ 24hr)

Moko Coffee Bar (Mòkè Wǎngbā; Map p262; ☎ 6525 3712, 6559 8464; 57 Dongsi Nandajie; per hr upstairs/downstairs Y4/15; ⌚ 24hr) No English sign, but it's next to a chemist. Downstairs rates include a drink.

Qian Yi Internet Café (Map pp268–9; ☎ 6705 1722; 3rd fl, Old Station Bldg; per hr Y20; ⌚ 9am-midnight) Outrageously expensive. A much cheaper internet café (Y4) exists on the same floor, but foreigners are not welcome.

LEGAL MATTERS

Anyone under the age of 18 is considered a minor in China, and the minimum driving age is also 18. The age of consent for marriage is 22 years for men and 20 years for women. There is no minimum age restricting the consumption of cigarettes or alcohol.

China's laws against the use of illegal drugs are harsh, and foreign nationals have been executed for drug offences (trafficking in more than 50g of heroin can result in the death penalty).

The Chinese criminal justice system does not ensure a fair trial, and defendants are not presumed innocent until proven guilty. Note that China conducts more judicial executions than the rest of the world combined. If arrested, most foreign citizens have the right to contact their embassy.

MAPS

As Běijīng is so huge and spread out, it's vital to get a decent map of town. English-language maps of Běijīng can be bought from newspaper kiosks and the **Foreign Languages Bookstore** (p164). They can also be picked up for free at most big hotels and branches of the **Beijing Tourist Information Center** (see p231).

Street vendors hawk cheap maps near subway stations around Tiananmen Square and Wangfujing Dajie – make sure you check they have English labelling before purchasing from pushy vendors. One of the better English-language maps is the Beijing Tourist Map (Y8), labelled in both English and Chinese, but it doesn't show much detail on the lesser streets and alleys. The Wangfujing Bookstore (north of Oriental Plaza) has a large range of (largely Chinese language) detailed maps and guides to Běijīng. Check the expat magazine *That's Beijing* (p227), which occasionally prints handy colour maps to popular bar and restaurant haunts around town.

MEDICAL SERVICES

As the national capital, Běijīng naturally sports some of China's best medical facilities and services. Your embassy can provide you with a list of recommended English-speaking doctors, dentists, hospitals and international clinics.

A consultation with a doctor in a private clinic will cost between Y200 and Y800, depending on where you go. It will cost Y10 to Y50 in a state hospital.

Bayley & Jackson Medical Center (Map p264; ☎ 8562 9998; www.bjhealthcare.com; 7 Ritan Donglu) Full range of medical and dental services; attractively located in a courtyard on Ritan Park.

Beijing Union Hospital Xiéhé Yīyuàn (Map p262; Xiéhé Yīyuàn; ☎ 6529 6114, emergency 6529 5284; 53 Dongdan Beidajie) A recommended Chinese hospital operating from a wonderful building off Wangfujing Dajie, with a wing reserved for foreigners in the back building. Open 24 hours with a full range of facilities for inpatient and outpatient care, plus a pharmacy.

Beijing United Family Hospital (Map pp258–9; ☎ 6433 3960, 24hr emergency hotline 6433 2345; www.unitedfamilyhospitals.com; 2 Jiangtai Lu; ⌚ 24hr) Can provide alternative medical treatments along with a comprehensive range of inpatient and outpatient care, as well as a critical care unit. Emergency room staffed by expat physicians.

Hong Kong International Medical Clinic (Map p264; ☎ 6553 2288; www.hkclinic.com; 9th fl Office Tower, Hong Kong Macau Center, Swissôtel, 2 Chaoyangmen Beidajie; ⌚ 9am-9pm) The clinic has a 24-hour medical and dental clinic, including obstetric/gynaecological services. The clinic has facilities for ultrasonic scanning, and immunisations can also be performed. Prices are more reasonable than at SOS.

International SOS (Map p264; ☎ clinic appointments 6462 9112, dental appointments 6462 0333, 24hr alarm centre 6462 9100; www.internationalsos.com; Bldg C, BITIC Ying Yi Bldg, 1 Xingfu Sancun Bei Jie, Cháoyáng; ⌚ 9am-6pm Mon-Fri) Offering 24-hour emergency medical care, this clinic is located behind the German embassy and has a high-quality clinic with English-speaking staff.

METRIC SYSTEM

China officially subscribes to the international metric system. In markets however, you're likely to encounter the traditional Chinese weights and measures system, which features the *liǎng* (两) and the *jīn* (斤). One *jīn* is 0.6kg (1.32lb). There are 16 *liǎng* to the *jīn*, so one *liǎng* is 37.5g (1.32oz).

MONEY

For information regarding exchange rates, see the Quick Reference section on the inside front cover. The City Life chapter (p16) gives you some idea of the costs you are likely to incur during your stay in Běijīng.

ATMs

A growing number of ATMs now accept foreign credit cards and bank cards. The network is not citywide, however, and you are more likely to find handy ATMs connected to Plus, Cirrus, Visa, Mastercard and Amex in and around the main shopping areas (such as along Wangfujing Dajie) and international hotels and their associated shopping arcades. Many large department stores also have useful ATMs. Most ATMs at banks other than the Bank of China and the Industrial and Commercial Bank of China accept only domestic cards. ATM screens that take international cards offer the choice of English or Chinese operation.

Useful ATMs can be found in the arrivals hall at **Capital Airport**. ATMs are also plentiful along **Wangfujing Dajie**, including a handy wall-mounted ATM at the **Bank of China** next to the main entrance to Sundongan Plaza. On the other side of the road you will find an ATM of the **Industrial and Commercial Bank of China** that takes foreign cards. A further ATM can be found at the Bank of China on the corner of Oriental Plaza (on the corner of Wangfujing Dajie and Dongchan'an Jie). Most top-end hotels, such as the **Peninsula Beijing** (p185) and the **Novotel Peace Hotel** (p184) have useful ATMs. The **Hong Kong and Shanghai Banking Corporation** (HSBC; ☎ 6526 0668; www .hsbc.com.cn; ground fl, Block A, COFCO Plaza, 8 Jianguomen Dajie) has a 24-hour ATM in Dōngchéng, as well as one just by Silk Street. An ATM can be found at **Citibank** (Map pp268–9; ☎ 6510 2933; www.citi bank.com; 16th fl, Tower 2, Bright China Chang'an Bldg, 7 Jianguomennei Dajie). For your nearest ATM, consult www.visa .com/pd/atm or www.mastercard.com/atm locator/index.jsp; both have comprehensive listings. For those without their own ATM card or credit card, a PIN-activated **Visa TravelMoney card** (☎ 1-877-394-2247) gives you access to pre-deposited cash through the ATM network.

Changing Money

Foreign currency and travellers cheques can be changed at large branches of banks such as the Bank of China, CITIC Industrial Bank, the Industrial and Commercial Bank of China and the China Construction Bank, at the airport, hotel money-changing counters and at several department stores, as long as you have your passport. You should be able to change foreign currency into Renminbi at foreign-exchange outlets and banks at large international airports outside China, but rates may be poor. Hotels usually give the official rate, but some will add a small commission. Some upmarket hotels will change money only for their own guests.

Useful branches of the Bank of China with foreign exchange counters include a branch next to Oriental Plaza on Wangfujing Dajie, in the Lufthansa Center and in the China World Trade Center.

As Renminbi (Y) is still not fully convertible on international markets, you need to have a few exchange receipts if you want to change any remaining Renminbi back into another currency at the end of your trip.

Credit Cards

Most tourist hotels and restaurants and some major department stores accept credit cards. Many travel agencies also now accept credit cards for air tickets (plus a 4% service charge).

It's possible to get a cash advance on credit cards at CITIC Bank (19 Jianguomenwai Dajie), or the Bank of China (Sundongan Plaza and Sanlitun branches), but there is a steep (4%) commission. You can also cash personal cheques if you have an Amex card at CITIC Industrial Bank (CITIC Bldg, Jianguomenwai Dajie) and large branches of the Bank of China.

Currency

The basic unit of Chinese currency is the *yuán* – which is designated in this book by a capital 'Y'. In spoken Chinese, the word *kuài* or *kuàiqián* is often substituted for *yuán*. Ten *jiǎo* – in spoken Chinese, it's pronounced *máo* – make up one *yuán*. Ten *fēn* make up one *jiǎo*, but these days *fēn* are very rare because they are worth next to nothing.

Renminbi (RMB), or 'people's money', is issued by the Bank of China. Paper notes are issued in denominations of one, two, five, 10, 20, 50 and 100 *yuán*; one, two and five *jiǎo*; and one, two and five *fēn*. Coins are in denominations of one *yuán*; one, two and five *jiǎo*; and one, two and five *fēn*.

Travellers Cheques

Besides security considerations, travellers cheques are useful to carry in China because the exchange rate is actually more favourable than the rate for cash. Cheques from most of the world's leading banks and issuing agencies are acceptable in Běijīng – stick with the major players such as Citibank, American Express (Amex) and Visa and you should be OK. Note that although cashing travellers cheques is easy in Běijīng, don't expect to find anywhere to cash your cheques in small towns elsewhere in China.

Amex (Map pp268–9; ☎ 6505 2838; Room 2313, Tower 1, China World Trade Center, 1 Jianguomenwai Dajie)

Citibank (Map pp268–9; ☎ 6510 2933; fax 6510 2932; 16th fl, Tower 2, Bright China Chang'an Bldg, 7 Jianguomennei Dajie)

MOVING TO/FROM BĚIJĪNG

If you're moving things like furniture or all your household goods, you'll need an international mover or freight forwarder. Only foreigners on working visas are permitted to move the contents of a flat or house abroad from Běijīng in one go. In Běijīng, contact one of the following international companies, but note that their rates are typically around US$500 to US$1000 per cubic metre:

Allied Pickfords (☎ 5870 1133; www.alliedpickfords .com.cn; Room 812, Bldg A, The Space International Centre, 8 Dongdaqiao Lu)

Asian Express (☎ 8580 1471/2/3; www.aemovers .com.hk; Room 1612, Tower D, SOHO New Town, 88 Jianguo Lu).

Crown Relocations (☎ 6585 0640; www.crownrelo.com; Room 201, West Tower, Golden Bridge Bldg, 1 Jianguomenwai Dajie, Cháoyáng)

Santa Fe (☎ 6497 0688; www.santaferelo.com; 2, Street No 8, Beijing Airport Logistics Zone)

NEWSPAPERS & MAGAZINES

Copies of popular imported English-language international magazines, such as *Time, Newsweek, Far Eastern Economic Review* and the *Economist* can be bought from the bookshops of four- and five-star hotels around Běijīng. These hotels also stock European magazines in French or German and foreign newspapers such as the *Times*, the *International Herald Tribune*, the *Asian Wall Street Journal*, the *Financial Times* and the *South China Morning Post*. The occasional censorship of touchy subjects (eg unrest in Xīnjiāng) generally involves the ripping out of pages. Most English-language newspapers and magazines are accessible online from Běijīng.

Běijīng has a lively galaxy of English-language rags available free at most five-star hotels and expat bars and restaurants. The slick and confident *That's Beijing* (www .thatsbj.com) is well designed, well written and the best of the bunch. Others include *Time Out Beijing, City Weekend* (www.city weekend.com.cn) and *Beijing This Month* (www.btmbeijing.com).

The *China Daily* (www.chinadaily.com .cn), the government's favourite English-language mouthpiece, is generally an unappetising blend of censorship and pro-government opinion, but it is improving and the weekend culture section, *Beijing Weekend*, is useful for arts listings, events and trips out of Běijīng. Among the countless other Chinese-language newspapers is the state's flagship paper, the *Renmin Ribao* (人民日报; People's Daily), and papers of more specialist leanings, such as the *Nongmin Ribao* (农民日报; Farmer's Daily).

For a country expected to shape the course of the 21st century, the media outlook in China (see p21) is grim indeed. The BBC has its excellent Chinese-language news website blocked around the clock and even the BBC news website (in English) is blocked.

Various embassies also have small libraries of newspapers and magazines in English and other languages. The Cultural and Educational Section of the British Embassy (Map p264; ☎ 6590 6903; www.britishcouncil .org.cn; 4th fl, Landmark Building Tower 1, 8 Dongsanhuan Beilu, Cháoyáng; ⊙ 9am-5pm Mon-Fri) is worth visiting.

PHARMACIES

Pharmacies (药店; *yàodiàn*) are identified by a green cross. Several sizeable pharmacies on Wangfujing Dajie stock both Chinese (中药; *zhōngyào*) and Western medicine (西药; *xīyào*). You do not necessarily need a prescription for the drug you are seeking in Běijīng, so ask at the pharmacy first. In other parts of China, however, you will probably need a prescription issued by a doctor. As with many other large shops in Běijīng, once you have chosen your item, you are issued with a receipt which you take to the till counter (收银台; *shòuyíntái*) to pay, and then return to the counter where you chose your medicine to collect your purchase. Note that many chemists are effectively 24-hour and have a small window or slit through which you can pay for and collect medicines through the night. Chemists stocking traditional Chinese medicine can be found all over town. The best known is **Tongrentang Yaodian** (Map pp268–9; ☎ 6308 5413; 24 Dazhalan Jie). Branches of **Watson's** (Map p264; 1st fl, Full Link Plaza, 19 Chaoyangmenwai Dajie; Map pp268–9; CC17, 19, CC21, 23 Oriental Plaza, 1 Dongchan'an Jie) also purvey medicines, but are more geared to selling cosmetics, sunscreens, deodorants and the like.

Quanxin Pharmacy (Quánxīn Dàyàofáng; Map p262; ☎ 652 4123; 153 Wangfujing Dajie; ☯ 8.30am-10pm) Large pharmacy opposite St Joseph's Church.

Wangfujing Medicine Shop (Wángfǔjīng Yīyào Shāngdiàn; Map p262; ☎ 6524 0122; 267 Wangfujing Dajie; ☯ 8.30am-9pm) Come here for a large range of Western and Chinese drugs.

PHOTOGRAPHY

Kodak Express outlets are ubiquitous in Běijīng, where you can burn digital images to a CD for Y15. There is a handy Kodak Express branch just off Tiananmen Square (Map pp268–9).

POST

Convenient post offices can be found in the CITIC building next to the Friendship Store, in the basement of the China World Trade Center, east of Wangfujing Dajie on Dongdan Ertiao, on the south side of Xichang'an Jie west of the Beijing Concert Hall and just east of the Jianguo Hotel Qianmen, on Yong'an Lu. You can also post letters via your hotel reception desk, or at green post boxes around town. Large post offices are generally open daily between 8.30am and 6pm. Check the Information sections of the maps at the rear of this book for locations.

Letters and parcels marked 'Poste Restante, Beijing Main Post Office' will arrive at the **International Post Office** (Map p264; ☎ 6512 8114; Jianguomen Beidajie; ☯ 8am-7pm Mon-Sat), 200m north of Jianguomen subway station. Outsize overseas parcels should be sent from here; smaller parcels (up to around 20kg) can go from smaller post offices. Both outgoing and incoming packages will be opened and inspected. If you're sending a parcel, don't seal the package until you've had it inspected.

Letters take around a week to reach most overseas destinations. China charges extra for registered mail, but offers cheaper postal rates for printed matter, small packets, parcels, bulk mailings and so on.

Express Mail Service (EMS) is available for domestic and international destinations. Many post offices offer EMS. The main **EMS office** (☎ 6512 9948; 7 Qianmen Dajie) can be found south of Tiananmen Square.

Courier Companies

Several private couriers in Běijīng offer international express posting of documents and parcels, and have reliable pick-up service as well as drop-off centres:

DHL (☎ 6466 2211/6466 5566, 800-810 8000; www.dhl.com; 45 Xinyuan Jie, Cháoyáng) Further branches in the China World Trade Center and COFCO Plaza.

Federal Express (FedEx; ☎ 6561 2003, 800-810 2338; Hanwei Bldg, 7 Guanghua Lu, Cháoyáng; office in Rm 107, No 1 Office Bldg, Oriental Plaza). FedEx also has self-service counters in Kodak Express shops around town.

United Parcel Service (UPS; ☎ 6505 5005; www.ups.com; Rm 1818, China World Tower 1, 1 Jianguomenwai Dajie).

RADIO

The BBC World Service can be picked up on 17760, 15278, 21660, 12010 and 9740 kHz. Reception can often be poor, however, and Voice of America (VOA) is often a bit clearer at 17820, 15425, 21840, 15250, 9760, 5880 and 6125 kHz. You can find

Directory

PRACTICALITIES

tuning information for the BBC on the web at www.bbc.co.uk/worldservice/tuning, for Radio Australia at www.abc.net.au/ra, and for VOA at www.voa.gov. Crystal clear programmes from the BBC World Service can be heard online: follow the links on www.bbc.co.uk/worldservice.

China Radio International (CRI) is China's overseas radio service, and it broadcasts in about 40 foreign languages, as well as in *pǔtōnghuà* and several local dialects.

SAFETY

Generally speaking, Běijīng is a very safe city compared to other similarly sized cities in the world. Serious crime against foreigners is rare, although it is increasing as Běijīng's population expands due to huge migration by the nation's poor in search of employment.

You need to guard against pickpockets, especially on public transport and crowded places such as train stations. If you want to avoid opening wallets or bags on the bus, keep a few coins or small notes ready in an accessible pocket before launching yourself into the crowd. A money belt is the safest way to carry valuables, particularly when travelling on buses and trains.

Hotels are usually safe places to leave your stuff and in the older establishments each floor has an attendant watching who goes in and out. Staying in a dormitory carries its own set of risks, and while there have been a few reports of thefts by staff, the culprits are more likely to be other foreigners. Use lockers as much as possible.

The greatest hazard may well be crossing the road, a manoeuvre that requires great alertness. Driving standards are poor overall, traffic comes from all directions, while a reluctance to give way in any situation means drivers constantly compete with each other to make progress around town. If right of way is uncertain, drivers tend to dig their heels in and maintain their course. Safe crossing points are indicated by zebra crossing markings and/or pedestrian lights, although cars are not obliged to stop at zebra crossings and rarely do so. The green 'cross now' light doesn't necessarily mean that traffic won't try to run you down, as cars can turn right on a red light. In other words, learn to look in three different directions at once and be prepared to sprint.

Carry several forms of ID with you, including your passport. You will always need your passport to check into Chinese hotels, regardless of budget. It's a good idea to make photocopies of the visa and information pages of your passport, in case of loss. This makes the job of replacing your passport much simpler and faster.

SCAMS

Foreigners at Tiananmen Square or wandering Wangfujing Dajie are routinely hounded by pesky 'art students' either practising their English or roping visitors into going to exhibitions of over-priced art. They will try to strike up a conversation with you, but while some travellers enjoy their company, others find their attentions irritating and feel pressurised into buying art. Also be alert to similar types loitering around Tiananmen Square luring foreigners to expensive teahouses where they are left to foot staggering bills. See the Getting Into Town boxed text (p210) for details of the Capital Airport taxi scam. Also beware of fraudsters trying to sell you departure tax (now included in the price of your ticket) at Capital Airport.

TAXES

Four- and five-star hotels add a service charge of 15%, and smarter restaurants levy a service charge of 10%.

TELEPHONE

Both international and domestic calls can be made easily from your hotel room or from public telephones. Local calls from hotel room phones are free, although international phone calls are expensive and it is preferable to buy a phonecard (see Phonecards). Public telephones are plentiful. If making a domestic phone call, public phones at newspaper stands (报刊亭; *bàokāntíng*) and hole-in-the-wall shops (小卖部; *xiǎomàibù*) are useful; make your call and pay the owner (a local call is around five *jiǎo*). Most public phones take IC cards (see Phonecards, right).

Domestic long-distance rates in China vary according to distance, but are cheap. Card-less international calls are expensive (Y8.2 per minute or Y2.2 for calls to Hong Kong and Macau), but calls made between midnight and 7am are 40% cheaper than at other times; it's far cheaper to use an IP card (see Phonecards, right). Domestic and international long-distance phone calls can also be made from main telecommunications offices.

The country code to use to access China is 86; the code for Hong Kong is 852, and Macau is 853. To call a number in Běijīng from abroad, dial the international access code (00 in the UK, 011 in the USA), dial the country code (86) and then the area code for Běijīng (010), dropping the first zero, and then dial the local number. For telephone calls within the same city, drop the area code (区号; qūhaò). If calling internationally from Běijīng or from China drop the first zero of the area or city code after dialling the international access code and then dial the number you wish to call.

Important city area codes within China include:

Běijīng	☎ 010
Chéngdū	☎ 028
Chóngqìng	☎ 023
Guǎngzhōu	☎ 020
Hángzhōu	☎ 0571
Harbin	☎ 0451
Hong Kong	☎ 852
Jǐ'nán	☎ 0531
Kūnmíng	☎ 0871
Nánjīng	☎ 025
Qīngdǎo	☎ 0532
Shànghǎi	☎ 021
Shíjiāzhuāng	☎ 0311
Tiānjīn	☎ 022
Xiàmén	☎ 0592

The English-language Běijīng Yellow Pages is available at most business centres, and you might find it provided in your hotel room; alternatively, you can go online at www.yellowpage.com.cn or pick up your own copy at 65 Jiāguomennei Dajie (☎ 6512 0400).

Mobile Phones

Mobile-phone shops (手机店; shǒujīdiàn) such as China Mobile and China Unicom sell SIM cards which cost from Y60 to Y100 (numbers containing '4's are avoided by the Chinese, making them cheaper), which include Y50 of credit. This can be topped up by buying a credit-charging card (充值卡; chōngzhí kǎ) for Y50 or Y100 worth of credits. Cards are also available from ubiquitous newspaper kiosks displaying the China Mobile sign.

The mobile phone you use in your home country should work (as long as it has not been locked by your network – check with your network); alternatively, buy a phone locally. The local per-minute, non-roaming city call charge for China Mobile is seven jiǎo if calling a landline and 1.50 jiǎo if calling another mobile phone. Receiving calls on your mobile are free from mobile phones and seven jiǎo from landline phones. Roaming charges cost an additional two jiǎo per minute, but the call receiving charge is the same. Overseas calls can be made for Y4.80 per minute plus the local charge per minute by dialling ☎ 17951 – then follow the instructions and add 00 before the country code. Otherwise you will be charged the IDD call charge plus seven jiǎo per minute.

If you have an English-speaking Chinese contact, mobile phones can be particularly useful for handing over to your non-English speaking taxi driver (or whoever you want to talk to). Just phone your friend, tell him/her what you want to say and hand the phone over to whoever you are trying to communicate with.

Phonecards

For domestic calls, IC (Integrated Circuit; IC 卡; IC kǎ) cards, available from kiosks, hole-in-the-wall shops, internet cafés and China Telecom offices, are prepaid cards in a variety of denominations that can be used in most public telephones.

Note that some IC cards can be used only in Běijīng (or locally, depending on where the card is purchased), while other cards can be used in phones throughout China, so check.

For international calls on a mobile phone or hotel phone, buy an IP (Internet Phone) card. International calls on IP cards (IP 卡; IP kǎ) are Y1.80 per minute to the USA or Canada, Y1.50 per minute to Hong Kong, Macau and Taiwan and Y3.20 to all other countries; domestic long-distance calls are Y0.30 per minute. Follow the instructions on the reverse; English-language service is usually available. IP cards come in various denominations, typically with a big discount (a Y100 card should cost around Y40). IP cards can be found at the same places as IC cards. Again, some IP cards can only be used locally, while others can be used nationwide, so it is important to buy the right card (and check the expiry date).

TELEVISION

The national TV outfit, Chinese Central Television (CCTV), has an English-language channel (CCTV 9) that is useful for news and programmes on cultural topics, but is markedly bland. Its news bulletins in English can be useful but only if you can't get hold of anything else, as there is the usual censorship and absence of true debate or objectivity. Most in-room TVs in hotels have CCTV 9. CCTV 4 also has some English programmes. Tourist hotels may have ESPN, Star Sports, CNN or BBC News 24. Sports programmes and live matches (eg English Premiership football) can be picked up on CCTV 5 (in Chinese) or on BJTV, otherwise you will have to find a bar with sports TV.

Satellite TV is simple to arrange for residents, with most customers going for pirate versions which cost around Y1600 for a one-off installation with no subsequent charge. Those purchasing the pirated version have to put up with periodic transmission loss, however, as broadcast codes are occasionally changed (requiring a few days to crack).

TIME

All of China runs on the same time as Běijīng, which is set eight hours ahead of GMT/UTC (there's no daylight saving during summer). When it's noon in Běijīng it's 4am in London, 5am in Frankfurt, Paris and Rome, noon in Hong Kong, 2pm in Melbourne, 4pm in Wellington, and, on the previous day, 8pm in Los Angeles and 11pm in Montreal and New York.

TIPPING

Běijīng is one of those wonderful cities where tipping is not the norm. This applies throughout China. Midrange restaurants and above have closed the gap with a service charge (服务费; fúwùfèi), however, so there is no need to indulge them with a tip. Porters at upmarket hotels will, of course, expect a tip. Taxi drivers certainly do not expect a tip and will often refuse.

TOILETS

Travellers on the road relate China toilet tales to each other like soldiers comparing old war wounds. Despite proud claims to have invented the first flushing toilet, China has some wicked loos, but in a country of 1.3 billion, that is perhaps unsurprising. Over the last decade the capital has made its toilets less of an assault course of foul smells and primitive appliances, but many remain sordid. Make a beeline for fast-food outlets, top-end hotels and department stores for more hygienic alternatives. Toilet paper is rarely provided in streetside public toilets so *always* keep a stash with you. In some Běijīng hotels and buildings, especially old ones, the sewage system can't handle paper. As a general rule, if you see a wastebasket next to the toilet, that's where you should throw the toilet paper; otherwise the loo could choke up and flood.

Hyperventilate before tackling toilets on the older trains, or enter with a strong cigarette.

Remember:

| men | 男 |
| women | 女 |

TOURIST INFORMATION

In a land where everything disconcertingly has its price and awareness of the needs of international visitors was always inadequate, China never got the hang of tourist offices. The local chain of **Beijing Tourist Information Centers** (Běijīng Lǚyóu Zīxún Fúwù Zhōngxīn; ⏰ 9am-5pm) – with uniform turquoise façades – is an attempt to get its act together. English skills there are limited, but you can grab a free tourist map of town, nab handfuls of free literature, at some branches (eg Cháoyáng), rustle up train tickets. Preparations for the 2008 Olympics should surely see an injection of investment and trained staff. Useful branches include:

Beijing Train Station (Map pp268–90; ☎ 6528 4848; 16 Laoqianju Hutong)

Capital Airport (☎ 6459 8148)

Cháoyáng (Map p264; ☎ 6417 6627, 6417 6656; chaoyang@bjta.gov.cn; 27 Sanlitun Beilu)

Dōngchéng (☎ 6512 3043, 6512 2991; dongcheng@bjta.gov.cn; 10 Dengshikou Xijie)

Fēngtái (☎ 6332 3983; fengtai@bjta.gov.cn; Zhongyan Hotel lobby, Guangwai Dajie)

Hǎidiàn (☎ 8262 2895; haidian@bjta.gov.cn; 40 Zhongguancun Dajie)

Xīchéng (Map pp266–7; ☎ 6616 0108, 6612 0110; xicheng@bjta.gov.cn; 1st fl, Keji Guangchang, Xidan Beidajie)

Xuānwǔ (Map pp266–7; ☎ 6351 0018; xuanwu@bjta.gov.cn; 3 Hufang Lu)

The **Beijing Tourism Hotline** (☎ 6513 0828; ⊗ 24hr) has English-speaking operators available (press '1' after dialling the number) to answer questions and hear complaints. **CITS** (China International Travel Service; Map p264; ☎ 8511 8522; www.cits.com.cn; Rm 1212, CITS Bldg, 1 Dongdan Beidajie) is more useful for booking tours.

Hotels can offer you advice or connect you with a suitable tour, and some have useful tourist information desks (such as the Fangyuan Hotel, p183) which can point you in the right direction.

Some bars also informally address themselves to the needs of travellers: Passby Bar (p143) has travel-oriented staff who are keen to help, as long as you order a drink or two.

TRAVELLERS WITH DISABILITIES

If you are wheelchair-bound or have a mobility disability, Běijīng will be a major obstacle course. Pavements are often crowded and in a dangerous condition, with high curbs preventing wheelchair access. Many streets can be crossed only via an underground or overhead walkway with many steps. You will also have to stick to the main roads, as cars and bicycles often occupy the pavements of smaller alleys and lanes, forcing pavement users on to the road. There are no lifts in the subway, where escalators usually only go up. Getting around temples and big sights such as the Forbidden City and the Summer Palace can be very trying for those in wheelchairs. A ramp may be found at the entrance to a sight, but there may be no further ramps within the complex you are visiting. It is recommended that you take a lightweight chair so you can collapse it easily for navigating around obstacles or loading into the back of taxis.

Those with sight, hearing or mobility disabilities must be extremely cautious of the traffic, which almost never yields to pedestrians. Most, but not all, hotels will have lifts, and while many top-end hotels do have rooms for those with disabilities as well as good wheelchair access, hotel restaurants may not.

VISAS

A visa is required for the People's Republic of China (PRC), but at the time of writing visas were not required for most Western nationals to visit Hong Kong or Macau.

For most travellers, the type of visa is an L, from the Chinese word for travel (lǚxíng). This letter is stamped right on the visa.

Visas are readily available from Chinese embassies and consulates in most Western and many other countries (see p220 for a list of these). A standard 30-day, single-entry visa from most Chinese embassies abroad can be issued in three to five working days. Express visas cost twice the usual fee. You normally pay up front for the visa, rather than on collection. You can get an application form in person at the embassy or consulate, or obtain one online from a consular website. A visa mailed to you will take up to three weeks. Rather than going through an embassy or consulate, you can also make arrangements at certain travel agencies. Visa applications require at least one photo.

When asked on the application form, try to list standard tourist destinations such as Běijīng and Chéngdé; if you are toying with the idea of going to Tibet or western Xīnjiāng, just leave it off the form as it might raise eyebrows; the list you give is not binding in any way.

A 30-day visa is activated on the date you enter China, and must be used within three months of the date of issue. The 60-day and 90-day visas are activated on the date they are issued. Although visas valid for more than 30 days were once difficult to obtain anywhere other than in Hong Kong,

90-day visas are now becoming easier to obtain abroad.

Be aware that political events can suddenly make visas more difficult to procure.

A Chinese visa covers virtually the whole of China, although some restricted areas exist (eg Yìxiàn in Ānhuī province) which will require an additional permit from the Public Security Bureau (PSB), at a cost. In addition to a visa, permits are also required for travel to Tibet.

When you check into a hotel, there is a question on the registration form asking what type of visa you hold. The letter specifying what type of visa you have is usually stamped on the visa itself. There are eight categories of visas, as follows:

Type	Description	Chinese name	
L	Travel	lǚxíng	旅行
F	Business or student (less than 6 months)	fǎngwèn	访问
D	Resident	dìngjū	定居
G	Transit	guòjìng	过境
X	Long-term student	xuéshēng	学生
Z	Working	gōngzuò	工作
J	Journalist	jìzhě	记者
C	Flight attendant	chéngwù	乘务

Getting a Visa in Hong Kong

Hong Kong is still a good place to pick up a visa for China.

Almost any travel agent can obtain one for you or you can apply directly to the **Visa Office of the People's Republic of China** (☎ 852-3413 2300; 7th fl, Lower Block, China Resources Centre, 26 Harbour Rd, Wan Chai; ☷ 9am-noon & 2-5pm Mon-Fri). Visas processed here in one/two/three days cost HK$400/300/150. Double/six-month multiple/one-year multiple visas are HK$220/400/600 (plus HK$150/250 if you require express/urgent service). Be aware that US and UK passport holders must pay considerably more for their visas. You must supply two photos, which can be taken at photo booths in the MTR (Mass Transit Railway) and at the visa office for HK$35.

Visas for China can be arranged by **China Travel Service** (CTS; ☎ 852-2522 0450; Ground fl, China Travel Bldg, 77 Queen's Rd Central; ☷ 9am-6pm Mon-Fri, 9am-5pm Sat, 9.30am-12.30pm & 2.30-5pm Sun) or more cheaply at many other

Hong Kong travel agencies, including **Phoenix Services Agency** (☎ 852-2722 7378; info@phoenixtrvl.com; Room 1404-5, 14th fl, Austin Tower, 22-26A Austin Av, Tsim Sha Tsui; ☷ 9am-6pm Mon-Fri, 9am-4pm Sat) and **Traveller Services** (☎ 852-2375 2222; www.taketraveller.com; Room 1813 Mirimar Tower, 132 Nathan Rd, Tsim Sha Tsui; ☷ 9am-6pm Mon-Fri, 9am-1pm Sat).

Residence Permit

The 'green card' is a residence permit, issued to English teachers, foreign expats and long-term students who live in China. Green cards are issued for a period of six months to one year and must be renewed annually. Besides needing all the right paperwork, you must also pass a health examination (for which there is a charge). If you lose your card, you'll pay a hefty fee to have it replaced.

Visa Extensions

The Foreign Affairs Branch of the local **Public Security Bureau** (PSB; Gōngānjú) – the police force – handles visa extensions.

The **PSB main office** (Běijīngshì Gōngānjú Chūrùjìng Guǎnlǐchù; Map p262; ☎ 8402 0101; 2 Andingmen Dongdajie; ☷ 8.30am-4.30pm Mon-Sat) is in Dōngchéng. The visa office is on the 2nd floor on the east side of the building – take the escalator up. You can also apply for a residence permit here.

Visa extensions vary in price, depending on your nationality. US travellers pay Y185, Australians pay Y100, Canadians pay Y165 and UK citizens pay Y160; and prices can go up or down. Expect to wait up to five days for your visa extension to be processed. You can obtain passport photographs here (Y30 for five).

First-time extensions of 30 days are easy to obtain and are issued on any tourist visa, but further extensions are harder to get and might give you only a further week. Offices of the PSB outside Běijīng might be more lenient and more willing to offer further extensions, but don't bank on it.

The penalty for overstaying your visa in China is up to Y500 per day. Some travellers have reported having trouble with officials who read the 'valid until' date on their visa incorrectly. For a one-month tourist (L) visa, the 'valid until' date is the date by which you must enter the country, not the date upon which your visa expires. Your visa expires the number of days for which your visa is valid after the date of entry into China (but note that you must enter China within three months of the date the visa was issued). Sixty- and 90-day visas are activated on the day they are issued.

Visa extensions can also be obtained for a fee through private visa services in Běijīng. The legality of these services is questionable, and most of them seem to operate through private connections with the PSB. Although some foreigners have used these services without incident, you are taking a risk. Look in the classified section of the expat mags for listings, or try to get a personal recommendation from someone.

WOMEN TRAVELLERS

Women travellers generally feel safe in Běijīng. Chinese men are not macho and respect for women is deeply ingrained in Chinese culture.

As with anywhere else, you will be taking a risk if you travel alone. A self-defence course can equip you with extra physical skills and boost your confidence before your trip. Taking a whistle or alarm with you would offer a measure of defence in any unpleasant encounter. Calling home regularly can reassure your family that you are safe.

If travelling to towns outside Běijīng, stick to hotels near the city centre. For further tips, consult www.oculartravel.com, which has a very useful section for women travellers. Another useful website is www .journeywoman.com.

Tampons (卫生棉条; *wèishēng miántiáo*) can be found almost everywhere. It may be advisable to take supplies of the pill (避孕药; *bìyùnyào*) although you will find brands like Marvelon at local pharmacies; morning after pills (紧急避孕药; *jǐnjí bìyùnyào*) are also available. Male condoms (保险套; *bǎoxiǎntào*) are widely available.

WORK

In recent years it has become easier for foreigners to find work in Běijīng, although Chinese-language skills will naturally increase your options.

Teaching jobs that pay by the hour are usually quite lucrative. If you have recognised ELT qualifications, such as TEFL and/or experience, teaching can be a rewarding and profitable way to earn a living in Běijīng. International schools offer salaries in the region of Y6000 to Y10,000 per month to qualified teachers, with accommodation often provided. More basic (and plentiful) teaching positions will offer upwards of around Y100 per hour. Schools regularly advertise in the English culture magazines, such as *That's Beijing*; you can visit its classified pages online at www .thatsbj.com.

There are also opportunities in translation, editing, the hotel industry, copywriting, acting, modelling, photography, bar work, sales and marketing and beyond. Most people find jobs in Běijīng through word of mouth, so networking is the key.

Language

Language

It's true – anyone can speak another language. Don't worry if you haven't studied languages before or that you studied a language at school for years and can't remember any of it. It doesn't even matter if you failed English grammar. After all, that's never affected your ability to speak English! And this is the key to picking up a language in another country. You just need to start speaking.

Learn a few key phrases before you go. Write them on pieces of paper and stick them on the fridge, by the bed or even on the computer – anywhere that you'll see them often.

You'll find that the people of Beijing appreciate travellers trying to speak a little Mandarin, no matter how muddled you may think you sound. So don't just stand there, say something! If you want to learn more Mandarin than we've included here, pick up a copy of Lonely Planet's comprehensive but user-friendly *Mandarin Phrasebook*.

PRONUNCIATION
Pinyin

In 1958 the Chinese adopted a system of writing their language using the Roman alphabet, known as *Pīnyīn*. Pinyin is often used on shop fronts, street signs and advertising billboards, but very few Chinese are able to read or write it.

A few consonants in Pinyin may cause confusion when compared to their counterparts in English:

c	as the 'ts' in 'bits'
ch	as in 'chop', but with the tongue curled back
q	as the 'ch' in 'cheese'
r	as the 's' in 'pleasure'
sh	as in 'ship', but with the tongue curled back
x	as the 'sh' in 'ship'
z	as the 'dz' sound in 'suds'
zh	as the 'j' in 'judge', but with the tongue curled back

Tones

Chinese is a language with a large number of words with the same pronunciation but a different meaning; what distinguishes them are 'tones' – rises and falls in the pitch of the voice on certain syllables. The word *ma*, for example, has four different meanings depending on tone:

high tone	mā	(mother)
rising tone	má	(hemp, numb)
falling-rising tone	mǎ	(horse)
falling tone	mà	(to scold, to swear)

Mastering tones is tricky for newcomers to Mandarin, but with a little practice it gets a lot easier.

SOCIAL
Meeting People

Hello.	Nǐ hǎo.	你好
Goodbye.	Zàijiàn.	再见
Please.	Qǐng.	请
Thank you.	Xièxie.	谢谢
Thank you very much.	Tài xièxie le.	太谢谢了
Yes.	Shìde.	是的
No. (don't have)	Méi yǒu.	没有
No. (not so)	Búshì.	不是
Do you speak English?	Nǐ huì shuō yīngyǔ ma?	你会说英语吗?
Do you understand?	Dǒng ma?	懂吗?
I understand.	Wǒ tīngdedǒng.	我听得懂
I don't understand.	Wǒ tīngbudǒng.	我听不懂

Could you please ...?
Nǐ néng bunéng ...?
你能不能 ...?

repeat that
chóngfù — 重复

speak more slowly
màn diǎnr shuō — 慢点儿说

write it down
xiě xiàlái — 写下来

Going Out

What's on ...?
... yǒu shénme yúlè huódòng?
... 有什么娱乐活动?

locally
běndì — 本地

this weekend
zhège zhōumò — 这个周末

today
jīntiān — 今天

tonight
jīntiān wǎnshang — 今天晚上

Where are the ...?
... zài nǎr?
... 在哪儿?

clubs
jùlèbù — 俱乐部

gay venues
tóngxìngliàn chángsuǒ — 同性恋场所

places to eat
chīfàn de dìfang — 吃饭的地方

pubs
jiǔbā — 酒吧

Is there a local entertainment guide?
Yǒu dāngdì yúlè zhǐnán ma?
有当地娱乐指南吗?

PRACTICAL
Question Words

Who?
Shuí? — 谁?

What?
Shénme? — 什么?

When?
Shénme shíhou? — 什么时候?

Where?
Nǎr? — 哪儿?

How?
Zěnme? — 怎么?

Numbers & Amounts

1	yī/yāo	一/幺
2	èr/liǎng	二/两
3	sān	三
4	sì	四
5	wǔ	五
6	liù	六
7	qī	七
8	bā	八
9	jiǔ	九
10	shí	十
11	shíyī	十一
12	shí'èr	十二
13	shísān	十三
14	shísì	十四
15	shíwǔ	十五
16	shíliù	十六
17	shíqī	十七
18	shíbā	十八
19	shíjiǔ	十九
20	èrshí	二十
21	èrshíyī	二十一
22	èrshí'èr	二十二
30	sānshí	三十
31	sānshíyì	三十一
40	sìshí	四十
50	wǔshí	五十
60	liùshí	六十
70	qīshí	七十
80	bāshí	八十
90	jiǔshí	九十
100	yìbǎi	一百
200	liángbǎi	两百
1000	yìqiān	一千
2000	liǎngqiān	两千
10,000	yíwàn	一万
20,000	liǎngwàn	两万
100,000	shíwàn	十万
200,000	èrshíwàn	二十万

Days

Monday	xīngqīyī	星期一
Tuesday	xīngqī'èr	星期二
Wednesday	xīngqīsān	星期三
Thursday	xīngqīsì	星期四
Friday	xīngqīwǔ	星期五
Saturday	xīngqīliù	星期六
Sunday	xīngqītiān	星期天

Banking

I'd like to ...
Wǒ xiǎng ... — 我想 ...

change money
huàn qián — 换钱

change travellers cheques
huàn lǚxíng zhīpiào — 换旅行支票

cash a cheque
zhīpiào — 支票

Excuse me, where's the nearest ...?
Qǐng wèn, zuìjìnde ... zài nǎr?
请问, 最近的 ... 在哪儿?

  automatic teller machine
  zìdòng guìyuánjī
  自动柜员机
  foreign exchange office
  wàihuì duìhuànchù
  外汇兑换处

Post

Where is the post office?
Yúojú zài nǎlǐ?
邮局在哪里?

I'd like to send a ...
Wǒ xiǎng jì ...
我想寄 ...

letter xìn	信
fax chuánzhēn	传真
package bāoguǒ	包裹
postcard míngxìnpiàn	明信片

I'd like to buy (a/an) ...
Wǒ xiǎng mǎi ...
我想买 ...

aerogram hángkōngyóujiǎn	航空邮简
envelope xìnfēng	信封
stamps yóupiào	邮票

Internet

Is there a local internet café?
Běndì yǒu wǎngbā ma?
本地有网吧吗?

Where can I get online?
Wǒ zài nǎr kěyǐ shàng wǎng?
我在哪儿可以上网?

Can I check my email account?
Wǒ chá yīxià zìjǐ de email hù, hǎo ma?
我查一下自己的email户, 好吗?

computer diànǎo	电脑
email diànzǐyóujiàn	电子邮件 (often called 'email')
internet yīntè wǎng/hùlián wǎng	因特网/互联网 (formal name)

Phone & Mobile Phones

I want to make ...
Wǒ xiǎng dǎ ...
我想打 ...

  a call (to ...)
  diànhuà (dào ...)
  打电话 (到 ...)
  a reverse-charge/collect call
  duìfāng fùfèi diànhuà
  对方付费电话

Where can I find a/an ...?
Nǎr yǒu ...
哪儿有 ...?
I'd like a/an ...
Wǒ xiǎng yào ...
我想要 ...

  adaptor plug
  zhuǎnjiēqī chātóu
  转接器插头
  charger for my phone
  diànhuà chōngdiànqì
  电话充电器
  mobile/cell phone for hire
  zūyòng yídòng diànhuà
  租用移动电话 or
  zūyòng shǒujī
  租用手机
  prepaid mobile/cell phone
  yùfù yídòng diànhuà
  预付移动电话 or
  yùfù shǒujī
  预付手机
  SIM card for your network
  nǐmen wǎngluò de SIM kǎ
  你们网络的SIM卡

I want to buy a phone card.
Wǒ xiǎng mǎi diànhuà kǎ.
我想买电话卡

Transport

What time does ... leave/arrive?
... jǐdiǎn kāi/dào?
... 几点开/到?

the bus qìchē	汽车
the train huǒchē	火车
the plane fēijī	飞机
the boat chuán	船

When is the ... bus?
... qìchē jǐdiǎn kāi?
... 汽车几点开?
　first
　tóubān　　　　　　　头班
　next
　xià yìbān　　　　　　下一班
　last
　mòbān　　　　　　　末班

Is this taxi available?
Zhèi chē lā rén ma?
这车拉人吗?
Please use the meter.
Dǎ biǎo.
打表

How much (is it) to ...?
Qù ... dūoshǎo qián?
去 ... 多少钱?
I want to go to ...
Wǒ yào qù ...
我要去 ...
　this address
　zhège dìzhǐ
　这个地址

FOOD
breakfast
zǎofàn　　　　　　　早饭
lunch
wǔfàn　　　　　　　午饭
dinner
wǎnfàn　　　　　　　晚饭
snack
xiǎochī　　　　　　　小吃
eat
chī　　　　　　　　　吃
drink
hē　　　　　　　　　喝

Can you recommend a ...?
Nǐ néng bunéng tuījiàn yíge ...?
你能不能推荐一个 ...?
　bar/pub
　jiǔbā/jiǔguǎn　　　酒吧/酒馆
　café
　kāfēiguǎn　　　　　咖啡馆
　restaurant
　fànguǎn　　　　　　餐馆

Is service/cover charge included in the bill?
Zhàngdān zhōng bāokuò fúwùfèi ma?
帐单中包括服务费吗?

For more detailed information on food and dining out, see p40.

EMERGENCIES
It's an emergency!
Zhèshì jǐnjí qíngkuàng!
这是紧急情况!
Could you help me please?
Nǐ néng bunéng bāng wǒ ge máng?
你能不能帮我个忙?
Call the police/a doctor/an ambulance!
Qǐng jiào jǐngchá/yīshēng/jiùhùchē!
请叫警察/医生/救护车!
Where's the police station?
Jǐngchájú zài nǎr?
警察局在哪儿?

HEALTH
Excuse me, where's the nearest ...?
Qǐng wèn, zuìjìnde ... zài nǎr?
请问, 最近的 ... 在哪儿?
　chemist
　yàodiàn　　　　　　药店
　chemist (night)
　yàodiàn (yèjiān)　　药店 (夜间)
　dentist
　yáyī　　　　　　　　牙医
　doctor
　yīshēng　　　　　　医生
　hospital
　yīyuàn　　　　　　　医院

Is there a doctor here who speaks English?
Zhèr yǒu huì jiǎng yīngyǔ de dàifu ma?
这儿有会讲英语的大夫吗?

Symptoms
I have (a/an) ...
Wǒ ...
我 ...
　diarrhoea
　lādùzi　　　　　　　拉肚子
　fever
　fāshāo　　　　　　　发烧
　headache
　tóuténg　　　　　　　头疼

GLOSSARY

apsaras – Buddhist celestial beings, similar to angels

arhat – Buddhist, especially a monk who has achieved enlightenment and passes to nirvana at death

běi – north; the other points of the compass are *nán* (south), *dōng* (east) and *xī* (west)

bīnguǎn – tourist hotel

bìxì – mythical tortoise-like dragons often depicted in Confucian temples

bìyùn tào – condom

Bodhisattva – one worthy of nirvana but who remains on earth to help others attain enlightenment

bówùguǎn – museum

bǔpiào – upgrade

CAAC – Civil Aviation Administration of China

cāntīng – restaurant

catty – unit of weight, one catty *(jīn)* equals 0.6kg

CCP – Chinese Communist Party, founded in Shànghǎi in 1921

Chángchéng – the Great Wall

cheongsam (Cantonese) – originating in Shànghǎi, a fashionable tight-fitting Chinese dress with a slit up the side

chop – see *name chop*

CITS – China International Travel Service; the organisation deals with China's foreign tourists

CTS – China Travel Service; CTS was originally set up to handle tourists from Hong Kong, Macau, Taiwan and overseas Chinese

CYTS – China Youth Travel Service

dǎ zhé – discounting

dàdào – boulevard

dàfàndiàn – large hotel

dàjiē – avenue

dānwèi – work unit, the cornerstone of China's social structure

dàshà – hotel, building

dàxué – university

dìtiě – subway

dìtiě zhàn – subway station

dōng – east; the other points of the compass are *běi* (north), *nán* (south) and *xī* (west)

dòngwùyuán – zoo

fàndiàn – hotel or restaurant

fēng – peak

fēng shuǐ – geomancy, literally 'wind and water', the art of using ancient principles to maximise the flow of *qì*, or vital energy

Fifth Generation – a generation of film directors who trained after the Cultural Revolution and whose political works revolutionised the film industry in the 1980s and '90s

gānxǐ – dry-cleaning

gé – pavilion, temple (Daoist)

gōng – palace

gōngfu – kungfu

gōnggòng qìchē – bus

gōngyì – crafts

gōngyuán – park

gùjū – house, home, residence

gǔwán – antiques

hé – river

hú – lake

huàjù – theatre

huàndēngpiàn – colour slide film

Huí – ethnic Chinese Muslims

hútòng – a narrow alleyway

jiāng – river

jiǎo – see *máo*

jiàotáng – church

jìcúnchù – left-luggage counters

jiē – street

jié – festival

jīn – see *catty*

jīngjù – Beijing opera

jiǔdiàn – hotel

jū – residence, home

kàngjūnsù – antibiotics

kǎoyādiàn – roast duck restaurant

kuài – colloquial term for the currency, *yuán*

Kuomintang – Chiang Kaishek's Nationalist Party, the dominant political force after the fall of the Qing dynasty

lama – a Buddhist priest of the Tantric or Lamaist school; it is a title bestowed on monks of particularly high spiritual attainment

lǎowài – foreigner

lín – forest

líng – tomb

lóu – tower

lù – road

lǚguǎn – cheap hotel

luóhàn – see *arhat*

máo – colloquial term for *jiǎo*, 10 of which equal one *kuài*

mén – gate

miào – temple

mù – tomb

name chop – a carved name seal that acts as a signature

nán – south; the other points of the compass are *běi* (north), *dōng* (east) and *xī* (west)

páilou – decorated archway

pedicab – pedal-powered tricycle with a seat to carry passengers

Pinyin – the official system for transliterating Chinese script into the Roman alphabet

PLA – People's Liberation Army

Politburo – the 25-member supreme policy-making authority of the CCP

PRC – People's Republic of China
PSB – Public Security Bureau; the arm of the police force set up to deal with foreigners
Pǔtōnghuà – the standard form of the Chinese language used since the beginning of the 20th century and based on the dialect of Běijīng

qì – flow of vital or universal energy
qiáo – bridge
qìgōng – exercise that channels *qì*
qílín – a hybrid animal that only appeared on earth in times of harmony
qīngzhēnsì – mosque

rénmín – people, people's
Renminbi – literally 'people's money', the formal name for the currency of China; shortened to RMB
ruǎn wò – soft sleeper
ruǎn zuò – soft seat

shān – hill, mountain
shāngdiàn – shop, store
shěng – province, provincial
shì – city
shìchǎng – market
Sixth Generation – a generation of film directors whose dour subject matter and harsh film style contrasts starkly against the lavish films of the Fifth Generation
sì – temple, monastery
sīchóu – silk
sìhéyuàn – courtyard house

tǎ – pagoda

tàijíquán – the graceful, flowing exercise that has its roots in China's martial arts; also known as taichi
tíng – pavilion
tripitaka – Buddhist scriptures

wǎngbā – internet café
wǔshù – martial arts

xī – west; the other points of the compass are *běi* (north), *nán* (south) and *dōng* (east)
xī yào – Western medicine
xiàn – county
xiàng – statue
xǐyī – laundry

yángróngshān – cashmere
yáng – positive, bright and masculine; the complementary principle to yín
yín – negative, dark and feminine; the complementary principle to yáng
yìng wò – hard sleeper
yìng zuò – hard seat
yuán – the Chinese unit of currency; also referred to as RMB (see also *Renminbi*)
Yuècài – Cantonese

zhāodàisuǒ – basic lodgings, a hotel or guesthouse
zhēng – 13- or 14-stringed harp
zhíwùyuán – botanic gardens
zhōng – middle, centre
zhōng yào – herbal medicine
zǒngtái – hotel reception

Behind the Scenes

THIS BOOK

This 7th edition of *Beijing* was written by Damian Harper and David Eimer. Julie Grundvig contributed to the Arts & Architecture and Food & Drink chapters. Jasper Becker wrote the History chapter, and Dr Trish Batchelor wrote the Health section in the Directory chapter. Lin Gu wrote the boxed text 'Home,' which appears in the City Life chapter. The interview with Wang Ruihai in the Life in Běijīng chapter was arranged with the help of the Culture and Communication Center for Facilitators (CCCF), a Chinese NGO that provides support and education to migrant workers (www.facilitator.ngo.cn). The 5th and 6th editions of *Beijing* were written by Damian Harper. This guidebook was commissioned in Lonely Planet's Melbourne office, and produced by the following:

Commissioning Editor Rebecca Chau

Coordinating Editor Nigel Chin

Coordinating Cartographer David Connolly

Coordinating Layout Designer Jessica Rose

Managing Editor Suzannah Shwer

Managing Cartographer Julie Sheridan

Assisting Editors Elisa Arduca, Gennifer Ciavarra, Kate Cody

Assisting Cartographers Damien Demaj, Owen Eszeki, Corey Hutchison, Anthony Phelan, Malisa Plesa, Andy Rojas

Cover Designer Nic Lehman

Project Manager Fabrice Rocher

Language Content Coordinator Quentin Frayne

Thanks to Carolyn Boicos, Dora Chai, Sally Darmody, Barbara Delissen, Ryan Evans, Lin Gu, Feng Guangju, Trent Holden, Graham Imeson, Laura Jane, Margot Kilgour, Rebecca Lalor, Chris LeeAck, Zhang Liang, Alison Lyall, Kate McDonald, Wayne Murphy, Paul Piaia, Lushan Charles Qin, Han Qing, Wang Ruihai, Cara Smith, Gina Tsarouhas, Gerard Walker, Celia Wood, Wendy Wright, Zan Xin and Zhen Ying.

Cover photographs National Grand Theater in Běijīng, Dennis Cox/Alamy (top); children gathering in Tiananmen Square, Jay Dickman/Corbis (bottom); Great Wall of China, Nicholas Pavloff/Lonely Planet Images (back).

Internal photographs p3 (top), p4 (top), p5 (top), p7 (top) & p8 (top) by David Eimer; p105, p106, p107 (left), p111 by Damian Harper; p2, p7 (bottom), p8 (bottom), p110, p169 (#3), p173 (#1), p175 (#3), p176 (#1 & #3) Andrew J Loiterton/Getty. All other photographs by Lonely Planet Images, and by Phil Weymouth except p6 (bottom), p172 (#3) Krzysztof Dydynski; p171 (#4) Manfred Gottschalk; p4 (bottom), p5 (bottom), p107 (right), p108, p109 (right), p174 (#1, #2 & #3), p175 (#1), p176 (#2) Ray Laskowitz; p171 (#2) Nicholas Pavloff; p169 (#1) Jean Robert.

All images are the copyright of the photographers unless otherwise indicated. Many of the images in this guide are available for licensing from Lonely Planet Images: www.lonelyplanetimages.com.

THANKS

DAMIAN HARPER

Thanks as ever to Dai Jiafu and Dai Jiale for their constant support and patience. All the help and advice of Liu Ji, Zang Yijie and Sun Demin was much appreciated. Thumbs up also to Rex Chen for his unfaltering good humour, resourcefulness and hospitality. Much gratitude also to Rebecca Chau and the editorial and cartographic staff at LP for putting this book together. Last but not least, heartfelt thanks to the convivial folk of Běijīng who make a visit to their city such a pleasure.

DAVID EIMER

Special thanks to Liu Lu for invaluable assistance and to Liu Qianwen for her reminiscences. Thanks also to the staff at Lonely Planet for their help and advice.

OUR READERS

Many thanks to the travellers who used the last edition and wrote to us with helpful hints, useful advice and interesting anecdotes:

Babatunde Adefila, Liz Avenell, Joachim Bergmann, Adriana Bishop, Nick Bonner, Grady Bourn, Leesa Bridson, Daniel Brown, Nigel Brown, Nicola Calabrese, Ken Chapman, Jian Chen, Aaron Dailey, Luke Dekoster, Karin Deraedt, Robert Doub, Fabian Duffe, Pascal Enz, Clemmie Evans, Stephen Evans, Hauck Evelyn, Eileen Gallagher, Domenic Georgantas, Patrick Gleeson, Bob Goldfarb, Alex Gray, Allison Green, Victoria Grierson, Neil Griffith, La Gyatso, Kelly Hardwick, Frederik Helbo, Ralf Hempel, Larissa Hoerzer, Andy Holder, Nikki Holloman, Michael Holm, Ben Inchi, Seba K, Andrea Kelleher, David Kerkhoff, Eugene Kim, Aik Hooi Kok, Anne Krogh, Pang Kullawan, Takeshi Kusuda, Elina Kyllönen, Truong B Lam, Becky Lister, Michael Lucht, Charlotte Lumley, Ally Macdonald, Trever Madsen, Jennifer Maile, Mikko Manninen, Catherine Manning, Peter John Martinez, Guido Mellicovsky, Omer Mendelson, Richard Merritt, Maurice Morgan, Sanjukta Mukherjee, Colin Mumford, Tony Ng, Helena Niku, Bonnie Nolen, Patrick Orhammar, Lars Pardo, Hirak Parikh, Julia Pearce, Sheridan Roberts, Martijn Roest, Aurelie Salvaire, Nicky Schram, Wendy Scorgie, Tracey Seslen, Destin Singleton, Julian Sirull, Carey Stevens, Mattias Stridh, Tom Thornton, Charles Tyler, Jos Vandendriessche, Manuel Guedes Viereira, David Wakelam, Dryden Watner, Tim Weeple, Alan Whyte, Jonathan Wise, Bin Yang, Cecilia Yong, Andrew Young

SEND US YOUR FEEDBACK

We love to hear from travelers – your comments keep us on our toes and help make our books better. Our well-traveled team reads every word on what you loved or loathed about this book. Although we cannot reply individually to postal submissions, we always guarantee that your feedback goes straight to the appropriate authors, in time for the next edition. Each person who sends us information is thanked in the next edition – and the most useful submissions are rewarded with a free book.

To send us your updates – and find out about Lonely Planet events, newsletters and travel news – visit our award-winning website: www.lonelyplanet.com/contact.

Note: We may edit, reproduce and incorporate your comments in Lonely Planet products such as guidebooks, websites and digital products, so let us know if you don't want your comments reproduced or your name acknowledged. For a copy of our privacy policy visit www.lonelyplanet.com/privacy.

Notes

Notes

Notes

Notes

Notes

Index

See also separate indexes for Eating (p255), Entertainment (p255), Shopping (p256) and Sleeping (p256).

000 map pages
000 photographs

000 map pages
000 photographs

Index

000 map pages
000 photographs

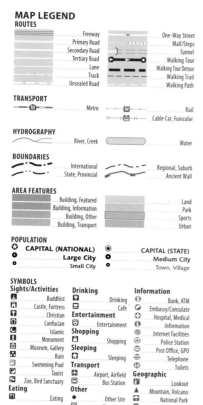

MAP LEGEND
ROUTES

Freeway
Primary Road
Secondary Road
Tertiary Road
Lane
Track
Unsealed Road

One-Way Street
Mall/Steps
Tunnel
Walking Tour
Walking Tour Detour
Walking Trail
Walking Path

TRANSPORT

Metro
Rail
Cable Car, Funicular

HYDROGRAPHY

River, Creek
Water

BOUNDARIES

International
State, Provincial
Regional, Suburb
Ancient Wall

AREA FEATURES

Building, Featured
Building, Information
Building, Other
Building, Transport
Land
Park
Sports
Urban

POPULATION

⊙ **CAPITAL (NATIONAL)**
● **Large City**
○ Small City

◉ CAPITAL (STATE)
● Medium City
○ Town, Village

SYMBOLS

Sights/Activities
Buddhist
Castle, Fortress
Christian
Confucian
Islamic
Monument
Museum, Gallery
Ruin
Swimming Pool
Taoist
Zoo, Bird Sanctuary
Eating
Eating

Drinking
Drinking
Café
Entertainment
Entertainment
Shopping
Shopping
Sleeping
Sleeping
Transport
Airport, Airfield
Bus Station
Other
Other Site
Picnic Area

Information
Bank, ATM
Embassy/Consulate
Hospital, Medical
Information
Internet Facilities
Police Station
Post Office, GPO
Telephone
Toilets
Geographic
Lookout
Mountain, Volcano
National Park
Waterfall

Maps

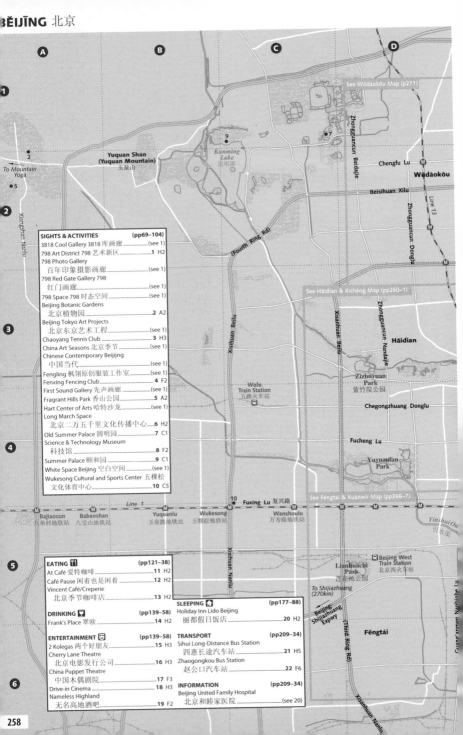

A   B   C   D

1

See Wǔdàokǒu Map (p271)

Zhōngguāncūn Běidàjiē

Chéngfǔ Lù

Wǔdàokǒu

Yuquan Shan
(Yuquan Mountain)
玉泉山

Kunming
Lake
昆明湖

9

To Mountain
Yoga

5

Běisìhuán Xīlù

Zhōngguāncūn Dōnglù

Line 13

Xiāngshān Nánlù

(Fourth Ring Rd)

2

See Hǎidiàn & Xīchéng Map (pp260–1)

Zhōngguāncūn Nándàjiē

Hǎidiàn

Zizhuyuan
Park
紫竹院公园

Chegongzhuang Donglu

Xīsānhuán Běilù

Wulu
Train Station
五路火车站

Fucheng Lu

Yuyuantan
Park

4

Line 1

10 Fuxing Lu 复兴路

Bajiacun
八角村地铁站

Babaoshan
八宝山地铁站

Yuquanlu
玉泉路地铁站

Wukesong
五棵松地铁站

Wanshoulu
万寿路地铁站

See Fēngtái & Xuānwǔ Map (pp266–7)

5

Lianhuachi
Park
莲花池公园

Beijing West
Train Station
北京西火车站

To Shijiazhuang
(270km)

Beijing-Shijiazhuang Expwy

Fēngtái

Xīsānhuán Nánlù

Third Ring Rd

6

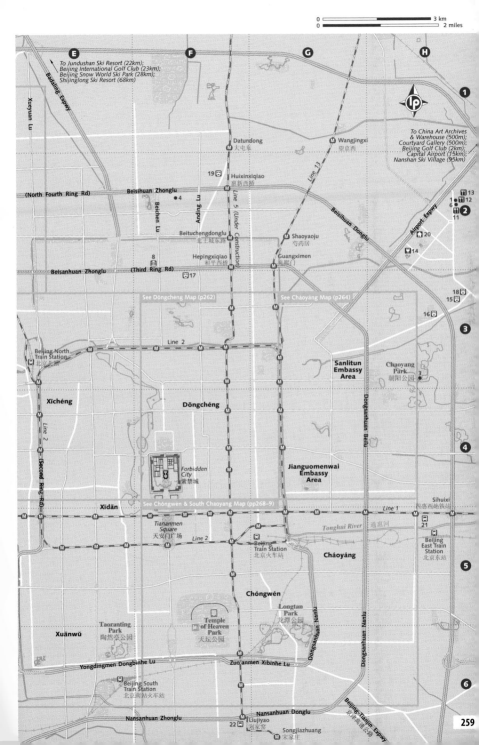

HĂIDIÀN & XĪCHÉNG 海淀和西城

CHÁOYÁNG 朝阳

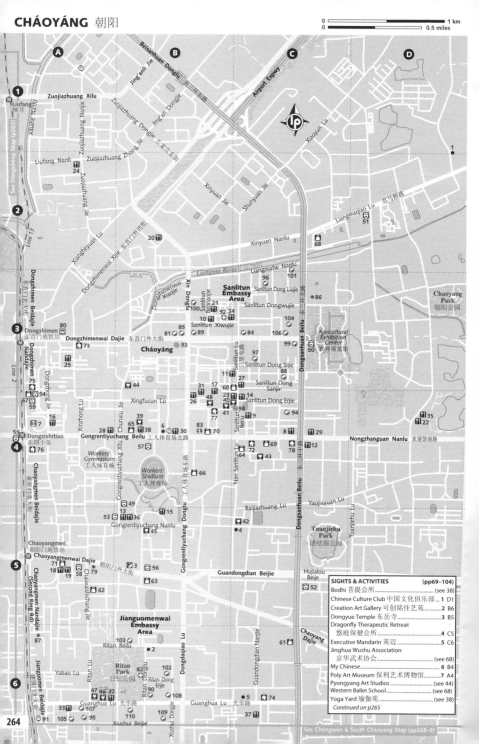

SIGHTS & ACTIVITIES (pp69–104)

Bodhi 菩提会所	(see 38)
Chinese Culture Club 中国文化俱乐部	1 D1
Creation Art Gallery 可创铭佳艺苑	2 B6
Dongyue Temple 东岳寺	3 B5
Dragonfly Therapeutic Retreat 悠庭保健会所	4 C5
Executive Mandarin 英迈	5 C6
Jinghua Wushu Association 京华武术协会	(see 68)
My Chinese	6 B4
Poly Art Museum 保利艺术博物馆	7 A4
Pyongyang Art Studios	(see 44)
Western Ballet School	(see 68)
Yoga Yard 瑜伽苑	(see 38)
Continued on p265	

264

See Haidian & Xicheng Map (pp260–1)

Fuxingmenwai Dajie

Fuxing Lu 复兴路

Gongzhufen 公主坟地铁站

Junshibowuguan 军事博物馆地铁站

Muxidi 木樨地地铁站

Yangfangdian Lu

Beifengwo Lu

Yushu On Silou

Baiyun Lu

Lianhuachi Donglu

Lianhuachi Park 莲花池公园

Lianhuachi Pond 莲花池

Lianhuachi Xilu

Xisanhuan Zhonglu 西三环中路

(Third Ring Rd)

Beijing West Train Station 北京西站

Nanfengwo Lu

Maliandao Beilu

Shoupaokou Beijie

NalHe порожкеск

Guang'anmenwai Dajie

Guang'an Lu 广安路

Maliandao Lu

Beijing-Shijiazhuang, Gaosu Gonglu 京石高速公路

(Third Ring Rd)

Fēngtái

Hongju Nanjie

Guang'anmen Train Station 广安门火车站

Sanluju Lu

Fengtai Beilu

SIGHTS & ACTIVITIES (pp69–104)

Capital Museum 首都博物馆	1 D1
China Millennium Monument 中华世纪坛	2 C1
Fayuan Temple 法源寺	3 G4
Military Museum 军事博物馆	4 C1
Niujie Mosque 牛街礼拜寺	5 F3
South Cathedral 南堂	6 G2
White Cloud Temple 白云观	7 D2

ENTERTAINMENT (pp139–58)

Beijing Concert Hall 北京音乐厅	8 H1
Huguang Guild Hall 湖广会馆	9 H3
Liyuan Theatre 梨园剧场	10 H3
Sanwei Bookstore 三味书屋	11 G1
Zhengyici Theatre 正乙祠剧场	12 H2

SHOPPING (pp159–68)

Cathay Bookshop 中国书店	13 H2
Róngbǎozhāi 荣宝斋	14 H2
Sogo 崇光百货	15 G3
Ten Fu's Tea 天福茗茶	16 H2
Xidan Bookshop 西单图书大厦	17 H2

SLEEPING (pp177–88)

Beijing Feiying International Youth Hostel 北京飞鹰青年旅社	18 F2
Far East Hotel 远东饭店	(see 19)

Far East International Youth Hostel 远东国际青年旅社	19 H3
Marco Polo Beijing 北京马哥孛罗酒店	20 G2
Qianmen Jianguo Hotel 前门建国饭店	(see 10)

TRANSPORT (pp209–34)

Air China 中国航空	(see 21)
Aviation Building (CAAC & Airport Bus) 民航营业大厦	21 G1
Lianhuachi Bus Station 莲花池长途汽车站	22 B3
Liuliqiao Long-Distance Bus Station 六里桥长途站	23 B4
Tour Buses 旅游汽车	(see 6)

INFORMATION (pp209–34)

Beijing Tourist Information Center 北京旅游咨询中心	24 H3
Beijing Tourist Information Center 北京旅游咨询中心	25 G1
Bicycle Rental 租自行车店	26 H3
Dayusu Internet Café 达宇速网吧	27 H3
Post Office 邮局	28 G1
Post Office 邮局	29 H3

A B C D

1

43 13 29
31
Nanchang Jie
南昌街
Zhongshan Park
中山公园
18
Narchizi Dajie
南池子大街
21 20 39
Nanheyan Dajie
南河沿大街
Tiananmen Dong
天安门东地铁站
Zhengyi Lu
正义路
36
Nanheyan Dajie
Taijichang Dajie
太基厂大街
66
Wangfujing
王府井
47 Dongdan Santiao
东单三条
55
67
7
65
Dongdan Beidajie
东单北大街
Chaoyangmennanxiao Jie →
63 84

Xichang'an Jie 西长安街 Dongchang'an Jie Jianguomennei Dajie
Tiananmen Xi
天安门西地铁站
Tiananmen
Square
天安门广场
45
19
24
10
Dongdan
东单地铁站
Wangfujing
王府井地铁站
25
12
Dongdan
Park
东单公园
Chongwennei Dajie
Beijingzhan Xijie
Line 2
81
85
62
83
Beijingzhan
Dongjie
Beijingzhan
北京站地铁站
Beijing Train
Station
北京火车站

9
Xijiaomin Xiang 西交民巷
77 17
Qianmen
前门地铁站
2
78
Dongjiaomin Xiang
16
15
70
Qianmen Dongdajie
28
Chongwenmen Xidajie   Line 2
73
Chongwenmen
崇文门地铁站
23
Chongwenmen Dongdajie

Qianmen Xidajie
53
2

44
Qianmen Xiheyan Jie
68
90
4
Xidamachang Jie
34
6
Dongdamochang Jie
Qinian Dajie 祈年大街
Dongxinglong Jie
32
Xihuashi Dajie
Beiyangshikou Jie
Donghuashi Dajie
Zhuying Hutong

79
49 57
54 59 37
Dahsilan Jie
大栅栏街
72
Liangshidian Jie
粮食店街
69
Post
Office
Zhushikou Dongdajie
Ciqikou
磁器口
Guangqumenei Dajie
Xingfu Dajie

26
Meishi Jie
33
3
Zhushikou Xidajie
Qianmen Dajie
珠市口西大街
Dongxiaoshi Jie
Chongwenmenwai Dajie
Dongxiaoshi Jie
52
Chóngwén
崇文

Tiantan Lu 天坛路
Tiyuguan Xlu
Temple
of Heaven
Park
天坛公园
Tiyuguan Lu

46
Beiwei Lu 北纬路
Nanwei Lu
Tianqiao Nandajie 天桥南大街
3
Xinnong Jie
Dongjing Lu
Beijing
Amusement
Park
北京游乐园
Longtan Lu

30
Xiannongtan Jie
Yongdingmennei Dajie
永定门内大街

22
Yongdingmen Dongjie 永定门东街
Tiantandongmen
天坛东门
Yongdingmen Dongbinhe Lu
Huicheng River (Li Ma Gou)
Zuo'anmen Xibinhe Lu

5

Jingtai Lu 景泰路
Puhuangyu
蒲黄榆

6

E ⊙89 Ritan 日 88 92
Xiushui Beijie 91
75 ⊟ 35 87
11● 8 38 Xiushui Nanjie
51 Jianhua **F** Xiushui Dongjie Dongdaqiao ⊟60 71 58 Jianguomenwai Dajie 建国门外大街 64⊟ 50
G CCTV Building
Guomao 国贸地铁站 **H**
Jianguomen 建国门地铁站 82 42⊟ ●80 41 永安里地铁站 Yonganli ●14 **1** Dawanglu 大望路地铁站 86⊟ **M**
1 🛈
Jingtong Kuaisu Gonglu 京通快速公路
27 🛈 ⊟76

2

Jianguomen Nandajie
Tonghui River 通惠河

Cháoyáng

Nanxiaoshikou Jie
Baijiao Lu
Guangqumen Nanbinhe Lu
Huashuo River City Park
Xizhaosi Jie
Guangqumenwai Dajie 广渠门外大街
Chuiyangliu Zhongjie
Guanghe Lu
Dongsanhuan Zhonglu 东三环中路
Guangqu Lu

3

Chuiyangliu Nanjie

Guangming Lu
Longtan Lu
🟦 Jingsong Lu 🟦
Nanmofang Lu

4
Zuo'anmennei Dajie
Longtan Park 龙潭公园
Jinsong Nanlu
Panjiayuan Donglu
Huawei Lu
61⊟

Panjiayuan Lu
56⊟

5
Huawei Nanlu
48⊟

Zuo'an Lu

6

Beijing-Tianjin Expwy 京津高速公路

269